# Forging *the* Modern World

# Forging *the* Modern World

## *A History*

James Carter          Richard Warren

New York   Oxford
OXFORD UNIVERSITY PRESS

Oxford University Press is a department of the University of Oxford.
It furthers the University's objective of excellence in research,
scholarship, and education by publishing worldwide.

Oxford   New York
Auckland   Cape Town   Dar es Salaam   Hong Kong   Karachi
Kuala Lumpur   Madrid   Melbourne   Mexico City   Nairobi
New Delhi   Shanghai   Taipei   Toronto

With offices in
Argentina   Austria   Brazil   Chile   Czech Republic   France   Greece
Guatemala   Hungary   Italy   Japan   Poland   Portugal   Singapore
South Korea   Switzerland   Thailand   Turkey   Ukraine   Vietnam

For titles covered by Section 112 of the US Higher Education
Opportunity Act, please visit www.oup.com/us/he for the
latest information about pricing and alternate formats.

Published by Oxford University Press
198 Madison Avenue, New York, New York 10016
http://www.oup.com

**Library of Congress Cataloging-in-Publication Data**
Carter, James Hugh.
  Forging the modern world : a history / James Carter, St. Joseph's University,
Richard Warren, St. Joseph's University.
    pages cm
  Includes index.
  ISBN 978-0-19-998856-3 (pbk., acid free : alk. paper)  1.  History, Modern. 2.  History,
Modern--20th century.  I. Warren, Richard A., 1961- II.  Title.
  D208.C337 2015
  909.08--dc23

                                                                          2015002228

**About the Cover**
The cover image is based on a Japanese woodblock print, probably produced in 1874 by Hiroshige III (1842–
1894), the year in which the first rail line in Japan opened between Tokyo and Yokohama. The image is appropriate to *Forging the Modern World* for several reasons: first, it highlights the interconnections among
different parts of the world in the modern era, depicting a scene of a Japanese port, with Japanese, Chinese,
American, and European observers on the shoreline, and (primarily) foreign vessels in the bay. Second, the
national flags displayed on the ships illustrate the central importance of the nation-state to the modern world
that emerges over the course of the book. Finally, the locomotive in the foreground emphasizes the key role
played by industrial technology in reshaping relationships among states and peoples.

Printing number: 9  8  7  6  5  4  3  2  1

Printed in the United States of America
on acid-free paper

# Brief Contents

Detailed Contents . . . . . . . . . . . . . . . . . . . . . . . . . . . . . . . . . . vii

List of Maps . . . . . . . . . . . . . . . . . . . . . . . . . . . . . . . . . . . . . . xi

Acknowledgments . . . . . . . . . . . . . . . . . . . . . . . . . . . . . . . . xiii

About the Authors . . . . . . . . . . . . . . . . . . . . . . . . . . . . . . . . . xv

**INTRODUCTION**    Forging the Modern World . . . . . . . . . . . . . . . . . 1

**CHAPTER 1**    The Many Worlds of the Fifteenth Century . . . . . . 19
1405–1510

**CHAPTER 2**    The New Global Interface . . . . . . . . . . . . . . . . 45
1486–1639

**CHAPTER 3**    The Paradoxes of Early Modern Empire . . . . . . . 67
1501–1661

**CHAPTER 4**    Production and Consumption in the
First Global Economy . . . . . . . . . . . . . . . . . . 91
1571–1701

**CHAPTER 5**    Global War and Imperial Reform . . . . . . . . . . 117
1655–1765

**CHAPTER 6**    A New Order for the Ages . . . . . . . . . . . . . . . 143
1755–1839

**CHAPTER 7**    The Engines of Industrialization . . . . . . . . . . . 173
1787–1868

CHAPTER 8     Modernity Organized . . . . . . . . . . . . . . . . . . 199
1840–1889

CHAPTER 9     Globalization and Its Discontents . . . . . . . . . 227
1878–1910

CHAPTER 10     Total War and Mass Society . . . . . . . . . . . . . 255
1905–1928

CHAPTER 11     The Ongoing Crisis of Global Order . . . . . . . . . 283
1919–1948

CHAPTER 12     Hot Wars, Cold Wars, and Decolonization . . . . . 311
1942–1975

CHAPTER 13     The Many Worlds of the Twenty-first Century . . . 337
1972–2012

Epilogue . . . . . . . . . . . . . . . . . . . . . . . . . . . . . . . . . . . . . . . . . 365
Credits . . . . . . . . . . . . . . . . . . . . . . . . . . . . . . . . . . . . . . . . . 371
Index . . . . . . . . . . . . . . . . . . . . . . . . . . . . . . . . . . . . . . . . . . 375

# Contents

List of Maps . . . . . . . . . . . . . . . . . . . . . . . . . . . . . . . . . . . . . . . . . xi

Acknowledgments . . . . . . . . . . . . . . . . . . . . . . . . . . . . . . . . . . . xiii

About the Authors . . . . . . . . . . . . . . . . . . . . . . . . . . . . . . . . . . . . . xv

**INTRODUCTION**  Forging the Modern World . . . . . . . . . . . . . . .1
- What is this Book About?     1
- The Modern World     2
- Sources and Methods     7
- Practicing History     12
- Time and Space     13
- Recommended Reading     15
- Historical Inquiry as a Hopeful Practice     16
- *A Few Good Books*     *17*

**CHAPTER 1**  The Many Worlds of the Fifteenth Century . . . . . 19
**1405–1510**
- Political and Economic Order on the Afro-Eurasian Supercontinent     21
- Collapse and Transformation in Afro-Eurasia     27
- American Empires of the Fifteenth Century     38
- Conclusion     43
- *A Few Good Books*     *43*

**CHAPTER 2**  The New Global Interface . . . . . . . . . . . . . . . 45
**1486–1639**
- The Conquest Era     48
- A World Connected     60
- Conclusion     64
- *A Few Good Books*     *65*

**CHAPTER 3**   The Paradoxes of Early Modern Empire . . . . . . . . 67
1501–1661

- The Words and Deeds of Empire Building                              69
- Tangled Loyalties and the European Wars of Religion                 79
- Collapse and Restoration of Empire in China: From Ming to Qing      83
- Conclusion                                                          88
*A Few Good Books*                                                    *89*

**CHAPTER 4**   Production and Consumption in the
First Global Economy . . . . . . . . . . . . . . . . . 91
1571–1701

- The World's Rural Economies                                         94
- The Sugar-Slave Plantation System                                   98
- Manufactured Goods and the Emerging Global Economy                  101
- The Silver Supply and the Global Economy                            106
- Political Economy                                                   112
- Conclusion                                                          113
*A Few Good Books*                                                    *115*

**CHAPTER 5**   Global War and Imperial Reform . . . . . . . . . . 117
1655–1765

- Consolidating the Center: Modernizing Monarchies                    120
- The Question of Control in the Atlantic Seaborne Empires            125
- The Path to World War Zero                                          131
- Conclusion                                                          139
*A Few Good Books*                                                    *141*

**CHAPTER 6**   A New Order for the Ages . . . . . . . . . . . . . . 143
1755–1839

- What Is Enlightenment?                                              146
- The Breakup of British North America                               148
- Revolution in France and Haiti                                     152
- The Collapse of the Iberian Empire in the Americas                 157
- A New Order for the Ages? The Idea of the Nation-State             163
- Freedom and Equality                                               167
- Conclusion                                                         169
*A Few Good Books*                                                    *171*

**CHAPTER 7**   The Engines of Industrialization . . . . . . . . . . . 173
1787–1868

- What Is Revolutionary about Industrialization?                     176
- Spinning the Industrial Revolution Story                           177

• The Transformation of Global Power Relations          188
• Conclusion                                            195
*A Few Good Books*                                      *197*

**CHAPTER 8**    Modernity Organized . . . . . . . . . . . . . . . . **199**
1840–1889

• Reform versus Revolution                              201
• Abolition, Immigration, and the Meaning of Free Labor 212
• Modernizing Japan                                     214
• The Second Industrial Revolution                      216
• Keeping Up: The World's Fair                          220
• Conclusion                                            223
*A Few Good Books*                                      *225*

**CHAPTER 9**    Globalization and Its Discontents . . . . . . . . . . **227**
1878–1910

• Redrawing the Map of the World                        229
• Questioning Empire                                    237
• Challenging the Modern Order at its Core              246
• Neocolonialism                                        250
• Conclusion                                            251
*A Few Good Books*                                      *252*

**CHAPTER 10**    Total War and Mass Society . . . . . . . . . . . . . **255**
1905–1928

• New Theories, Grand Strategy                          258
• Mass Unrest in Russia, China, and Mexico              259
• A Great War                                           262
• Negotiating the Future in the Shadow of the Great War 270
• Which Way Forward?                                    276
• Conclusion                                            279
*A Few Good Books*                                      *281*

**CHAPTER 11**    The Ongoing Crisis of Global Order . . . . . . . . . **283**
1919–1948

• Struggles over Political Order in the Middle East and Asia   286
• A Communist Future?                                   290
• The Global Economy in the 1920s                       292
• The Collapse of the Post-War Order                    294
• War Without Limits                                    302
• Unraveling Empire as a Key to the Future              306
• Conclusion                                            308
*A Few Good Books*                                      *309*

**CHAPTER 12**     Hot Wars, Cold Wars, and Decolonization . . . . . 311
1942–1975

- Uncomfortable Allies Plan a New Order                          314
- Decolonization                                                 321
- Economic Development and Nonalignment: Three Worlds?           328
- Conclusion                                                     333
- *A Few Good Books*                                             *334*

**CHAPTER 13**     The Many Worlds of the Twenty-first Century . . . 337
1972–2012

- The Cold War and 1970s Political Realism                       339
- Transitions in the Communist World in the 1980s               346
- Towards a New Global Order                                     350
- Economic Integration                                          354
- Conclusion                                                     362
- *A Few Good Books*                                             *363*

Epilogue . . . . . . . . . . . . . . . . . . . . . . . . . . . . . . . . . . . . . . . . . . . . . . . 365
Credits . . . . . . . . . . . . . . . . . . . . . . . . . . . . . . . . . . . . . . . . . . . . . . 371
Index . . . . . . . . . . . . . . . . . . . . . . . . . . . . . . . . . . . . . . . . . . . . . . . 375

# List of Maps

MAP 1.1   Afro-Eurasian Trading Networks in the Fifteenth Century . . . . . . 20

MAP 1.2   Food Production Strategies in the Fifteenth Century. . . . . . . . . . 26

MAP 1.3   The Aztec Empire, ca. 1520. . . . . . . . . . . . . . . . . . . . . . 40

MAP 1.4   The Inca Empire ca. 1525 . . . . . . . . . . . . . . . . . . . . . . 41

MAP 2.1   Voyages of Exploration, 1485–1600 . . . . . . . . . . . . . . . . . 46

MAP 2.2   The Columbian Exchange. . . . . . . . . . . . . . . . . . . . . . . 54

MAP 2.3   European Activity in Asia, ca. 1650. . . . . . . . . . . . . . . . . . 61

MAP 3.1   Early Modern Afro-Eurasian Land Empires . . . . . . . . . . . . . . 68

MAP 3.2   The Islamic World in 1500. . . . . . . . . . . . . . . . . . . . . . . 73

MAP 3.3   Major Fortifications and Battles in Europe, 1450–1750 . . . . . . . . 80

MAP 4.1   Global Trade in the Seventeenth Century. . . . . . . . . . . . . . . 92

MAP 4.2   The Migration of Sugar Cane Cultivation . . . . . . . . . . . . . . . 99

MAP 4.3   Principal Commodities in Asian Trade, 1600–1750 . . . . . . . . . . . 103

MAP 5.1   Volume and Direction of the Transatlantic Slave Trade . . . . . . . . 118

MAP 5.2   China from the Ming to the Qing Dynasties . . . . . . . . . . . . . . 124

MAP 5.3   (a) The Seven Years' War; (b) The British Empire in 1763 . . . . . . . 136

MAP 6.1   Empires and Trade, ca. 1770. . . . . . . . . . . . . . . . . . . . . . 144

MAP 6.2   Empires and States in the Western Hemisphere, ca. 1830 . . . . . . . 160

MAP 6.3   Western Eurasia after Napoleon . . . . . . . . . . . . . . . . . . . . 165

MAP 7.1   World Population Growth, 1700–1900. . . . . . . . . . . . . . . . . 174

MAP 7.2   Industrialization in Britain to 1850. . . . . . . . . . . . . . . . . . 178

MAP 7.3   US Cotton Production and the Enslaved Population . . . . . . . . . . 183

MAP 8.1   Major Population Movements, 1500–1914 . . . . . . . . . . . . . . . 200

MAP 8.2   Germany: From Confederation to Empire . . . . . . . . . . . . . . . 206

MAP 8.3    Contraction of the Ottoman Empire . . . . . . . . . . . . . . . . . . . . . 208

MAP 9.1    Empires and World Trade, 1870–1914 . . . . . . . . . . . . . . . . . . . 228

MAP 9.2    The Expansion of Japanese Influence, 1870s–1930s . . . . . . . . . . 240

MAP 9.3    Sovereignty Claims in Africa, Early Twentieth Century. . . . . . . 245

MAP 10.1   Major Fields of Battle, 1914–45 . . . . . . . . . . . . . . . . . . . . . . . 256

MAP 10.2   (a) Europe in 1914; (b) Western Eurasia, 1914–23 . . . . . . . . . . 271

MAP 10.3   Revolution and Civil War in Russia. . . . . . . . . . . . . . . . . . . . . 278

MAP 11.1   Colonies and Mandates, 1939. . . . . . . . . . . . . . . . . . . . . . . . . 284

MAP 11.2   Countries on the Gold Standard, 1929–34 . . . . . . . . . . . . . . . . 296

MAP 11.3   Japan in China, 1931–45 . . . . . . . . . . . . . . . . . . . . . . . . . . . . 303

MAP 12.1   The Cold War. . . . . . . . . . . . . . . . . . . . . . . . . . . . . . . . . . . . 312

MAP 12.2   The Partition of India . . . . . . . . . . . . . . . . . . . . . . . . . . . . . . 322

MAP 12.3   Decolonization in Africa and Asia, 1945–75 . . . . . . . . . . . . . . 327

MAP 13.1   The World in 2015 . . . . . . . . . . . . . . . . . . . . . . . . . . . . . . . . 338

MAP 13.2   The Oil Crisis, 1973–74 . . . . . . . . . . . . . . . . . . . . . . . . . . . . . 342

MAP 13.3   The Global Distribution of Wealth in the Early
           Twenty-first Century . . . . . . . . . . . . . . . . . . . . . . . . . . . . . . 358

# Acknowledgments

We are fortunate to enjoy in our professional lives the generous encouragement and insightful intellectual support of many fellow teachers and scholars. We are particularly indebted to our past and present colleagues at Saint Joseph's University: Amber Abbas, Lisa Baglione, Melissa Chakars, Christopher Close, Emily Hage, Jane Hooper, Erik Huneke, Kazuya Fukuoka, Susan Liebell, Elizabeth Morgan, and Brian Yates all read numerous drafts in various stages of disarray. Thank you also to Brian Ulrich, Shippensburg University; Peter Worthing, Texas Christian University; Michael G. Vann, California State University, Sacramento; Erin E. O'Connor, Bridgewater State University; William E. Burns, George Washington University; James De Lorenzi, CUNY John Jay College; Bedross Der Matossian, University of Nebraska/Lincoln; Cecilia Miller, Wesleyan University; Isa Blumi, Centre for Area Studies, Leipzig University; Andrew D. Devenney, Grand Valley State University; Robert Cliver, Humboldt State University; Thomas Sanders, US Naval Academy; Chad Ross, East Carolina University; and the anonymous reviewers of our manuscript.

For help with particular queries, we'd like to thank Michael Chang, Jane Hooper, Jeffrey Hyson, Susan Liebell, Randall Miller, Bryan McCann, and Fritz Schwaller.

Several sections of students in History 154 "road-tested" drafts of the manuscript, and their comments and reactions helped make it a better book.

Administrative support from Susan McFadden and Denise Thomas helped make sure things got where they needed to go.

Kelsey Kostelnik and Dale Pappas, both History majors at Saint Joseph's University, provided assistance during the research and writing phases of the book.

Charles Cavaliere, our editor at Oxford University Press, has been impassioned and enthusiastic about this project from its inception. It has been a delight to work with the entire staff at the Press.

Finally, the lines between work and home are rarely bright these days, and this project has been no exception. Rich feels particularly thankful for the support he received from Suzanne Cohen and Ben, Rose, and Nate Warren, each of whom contributed to the completion of this book in many ways. Jay wants to thank Susan Liebell, for contributing so much to this project both personally and professionally, to Mariel and Charlotte, for reminding how important it is to teach and why it matters, and to, Adam, Julia, and Eli for many kinds of support.

Finally, and as always, any errors of fact or interpretation remain solely the authors' responsibility.

# About the Authors

J ames Carter is Professor of History at Saint Joseph's University, in Philadelphia, and holds a PhD in Modern Chinese history from Yale University. He is the author of *Creating a Chinese Harbin* (Cornell, 2002) and *Heart of Buddha, Heart of China* (Oxford, 2010), among other publications. When not teaching Forging the Modern World, he writes about the history of cultural interactions between China and the West.

R ichard Warren is Professor of History at Saint Joseph's University, where he has served on the faculty since 1995. He is the author of numerous works on the political culture of modern Mexico, including *Vagrants and Citizens: Politics and the Masses in Mexico City from Colony to Republic* (Scholarly Resources, 2001).

# Introduction: Forging the Modern World

This is a book about history. It's important to point out from the start that when we say history, we don't mean "the past." Despite science fiction plots and the musings of some physicists about the possibilities of time travel, we're comfortable saying that the earth's past cannot change: what happened once cannot happen again. History, though—our understanding of the past—changes all the time. New sources are found, new methodologies develop, and new concerns about the human experience emerge as subjects for investigation. New histories result, and this is one of them.

The history that is *Forging the Modern World* emerged from a question: if we had only one history course that we could teach every university student, what would that course look like? Our answer had two key parts. The first was that we wanted to help students understand the development of the most important structures through which people around the world relate to each other: both the structures *and* the people who act within them are critical to the story we wanted to tell. The second was to pull back the curtain on what historical inquiry is so that our students could better understand the distinction between the past and history and could learn to analyze historical arguments (including those made by their instructors).

When we got the opportunity to design a course based on these ideas, we did not intend to write a book. However, conversations with colleagues and students led us to write one that would reflect the goals of the new course. You have before you the result. It's a relatively short book with ambitious goals that tries to stick to some basic ideas: focus on a limited set of arguments based on the best available evidence; explain assumptions and terms clearly; and trust that readers will use this book as a starting point, rather than an endpoint, in the exploration of world history.

## What is this Book About?

Why do we call this book—and the course that produced it—"Forging the Modern World"? The title is an important place to start understanding anything you read, watch, or hear; so why did we choose these words: forging, modern, and world? The last word, "World," indicates that we are writing a history of the entire world, as a unit, not of any particular place. We don't mention all areas evenly: some parts of the world get more attention than others, and we leave out many important events. Nevertheless, the argument we try to make is one that applies to the entire globe.

"Forging," which has become shorthand for the course itself, is the least common word in the title. We like it because it conveys the sense of active creation that applies to both historical actors and historians like ourselves. A smith in a forge takes raw materials and uses skill and hard work to shape them—within limits—into something new. In this same way, people in different times and places have shaped their world through their decisions and actions. Karl Marx, whom we meet later in the book, once wrote "Men make their own history, but they do not make it as they please; they do not make it under self-selected circumstances, but under circumstances existing already, given and transmitted from the past." In other words, everyone affects the world, but circumstances limit how and how much. This book looks at the decisions, actions, and contexts of people in the world and how those things created—*forged*—the modern world.

We, as authors, are forging something too: creating a history out of sources, interpretations, our own experience and training, and the goals of the book. We're also limited. We don't have access to every source, and we're not experts in every part of the world or every time period—not even close. Within these limits, we've crafted an argument and supported it with sources, forging our own modern world. There are other ways it could have been created. You may not agree with every choice we have made in the way we present our evidence. If you're reading this in a class, it is certain that your instructor and classmates will disagree with some of the decisions we made. We think our arguments are sound, but it's just as important to make the point that historical arguments are not received truths that exist outside of time and space: they are created by historians.

## The Modern World

And what about "modern"? In everyday speech, this word means something like "new" or "current." A radio in 1920, a television in 1940, a desktop computer in 1980—each of these was considered modern, although none of them are looked at that way now. The term "modern" in our title refers to something else though. Starting sometime in the last few hundred years (exactly when is hard to pin down, as it happened at different times in different places), the concept of modernity came to be used to define characteristics of certain societies that distinguished them from those that existed in earlier eras, and particular characteristics of the world as a whole that distinguished a new historical era from what came before. Coming up with a precise definition of "modern" that applies to all places and in all circumstances is impossible; and we argue instead that there is a con-stellation of features that, taken as a whole, represent the modern world. Some are more, or less, present in any given place or time, but overall these seem to us a good list of what separates modern societies from what came before.

It has been said that there is nothing new under the sun, implying that some struggles and joys humans experience today are no different than what people have experienced throughout time. We ourselves, as authors, can be accused of "presentism": seeing the past through the lens of the present. We'd respond in part by saying that the present is the only place where humans actually live—we're stuck here, at least for now! But less abstractly, it does not diminish the grandeur, complexity, and variety of the distant past to say that in fundamental ways—politically, economically, and socially—human society looks very different today than it did only a short time ago. What are some of these essential differences?

## A Belief in Progress

A fundamental (and tricky) feature of "modern" societies is the belief among people, mostly elites, that they were thinking and acting in ways that were dis-tinct—not just different but fundamentally changed—from their predecessors. If people correctly understood what needed to be done and how it could be achieved, these changes would move society toward a better future. In modern societies, people have tended to believe that human action could and, with proper under-standing of what needed to be done, *would* improve societies.

One way to make this clear is to think about the way the term "backward" came to be used to criticize other societies (or policies in one's own society). The belief in progress was tied to ideas about technology and material resources: modern societies had both the physical stuff and the ways of thinking to create progress, while "pre-modern" societies would not progress until they acquired both of these things. If you didn't have the right technology, or the right mindset, to move forward to the next stage, then you were behind, facing or moving "back-ward." The idea that there is a single path and direction through history and toward the future, and that all societies are moving along it like pieces on a game board, is a common feature of how modern people view the world. This optimistic outlook overlooks many of the disastrous events and outcomes of world history over the last centuries. As we will explore in this book, those who possess political and economic power tend to overestimate the universality of their claims to truth and the justice of their decisions while dismissing (perhaps as "backward") those who disagree with them, especially those who are poor or culturally different.

## Production of Knowledge

To support this position, modern people used particular forms of knowledge to assert that their ways of understanding the world were fundamentally superior to those of earlier generations. Science became the quintessentially modern form of knowledge. Observation, hypothesis, and experiment produced results from which to better understand cause-and-effect relationships rooted in the natural world, not in the supernatural, spiritual, or religious realms that had been primary in earlier eras. Modern people came to think of themselves as practicing rational inquiry and using the scientific method to solve all kinds of problems, while pre-modern peoples were governed more by superstition and tradition. That isn't to say that modern people were always rational, or even that they were more rational than people in the past, but rather that a general belief emerged that the world is governed by rules that can (in theory) be understood and applied equally to all things.

These ideas could be applied not only to the natural world but to the social world as well. Egypt five thousand years ago, or China three thousand years ago, or Greece twenty-five hundred years ago, were technologically, socially, and politically sophisticated societies but they were not "modern" because those in power did not typically base their decisions—or justify their rule or political organization—on the methods and techniques of scientific inquiry. Explanations for the social order, or government, or natural phenomena were often sought in supernatural authorities, in the inertia of custom or tradition, or in the private deliberations of an elite few. In contrast, by the middle of the nineteenth century, those with the greatest amounts of economic and political power throughout most of the world tended to make political and economic decisions based on claims of progress and reason, and a belief that the world is understandable through rational, scientific inquiry.

## Global Interconnections

Connections between and among different parts of the world—even parts far away from one another—are not new. Ancient Rome and Ancient China, for instance, traded with one another more than two thousand years ago. However, the quantity and quality of global connections have increased sharply in the last several centuries. In 1400, direct communication between China and North America was nonexistent. In 1600, letters from India to Europe took months to reach their destination, if they arrived at all. Just a few decades ago, communication beyond one's own town was frequently slow, expensive, or both.

Today, as we finish writing this book, we will receive dozens of emails, texts, and maybe even phone calls from around the world, all instantly delivered at low cost. This instant communication has enormous impact. Stock markets in New York rise and fall based on news from Beijing. Factory workers in Vietnam might be laid off because of an economic downturn in the United States or offered more work when reports arrive of a natural disaster in Indonesia. Gasoline prices in London can rise overnight on word of political unrest in Venezuela. In our global village, what happens *anywhere* can affect people and places *everywhere*.

Alongside increased global communication, patterns of mobility have also changed. Accelerating movement across the world fundamentally altered how people live. In one day, many of us travel farther than most people moved in their entire lives two centuries ago. This mobility matters: clothes at your local store cost less than they did a few decades ago because they can be produced at lower cost in other countries and shipped cheaply to the United States. Likewise, jobs at factories in the United States or Europe might disappear when their products can be made less expensively in another country. Workers may move thousands of miles in pursuit of new jobs. The effects of this great mobility can degrade the natural environment and disrupt the social one. Taken together, the movement of ideas, goods, and people across the globe are essential parts of how most people experience the modern world.

## Production and Distribution of Resources

The interconnectedness of our world changes how resources are produced and distributed. Economic, social, cultural, and intellectual resources have never been evenly distributed across the planet; we will analyze the reasons why. In 1400, material resources were arranged much differently than they are in the modern world. Differences in climate, geography, and technology made certain goods and commodities uniquely available in specific places. China was the main place in the world that produced silk and porcelain. The best cotton textiles came from India. Spices such as pepper and cinnamon were unique to Southeast Asia. Gold was concentrated in Africa and India.

Reflecting this distribution of resources, the wealthiest parts of the world then were probably in East and South Asia; the world's richest man was probably the Emperor of Mali in Africa. This distribution influenced the growth of trade routes crisscrossing the Indian Ocean to connect the unique products and commodities found along its rim with consumers. Overland trade routes brought the wealth of the Indian Ocean to the Asian, African, and European interiors. Other resources, too, were differently distributed than they are today. China had a distinct advantage over other regions in shipbuilding and engineering. Islamic empires generated new insights in mathematics and astronomy. Indigenous societies in the Americas produced agricultural surpluses without the benefit of imported technologies.

By the twentieth century, that pattern had changed. Material wealth was concentrated in North America and Western Europe, where the world's richest nations were found. The gap between the amounts of wealth controlled by residents of some regions compared to others had also increased dramatically so that the wealth of the average person in a rich country could be one hundred times that of an average person in a poor country. These same wealthy states exercised political control over much of the world and dominated scientific and cultural production as well. What changed? How? Why? Partly, political elites made decisions about how they wished to preserve their power. Partly, individuals and groups pursued their interests given the best information available to them. Both of these actions often led to unintended consequences in the long-term distribution of resources.

## Economic Organization

Technologies and economic productivity changed too, at different rates in different places, much of it having to do with circumstance. Although manufactured goods like porcelain or textiles were important to pre-modern long-distance trading networks, most economic production was on a small scale, locally produced and consumed. The power to grow crops, acquire commodities, finish goods, and transport it all to market was provided by human or animal muscle, wind or water power. Most producers were only indirectly linked to global, or even regional, economies. Barter was common; sophisticated economic transactions were not.

By the twentieth century, most goods—industrial and agricultural— were mass produced using machines powered by fossil fuels. Coal was of limited use in pre-industrial societies, but once steam engines spread, improving productivity, some coal-rich regions became economic powerhouses. Access to coal became a vital strategic and economic factor, although certainly not the only one, that explains where and how industrialization occurred.

For reasons and in ways we will demonstrate, political and economic elites in the industrializing zones of Europe and North America used emerging disparities in technology to redistribute wealth from other parts of the world to themselves and their countries. India, Africa, and Southeast Asia still produced great wealth in the nineteenth century, but more of it came to be controlled by the populations of Europe and North America. Further shifts in the amount and distribution of the world's wealth characterized the twentieth century and this continues to our own day, as an accelerating pace of economic and technological change became one of the defining features of the modern world. Charting and explaining these shifts is thus another of this book's main aims.

## Political Organization

Try boarding a plane traveling from Atlanta to Tokyo without a passport: you'll fail. A valid passport, issued by a recognized nation-state, enables you to travel because citizenship—belonging to a nation-state—is an essential component of modern identity. Today, the landmass of the entire world is divided up into nation-states. The only exception, Antarctica, is unclaimed by any nation—by an agreement among nations. The ability to live, work, travel, raise children, receive medical care, express yourself, and communicate with others is influenced by citizenship. Nearly every aspect of life on earth today depends on nation-states and the relations among them.

Six hundred years ago, there were no nation-states of the kind that exist in our time. Political organization in the world varied greatly, including large empires and kingdoms, smaller principalities or duchies, free cities and city states, and many others. Even if you lived in one of the large empires like Ming China or Mali connections to your family and village were still tangible in ways that more abstract associations to a larger political entity could never be. There is nothing natural or inevitable about the rise of nation-states, but they are a fundamental fixture of the modern world. Defining and understanding the characteristics, origins, development, and consequences of nation-states is essential to understanding modernity. This book traces the ebb and flow of political organization over several centuries, through waves of empire building and reorganization, and finally—and only in the twentieth century—to the domination of nation-states that characterizes the modern world.

## Sources and Methods

This book is not "the" history of the modern world; it is one among many possible histories to be written on the topic. There are many different arguments to be made about the past, depending on an author's goals, perspectives, and sources. This is why so many books—so many histories—may be written about a single event. Thousands of books have been written about the US Civil War, but they differ dramatically from one another. Books written today about the war differ from ones written fifty or one hundred years ago. Books about military tactics are not like economic studies or ones focusing on the role of slavery as a cause of the war. Even two books on the same subject, written at the same time, may be quite different. Can only one be "true" or "right"?

The differences among historical works come from how historians make history. (Yes, historians make history—though they do not make it up.) Like the forging imagery of the title, the historian combines raw materials and expertise to create histories. The historian's raw materials are the records that people have left behind; and the forging process is how those records are acquired, analyzed, and put together. There are many different ways to do this. Some are more interesting, more creative, and more complex than others (and some of them don't work at all), but they all require the historian to gather and interpret sources and to construct an argument about the past from them. Before we go further, then, let's explain what we mean by evidence and by argument and look at some of the factors involved in putting them together.

Historical evidence is anything that helps us understand the past. For the most part, historians work with two kinds of evidence: primary and secondary sources. (A third category, tertiary sources, usually refers to reference works like dictionaries and encyclopedias.) Primary and secondary sources are used differently, although they can overlap, and sometimes it can be hard to distinguish between them. In some cases, the same source can be *either* primary or secondary, depending on how it is used.

Primary sources are typically produced in the time period being studied. Written documents are the most common kind, but photographs, paintings, sound recordings or music, buildings, and other objects can also be primary sources. Written primary sources include letters, government documents, memoirs, diaries, or any other document produced at, or near, the time of the events under scrutiny. A good rule of thumb for deciding what constitutes written primary sources is that they are generated by people who do not know how the subjects they are writing about will turn out at the moment they are writing. It is also important to understand that historians are limited by primary sources or their absence: a great idea about the past cannot be turned into history unless primary sources can be located and examined. Given that much of the record of the past has disappeared without a trace, and that many people, even entire societies, left little evidence of their time on earth, one begins to understand the limits of history.

Secondary sources can, like primary sources, be sounds, images, the printed word, or other kinds of objects. Usually these are not produced at the time being studied but sometime later, and they typically use primary sources (and other secondary sources) to make their arguments. The most common of these would be books or essays. Most of the books in the history section of bookstores or online retailers are secondary sources: works of history that interpret primary sources to make an argument. Historical arguments begin when researchers ask questions about the past and then search for and collect both primary and secondary sources, analyze those sources, compare the results of their research to the work of others who have asked similar questions, and then offer their conclusions about the best way to answer the question.

An example can illustrate both different kinds of sources and how historical arguments get conducted. Let's take the sinking of the *Titanic* in 1912, an event that has been studied in many different ways for more than a century. A letter written by a passenger the night the ship sank, or the captain's log of one of the rescue ships, would be primary sources. So would the distress calls and other communications among different ships on the North Atlantic that night as well as blueprints and plans for the vessel, weather reports from that evening, photographs of survivors, passenger lists, artifacts from the ship—or the ship itself. All of these primary sources can help us understand the events of that night, their causes and effects.

When historians gather these sources and make arguments about what happened and why, they produce secondary sources. The first book about *Titanic* came out within a year of the sinking, and hundreds have been printed since then. Each uses some of the sources available to make an argument. No single work could use all of the potential sources that exist at any given moment, and sometimes new sources are discovered. In addition, the interests of authors and the audience for books about history also change over time. Some authors and audiences are interested in the history of shipbuilding and technology and others in the social lives of the passengers. The discovery of the ship's wreckage in the 1990s led to new theories about how the ship sank. Histories written before that would be different because their authors did not have access to this source. The release of a successful fictionalized movie about the ship's passengers spurred a new round of research and writing on the real event and drove up sales of different kinds of books about it.

To understand better the idea that sources might be either primary or secondary sources, depending on their use, let us take the example of books written about the history of Native Americans. These books might be used as secondary sources for understanding the expansion of the United States in the nineteenth century because these books use primary sources and the authors' analytical skills to make arguments about that topic. However, if we take a different topic— say, how portrayals of Native Americans changed over a certain period of time— history books themselves could become primary sources.

Which are more useful for understanding the past—primary or secondary sources? The answer depends on what you are looking for. People sometimes assume that primary sources are better or more accurate than secondary sources and that is why they are called "primary" sources. This interpretation misunderstands the distinction between primary and secondary sources. Primary sources often convey immediacy with a literary quality that secondary sources lack; but even the most detailed and beautifully written eyewitness accounts contain a very limited perspective on events, often lack important information available to others living at the time, and may even be untrue by design or unintended error. As an example of the challenge of primary sources, let's think again about the US Civil War.

If you were to read, as we did, the diary of a Confederate soldier who participated in the Battle of Gettysburg, you would discover that on July 1, 1863, his unit took 3,000 prisoners and drove the Union soldiers out of the town. If you stopped your research here, you might conclude that the Confederate Army was on its way to a quick victory (and many people did think this was the case at the end of the battle's first day). But this source gives only a brief portrait of events that this soldier believed to be true at the time of writing, followed by a compelling description of what it was like for him to participate in battle. Despite what this source describes, the Union Army won the battle, turning the tide of the war in its favor. This primary source might tell us many things of value about how a soldier lived and fought and thought, but this snapshot of one day's events does not reveal the bigger picture.

Using multiple primary sources and comparing them with one another helps get a more complete picture, but does not solve the problem of understanding the past in and of itself. To illustrate this limitation, let us imagine that you want to write the history of a college's sophomore class experience. If every person in that class—hundreds or thousands of students—kept a diary of what life at that university was like, they would produce a wealth of primary sources. Yet, even if they all tried to tell the truth, there would be major disagreements. What one student found unbearable (location, food, Greek life, academic requirements, sports), another may describe as the best part of college. If you rely on just one of these sources, you may get a view of college life that is unrecognizable to another student. Yet all of these diaries are eyewitness, first-person accounts: primary sources. The historian's challenge is deciding how to use all of these sources to understand life at this college, assessing the collective experience of students, rather than trying to figure out which individual perspective is the singular historical truth.

The diaries of college sophomores would certainly include entries whose accuracy or objectivity you might doubt. There is much to think about in approaching this issue of bias in sources. The concept of bias is important but often misunderstood. Sometimes, a source will be clearly biased, that is, skewed to a predetermined conclusion regardless of any consideration of the evidence. Adolf Hitler's writing about racial difference would be a clear example of this type of bias: if we understand Hitler's assumptions, we should know, as readers, not to accept his opinions on Jewish culture at face value. More often, though, bias refers to unintentional assumptions and presuppositions that shape how an author interprets events. A newspaper report from the United States in the 1950s might contain observations or use assumptions—about different races, ethnicities, political or social groups, for instance—that would seem odd or even outrageous in the twenty-first century, but they might have been typical for the time. In the same way, a French missionary's account of Native American society written in the 1600s would most certainly describe Huron social practices in ways that were influenced by the author's French and Catholic upbringing. These sources can be valuable for the historian, but to take advantage of them, one has to work hard to account for how each author's worldview affects what was written and how it was written.  In this way, a source might be less valuable for learning about Huron social organization than for understanding French missionary attitudes towards Native Americans. Bias is less often a conscious attempt by an author to lie and more often the way in which deeply held perspectives and expectations shape the way an author writes.

*All* sources are biased. It is impossible to be human and not have presuppositions or a point of view. It's tempting, because of this, to throw up our hands and say that all sources are just opinions. But the fact that all sources contain bias does not make them invalid or useless...or equal. One of our jobs as readers is to assess these sources and their biases, how important those biases are, and how they affect what knowledge and information we can glean from the sources. We try always to learn as much as possible about who created sources and what their motivations were—goals, audience, background, worldview, and so forth. For primary sources, we often do what is called "close reading," collecting everything possible from the sources themselves. For written sources, we take note of the organization, vocabulary, symbols, references, arguments, and suppositions. As we gather information about individual sources, we begin to compare them with other sources to build the base of evidence from which we will draw our own arguments and conclusions.

Just as all sources are biased, all readers are biased as well; and, as with sources, this bias is not simply a bad thing. Our biases are the sum total of all the life experiences that we carry with us, including our ability to form thoughts with language. They are the things that allow us to learn in the first place. But, reader bias can also affect how we evaluate sources in negative ways. For instance, if you know the race, gender, age, nationality, or social class of an author, do you take him or her less (or more) seriously? In the same way that we must make sure we understand the limits within which our sources are working, we need to undertake the (much harder) work of understanding our own limits as readers. Good historical inquiry means examining our own assumptions and preconceptions about the past and adjusting them if new evidence suggests that they need adjusting.

In this process, secondary sources become essential to historical inquiry. The authors of secondary sources benefit from hindsight, which can offer a perspective that primary sources lack. Secondary sources can combine, evaluate, and synthesize primary sources and weigh them against other secondary sources. A good secondary source provides balance, insight, and convincing analysis. Nonetheless, historians need to approach secondary sources with as much care as primary sources. They need to analyze the creator of the source and the context and motivations under which it was created. What do authors claim they are going to prove? Does the evidence they present adequately support the argument? For example, an author may present a portrait of life in the United States during the Great Depression using examples almost entirely from Chicago. The book may be a compelling analysis of life in Chicago, but we must be cautious about leaping to the conclusion that this study can apply to life in *all* cities during the same time period, or to other time periods and places. In secondary sources, we also look for transparency and reproducibility. Credible historical writing makes it easy for the reader to figure out what sources the author used, how they are used, and where those sources came from. Often that information is contained in notes, a bibliography, and perhaps even a separate discussion of how sources were located and used. Other researchers and readers can then track down the author's sources for themselves to confirm their content and verify that the author is using the sources responsibly. Casual readers often skip the documentation contained in notes and bibliographies, but they can be a key means to assess the value of secondary sources.

Not all books about the past are works of history as we understand the term. For instance, if an author's main idea can never be proved wrong, the book is not really a history. What does that mean? History depends on evidence and analysis. If an author makes the argument, for example, that God wanted the United States to become independent from Great Britain and that's why the War of Independence turned out the way it did, or that the residents of the Maya city state of Palenque were space travelers who abandoned earth one thousand years ago, these claims are not based on the kinds of evidence historians use. There are no documents that articulate God's preference in the War of Independence or the itineraries of extraterrestrials (at least not yet). Without a way to prove or disprove these claims using historical research methods, these are not historical arguments.

## Practicing History

All these concerns and qualifications have the potential to overwhelm readers looking for an introduction to world history so we decided that much of the work we've done collecting, assessing, and interpreting sources should be moved to the background rather than the foreground. Throughout the book, we provide readers with what we think are the best interpretations of all the evidence available, but we do not provide a very detailed roadmap of how we arrived at these conclusions. In the language of math tests, we haven't always "shown our work" and there are very few footnotes in the book. This simplicity is important, but we also want to emphasize that history is created by historians, so in each chapter we've focused on a case or two to show in detail the way historians work with primary and secondary sources.

Sometimes we've done this by highlighting recent historical research that has challenged, changed, or enhanced our understanding of the past and thus made new history. For example, we present details about newly discovered sources (like data from slave cemeteries in the Caribbean, or declassified documents from the Cold War) or especially innovative interpretations of sources. In these sections we've carefully cited the work of our colleagues, enabling readers to find their original research for more information or further explanation.

In other places, we've taken an issue on which historians disagree and laid out the terms of the debate. We will take a side in some of these debates; in others we will just point out the different arguments and why historians disagree. Our goal here is to illustrate how even scholars with access to the same sources can come to different conclusions on a topic. These tend to be big and controversial topics, often with contemporary political considerations and with great implications for our understanding of the past and the present. Some examples include the importance of slavery to the Industrial Revolution, or the scale of population decline after Europeans arrived in the Americas. In these cases, we present some of the competing arguments and cite books and articles where readers can learn more about them. These footnotes are not comprehensive but are designed to point readers to important original sources for the debates we describe.

By taking this approach we risk giving the impression that these are the only areas where history is controversial or innovative. This is certainly not so. Everything we know about the past is the product of historical research, and almost every sentence in the book could have been footnoted and expanded on. By highlighting just a few instances of how historians practice their craft, we hope to demonstrate that history is not a series of received truths while still writing a concise and readable introduction to a vast topic.

## Time and Space

In thinking about history, we often refer to memorable chronological markers—important years, days, generations, or epochs: 1492; 1776; December 7, 1941; and "the sixties," for example. However, the study of world history challenges us to recognize both the power and the limits of convenient chronological markers. Let's take 1776 and the Declaration of Independence as an example. The declaration didn't start or end a war. That summer day when the declaration was signed, it certainly didn't matter to the Emperor of China or the Sultan of the Ottoman Empire or even to many people living in North America. This event clearly matters somehow for world history, but knowing exactly how, for whom, and when means that our job barely begins with knowing that the US Declaration of Independence was signed in 1776.

And what is 1776 anyway? What most people in Philadelphia, where the Declaration was signed, called 1776 AD—*Anno Domini,* Latin for "In the Year of

Our Lord"—was the year 5536 in the Hebrew calendar, 1768 in Ethiopia, 1154 in Persia, 1189 by the Islamic calendar, 2320 by the Buddhist calendar, An'ei 5 in Japan, and Qianlong 41 (or the Wood Goat year 4472) in China, just to name a few. Christian thinkers developed the designation *Anno Domini* about 1,500 years ago as a means of dating events from the presumed birth of Jesus Christ, adding this to a calendar system first adopted by the Romans. In English, dates preceding the presumed birth of Christ came to be designated BC: "Before Christ."

All calendars are frames of reference, marking time from some important past event—perhaps the reign of a ruler, the mythical beginning of time, or a religious event. Most of the world, for most of its history, has not been Christian, so perhaps this calendar is not the optimal way to organize historical time. For that matter, not even all Christian calendars agree (and contemporary evidence suggests that Jesus was most likely born sometime between 3 BC and 1 AD).

To further complicate matters, different calendars measure the year differently. Whereas many calendars measure the moon's orbit around the earth, others keep track of the earth's orbit around the sun, or a combination of the two. Years can last anywhere from (about) 354 days to (about) 365 days. Without agreement on how long a year is or when to start counting them, the task of a historian seems pretty difficult. Fortunately, we don't need to weigh in on any astronomical, mathematical, or theological debates about time. For this book, we consider the calendar a tool that allows us to establish when events happened in relation to each other. What is most important about the dates in this book is their usefulness to readers. So, how will we mark time in this book?

We have chosen to note dates throughout this book using the Gregorian calendar, a sixteenth-century revision of Julius Caesar's solar calendar, which has grown since the eighteenth century to become one of the most widely accepted international standards for communications about time. As an acknowledgment of this shared past and common experience, we will refer to most dates in this book as belonging to the Common Era, written as CE, rather than AD (retaining the convenience of the Gregorian dating system without its religious overtones). However, in this book, because nearly all the dates we mention are from the Common Era, we will not typically use any letters after the numerical date. On those occasions when we note events prior to the Common Era, we will use the label BCE—Before the Common Era. If you are accustomed to seeing dates with the labels AD and BC attached to them, keep in mind that the dates themselves are not changed, just the way they are labeled: an attempt to recognize difference while still embracing the links and shared experiences among people and places.

A similar concern about the portability of dates across cultures and countries shapes the construction of the book's chapters. Time periods like "Victorian Era" or the "Age of Revolution" depend upon specific geographical, social, and cultural limits: they aren't universal. One way that we attempt to align our readers with the global context of this book is by creating less familiar starting and ending points for each chapter and to overlap them from chapter to chapter. Each chapter begins with a pair of vignettes, marking a start and end date for the chapter. The main importance of the events and people of those vignettes is symbolic, tying together the themes around which we have constructed that chapter. By overlapping the dates each chapter covers, we want to emphasize that history is not a linear progression of events: it's a series of interrelated and variable events that affect different parts of the world at different times and in different ways. The dates, and the vignettes that go with them, alert readers to themes that will be addressed, and also foreground our intention to move away from any effort to create in each chapter a self-contained historical epoch.

World history also challenges our ideas about geography. Different groups used different names to refer to the same place, place names changed over time, and even geographic markers that may appear objective are themselves historical artifacts injected with cultural and ideological meaning. Think about the term "Middle East," for example, which is used daily in the US media to describe a vast and vaguely defined part of the world that is sometimes stretched from the eastern Mediterranean to the Arabian Sea and beyond. The term entered common usage only in the early twentieth century and only in some parts of the world. We have tried to balance historical accuracy in using place names with the need to help our readers find things on maps so that they may be compared over time. This means that, at times, we will use multiple terms to refer to the same place, or that we will use terms that carry heavy, even controversial, cultural and ideological meaning.

Generally, we use the current common Anglicized spellings of cities, countries, and other political geography, omitting accents and diacritics unless they are present in the English usage (for example, Mexico does not have an accent, but Potosí does). For Chinese, we generally employ the Pinyin form of naming. We have taken a similar approach to the labels we attach to people and things throughout the book. For proper names and transliterations, we have attempted to adhere to conventions that would make the text both acceptable to specialists and accessible to non-specialists. But it would be fair for any of our readers to question the choices we made about naming and spelling, and to decide if they would have made different ones, and if so, why. Our hope is that questions about naming conventions proceed hand in hand with other discussions about the nature of historical events and processes.

## Recommended Reading

Writing this book has reminded us of our limits as researchers and writers. We have read remarkable works by our colleagues past and present, which push the boundaries of historical inquiry, from microhistory (the intensive study of a single place or issue) to "Big" or "Deep" history (which asks questions on enormous chronological and geographical scales). We have read masterful monographs and benefited from the ambitious projects of scholars who have turned their attentions to grand historical questions. We could not have finished this project were it not for the trust we place in our readers, especially the students and instructors who will use this book, knowing that they will understand that any individual text can only be a starting point for engaging the history of the modern world. We assume that you will have ready access to the Internet while you read this book. We encourage you to use it to find out more about the people, events, and arguments we present while you are working your way through the chapters that follow. We also want you to read what our colleagues have written, especially those who have different approaches and draw different conclusions from our own. To help our readers, we end each chapter with a list of "a few good books" related to themes addressed in the chapter. By no means comprehensive, the lists are simply attempts to point readers to engaging, thought-provoking works so that they can continue the journey of historical inquiry.

## Historical Inquiry as a Hopeful Practice

For us, being historians is an exercise in hope. Broad trends, covering large areas and long periods of time, are the stuff of world history. The enormous, abstract forces that shape history can make individual lives seem insignificant and individual actions appear irrelevant. Yet, a premise of this book is that historical outcomes happen because (although not *only* because) of human agency—people make choices. Given our interest in the place of human agency in history, you will find in the pages that follow both analysis of large abstract processes and many stories about individual actions and decisions. Sometimes, the actions of one individual can have enormous consequences. More often, groups of people bring about change. Human beings are not just passengers on a planet hurtling through space. The modern world is, within a set of material limits, a human creation.

In counterpoint, rarely are single human beings responsible for fundamental changes in world history. When Christopher Columbus (1451–1506) sailed from Spain to the Caribbean, he set in motion changes far beyond anyone's expectations at the time. The specific choices he made mattered enormously, but he was not the only person of similar background and motivation travelling in the Atlantic Ocean during that time period. If Columbus had not embarked on, or survived, his transatlantic crossing, someone else would have, sooner or later. Columbus's actions changed the world, yet it would be wrong to conclude that had he not lived the Americas and Afro-Eurasia would have remained unknown to one another. To take another aspect of this phenomenon, we can look at the case of Mohandas K. Gandhi (1869–1948), the activist for Indian independence. One of the most famous quotes about historical agency ever is attributed to Gandhi—"Be the change that you wish to see in the world"—and we can certainly say that the transition to independent nation-states in South Asia was shaped in large part by Gandhi's hand; but the thoughts and actions of millions of others also contributed to this particular historical outcome. A single person can change the world, to be sure, but always in the context of other events and other people.

This discussion of agency leads us to one last distinguishing characteristic of historical inquiry: the concept of contingency. We believe that our job as historians is to present the possibilities that existed in any given historical situation, not derive laws that can predict the future. We believe that the path that led to the predominant models of political organization and economic activity in the modern world could not have been predicted but that they can be explained. To do so requires us to consider the entire world, even if we do not cover all parts of it equally, or equally well. It would be a fool's errand to try to account for every event that contributed to these outcomes. These pages don't detail every event—even every important event—that has occurred across the globe, nor do they emphasize equally each of the world's regions and distinct histories. Nonetheless, our geographic scope is global. We are trying to explain how a world of distinct human traditions became increasingly interconnected, what the connections looked like, and why some connections, and not others, came to predominate in the modern world.

## A Few Good Books

Joyce Oldham Appleby, Lynn Avery Hunt, and Margaret C. Jacob. *Telling the Truth about History.* New York: W.W. Norton and Co., 1995.

Marc Bloch. *The Historian's Craft: Reflections on the Nature and Uses of History and the Techniques and Methods of Those Who Write It.* New York: Vintage, 1964.

R. G. Collingwood. *The Idea of History.* Reprint. Oxford, England: Oxford University Press, 2004.

Jared Diamond. *Guns, Germs, and Steel: The Fates of Human Societies.* New York: W.W. Norton and Co., 1997.

Mark T. Gilderhus. *History and Historians: A Historiographical Introduction.* 7th edition. Upper Saddle River, NJ: Pearson, 2009.

J. R. McNeill and William H. McNeill. *The Human Web. A Bird's-Eye View of World History.* New York: W.W. Norton and Co., 2003.

**(RIGHT) TRIBUTE GIRAFFE FROM BENGAL WITH KEEPER, CHINA.** The Chinese fleets led by Zheng He obtained a giraffe in India in 1414, but the transaction illustrates much wider trade networks connecting East Asia, South Asia, and East Africa. The animal had come originally from Malindi, in today's Kenya, as a gift to the court in Bengal. Zheng He purchased the animal and shipped it back to the Chinese emperor. Silk scroll paintings like this one memorialized the splendor of the royal menagerie.

**(BOTTOM) AFONSO DE ALBUQUERQUE'S RHINOCEROS AS IMAGINED BY ALBRECHT DÜRER.** Albrecht Dürer (1471–1528) produced this woodcut in Nuremberg, in today's Germany, based on reports, and perhaps drawings, of the rhinoceros that Afonso de Albuquerque sent to Portugal from South Asia. Dürer never saw the live animal, yet for hundreds of years this drawing became the idea of what rhinos looked like for many Europeans.

# The Many Worlds of the Fifteenth Century

## 1405–1510

On a hot July morning in 1405, a fleet of some three hundred vessels weighed anchor from the Chinese city of Nanjing, then the most populous city in the world. Sailing down the Yangzi River past Suzhou—a city that reminded the thirteenth-century merchant Marco Polo (1254–1324) of his home in Venice on the Italian peninsula—this "treasure fleet" included the largest ships ever built, bigger than any humans would build for another five hundred years. Admiral Zheng He (1371–1433), a Muslim from the southwestern region of the empire, led the fleet into the South China Sea and across Southeast Asia before reaching the kingdom of Calicut in southwestern India, long a trade destination for the Chinese. The fleet returned to Calicut three years later where crew members witnessed the installation of a new hereditary Hindu ruler. Between 1405 and 1433, seven voyages brought thousands of Chinese sailors across the Indian Ocean as far as East Africa and Arabia. The voyages' commercial, diplomatic, and strategic accomplishments are symbolized by the gift of a giraffe for the Emperor's menagerie, acquired in Bengal from African emissaries on their own trade mission. China's Yongle Emperor (1360–1424) spon- sored these impressive voyages to project the dynasty's political and economic authority, both within its own empire and abroad, but in the early 1430s, the voyages of the Chinese treasure fleets ceased.

During the same era, on the far western tip of Europe, Prince Henry (1394–1460), a son of the Portuguese king, financed a series of expeditions into the Atlantic Ocean. Over the course of the fifteenth century, Portuguese seafaring led to the establishment of plantations on islands in the Atlantic Ocean and trading posts on the west coast of Africa. The wealth these expeditions brought directly to Portugal, including gold from Africa and sugar from Madeira Island, inspired additional expe- ditions. By the end of the fifteenth century, Portuguese navigators had rounded the southern tip of Africa and reached the same Kingdom of Calicut that Zheng He had visited—from the opposite direction—earlier in the century.

**MAP 1.1** Afro-Eurasian Trading Networks in the Fifteenth Century

Portuguese vessels were small compared to the immense Chinese ships, but Portuguese caravels could withstand the rigors of the open ocean while remaining maneuverable in shallow coastal waters. In 1497, four ships with fewer than two hundred men left Portugal under Vasco da Gama's command and became the first Europeans to round the Cape of Good Hope, Africa's southern tip, and cross from the Atlantic to the Indian Ocean. Over the following years, the Portuguese traveled this route regularly and hoped to establish a permanent outpost in the Indian Ocean. In 1510, the Portuguese nobleman Afonso de Albuquerque (1453–1515) seized Goa, north of Calicut, which became the base for Portuguese attempts to gain a greater share of wealth from the world's most lucrative commercial crossroads and to spread Christianity in Asia. Like Zheng He, Afonso de Albuquerque acquired animal gifts in exchanges with local rulers. The Muslim ruler of Cambay (in today's Gujarat, in India), Sultan Muzaffar II, provided him with a rhinoceros, which the Portuguese explorer sent back to Lisbon as a symbol of the scope of his endeavors. The rhino caused a great sensation when it arrived in Lisbon but died on the route to Rome when King Manuel attempted to regift the beast to Pope Leo X.

---

These stories of seafarers separated by decades converging on South Asia from opposite directions introduce key places, structures, events, and relationships among regional economies and political structures that we analyze in this chapter. Although it is common to divide the world's landmass into six or seven continents, we first explain why it makes historical sense to consider Europe, Asia, and Africa as a single Afro-Eurasian supercontinent across which ideas, commodities, and peoples flowed for thousands of years. We then detail some of the major political, military, and economic relationships on the supercontinent in the fifteenth century. In the last section of the chapter, we focus on the political and economic systems of the Western Hemisphere, which developed without any sustained or significant contact with the supercontinent until the very end of the fifteenth century.

## Political and Economic Order on the Afro-Eurasian Supercontinent

The Ming voyages were impressive—picture that huge ship on the high seas hauling a giraffe back to China—but their significance must not be misunderstood. They occurred in the context of a long history of interactions among peoples and cultures across the Afro-Eurasia landmass and its surrounding oceans. Trade networks traversed the South China Sea and Indian Ocean long before Zheng He sailed and survived long after he stopped. Chinese traders had first sailed the Indian Ocean as early as the seventh century and already dominated the South China Sea when the treasure fleet launched. Southeast Asian, Indian, and Arab merchants connected the Indian Ocean trade networks to the Mediterranean Sea and East African ports. Overland routes connected the long-distance oceanic trade to the interiors of Europe, Asia, and Africa and linked southern and northern seaborne trade as well.

Evidence of these connections includes written records and other primary sources going back many centuries. Roman coins, minted from precious metals mined in Britain, have been discovered on the coasts of South Asia. Records of the Roman Senate include discussion of the trade in Chinese silks. Archaeological excavations have uncovered extensive stores of ivory in Roman ruins, and new techniques from materials science allow researchers to identify what kind of animals (elephant, walrus, or hippopotamus) the ivory came from. Roman authors from the first century of the Common Era, such as Juvenal and Pliny the Elder, augment our understanding of ivory's place in Roman culture with their descriptions of its use and status value. Artifacts found across Africa and Asia reveal extensive trade in precious metals, iron, pottery, lead, ivory, and other commodities between these regions. As we noted in our Introduction, this trade was driven by the unique technological, climatic, and geographical traits of different regions—requiring traders to travel to China for silk and porcelain, Southeast Asia for spices, Africa for gold and ivory, and India for cotton textiles. Chroniclers like Abu al Hasan al Masudi (896–956), Muhammad al Idrisi (ca. 1100–1165), and others describe these networks. These sources and others suggest how the size, shape, and variety of political and social systems across Afro-Eurasia—as well as the trade that flowed through them—changed significantly over the course of centuries. Rather than attempt to convey their full scope and variety, the following paragraphs define key terms and explain concepts of political and economic order generally before analyzing the fifteenth century more specifically.

## Key Concepts of Political Order

Four key terms related to political order are used throughout this book: "state," "sovereignty," "legitimacy," and "empire." What we write here just scratches the surface of rich and complex issues, but these words are used so often and in so many contexts that they can lose precision and value if we don't clarify how we plan to use them. Consider the word "state" first. A state is the organized exercise of power over the people who live in a certain territory. If you focus on *what* governments do—make and enforce laws, raise armies, declare wars, and collect taxes—rather than *how* any particular government does these things or claims the right to do them, then you've got the basic idea of what a state is. To think about and discuss states is to think about and discuss the accumulation, preservation, and use of the power to do these things.

Individuals or groups attempting to act like a state are claiming *sovereignty*; and if they succeed, they are exercising sovereignty. Sovereignty means an individual or group has the ability to make and enforce rules within a given territory and/or among a group of people. To retain sovereignty, those who claim it (whether called emperor, shah, sultan, queen, or president) must strive continuously to maintain it against continuous threat—both from within the territory over which they claim sovereignty and from challengers who live in territory beyond a sovereign's current claims.

Some have compared the building and maintenance of a sovereign state to the kinds of organized crime activities familiar to viewers of the *Godfather* movies of the 1970s or the television series *The Sopranos* (1999–2007). In this analogy, those who build states and exercise sovereignty might be compared to those who organize protection rackets, offering to reduce the disruptions of the daily lives of ordinary people in exchange for sacrificing some surplus to the local tough guys. This analogy is limited, but it helps us to think about the place of violence—its threat and its use—in the construction of states.

One essential difference separating a sovereign state from an organized crime syndicate is *legitimacy*. Exercising sovereignty is about more than just enforcing your will through violence. To be legitimate, a ruler must show not only the ability to rule but also justify his or her claim. Relying on sheer physical force to subdue a territory and its residents is unsustainable over the long term for any ruler (which is why mob bosses are, sooner or later, overthrown by their rivals or their lieutenants). States, therefore, tend to survive by delivering benefits to enough people to reduce the need for massive or constant physical violence imposed on the entire population. For example, enduring political systems such as Rome under the Five Good Emperors (96 CE–180 CE) or Han Dynasty China (206 BCE–220 CE) made long-distance travel and commerce easier in many ways. The rulers of these states built infrastructure to collect and redistribute resources while maintaining control over territories and people through the use of legal systems as much as armies. Those who claim sovereignty link these demonstrations of how they *can* exercise power to claims of why they *should* be able to do so. This is a claim of legitimacy, which is a condition of political order by which the exercise of power is considered correct or appropriate.

Finally, across the centuries and around the world, the successful assertion of sovereignty over large expanses of territory in which ethnically, culturally, and religiously diverse peoples live has led to a particular kind of state—an *empire*. Empires are states in which those who rule act as if both their sovereignty and legitimacy can be limited only by practical considerations, such as natural obstacles. They believe that, with the right combination of will, guile, military might, and/or divine providence, they can expand their control over territories almost without limit, regardless of the preexisting conditions in any of the territories over which the ruler wishes to exercise sovereignty. Empires create imbalances among the various peoples and territories under the sovereign's authority, with some receiving greater benefits from the political and economic system than others. These "others" are often the most frequent target of the state's use of violence to maintain sovereignty.

## The Polycentric Supercontinent

No single region, state, individual, or group ever dominated the vast supercontinent entirely. Many ethnic, linguistic, and religious groups lived close together, sometimes under the authority of a single ruler; but most people experienced primarily the authority of regional or local leaders who made and enforced laws and distributed resources such as agricultural land, gold, salt, wood, and human labor. Competition was fierce over the wealth of commercial centers and the legitimating power of religious ones.

Religion, one of the tools empires used to build their states, often played a vital role. This was especially true of Christianity and Islam, both because these religions were extraordinarily successful in attracting followers and also (related to this) because both faiths encourage—some would say require—their followers to spread their religion by converting nonbelievers. From the fourth century on, Christianity became important to empire builders as a faith tradition that could support claims of political authority; Islam emerged with similar characteristics during the seventh century. Both Christianity and Islam held out the possibility of conversion to all peoples, yet no attempts to create a universal community of believers with a single authority for all Christians or all Muslims proved sustainable, as questions of faith and leadership of the faithful in both spiritual and temporal matters created enduring rifts among both Christians and Muslims. Whereas claims of authority over all Christians or all Muslims persisted—leading to concepts like "Christendom" and "dar al-Islam," which claimed to encompass the community of all believers—in reality, neither Christians nor Muslims achieved consensus within their faiths on fundamental theological questions, much less did believers agree on the channels through which faith should influence political order. As a result, we need to recognize that although Christians and Muslims carried on long and bloody wars against each other, it is also true that Muslims fought other Muslims and Christians other Christians in shifting alliances to control resources and territory.

Across the supercontinent, Christian and Muslim rulers also competed with political leaders who relied on other religious traditions—Hinduism, Buddhism, and many others—for their own claims to rule. Religious diversity, like linguistic and cultural diversity, characterized the physical space of Afro-Eurasia, complicating the ways sovereigns could use religion to claim and exercise power.

## The Biological Old Regime

Even at moments of intense warfare or political fragmentation, ethnic and religious networks facilitated the movement of goods and people across Afro-Eurasia. Although most of the travelers along these networks are unknown to us today, a few left records, helping us see the connections among different parts of the supercontinent. A rabbi named Benjamin (1130–1173) from the town of Tudela (in today's Spain) left a record of his travels across the Mediterranean world, down the Persian Gulf, into the Indian Ocean, and back again over the course of eight years. Almost two centuries later, Ibn Battuta (1304–ca.1368) was born in Morocco, not far from Tudela by today's standards. Ibn Battuta traveled more than seventy thousand miles, over the course of decades, throughout North Africa, across the Arabian Peninsula, through Central and South Asia (including Calicut), and all the way to China. Each of these travelers carried a kind of cultural passport rather than a political one. Benjamin sought out Jewish communities as he moved across the Mediterranean world. Ibn Battuta, trained as a scholar of Islamic law, found that his education and religion opened doors and opportunities for him throughout his remarkable journey.

Although separated by almost two hundred years, many facets of life in Afro-Eurasia had changed little between the travels of Benjamin of Tudela and those of Ibn Battuta. It took Benjamin nine days to travel 150 miles from Al-Anbar to Baghdad (in present-day Iraq), one of the great centers of Islamic culture and also home to forty thousand Jews. Two centuries later, Ibn Battuta could travel no faster. There had been few innovations in technology or major changes in the productivity of human labor in Afro-Eurasia in the intervening years. Many of the fundamental rhythms and constraints of daily life had remained steady, rooted in a relationship between energy and human productivity that had changed little since humans first began sedentary agricultural practices and domesticating animals thousands of years earlier.

Most human societies depended on agriculture; and agricultural output depended on the amount and quality of land under cultivation, the number of laborers working the land, climate, and weather. Few technological innovations had yielded significant growth in agricultural productivity. Techniques were not well developed for the long-term storage of food or for its rapid transit from places of plenty to places of need (although there were some impressive exceptions, like the Chinese state granary system that stored and distributed grain in times of famine). Most of the world's population spent most of its time and energy producing food.

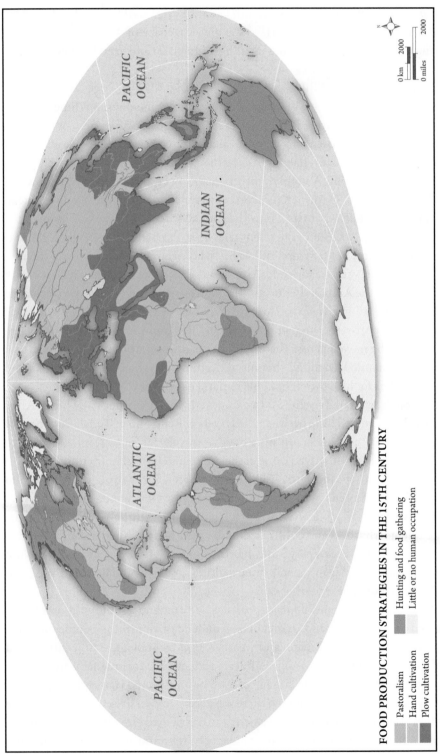

### FOOD PRODUCTION STRATEGIES IN THE 15TH CENTURY

Pastoralism

Hand cultivation

Plow cultivation

Hunting and food gathering

Little or no human occupation

**MAP 1.2** Food Production Strategies in the Fifteenth Century

Bad harvests led to famine. Contagious diseases, of mysterious origin and unknown cure, attacked regularly. Scholars like Robert Marks refer to these realities, with their enduring constraints on population and productivity growth, as the biological old regime.[1] To call this the "old regime," however, is hindsight. For the people who lived under its limits in the twelfth or fourteenth century, there was no foreshadowing that any "new regime" would ever replace their ways of life.

## Collapse and Transformation in Afro-Eurasia

The biological old regime's existence did not mean that things never changed. In the early 1200s (between Benjamin of Tudela's death and Ibn Battuta's birth), the Mongol chieftain Chinggis Khan (ca. 1162–1227) and his heirs, descended from nomads of the Eurasian steppe, built the largest empire ever on the landmass of Afro-Eurasia. The imposition of Mongol authority over territories from Korea to central Europe came at a high price in lives and resources and many works of history, particularly older publications, portray the Mongols primarily as destroyers of order, ending the reign of the Islamic Abbasid Caliphate in Baghdad in 1258 and overthrowing the Chinese Song Dynasty in 1279. Because the societies the Mongols conquered—like China and Baghdad—kept more written records than did the Mongols, much of our understanding of the Mongol conquest came from these conquered peoples, who emphasized the destruction and disruption of the Mongols. More recent scholarship balances this view with what the Mongols built in its place. Some even use the term *Pax Mongolica* (Mongolian Peace) to characterize the Mongol Empire at its height, as people, goods, and ideas flowed back and forth across Eurasia, using routes protected by the Mongol military's highly skilled horsemen.

Unity across such a large and diverse empire did not endure, however. From one generation to the next, Mongol elites divided the empire into multiple states with different sovereigns. Over time, succession struggles within each dynasty and rebellion against the Mongols became more frequent. Baghdad, the great Muslim cultural center that attracted both Benjamin and Ibn Battuta, was sacked several times. The descendants of the Mongols who ended the Abbasid Caliphate subsequently converted to Islam themselves and were trying to restore Baghdad to its former glory at the time of Ibn Battuta's visit in 1327. In China, rebel armies fought the Mongols, laying the groundwork for the rise of the Ming Dynasty in the 1360s.

At the northwestern end of the supercontinent, the fourteenth century brought a series of crises. The ruling elites of the kingdoms of England and France engaged in a seemingly endless cycle of battles that came to be known as the

---

[1]   Robert Marks, *The Origins of the Modern World*, 3rd ed. (Lanham, MD: Rowman & Littlefield, 2015).

Hundred Years' War (1337–1453). Armies and leaders from across Europe joined the fighting intermittently. Unconnected to these military battles, but more important in shaping lives across a wider landscape, a cooling trend affected agricultural production. Ongoing warfare and the changing climate led to frequent and widespread food shortages in the fourteenth century. Deprivation, religious disputes, and discontent with rulers drove popular revolts across Europe. Then, in the middle of the century, a devastating epidemic struck: the Black Death.

Bubonic plague—known as the Black Death because of its symptoms and lethality—spread from China through oceanic and overland trade networks across much of Afro-Eurasia. It is difficult to tally the toll from the Black Death. In 1348, a land-owner in Florence estimated ninety-six thousand plague-related deaths in his state between March and October of that year alone. Historians estimate that the population of Europe fell from eighty to sixty million during the era of the Black Death. Disease and warfare contributed to a population decline of as much as 40 percent in China between 1200 and 1400. Millions died across the rest of the supercontinent as well, although accurate numbers would be impossible to acquire, and the death toll varied dramatically from place to place. As we review the political, economic, and cultural geography of Afro-Eurasia in the fifteenth century, we need to keep in mind that both rulers and common people were responding to these multiple upheavals of the previous century.

## The Ming Dynasty in China

In the fifteenth century, China was the wealthiest and most populous empire in the world. The ruling Ming Dynasty had come to power in 1368 after defeating the Mongol Yuan Dynasty in a violent war. The new emperor chose a dynastic name—Ming, meaning "Bright"—to send a message that this dynasty, returning an ethnically Chinese group (the Han) to the Dragon Throne after two centuries, would serve as a beacon to the world. Rebuilding after decades of war, plague, and political infighting at court, the Yongle Emperor moved the Ming capital to Beijing in the early 1400s. The imperial palace (still standing as the largest complex of its kind in the world) embodied the new dynasty's power. More than just a residence, the "Forbidden City" comprised one thousand buildings where tens of thousands of people could live and work, including all the offices of the central government as well as the imperial household.

Despite grand titles and projects, one must be careful not to overestimate the power of any ruler in this era, even the Ming emperor. The power of individual rulers and the strength of the empire varied over time, but most scholars contend that there weren't enough government officials to collect direct tax revenue or regularly interact in other ways with the population across such a large landmass. More important to most people's lives than the imperial government was a local social hierarchy that regulated life according to age, gender, and occupational status. China's strength lay in its commercial vigor and regional autonomy, which yielded an economy that could produce and distribute staple foods within the empire as well as luxury goods like silk and porcelain. As long-distance trade routes recovered from the disruptions of the Black Death, porcelain bowls and silk robes from Chinese kilns and looms appeared again in grand residences, including royal palaces, across Afro-Eurasia.

Even with an inefficient tax system and an inadequate number of imperial officials, the expansive economy provided early Ming emperors with extraordinary resources. The scale and scope of Zheng He's maritime endeavors, introduced at the start of this chapter, reflect the wealth and ambition of the early Ming. The fleet featured the world's most advanced naval technology. The largest ships were perhaps four hundred feet long with four decks and luxury cabins for the officers and the merchants who accompanied the voyages. Capable of carrying five hundred tons, they were faster on the high seas, but less agile in shallow water, than the Spanish and Portuguese ships that would enter the Indian and Pacific Ocean trade in the next century. The Chinese vessels were double hulled—a feature of Chinese naval architecture since at least the Song Dynasty (960–1279)—with as many as a dozen watertight compartments.

After Zheng He's first three voyages (1405–1412) had satisfied the Yongle Emperor that no rivals to the throne threatened him, later voyages proceeded beyond the tip of South Asia, reaching the Arabian Sea, the Persian Gulf, and East Africa. The Chinese fleets exchanged ambassadors and goods with states throughout. The fourth voyage (1413–1415) went as far as Aden and Hormuz on the Persian Gulf, as did the fifth. The seventh voyage, an armada of four hundred vessels and almost twenty-eight thousand men, traveled down the East Coast of Africa as far south as Malindi (in modern Kenya), perhaps farther. A small expedition visited Mecca, the holy city of Islam on the Arabian Peninsula.

## Debating the Voyages of Zheng He

In recent decades, the voyages of Zheng He have received significant scholarly and popular attention. Like many historical questions, political and economic interests can influence scholarship. In our own time, senior Chinese governmental officials invoke Zheng He as a precedent for China's "peaceful rise" to great power status, emphasizing that during his "friendly diplomatic activities . . . Zheng He did not occupy a single piece of land, or seize any wealth from other countries."[2] Scholars who support this view include Tan Ta Sen, President of the International

2    Xu Zuyuan (People's Republic of China [PRC] Vice-Minister of Communications), July 2004, quoted in Geoff Wade, "The Zheng He Voyages: A Reassessment," *Journal of the Malaysian Branch of the Royal Asiatic Society* 78, no. 1 (2005): 38.

**AN ARTIST'S RENDITION COMPARING THE VESSELS COMMANDED BY ZHENG HE AND VASCO DA GAMA.** China had the world's most advanced naval technology in the fifteenth century, capable of producing vessels far larger and faster than those made in Europe. The smaller European ships had some advantages, though, particularly in shallow coastal waters.

Zheng He Society who has published widely in English and Chinese on the non-violent nature of the treasure fleet. The possibility that this type of expansion, led by Chinese, might have shaped the world much differently than the often violent colonial expansions that European nations—led by Spain and Portugal—would undertake from the end of the fifteenth century onward has been picked up by many authors, some even arguing that Zheng He's cooperative approach to international exploration has lessons for today's business world.

Other historians, though, question this depiction. Tansen Sen, among others, has established that rather than being a dramatic turn toward the oceans, Zheng He's voyages continued a trend of Chinese maritime ascendancy in the Indian Ocean and South China Sea. Challenging their depiction as peaceful missions supporting trade and exploration, Geoff Wade, using evidence from Ming dynasty official histories, points to violence, or threats of violence, by Zheng He's fleets in what is today Vietnam, Malaysia, Myanmar, Indonesia, Sri Lanka, Somalia, India, and Thailand. Wade sees the construction of Chinese garrisons and trading bases, as well as the imposition of Chinese will on Southeast Asian states, as similar to European imperialism a century later. Other scholars stop short of the label "proto-colonial" that Wade uses, suggesting that the Ming actions were focused on spreading the idea of a Chinese world order rather than occupying or controlling territory.[3]

The voyages were suspended in the mid-1420s and stopped for good in 1433. No primary source explains fully the decision to suspend the program and then end it after allowing one final voyage. No natural disaster destroyed the fleet or the resources that supported it. In the absence of such direct evidence from primary sources, historians turn to context to find plausible explanations. At least half a dozen factors have been suggested as contributing to this decision. Imperial sponsorship of large maritime expeditions was controversial at the Ming court, where the official ideology of Confucianism—named for the Chinese political philosopher Confucius (479–551 BCE)—mistrusted commercial motives. Confucian texts, knowledge of which was essential for serving in the imperial bureaucracy, declared that "The Great Man understands what is right; the Small Man understands what is profitable." Some traditional officials and imperial servants were suspicious of Zheng He, a Muslim eunuch, and his supporters at court. His death in 1433 made it easier to scuttle the program permanently at that time. The reconstruction of the Grand Canal, an interior waterway linking the Yangzi Delta with North China, meant that costly seaborne excursions were no longer as important. As the fifteenth century progressed, defense priorities against the Mongols and other inner Asian groups took precedence over sea power. The practical challenges to maintaining an Indian Ocean imperial navy were exacerbated when the Ming Dynasty relocated its capital from Nanjing to Beijing, further north and without direct access to the sea.

The end of the treasure fleet just decades before the arrival of Portuguese ships in the Indian Ocean leads to this question: what might have happened had the Chinese not retreated from their naval adventures? In her work on Zheng He's voyages, Louise Levathes writes, "Half the world was in China's grasp, and with such a formidable navy the other half was easily within reach, had China wanted it. China could have become the great colonial power, a hundred years before the great age of European exploration and expansion." If Zheng He had encountered Vasco da Gama, Levathes asks rhetorically, "Seeing the battered Portuguese boats, would the

---

[3]  The standard account of Zheng He's voyages in English is Louise Levathes, *When China Ruled the Seas: The Treasure Fleet of the Dragon Throne, 1405–1433* (London: Oxford University Press, 1997). The views of Zheng He's voyages as expansionist and proto-imperialist are expressed in Geoff Wade, "The Zheng He Voyages: A Reassessment," *Journal of the Malaysian Branch of the Royal Asiatic Society* 78, no. 1 (2005): 37–58; and Tansen Sen, "Maritime Interactions between China and India: Coastal India and the Ascendancy of Chinese Maritime Power in the Indian Ocean," *Journal of Central Eurasian Studies* 2 (May 2011): 41–82. Leading those supporting the view of Zheng He as a peaceful ambassador for trade is Tan Ta Sen, *Cheng Ho and Islam in Southeast Asia* (Singapore: Institute for Southeast Asian Studies, 2009), and Hum Sin Hoon, *Zheng He's Art of Collaboration: Understanding the Legendary Chinese Admiral from a Management Perspective* (Singapore: Institute for Southeast Asian Studies, 2012).

Chinese admiral have been tempted to crush these snails in his path, preventing the Europeans from opening an east-west trade route?"[4] This question is a great parlor game, and we encourage you to imagine an answer if you are so inclined, but history is a web of contingent and interrelated events so that one cannot really ever know what would have happened had the treasure fleet voyages continued. Such speculation can draw one into the Fallacy of Predetermined Outcomes, sometimes known as the Historians' Fallacy. In any historical event, there are too many variables at play to allow us to predict accurately what would have happened if we were to change only one of them. We can never really know what *would* have happened but only do our best to understand what *did* happen and why.

Although the Chinese state withdrew from its ambitious maritime program, Chinese merchants remained active in overseas trade and established communities in today's Vietnam, Indonesia, Thailand, Malaysia, and the Philippines. Whereas the end of the Ming Dynasty's Indian Ocean fleet after Zheng He died at sea returning from Africa in 1433 changed the political and military profile of the region, robust overseas trade continued.

## The Struggle over Central and South Asia

To the west and south of China during the fifteenth century, several key factors influenced political and economic events: the continued role of the Mongol rulers' descendants; the potential of Islam to build bridges across the region; the robust economic output of South and Southeast Asia; and the ability of Hindu and Buddhist institutions to underpin numerous states across South and Southeast Asia. One sees many of these factors at play in the history of the Timurid dynasty, founded by Timur, also known as Tamerlane (1336–1405). A Muslim descendant of Mongol rulers, Timur built a vast empire populated by Mongols, Persians, Kazakhs, Turks, and others. Functionally, the empire was trilingual. Persian was the language of state and among urban dwellers, while many rural dwellers spoke Chagatai, a now-extinct Turkic language. Arabic, the language of the Qur'an, the holy book of Islam, served as the language of literature and intellectual life.

Timur's ambitions led him into wars from China to Eastern Europe and into South Asia, including conflicts with other Muslim rulers. The Indian subcontinent had been spared many of the effects of the Black Death; its dynamic economy, producing valuable textiles and spices, was an attractive target. The Muslim leaders of the Delhi Sultanate had repulsed earlier Mongol raiders, but Timur's persistence, and the expense of fighting him off, proved too much. In 1398, Timur sacked the city of Delhi and temporarily annexed the entire region. The brutal summer heat dissuaded Timur from establishing a capital there, but incursions

---

[4]    Levathes, *When China Ruled the Seas*, 20–21.

from the north became regular features of the South Asian political landscape during the next century. Timur's descendants could not hold the empire together; but in the sixteenth century, one of them did succeed in creating a new South Asian Muslim empire, the Mughal, which would endure into the nineteenth century. Frequent disputes were common between and within the region's Islamic states, with combatants often dividing along both Sunni-Shi`a lines and long-settled communities versus more recent immigrants.

From the fourteenth century through the seventeenth century, significant territory in South Asia was ruled by a Hindu dynasty, the Vijayanagara, determined to keep the power of Muslim rulers from spreading south and also to keep other Hindu kingdoms in check. In this multifaceted struggle, the Vijayanagara rulers were aided by Muslim mercenaries who trained Hindu warriors in new military strategies and tactics. This training would then be used against the Portuguese incursions of the sixteenth century. These complex interactions illustrate the limitations of understanding conflict and expansion as primarily religious in nature.

## The Ottoman Empire as a Key Afro-Eurasia Link

While one end of the Indian Ocean trade network was anchored in China, the other was in the eastern edge of the Mediterranean Sea, where land and sea routes linking this trade to the far reaches of western Eurasia and Africa came together. Beginning in the late thirteenth century, under the leadership of a Sultan who claimed both secular and religious legitimacy, the Ottoman Turks began to expand and consolidate military and administrative control across Anatolia and the Balkans. Straddling the often-arbitrary dividing line between Asia and Europe, the Ottoman Empire is a good example of a new level of Afro-Eurasian statecraft, which we can see illustrated in the career of one of the Ottomans' most important sultans, Mehmed II, known as the Conqueror.

Mehmed II (1432–1481) was born a year before Zheng He's death. Like Zheng He, he was Muslim, but neither was Arab (neither was from the Arabian Peninsula or its surrounding territories, and neither one spoke Arabic as his native language). The ethnic diversity within Islam reminds us that Islam—like Christianity—had evolved into a religion open to all rather than limited to a specific ethnic or linguistic group. As in Christianity at this time, followers of Islam were taught to spread and defend their faith, using force if necessary. Islam was essential to Mehmed's education as a ruler, and he embraced these roles of expanding and defending the faith in the Sunni tradition. Indeed, his first challenge on ascending the Ottoman throne at age twelve was to defend his empire from invading Hungarian Christians. As sultan, Mehmed orchestrated the conquest of Constantinople, one of the world's largest cities and a center of Christian authority since the fourth century. Using superior weapons and naval technology, Mehmed's army and navy besieged the city, capturing it on May 29, 1453.

Mehmed and his successors also engaged in war against other Muslim king-doms, emerging by the early sixteenth century as rulers of one of the largest and most powerful empires in the world and gaining control of the holiest sites of Islam, the cities of Mecca and Medina on the Arabian Peninsula. These military victories in the Muslim holy land also made the Ottoman sultan, beginning with Selim I (ca. 1465–1520), the caliph. According to Sunni tradition, the caliph is the successor to the Prophet Muhammad and the main interpreter and enforcer of Islamic law and practice for the entire community of believers. (Although their histories and traditions diverge considerably, a key difference between Sunni Islam and Shiʿa Islam is that Shiʿa Muslims believe that the Prophet Muhammad appointed his son-in-law and cousin, Ali, to be his successor and the first caliph. Shiʿa Muslims would thus not recognize Sunni claims about a caliphate.)

As the Ottoman Empire expanded, its rulers considered the potential costs of enforcing religious authority across such a diverse landscape, even within the Is-lamic community, with its multiple traditions of belief and practice. Mehmed II established separate communities, called "millets," organized by religious tradi-tion, whether it be Muslim, Christian or Jewish. For each community, a religious leader appointed by, and therefore most likely loyal to, the Ottoman government made most legal and political decisions, including those related to education and local administration. Mehmed's successors maintained this tradition.

As it grew in this strategic location linking South Asia, the Eastern Mediter-ranean, and Europe, the Ottoman Empire could be either a bridge or a barrier for stitching together the northern regions of the supercontinent. The Ottomans par-ticipated actively in diplomatic and trade relations, as well as periodic wars, with Poland, Sweden, Finland, and others. Russia and the Ottoman Empire had a par-ticularly contentious relationship, as both were expanding, building up resources to defend new territories under imperial control, and focusing on their interests in the Black Sea. Between the sixteenth and nineteenth centuries, Russia was at war with the Ottoman Empire more than any other state.

In bringing the supercontinent's north into view, we need to understand that from the mid-thirteenth century, much of the trade across the north—rich in timber, preserved fish, salt, grains, and other valuable commodities—was domi-nated by the members of the Hanseatic League, or Hansa, a commercial and de-fense arrangement among merchant guilds concentrated in central European cities, but with members as far away as modern-day England and Russia. In some ways, the Hansa acted like a state. For example, the league went to war with the Kingdom of Denmark in the fourteenth century and England in the fifteenth century. Actions like these led to tensions between the Hansa and rulers (includ-ing England's Queen Elizabeth I (1533–1603) and Russia's Grand Prince Ivan III (1440–1505)) who claimed sovereignty over cities where these merchants

operated. Over time, the merchants of the Hansa ceded their claims of sovereignty and focused on commerce, or had their resources confiscated and destroyed.
However, in central Europe especially, sovereignty contested among many groups,
rather than concentrated under a single central authority, continued well beyond
the sixteenth century.

## Placing Africa within Afro-Eurasia

Peoples and resources of many African regions were essential components of
the political and economic networks that spanned the supercontinent. North
African cities like Tangier, Fez, Tunis, and Cairo connected the Mediterranean
world and Central Asia to an extensive commercial network in West and Central
Africa, and all were part of *dar al-Islam* (the "Abode of Islam"), territories in which
Muslims resided and practiced their faith and where Arabic was understood by
those with some education, including as a language of trade. The rulers of Mali,
a large fourteenth-century empire in West Africa, claimed a lineage back to one
of the Prophet Muhammad's early companions in the faith.

Like other Muslim rulers, Mali's Mansa Musa I (ca. 1280–ca. 1337) completed
the *hajj*—the pilgrimage to Mecca that was a central feature of Islamic practice.
Perhaps the wealthiest man in the world at the time due to Mali's extensive gold

**THE EMPEROR OF MALI.** This image is found in the Catalan Atlas of 1375, created by Abraham Cresques, a Jew from the
region of Catalonia. The text, in the Catalan language, identifies the image as that of the sovereign "Musse Melly"
(perhaps Musa of Mali), "the richest and noblest of all these lands due to the abundance of gold" he controlled.

and salt reserves, some scholars believe that he spent so much during his 1325 hajj to Mecca that he single-handedly affected the price of goods across the supercontinent during his travels. Because this pilgrimage was a pillar of Islamic faith, Mecca during the season of the hajj brought together people from across the Islamic world, from Spain to the South China Sea. Mansa Musa's wealth and the possibility of patronage helped invigorate the links of trade and scholarship between the Mediterranean and the states of the Sahara and West Africa. The open expanses of the Sahara, sometimes portrayed as a vast barrier separating peoples, can better be understood during this time as a highway linking different parts of Africa. The gold of Mali lured merchants and explorers much like the wealth of the Americas would two centuries later. New maps, produced in the 1300s, depicted the roads linking Mali and the Mediterranean coast, often with a gold nugget to represent Mali. Mansa Musa brought an Arabic library and religious scholars to the city of Timbuktu, as well as an architect to design mosques and a royal palace. Timbuktu became one of the most important commercial, religious, and political centers, not just of Africa but of Afro-Eurasia, linked by roads across the Sahara to the sea.

Although the neighboring Songhai Kingdom eclipsed Mali's power (and took control of Timbuktu) by 1400, the region remained a vital center of Islamic learning and scholarship. Sonni Ali (d. 1492) expanded the Songhai Empire by conquering neighboring states, making it perhaps the largest West African empire to have ever existed, covering almost nine hundred thousand square miles. The Songhai state revitalized Timbuktu, encouraging education, contemplation, and the production and collection of texts. Scholars from other Islamic kingdoms consulted with Timbuktu experts on key questions of Muslim belief and practice. The deep historical connections and dynamic relationship between Islam and Africa lead some scholars to write of an "Africanization of Islam" as much as an "Islamicization of Africa" over the centuries.

As with many of the other empires we have seen, Songhai at its height (in the late fifteenth and early sixteenth centuries) depended on a combination of bursts of power from the armies of the ruler and a daily regimen of great local autonomy. As long as tax revenue flowed to the central government and Songhai sovereignty was acknowledged (e.g., when decisions about war and peace were to be made), the provinces of the empire were to a great extent self-governing. The empire thrived on the wealth of the goldfields and the trans-Saharan caravan trade until internal divisions and an invading military force from North Africa split the empire apart at the end of the sixteenth century.

No large state like Mali or Songhai developed in East Africa. In these regions, multiple states actively participated in diverse trade networks across the Indian Ocean to South and East Asia. Trade in ivory, copper, and salt supported states like the Kingdom of Mutapa, but their ruling elites maintained religious traditions other than Islam. In the Horn of Africa, Christian dynasties continued to claim sovereignty over Ethiopia. From the late thirteenth century until the early sixteenth century, under the authority of a ruling dynasty that claimed a lineage back to King Solomon, Ethiopia enjoyed prosperous commercial relations with European merchants seeking alternatives to Islamic trading networks. In the rest of Africa, in the fifteenth century, most states, using the preceding definition, encompassed rulers making and enforcing sovereignty claims over only relatively small territories where production of surplus to be taxed or traded was much less than it was in these larger states.

## The Changing Political and Economic Profile of the Iberian Peninsula

Tangier, Ibn Battuta's birthplace, is a short boat ride across the narrowest point of the Mediterranean Sea to the westernmost territories of the European mainland on the Iberian Peninsula. Today divided between Spain and Portugal, fifteenth-century Iberia comprised five large states (and a number of smaller ones). Four of these states were ruled by Christian dynasties, but Muslims ruled the fifth. Many Muslims and Jews lived in the other four territories as well. A closer look at the history of this region can help us understand the emergence of a new political order in Europe after the Black Death, with larger, more powerful and effective central states under the authority of hereditary monarchs.

King John I (1357–1433) and his successors are good examples of the monarchs who worked to change the relationships between territory, sovereignty, and material resources in the western regions of the supercontinent from the fourteenth into the sixteenth centuries. The Portuguese sovereigns used warfare, strategic marriages, increased revenue, and religious zeal to consolidate their power. They expanded long-distance commerce and oceangoing exploration in the fifteenth century. Establishing a presence in the North African city of Ceuta, seized from its Muslim ruler in 1415, the Portuguese then claimed a number of islands in the Atlantic Ocean in the 1430s, and soon thereafter began to establish *feitorias*, fortified trading posts, on the west coast of Africa: first on an island off the coast of present-day Mauritania (1445) and then on the coast in present day Ghana (1482), both close to the Songhai Empire. Over the course of the fifteenth and sixteenth centuries, the Portuguese established approximately fifty *feitorias* across Afro-Eurasia, from Ghana to Goa to Macau, just off the Chinese mainland.

The conquest of Constantinople by Ottoman Sultan Mehmed II catalyzed the Christian rulers of Iberia to action. Over the second half of the fifteenth century, the rulers of the Christian kingdoms—Portugal, Castile, Aragon, and Navarre—declared a new round of warfare on Islam and each other. In 1469, Isabella I of Castile (1451–1504) and Ferdinand II of Aragon (1452–1616) married, beginning a long process of creating a new kingdom (Spain). Along with their well-known contributions to Christopher Columbus's sea voyages, they also declared a "reconquest" of the peninsula from Islamic rulers and demanded that all Muslims and Jews in their kingdoms convert to Christianity or leave. So it was with both religious fervor and commercial goals that Christopher Columbus and his crews set off into the Atlantic Ocean. What these men found in the last decade of the fifteenth century on the other side of the ocean was something no one on the supercontinent was prepared for.

## American Empires of the Fifteenth Century

All the landmasses of the earth were at one time connected to each other, drifting apart about two hundred million years ago. Humans migrated to the landmass of North and South America relatively recently; and the human, animal, and microbial populations there evolved in relative isolation from Afro-Eurasia for thousands of years. When the Americas rejoined Afro-Eurasia—metaphorically speaking—at the end of the fifteenth century, a remarkable new chapter in human history began.

Although history did not begin for the Americas in 1492, a number of factors render difficult the study of the hemisphere's past prior to that year. First, the indigenous peoples of the Americas kept records in ways that were very different from the Afro-Eurasian empires. It is only in the last few decades that scholars have had any success in interpreting the evidence woven into the cloth memory devices of the Andes called *khipus* or the region's highly decorated drinking vessels called *keros*.

In addition, much of the material record of the indigenous past has been reclaimed by nature. New techniques, for example, infrared aerial photography, have yielded many surprises about the dimensions and infrastructure of societies from Central America to the Amazon but scholars are still in the early stages of linking these to evidence gathered from oral histories, ethnographies, and archival work. Another factor is that the first Europeans who came to the Americas often destroyed the records and other artifacts that did exist. For example, in 1562, a Catholic priest named Diego de Landa (1524–1579) burned twenty handwritten books and thousands of artifacts of the Maya people of the Yucatán peninsula, which he deemed to be the work of the devil. Despite these obstacles (which hold true for other parts of the earth as well), researchers have been able to piece together many aspects of life in the Americas prior to the arrival of Europeans, with significant growth over the last four decades in our understanding of these societies.

### The Aztecs

Two important changes in the political organization of the Americas in the fifteenth century need attention in this chapter about trade networks in a polycentric world.

**KHIPU FROM THE INCA EMPIRE.** Khipus are knotted textiles used by the Inca. Approximately six hundred khipus have been discovered to date. Researchers have noted their intricate mathematical structures but are still working to understand fully how they served to record and transmit information.

Both involve the growth of empire. The first was in the Valley of Mexico, where a migrant group from the north transformed itself in several generations from mercenaries at the service of other city states to the most powerful state in one of the most densely populated, culturally diverse, and economically productive regions in the hemisphere. In the first decades of the fourteenth century, the Mexica (often called Aztecs) founded a city called Tenochtitlan (today's Mexico City). By the 1370s, they were claiming their ruler was a descendant of a legendary leader from another central Mexican state of an earlier era. By the 1420s, Tenochtitlan was the dominant state in a powerful alliance of tribute collectors that spread its claims ever further across Mesoamerica.

Tenochtitlan grew into one of the world's largest cities with one of its greatest and most diverse markets for goods. The wide variety of products and significant supply were available to tributary states as well, but at a cost. As the Mexica increasingly relied on their war machine to generate wealth through tribute, internal hierarchies within Mexica society solidified. The ruler, known as the *tlatoani* or chief speaker, began to take on god-like aspects—he could not be touched or looked at directly. War became glorified and captured prisoners were sacrificed to the gods. Religious specialists rewrote Mexica history, burning records that contradicted the story they now wanted to tell about their society.

Over the course of the fifteenth century, the Mexica built a system of tributary states that delivered human and material resources to them, which in turn fed

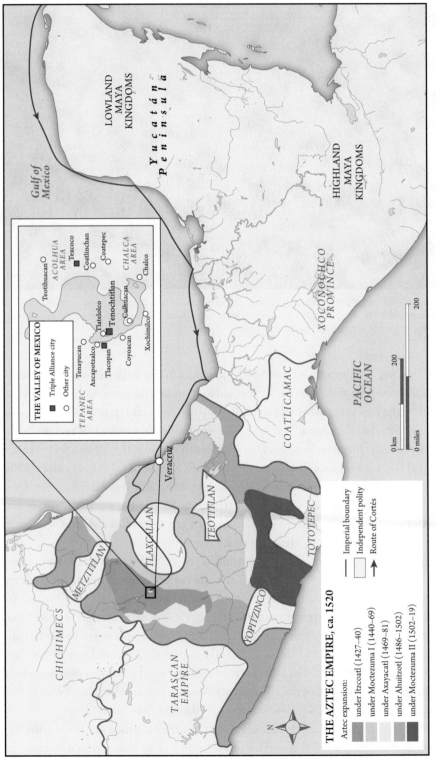

**THE AZTEC EMPIRE, ca. 1520**

Aztec expansion:
- under Itzcoatl (1427–40)
- under Moctezuma I (1440–69)
- under Axayacatl (1469–81)
- under Ahuitzotl (1486–1502)
- under Moctezuma II (1502–19)

— Imperial boundary
Independent polity
→ Route of Cortés

**THE VALLEY OF MEXICO**
■ Triple Alliance city
○ Other city

Teotihuacan ○
*ACOLHUA AREA*
Texcoco ■
Coatlinchan ■
Coatepec ○
*CHALCA AREA*
Chalco ○
Tlatelolco ○
Tenochtitlan ■
Culhuacan ○
Tenayucan ○
*TEPANEC AREA*
Azcapotzalco ○
Tlacopan ■
Coyoacan ○
Xochimilco ○

Gulf of Mexico

LOWLAND MAYA KINGDOMS

*Yucatán Peninsula*

HIGHLAND MAYA KINGDOMS

XOCONOCHCO PROVINCE

PACIFIC OCEAN

COATLICAMAC

TOTOTEPEC

YOPITZINCO

TEOTITLAN

Veracruz

TLAXCALLAN

METZTITLAN

CHICHIMECS

TARASCAN EMPIRE

N

0 km    200
0 miles  200

MAP 1.3  The Aztec Empire, ca. 1520

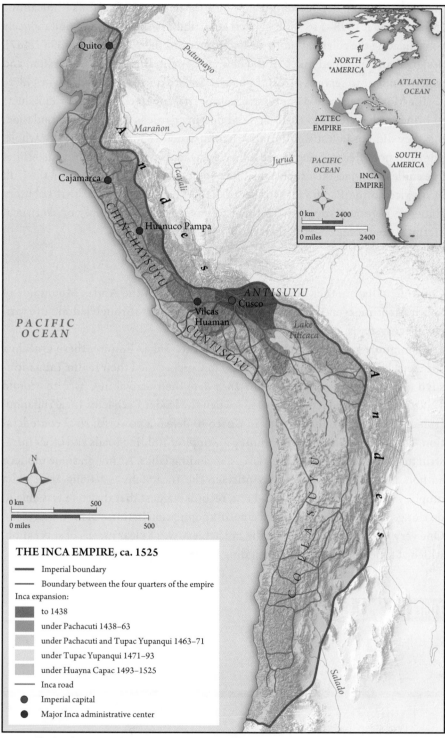

PACIFIC
OCEAN

Quito

Putumayo

Marañon

Cajamarca

Huanuco Pampa

CHINCHAYSUYU

Ucayali

Juruá

ANTISUYU

Cusco

Vilcas
Huaman

CUNTISUYU

Lake
Titicaca

A
n
d
e
s

COLLASUYU

Salado

NORTH
AMERICA

ATLANTIC
OCEAN

AZTEC
EMPIRE

PACIFIC
OCEAN

SOUTH
AMERICA

INCA
EMPIRE

N

0 km    2400

0 miles    2400

N

0 km    500

0 miles    500

### THE INCA EMPIRE, ca. 1525

——— Imperial boundary

——— Boundary between the four quarters of the empire

Inca expansion:

- to 1438
- under Pachacuti 1438–63
- under Pachacuti and Tupac Yupanqui 1463–71
- under Tupac Yupanqui 1471–93
- under Huayna Capac 1493–1525

——— Inca road

● Imperial capital

● Major Inca administrative center

**MAP 1.4**  The Inca Empire, ca. 1525

further expansion. Between 1440 and 1469, the *tlatoani* Moctezuma Ilhuicamina (Moctezuma I, 1398–1469) subjugated new tributary states while simultaneously consolidating the ruler's authority. Moctezuma's brother, Tlacaelel I (1398–1487), designed and enforced much of the new, more centralized, political system and would continue to serve as a trusted guide to Mexica rulers until his death in 1487.

The Mexica performed impressive feats of civil engineering, such as aqueducts to bring fresh water into their city and floating gardens to feed the population, but they did not invest significantly in infrastructure for the region as a whole. They did not offer to bring peace either. Instead, the Mexica offered something like endless conquest to other states and peoples in central Mexico, from the Gulf of Mexico to the Pacific Ocean, because the Mexica demanded that tributary states go regularly to war with them to ensure a steady supply of sacrificial victims, a key component of their ritual practices.

## The Inca

Coincidentally, another new empire was emerging in the Andes Mountains of South America, eventually stretching over 3,000 miles through a dramatic variety of ecosystems.

Commonly known in English as the Inca (or Inka) Empire, these Quechua speakers, building from their power base in Cusco, called their realm Tahuantin-suyu ("land of the four parts"). The Inca date their arrival in Cusco to around 1200, gaining regional power in 1438 when the leader Pachacuti Inca Yupanqui (ruled 1438–1471) rallied troops in Cusco to defeat a powerful rival confederation. The Inca then invested in running an empire, building roads and other infrastructure, and redistributing resources, including labor. Although some modern authors and audiences have romanticized the Inca state as having achieved a utopia, which it most certainly did not, records suggest that the state was able to do things like provide relief to the empire's population in times of food shortages. One very important thing that it did not achieve was a clear means of succession, which at times led to disputes, including warfare, over rulership.

## TIMELINE

**1368**
Ming dynasty assumes power in China

**1405–1433**
Voyages of Zheng He

**1432–1481**
Reign of Mehmed II, Ottoman sultan

**1405**
Death of Tamerlane

**1415**
Portuguese seize North African city of Ceuta

## Conclusion

As we noted in the Introduction, this book does not catalog all—or even most—of the events of world history from 1400 to the present. Estimates of the global population at the end of the fifteenth century range from about four hundred million to five hundred million people. Missing from this chapter is analysis of the political, social, and economic lives of most of them, with their own histories: village dwelling agriculturalists of North America, pastoralists of the Eurasian steppes, hunter-gatherers of Africa and Australia. At times, further on in the book, we will add additional information about other peoples and places, as they contribute to our analysis of how the structures that define the world we live in emerged. For now, we thought it most important to identify major circuits for the generation of surplus and long-distance exchange; explain the motivations and actions that brought the world's peoples to the edge of a new global interface in the late fifteenth century; and to provide a context for understanding how that next chapter in world history would play out, to which we turn now.

## A Few Good Books

Janet L. Abu-Lughod. Before European Hegemony: The World System A.D. 1250–1350. New York: Oxford University Press, 1989.

Ross Dunn. The Adventures of Ibn Battuta: A Muslim Traveler of the Fourteenth Century. Berkeley: University of California Press, 2012.

Halil Inalcik. The Ottoman Empire: The Classical Age, 1300–1600. New York: Phoenix Press, 1993.

Louise Levathes. When China Ruled the Seas: The Treasure Fleet of the Dragon Throne, 1405–1433. New York: Oxford University Press, 1997.

Charles Mann. 1491: New Revelations of the Americas before Columbus. New York: Vintage, 2006.

David O. Morgan. The Mongols, 2nd Ed. Malden, MA: Blackwell Publishing, 2007.

*For additional resources, including maps, primary sources, visuals, web links, and quizzes, please go to* **www.oup.com/us/carter**

**1438**
Inca assume regional power in Andes

**1497**
Vasco da Gama rounds Cape of Good Hope and reaches India

**1510**
Portuguese seize South Asia trading center of Goa

**1453**
Constantinople falls to the Ottomans; end of Hundred Years' War

**ca. 1500**
Height of Songhai Empire, West Africa

(RIGHT) A ROSTER OF CITY STATES SUB-JECTED BY THE AZTECS UNDER THE RULE OF AHUITZOTL. This is a page from the Codex Mendoza, which contains both pictograms and Spanish-language commentary. Produced in the 1540s, two decades after the empire fell, this book, painted on indigenous paper, contains over seventy pages of text and images depicting the history and daily life of the Aztecs and their relationship to other peoples in Central Mexico from the four-teenth to the sixteenth century.

(BOTTOM) A JAPANESE PERSPECTIVE OF DEJIMA, THE DUTCH TRADING POST AT NAGASAKI. Japanese leaders restricted most overseas trade to a single port, at Nagasaki, from the seventeenth century to the nine-teenth century. Dejima, an artificial island in Nagasaki harbor, served as the most impor-tant link between Japan and Europe for more than two hundred years. This painting, ca. 1800, is an example of *megane-e*, produced to be used in an optical device that would give viewers the illusion of depth in the picture. Originally made in Holland, these devices were most likely first imported through Nagasaki in the early eighteenth century.

# The New Global Interface

## 1486–1639

I n 1486, a man named Ahuitzotl assumed power in the Mexica capital of Tenochtitlan. The following year, he presided over a rededication of the city's main
temple, constructed to honor the gods of war and rain. Thousands of human sacrifices were offered, and Ahuitzotl—military, political, and religious leader—spilled
his own blood as part of the rituals. As we saw in Chapter 1, the Mexica had already
transformed their world. Over the preceding half-century, from their power base in
the Valley of Mexico, they had gained supremacy in a "Triple Alliance" of city states
that now dominated one of the most densely populated and wealthiest regions in the
Western Hemisphere.

Mexica expansion had stagnated in the early fifteenth century, but Ahuitzotl was
determined to reignite it, launching more than forty military campaigns, from the
Gulf Coast to the Pacific Ocean and south to the present-day border between Mexico
and Guatemala. These campaigns to subdue "all other nations" would continue
under Ahuitzotl's successors into the sixteenth century, but events soon showed
that the Mexica, like every other society on the planet, understood neither how big
the world was nor how many "other nations" it encompassed. Less than a decade
after Ahuitzotl came to power, a new and cataclysmic chapter in global history
began when a small group of Europeans, led by a Genoese navigator looking for
Japan, landed in the Caribbean.

Ahuitzotl ruled a great empire in the last years of isolation from a truly global
flow of goods, people, and information. A century later, Japanese rulers struggled
with the mounting consequences of this wave of globalization. European merchants
and firearms first arrived in Japan in the early 1540s, followed soon after by Catholic missionaries. Over the following century, merchants and missionaries operated
with the permission of regional leaders, some of whom converted to Christianity.
Complex alliances grew and fractured over time as the leaders who wanted to unify

**VOYAGES OF EXPLORATION,
1485–1600**

1487    Date of First Portuguese Landing

Davis    Name of explorer with date
         of voyage

→    Explorers on behalf of Spain

→    Explorers on behalf of Portugal

→    Explorers on behalf of France

→    Explorers on behalf of England

→    Explorers on behalf of the Dutch

- - -    The world known to
         Europeans ca. 1450

**MAP 2.1** Voyages of Exploration, 1485–1600

central authority in Japan determined (not without cause) that the activities of Christian missionaries were tied to European empires that could threaten their power, either directly or by arming and supporting their rivals. To limit foreign influence, Toyotomi Hideyoshi (1536–1598) expelled Christian missionaries and limited the spread of Christianity by regional authorities. When the Tokugawa clan acquired the title of Shogun—the supreme military ruler in Japan—in the early 1600s, it extended these limitations with a series of proclamations, most notably under the Shogun Tokugawa Iemitsu (1604–1651). In 1639, Portuguese contact with Japan was banned completely. The Sakoku Rei (Closed Country Edicts) also forbade Japanese from leaving the islands (and from returning to the islands if they did leave) and tightly controlled all contact between foreigners and Japanese. European trade was limited to just one delegation per year, at the port of Nagasaki. Trade with China and Korea was more open but still carefully regulated. Japanese rulers enforced strict limits on foreign interactions—commercial, religious, or otherwise—into the middle of the nineteenth century.

---

This chapter explains the emergence of, and responses to, the increasing flow of commodities, peoples, and ideas in all directions among the Americas, Europe, Africa, and Asia beginning at the end of the fifteenth century. Although interactions among different parts of the world had long been a consistent feature of human societies, in the decades after Christopher Columbus (1451–1506) made landfall in the Caribbean in 1492, ideas, animals, germs, and commodities began to move around the world in unprecedented ways. Thus began the "Columbian Exchange," which fundamentally changed the entire world.

In the first section of the chapter, we present the interactions between indigenous peoples and invaders in the first decades after Europeans arrived in the Western Hemisphere. In the chapter's second part, we introduce the concept of the Columbian Exchange as a way to understand changes in both the nature and scale of how and where goods were produced, traded, and integrated into the human experience. Understanding this concept is key to the next sections of the chapter in which we explain how different individuals and groups attempted to make sense of and use the resources of the Americas to their own advantage. First, we look at how the Spanish crown asserted greater control over resources in the Americas and the consequences of those actions. Then we turn to the efforts by other Europeans to challenge Spanish and Portuguese claims to control the Western Hemisphere. In the last part of the chapter, we integrate events in other parts of the world to attain a broader perspective on the new global interface.

# The Conquest Era

In 1492, the expanding empires of the Mexica and the Incas had no contact with each other, nor did either have contact with or any understanding of myriad other societies of the Western Hemisphere, from the whale hunters of the Arctic Circle, to the People of the Long House who lived in today's New York State, to hunter-gatherers in the Amazon basin. Europeans certainly had no detailed knowledge of the Western Hemisphere, its peoples, their economic and political structures, and their ideologies and religions. No one anywhere on the planet had a clue about the transformation that bringing these worlds together was about to set off.

The first contact with village-dwelling indigenous peoples living on islands off the coast of North America flummoxed Christopher Columbus and his crew. Numerous sponsors, including merchants from his native Genoa and the Iberian monarchs Ferdinand and Isabella, had financed a voyage to Asia, hoping to learn of the possibilities for trade and Christian evangelization there. It soon became apparent that what Columbus stumbled on challenged European conceptions of how the world fit together. Most Europeans who were interested in such things at the time believed that there was one great sea on the earth, with Europe on its eastern shore and Asia—China, Japan, and India—on its west. Columbus went to his grave believing that the Asian mainland was much closer to where he had landed than it actually was. Subsequent generations of seafarers continued to search for a "western passage" to Asia.

When he returned to Spain, Columbus convinced Queen Isabella to sponsor additional voyages across the Atlantic. In 1493, he returned to the Caribbean with over one thousand sailors, artisans, and soldiers and attempted to establish a fortified trading post. This failed; the indigenous population had neither the interest nor the surplus to engage in commerce, and some Caribbean peoples resisted the strangers furiously. Those who arrived with Columbus and remained grew impatient with promises of future wealth from trade and began to look for ways that could make them rich more quickly. Borrowing from experiences, understandings, and self-serving interpretations of the Iberian and Christian traditions, they distributed among themselves mineral and land rights, growing rich not through commerce but by exploiting the wealth of the land and the indigenous people by implementing a system of *encomiendas*. Encomiendas gave Spanish "trustees" the responsibility to Christianize and care for indigenous peoples, along with the right to exploit their labor, creating a system similar to feudalism with the Spaniard as a lord protecting and profiting from those under his protection. The potential profits to be gained from this right to labor made the encomiendas immensely valuable, and they were distributed as rewards to men expanding the Spanish presence in the Americas over the next half-century.

The Spanish monarchs, too, grew impatient, and replaced Columbus with a new governor to oversee royal interests in the Americas, including the extraction of tribute payments from indigenous taxpayers. Concern over the spiritual dimension of their rule in the new world led the crown to send more priests and also to instruct the governor to "ensure that the Indians are well treated." These various systems, implemented from the very first years of the Spanish presence in the Americas, illustrate that long before Europeans became aware that tens of millions of people lived on the American mainland, Spaniards in the Americas, and their rulers in Spain, had decided that relationships with the indigenous population held the key to their enterprises in the Americas. Yet, the objects of their political, economic, and spiritual desire had their own thoughts and motivations. Some indigenous peoples embraced a new faith and new rulers; others rejected them. (And all manner of people, regardless of their choices, would soon die in numbers heartbreaking to contemplate.)

Searching for additional resources and population centers, Spaniards established settlements across the Caribbean—Hispaniola, Jamaica, Puerto Rico, Cuba—and explored the coastline from present-day Venezuela to the Yucatán peninsula to Florida. Encomiendas and land grants were distributed, populations continued to decline, and new arrivals and anxious veterans spurred further exploration and settlement. Disputes over chain of command were common, as the rights to move, explore, and conquer were in theory separate and controlled from above. Defiance was often the order of the day. When the governor of Cuba, for instance, had second thoughts about sending Hernán Cortés (1485–1547) on an expedition in 1519, Cortés left before the governor's agents could stop him. Cortés spent the rest of his life in disputes over the legitimacy of his subsequent actions. When another group of adventurers subverted the Inca Empire a decade later, they too argued among themselves and with representatives of the crown, leading to armed conflict and the assassination of royal officials at the hands of Spanish rebels.

This relationship between sovereigns and globalization is worth dwelling on for a moment. Individuals were supposed to be subject to political and spiritual authorities (often the same person), but sixteenth-century transportation and communications systems were not suited to the great distances now separating monarchs from their dominions. It could take four months to sail from Spain to the port city of Veracruz (founded by Cortés on the Mexican mainland in 1519). Movement within the vast expanses of the Americas claimed by the Spanish crown was just as slow. Seven weeks of arduous travel were required to move silver from the legendary mines of Potosí (in present-day Bolivia) to Portobelo (in Panama), the staging area for its movement across the Atlantic to the royal treasury. Decisions made in centers of power were rarely implemented quickly or as intended.

The stakes of these disputes among Europeans rose in the second phase of conquest, from 1519 into the middle of the sixteenth century, as first Cortés's crew and then others encountered, fought, allied with, and gained control over large populations in resource-rich territories of the hemisphere. In 1519, an uneasy encounter between Cortés and Moctezuma II (1466–1520), the ruler of Tenochtitlan, became a war that ended two years later with Cortés in control of the city and its environs. In the meantime, Spaniards were moving down the Pacific coast into South America. Arriving at the heart of the Inca Empire in the midst of a civil war, the Spaniards kidnapped the ruler Atahualpa (1497–1533) and later killed him. Like their counterparts in Mexico, this small group of Spaniards, led by the Pizarro brothers, swiftly undermined Inca authority in much of the Andes; and from 1532 on, they began to reorganize the region.

These events are the ones most closely associated in our contemporary popular culture with the Spanish Conquest. They are also poorly understood and

**THE SPANIARDS AND THEIR INDIGENOUS ALLIES PREPARE TO TAKE TENOCHTITLAN.** This image is from a reproduction of the *Lienzo de Tlaxcala*, prepared by order of the indigenous city council of Tlaxcala in the 1550s. The council commissioned the work to demonstrate to Emperor Charles V the important role that the Spanish king's indigenous vassals played alongside Hernán Cortés in conquering the Aztecs.

subject to great mythologizing, so we offer several observations about how and why things turned out as they did. By the time Cortés founded Veracruz in 1519, Spanish goals and motivations had shifted away from the trading-post model of the Portuguese *feitoria* to a more complete form of sovereignty that went well beyond the exchange of merchandise. In pursuing their goals, the Spanish had some advantages. Their guns were impressive noisemakers but they were inaccurate and slow to reload; the real technological advantage lay in steel swords and horses. Spanish motivations and limitations diverged from those of the indigenous populations. For indigenous leaders and warriors, concern for the survival of families and communities influenced their decisions; Spanish risk takers did not have to include such factors in their calculations when preparing strategies and executing tactics.

Also, the conflict was not simply one of Europeans on one side and indigenous Americans on the other. By the time the Spaniards made their final assaults on the power structures of the largest American empires, they had thousands of allies. Almost two years passed between Cortés's arrival at Tenochtitlan and the surrender of the city in August 1521. During the final siege of the city, which was nestled in the middle of a lake and crisscrossed by canals, the Spaniards had tens of thousands of laborers build thirteen ships (each over forty feet long); squadrons of canoe-borne warriors to enforce an embargo on food and other goods entering the capital city; and at least twenty-five thousand indigenous soldiers who now thought of themselves as vassals of the Spanish crown. In Peru, regional indigenous leaders, hostile to Inca expansion and sensitive to the shifting balance of military power in the Andes, made tense alliances with Spaniards, pursuing what they perceived to be their own best interests and those of their people.

Disease-causing microorganisms were the conquerors' invisible allies. Smallpox outbreaks accompanied the arrival of Spaniards in the midst of the Aztec and Inca empires, devastating their labor and military forces, undermining morale, and eliminating key leaders. Moctezuma's successor, Cuitlahuac (1476–1520), succumbed to the disease while the Spaniards were regrouping after a failed attack on Tenochtitlan. The succession crisis among the Inca that facilitated Spanish conquest of the Andes resulted when both the current ruler and his immediate heir died of smallpox, leaving more distant claimants to power at loggerheads. Spaniards were aware of their reliance on indigenous peoples, often for their very survival in unfamiliar environments. They neither planned nor pursued a strategy of genocide, but their war against Aztec and Inca authority exacerbated the conditions that spread disease and death, as depleted populations were congregated into new communities, encomiendas were allocated, and complex indigenous systems for the production and distribution of foodstuffs and other goods collapsed.

## The Great Dying

There is no question that the European conquest devastated the indigenous population of the Americas. Debates over the nature and extent of population decline in the Americas after European contact first emerged in the sixteenth century when Spanish priests like Antonio de Montesinos (ca. 1470 – ca. 1545) and Bartolomé de las Casas (1474–1566) decried the abuses committed against indigenous peoples by Spanish conquistadors. Trying to understand the scope and scale of the cataclysmic changes in the population of the Americas, scholars have focused on several connected issues: the size of the Western Hemisphere's population prior to the arrival of Europeans; the different causes of population decline; and how the causes and effects of population decline (and recovery) varied by region.

There is no direct evidence, even of questionable reliability, with which to start the task. Archives, the traditional workshop for the historian's craft, are of very limited use. The comprehensive censuses and tax rolls that in modern states provide detailed records about population do not exist. The written record from the post-contact era, which includes the memoirs of conquistadors and priests, provides descriptions of indigenous populations from small villages to large cities in only vague and impressionistic ways. Indigenous documents, such as maps and tributary records, are fragmentary. Guessing and estimating from these traces, early twentieth-century scholars debated whether the total population of the Americas in 1492 reached even ten million. Subsequent researchers assailed these estimates as ridiculously low, contributing (intentionally or not) to demographic justifications of the conquest: an expanding European population making more efficient use of resources "underutilized" by a relatively small indigenous population. The journal *Current Anthropology* published a special edition in 1966 on "Estimating Aboriginal American Population," which featured two articles and almost twenty-five comments and replies from scholars involved in the search for new ways to answer this vexing question.

Over the next decades, answers to the population question relied on growing confidence in interdisciplinary research methods that attempted to integrate things like estimates of the agricultural carrying capacity of land, anthropological interpretations of indigenous social organization and production techniques, statistical extrapolation, and the analysis of additional archival records, like those for births, baptisms, deaths, and burials in the early colonial period. Using these methods, some authors estimated a pre-contact population as high as one hundred million, although the most influential revisions were about half that number—forty to sixty million people. Scholarly critics of these new estimates suggested that the researchers who produced them were too optimistic in their assessments of things like the productive capacity of indigenous societies, or too negative in their estimates of the spread and virulence of European diseases.

The debate continues. Why does this matter? One of the most important issues underlying this long debate over the size of the pre-contact population has been the effort to understand better the long-term impact of the arrival of Europeans. On this question, there will likely never be consensus on the exact scale of devastation, yet the overwhelming force of evidence subject to both qualitative and quantitative analysis leads to several conclusions. Almost the entire indigenous population of the Caribbean died within decades of the Europeans' arrival. On the mainland, the rates of population decline varied greatly from place to place. The preponderance of evidence points to disease and the disruption of indigenous political, economic, and social systems as the main causes of demographic decline. The overall indigenous population fell to perhaps four or five million during the first century of contact, a decline of some 90 percent from the most widely accepted estimates. Even if one were to accept the very lowest pre-contact estimates (which we do not), the scale of the catastrophe is hard to imagine.[1]

## The Columbian Exchange

The great dying is the grisliest manifestation of the bringing together of Afro-Eurasia and the Americas that scholars call the Columbian Exchange. This term also refers to the transfer of agricultural commodities originating in the Americas that came to be grown or consumed around the world, a process that began with Columbus's return to Europe. The list is long and stunning in its impact. Over time, many of these products even came to be associated with distinctive European, African, and Asian traditions. Consider, for example, that tomatoes didn't exist in Italy prior to the 1500s. These, along with potatoes, peanuts, peppers, cassava, and corn are among the crops that originated in the Americas and then spread around the world to transform the diet of much of the world's population. Other plant products, such as chocolate, vanilla, and tobacco, changed consumption habits in similarly profound ways. The idea of the Columbian Exchange can also apply to the precious metals that began to flow out of the Americas to other parts of the world, transforming the global economy. A third way the term can be used is to describe how things from the Old World were brought to the

---

[1]　Henry F. Dobyns, "An Appraisal of Techniques with a New Hemispheric Estimate," *Current Anthropology* 7, no. 4 (1966): 395–416; H. Paul Thompson, "A Technique Using Anthropological and Biological Data," *Current Anthropology* 7, no. 4 (1966): 417–449; "Comments and Replies," *Current Anthropology* 7, no. 4 (1966): 425–499; Angel Rosenblat, *La población de América en 1492: Viejos y nuevos cálculos* (Mexico City: El Colegio de México, 1967); William M. Denevan, ed., *The Native Population of the Americas in 1492*, 2nd ed. (Madison: University of Wisconsin Press, 1992); Ann Ramenofsky, *Vectors of Death: The Archaeology of European Contact* (Albuquerque: University of New Mexico Press, 1988); David Henige, *Numbers from Nowhere: The American Indian Contact Population Debate* (Norman: University of Oklahoma Press, 1998); Massimo Livi Bacci. "The Depopulation of Hispanic America after the Conquest," *Population and Development Review* 32, no. 2 (June 2006): 199–232.

### THE COLUMBIAN EXCHANGE

**From Eurasia to the Americas**

| | |
| --- | --- |
| almonds | measles |
| apples | meningitis |
| bananas | oats |
| barley | olives |
| cattle | onions |
| cherries | oranges |
| chicken pox | peaches |
| chickens | pears |
| coconuts | pigs |
| coffee | plums |
| dandelions | rice |
| diphtheria | sheep |
| grapes | smallpox |
| honeybees | sugar |
| horses | turnip |
| influenza | typhus |
| lemons | wheat |
| malaria | whooping cough |

**From Africa to the Americas**

African rice
collard greens
okra
palm oil
yams

**From the Americas to Africa and Eurasia**

avocado
beans
cacao
cassava (manioc)
chili peppers
corn
maize
peanuts
peppers
pineapples
potatoes
pumpkins
quinine
squash
sweet potatoes
syphilis
tobacco
tomatoes
turkeys
vanilla

ASIA

EUROPE

AFRICA

NORTH AMERICA

SOUTH AMERICA

ATLANTIC OCEAN

N

0 km          1000
0 miles          1000

**MAP 2.2** The Columbian Exchange

New—domesticated farm animals are one example. Columbus himself brought Afro-Eurasian crops and seeds, including wheat, onions, radishes, and sugar cane on his second voyage in 1493. By 1600, most of the major domesticated Afro-Eurasian crops were grown in the Americas. Rice, and the techniques for its production, arrived from Africa in the 1600s.

The Columbian Exchange produced fundamental demographic, economic, and environmental transformation around the world. New World crops did not simply enter Afro-Eurasian diets; they fueled population growth and agricultural upheaval. Sheep and cows brought new sources of wool and protein to the Americas, but they were also a plague on the land, consuming native grasses and trampling the ground to bare wasteland. Horses were never supposed to get into the hands of the hostile indigenous groups on the northern edges of Spanish settlements; yet they did, transforming the society and politics of the North American Great Plains long before Europe's human settlers arrived in large numbers. Rats, earthworms, snakes, mosquitoes, honeybees, and all manner of other living things went along for the ride around the world.

The exchange also precipitated a great demographic transformation, including not only the microbe-induced dying off of the indigenous population but a great migration to the Americas from Europe and, especially, Africa. About a quarter-million Europeans migrated to the Spanish Americas between 1492 and 1650, and similar numbers migrated to territory controlled by England. Fewer traveled to the Portuguese and French outposts in the hemisphere. French migration to the Americas was only a trickle into the seventeenth century. During the same period, Brazil took a back seat to Portuguese interests in Asia, although the Portuguese developed sugar plantations along the Brazilian coast in the second half of the sixteenth century. By 1600 about thirty thousand Europeans and fifteen thousand enslaved Africans resided in the territory claimed by Portugal, out of a total population of perhaps one hundred thousand. Peoples of African origin arrived on the very first vessels to reach the New World from the Old; but over time, the number of enslaved Africans in the New World far outnumbered those who arrived of their own volition. Overall, by 1600, about two hundred seventy-five thousand Africans had been enslaved and transported to the Caribbean islands and mainland Americas. That number would skyrocket over the next two hundred years before declining again in the nineteenth century.

This immigration profoundly shaped the Americas. Despite moral, social, and religious proscriptions, the migrants, overwhelmingly men, reproduced with indigenous women. Their children formed their own relationships across ethnic and racial lines. Over time, cultures and societies combining features of distinct peoples and traditions—African, European, and indigenous—would become a signal characteristic of the Americas.

One final clarification of the Columbian Exchange is necessary: the perception that this was a process that linked only Europe and Africa to the Americas is off-base. Asia was the goal that brought Europeans to the Americas, and the intricate links that developed between Asia and the Western Hemisphere exemplify the true globalization that emerged in the sixteenth century. The migration of plants in each direction—sugar to the west, peppers to the east—is often noted, but the Asia/Pacific connection to the Americas is much more comprehensive than that. China's economy devoured American silver. The mines of Spanish America produced 85 percent of the world's silver between 1500 and 1800, and China absorbed 40 percent of that. In exchange, Chinese goods were shipped to the port of Acapulco, on the Pacific coast of Mexico (which the Spaniards called "New Spain") on a regular basis beginning in the 1570s. By the 1580s, Asian products were the main commodities exchanged between the two Spanish viceroyalties in the Americas. At this same time, both free and unfree migrants from Asia, although fewer than those from Europe and Africa, had a substantial impact in the Americas. The Spanish crown struggled to collect tax revenues from the burgeoning direct trade between Asia and the Americas and to control the terms under which it was conducted, while local subjects on both sides of the Pacific Ocean undermined the efforts of the distant monarchs. The struggle among priests, settlers, merchants, and royal officials over the management of and profit from the Americas accelerated over the course of the sixteenth century.

## Moving from Conquest Society to Colonial Society

Focus on the actions of conquistadors like Cortés and Pizarro, as dramatic as these were, can lead audiences to conclude that the conquest ended with the fall of Cusco in the 1530s; but vast expanses of the Americas and millions of people lay beyond central Mexico and the Andes. Much of North America remained outside the Spaniards' grasp, as did the interior regions of Central and South America. A remnant of the Inca Empire, based in the city of Vilcabamba, continued to fight the Spanish until 1572. Even places that Spaniards thought were under their control proved volatile: a 1541 revolt northwest of Mexico City (the Spanish capital, built on the ruins of Tenochtitlan), required the reconquest of the region, completed with indigenous forces loyal to the Spanish. In 1560, an Andean resistance movement (the *Taki Onqoy*) called for the complete elimination of Spaniards and their culture. Throughout Spanish America, conflict and accommodation would always coexist.

From the first moments of this encounter with indigenous peoples in the Americas, questions abounded about what this "New World" meant, many of them reflecting the influence of Bible stories on European society during this era.

Was this where the gifts of the Magi to the Christ child originated? Was the Garden of Eden upriver somewhere? Had the indigenous people's gold come from King Solomon's mines? The Bible stated that Christ's disciples had spread the gospel to the *entire* world, so which of them had brought the good news to the Americas, and why was there so little trace of that effort?

Questions such as these contributed to fierce disputes within Spain over how to relate to the Americas and its peoples. Like most of the rulers we have introduced so far, the Spanish monarchy based its authority on the contention that the will of the ruler aligned with divine objectives: what would God want someone ruling in his name to do? Trying to answer this question led to debates about the relationship between conquest, legitimacy, religion, and justice that began with Columbus's landfall in 1492. These debates focused on questions about the nature of indigenous societies and how to deal with them. Europeans had limited, but multiple, tools and techniques for answering these questions. St. Augustine (354–430), one of the pillars of medieval Christian political thought, wrote "remove justice, and what are kingdoms but bands of criminals on a large scale?" However, many voices with diverse interests argued over the meaning of justice as it related to the peoples of the Americas. Some, like the scholar Juan Ginés de Sepúlveda (1489–1573), argued that the indigenous peoples were natural slaves and therefore the Spaniards had a right, even a duty, to subjugate them. Others, especially priests with some experience in the Caribbean, such as the former *encomendero* Bartolomé de las Casas, insisted that the mistreatment of the indigenous peoples jeopardized not only individual sinners but also the rule of sovereigns who implicitly or explicitly tolerated such behavior. However, even the most critical priests did not reject the Spanish monarchs' claim of sovereignty over the Americas. They just advocated a different kind of stewardship over the rich lands and peoples to which God had drawn them.

The Spanish crown wrestled with how to balance justice, the riches of the conquest, and the maintenance of royal authority in distant lands among diverse peoples. In 1512, the crown issued the Laws of Burgos, which required those holding encomiendas to provide Catholic religious instruction, food, and clothing to their indigenous charges, and they banned certain types of corporal punishment. The following year, Spanish jurists drew up a legal document known as the *Requerimiento* (Requirement). This text was to be read at the time of encounter with any new indigenous groups, offering the opportunity to accept Christianity and the authority of the Spanish crown peacefully or refuse and jeopardize life, property, and freedom. Similar pronouncements were used during the long conflict between Christian and Muslim forces on the Iberian Peninsula.

Even at the time it was first issued, critics called the Requerimiento absurd, as it presumed the indigenous people could understand the decree. It was supposed to be translated into the local language, but it was difficult, if not impossible, to translate the political and theological implications of the text adequately. Besides, it was often read in Spanish anyway. In practice, even the barest threads of justice unraveled, as the Requerimiento was pronounced at times in the midst of empty villages, recited to trees, or accompanied by the burning of huts. The ritual may have assuaged the consciences of some Spaniards, but it did not offer the indigenous peoples genuine options.

The stakes of this struggle among goals and actors rose as the expansion of New Spain and Peru increased the number of people under Spanish rule to tens of millions by the end of the 1530s. In 1542, the crown issued a set of "New Laws" that banned the distribution of new encomiendas and the enslavement of indigenous persons and created additional political infrastructure in the Americas. In effect, the crown declared the conquest complete. Disgruntled encomenderos assassinated the first Viceroy to arrive in Peru with this news. Lacking the support among settlers and the ability to impose such reforms from above, the crown backed off on many of the reform's key features. Throughout the subsequent two hundred fifty years of Spanish rule in the Americas, Spanish monarchs and their advisers strove to balance material interests, royal dependence on local power brokers in the Americas, and a sense of religious obligation.

## Competition from Other European Powers

Although debates about divine and earthly justice were sincere and fierce, Europeans did not colonize the Western Hemisphere primarily because of theology. As soon as word of Columbus's voyages reached Europe, rivals hotly contested Spain's claims to dominion over the peoples, territories, and resources of the New World. Pope Alexander VI (1431–1503) brokered the Treaty of Tordesillas in 1494, drawing an imaginary line from north to south in the middle of the Atlantic Ocean, giving that which fell to the east to Portugal and that which fell to the west to Spain (the line crosses the South American mainland, explaining why Portugal claimed Brazil and Spain the rest of South America). Eager to stake their own claims, other European sovereigns sponsored expeditions into the Atlantic world. The English king dispatched Giovanni Caboto (John Cabot, ca. 1450–ca. 1499) in 1497 to find the passage to Asia that had eluded Columbus. Far to the north of Columbus's expeditions, Cabot claimed territory from Newfoundland to the Chesapeake Bay for England. In the early sixteenth century, Giovanni Verrazzano (1485–1528)—like Columbus and Cabot, another seafarer from the Italian peninsula—sailed the eastern seaboard from Florida to Newfoundland and proclaimed vast expanses of territory "New France." The overlapping French and English claims foreshadowed important conflicts to come, but neither kingdom paid North America much attention for most of the sixteenth century. Similarly, the Portuguese focused on protecting their trade routes to West Africa and around the Cape of Good Hope to the Indian Ocean. For a century after Columbus's voyage, it was primarily the people of Spain and their monarchs who invested time, energy, and resources connecting the New World to the Old.

As the sixteenth century gave way to the seventeenth, however, the English, French, and Dutch began to challenge the Spanish and Portuguese in global oceanic trade. They also employed a new model of enterprise—the joint stock company—that spread the high risks of global commerce among investors who would purchase from their sovereign the exclusive right to trade in a particular region. English companies received charters to trade, explore, and settle Jamestown (1607) and the Plymouth Colony (1620) on the east coast of North America. The French, trading guns for furs in the northern reaches of the continent, established Québec in 1608. The Dutch chartered the West India Company in the 1620s and built Fort Amsterdam on the tip of Manhattan Island to defend their interests. Even the Swedes established short-lived New Sweden in what is today Delaware, but were soon overrun by the Dutch. From these points of entry, contact, alliances, and conflicts developed among various combinations of Europeans and indigenous groups.

By 1546, when rebel encomenderos beheaded the first Viceroy of Peru, interactions among Europeans and between Europeans and the broader world had gained greater urgency and complexity as disputes over fundamental issues of Christian faith and practice fragmented the world of Christian believers. Those who remained supportive of and loyal to the traditions and teachings advocated by the papacy became known as Roman Catholics. The protesters (hence "Protestants"), drawn to the ideas of Martin Luther (1483–1546), Huldrych Zwingli (1484–1531), John Calvin (1509–1564), and others, rejected the structures and practices of Roman Catholic tradition. The link between religion and claims to political sovereignty led to wars and rebellions that disrupted relationships between sovereigns and subjects in territories ruled by Christians. We will discuss the impact of this upheaval on the formation of early modern states in a subsequent chapter; but for now, it is important to note the extent to which these conflicts affected emerging globalization and European migration. First, religious groups out of favor with political power holders left Europe for other parts of the world, from southern Africa (French Protestants in the Dutch Cape colony) to New England (the Puritans). Second, the emergence of Protestant Christianity spurred a reforming spirit within Roman Catholicism, inspiring new generations of missionaries—especially Dominican, Franciscan, and Jesuit priests—who believed that God had bestowed the fruits of the world on them for the express purpose of providing the means to save millions of souls, whether from heathenism; rival religions like Islam; or, now, Protestantism.

CALECHVT CELEBERRI MVM INDIÆ EMPORIVM.

**THE PORT AT CALICUT.** This 1572 image shows Portuguese and other vessels in the harbor. Elephants, like the one on the right side of the image, were used for heavy lifting, such as moving timber for ship repairs. Calicut (not to be confused with Calcutta) had been an important trading hub in southern India since at least the twelfth century. Zheng He's Chinese fleet and Vasco da Gama's Portuguese ships both landed there in the fifteenth century, about ninety years apart. Portugal, France, Britain, and the Netherlands competed with Indian states for control of the city, which gave its name to the popular "calico" cloths (see Chapter 4, p. 90 [Image 2]).

## A World Connected

Pushing out from their anchorage at Goa, in southern India, Portuguese forces took control in 1511 of Malacca, a key point of exchange between Chinese and Islamic trading networks. Through the middle decades of the sixteenth century, Portuguese traders engaged in the vibrant commerce of the Indian Ocean and South China Sea, contending with smugglers, pirates, and Chinese imperial policy. During the sixteenth century, trade through Southeast Asia grew rapidly. Tax revenues, collected in return for the protection of this trade, helped centralize military power, purchase gunships and muskets, and hire Muslim and Portuguese mercenaries—all to support "port-states," safe harbors for trade in the places known today as the Philippines, Indonesia, Vietnam, Cambodia, Thailand, Myanmar, and Malaysia. Muslim rulers claimed sovereignty over some of these territories, collecting tribute in return for military protection; but local populations usually experienced little change in their daily lives and cultures imposed by different rulers. Contending with the Portuguese for control of trading routes and resources, the sultans of Southeast Asia turned to Suleiman, ruler of the Ottomans and protector of the Islamic faith, who sent materiel and perhaps even supported a military academy in the sultanate of Aceh, on the Indonesian island of Sumatra.

### Iberia in the Pacific

The Iberian presence in the Pacific also grew in the sixteenth century. The arrival of American silver in China prompted Chinese officials to sanction trade with

**EUROPEAN ACTIVITY IN ASIA, ca. 1650**

Dutch | British
Portuguese | Danish
Spanish

**MAP 2.3** European Activity in Asia, ca. 1650

**AN ARTIST'S RENDERING OF THE GLOBAL MISSIONARY INITIATIVES OF THE SOCIETY OF JESUS (JESUITS).** The Society of Jesus commissioned this painting in the seventeenth century for the Church of San Pedro in Lima (Peru). The Jesuits used art as a key means to convey their image as a global Catholic missionary enterprise. Notice the variety of clothes and phenotypes portrayed. The Jesuit missionaries, displayed in the center of the painting, bring the New Testament message, excerpted in Latin from the Gospels of Mark, Luke, and the Acts of the Apostles.

the Europeans, leading to the establishment of a permanent Portuguese enclave at Macau, on the South China coast, in 1557. In the 1560s, a Spanish expedition, launched from the Pacific coast of Mexico, established a permanent commercial and administrative settlement on the islands now called the Philippines, named after the Spanish monarch Philip II (1527–1598). From these bases, the Spanish and Portuguese conducted trade throughout maritime Asia, although China and Japan remained their primary objectives. With the merchants and sailors came priests, who, as in the Americas, attempted Roman Catholic evangelization of the region's peoples.

The Spanish and Portuguese recognized the great diversity of political and social power structures in Asia and tried to act accordingly. Miguel López de Legazpi (1502–1572), leader of the Spanish expedition to the Philippines, remarked that "the inhabitants of these islands are not subjected to any law, king or lord," which meant that the islands, with their natural and human resources, were not organized in a way that could prevent Spanish dominion over them. His sovereign, Philip II, wanted to use this island base as the foundation for a new diplomatic relationship with the Chinese emperor. Chinese pirates, captured by the Spanish, were returned to Chinese imperial officials, priestly emissaries were dispatched, and gifts were exchanged; but officials in Mexico and the Philippines who advocated military intimidation rather than negotiation undermined Philip's efforts. Sovereign-to-sovereign diplomacy did not materialize, although Jesuit missionaries were ultimately permitted to enter Beijing, the imperial capital. The Jesuit Matteo Ricci (1552–1610) became the first European invited to the Forbidden City, although he never met the Emperor. The Jesuits, through their strategies of adopting local customs, learning the local language, and interpreting Christian doctrine in the context of local practices, won converts to Catholicism—tens of thousands in the early 1600s—including some members of the imperial court. Still, this was a tiny fraction of the total population, and any momentum these Christian missionaries had at the Ming court flagged as the dynasty declined into rebellion and disorder in the 1640s.

## Japan and the Dutch

In Japan, as noted in the introduction to this chapter, rulers interested in strengthening their control were even more vigilant in limiting the activities of foreigners. Under the government of the Tokugawa family (the military government was called a Shogunate), the Portuguese first were isolated on an artificial island (Dejima) built in the harbor at Nagasaki, and later barred from trade entirely when they were blamed in part for a large-scale uprising of mostly Catholic peasants, the Shimabara Rebellion (1637–1638). In 1641, the Dutch became the only European merchants legally permitted to import goods to Japan through Dejima. Dutch commercial success in Japan was based in part on the fact that the Dutch Protestants were not committed to Christian evangelization as part of their global engagements in the same way as the (Catholic) Spanish and Portuguese were.

The Dutch success illustrates how competition for trade among European powers strengthened the position of Asian rulers against the Spanish and Portuguese and contributed to the decline of these Iberian powers in relation to other kingdoms. From this period forward, Britain, French, and Dutch merchants and seafarers would be the most important Europeans in the region. The British and Dutch East India Companies, both established in the first decade of the seventeenth century, would dominate European-Asian economic relations over the next one hundred fifty years, particularly in South and Southeast Asia. The French, too, established trading posts in West Africa (Senegal), South Asia (Pondicherry), and the Indian Ocean (Île de Bourbon) during this period.

## Conclusion

First setting eyes on Tenochtitlan, Bernal Díaz del Castillo wondered if he was seeing a mirage. Arriving with Cortés, Díaz cast his gaze on a city that appeared to him straight out of medieval legends. His memoir of the conquest, written as an old man back in Spain, continued to couch the activities of Cortés and his band in the terms of these epic tales. Understanding the full scope of this era, and its importance, requires overcoming enduring misconceptions that emerge from relying on the perspective of conquistadors like Bernal Díaz or those who place these men as the only protagonists who mattered in shaping historical outcomes. In this chapter, we have tried to provide a broader perspective. Even so, through much of the sixteenth century, Spanish and Portuguese institutions, individuals, and ideas mediated the connection between the Western Hemisphere and the rest of the world. Because Iberia—Spain and Portugal—was already part of the European-Asian-African network, the Western Hemisphere was immediately linked into that complex. Yet, this joining of the hemispheres with Iberian political, economic, and cultural thread is not the whole story. Other changes of global significance in the sixteenth century also wove the globe together. German and English religious dissidents, Chinese potters, Islamic sultans, Hindu

**TIMELINE**

**1486**
Ahuitzotl assumes
power in Tenochtitlan

**1492–1600**
275,000 enslaved
Africans transported
to the Americas

**1511**
Portuguese
seize Malacca

**1521**
Tenochtitlan
surrenders to
Hernán Cortés

**1492**
Christopher Columbus makes
landfall in the Caribbean, beginning
the Columbian Exchange

**1500–1600**
Indigenous population of
the Americas declines by
approximately 90 percent

**1512**
Spanish Crown issues Laws of Burgos
outlining legal obligations of
conquistadors toward indigenous peoples

textile workers, Japanese officials, and Dutch merchants joined Spanish priests, Portuguese sailors, Aztec warriors, and Inca mine workers in the new era of globalization, to which we will devote further attention in the following two chapters. First, we will describe how this emerging global economy worked. Then, we will see the ways in which rulers attempted to muster both old and new resources to gain and maintain power.

## A Few Good Books

Giancarlo Casale. *The Ottoman Age of Exploration*. New York: Oxford University Press, 2010.

Inga Clendinnen. *Ambivalent Conquests: Maya and Spaniard in Yucatán*. 2nd ed. Cambridge: Cambridge University Press, 2003.

Alfred W. Crosby, Jr. *The Columbian Exchange: Biological and Cultural Consequences of 1492*. 30th Anniversary Edition. Westport, CT: Praeger Publishers, 2003.

Matthew Restall. *Seven Myths of the Spanish Conquest*. New York: Oxford University Press, 2003.

Charles Mann. *1493: Uncovering the New World Columbus Created*. New York: Alfred A. Knopf, 2011.

Jonathan D. Spence. *The Memory Palace of Matteo Ricci*. New York: Penguin, 1985.

A. J. R. Russell-Wood. *The Portuguese Empire, 1415–1808: A World on the Move*. Baltimore: Johns Hopkins University Press, 1998.

*For additional resources, including maps, primary sources, visuals, web links, and quizzes, please go to* **www.oup.com/us/carter**

**1533**
Spanish conquistadors execute Inca ruler Atahualpa

**1557**
Portuguese establish permanent trading port at Macau, China

**1639**
Portuguese banned from Japan

**1542**
Spanish Crown attempts to assert greater control over the Americas with "New Laws"

**1607**
Jamestown colony founded by English

**1641**
Dutch become only European merchants legally permitted to import goods to Japan

(TOP) MASJID-I-SHAH, ISFAHAN, PERSIA (IRAN). Begun by Shah Abbas in the early seventeenth century, the mosque was a testament to the ambitions and wealth of the Safavid rulers who built the capital of their empire at Isfahan. This photograph, ca. 1900, was taken by Percy Molesworth Sykes, a British military officer and diplomat, stationed in the region.

(RIGHT) THE KANGXI EMPEROR OF QING DYNASTY CHINA. Seen here in a formal imperial portrait painted on silk, the Kangxi Emperor ruled from 1661 to 1722, longer than any other Emperor of China up to that time. Under his rule, the Manchu Qing Dynasty consolidated its conquest of China and expanded its borders in central and southeast Asia.

# The Paradoxes of Early Modern Empire

## 1501–1661

In 1501, the army of a young religious visionary named Ismail (1487–1524) captured the city of Tabriz, about four hundred miles northeast of Tehran (in present-day Iran). Just fourteen years old, Ismail rose to power with the military aid of the *Qizilbash*, warrior horsemen with roots in Azerbaijan and Anatolia. Ismail believed he was the "Shadow of God," divinely ordained to impose the practices of Shi`a Islamic belief, and his warriors adopted the battle cry, "My spiritual leader and master, for whom I sacrifice myself!" Assuming the title Shah, a Persian title that dated back almost two thousand years, Ismail established the Safavid Empire. Under Ismail and his descendants, who also embraced the principle of divinely inspired rule, the empire survived for over two centuries. Royal workshops produced high-quality textiles for the imperial court but also for export, delivering income to the royal treasury. A sophisticated administrative structure maintained the imperial court's power. At the end of the sixteenth century, Ismail's descendant Shah Abbas (1571–1629) moved the capital to Isfahan and added an entirely new city to the existing urban complex, building a grand mosque, an imperial palace, and a giant commercial center (bazaar). Isfahan grew into one of the most dynamic economic and cultural hubs of the early modern world.

One hundred and sixty years after Ismail captured Tabriz, a Manchu prince who would rule as the Kangxi Emperor (1654–1722) succeeded to the throne in China, beginning the longest individual reign in China's history. Every new ruler faces challenges, but these circumstances were particularly difficult. When he took the throne in 1661, Kangxi was only seven years old. He began ruling in his own right (without supervising regents) just six years later. Like all rulers of the Qing (pronounced "ching") Dynasty, he was not Chinese but Manchu, a linguistically and culturally distinct people who had conquered China from the north only two decades before. Many Chinese, especially those loyal to the preceding Ming Dynasty, still regarded the Manchus with hostility, and the Kangxi Emperor worked hard to establish and maintain his

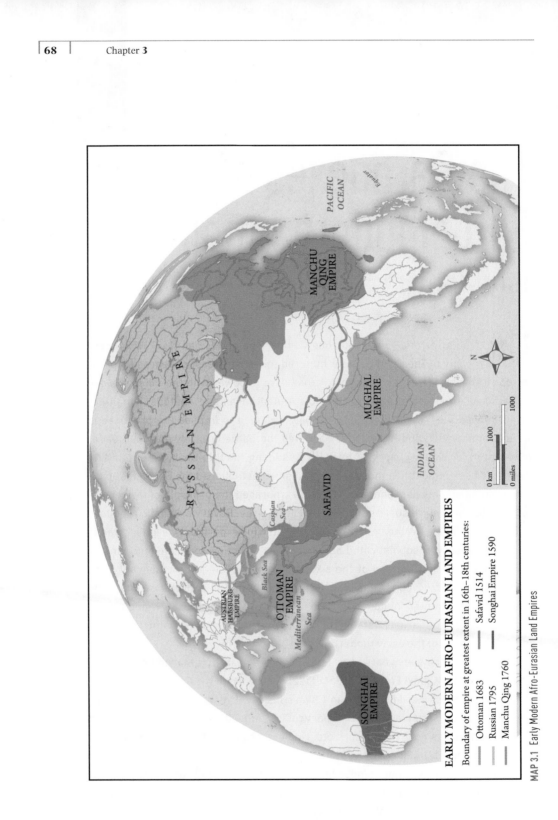

## EARLY MODERN AFRO-EURASIAN LAND EMPIRES

Boundary of empire at greatest extent in 16th–18th centuries:

Ottoman 1683

Russian 1795

Manchu Qing 1760

Safavid 1514

Songhai Empire 1590

**MAP 3.1** Early Modern Afro-Eurasian Land Empires

legitimacy. He made six tours of the south (for centuries the traditional center of Chinese culture), learning about local conditions, demonstrating to officials his active leadership, and publicizing his concern for the people. He also issued a "Sacred Edict"—to be read in every village by local officials—that encouraged filial respect, generosity, frugality, and loyalty. These were Confucian principles that had been the official foundation of Chinese statecraft for centuries, showing that although the Qing rulers were Manchu, they were familiar with the values that Chinese emperors had invoked for centuries to maintain a stable and well-ordered society. The Kangxi Emperor also worked to win over the Chinese scholars needed to run the bureaucracy. He sponsored a special examination to select authors to write the history of the Ming dynasty and set others to work compiling a dictionary (still used today) and an encyclopedia of five thousand volumes. Combined with military expansion into Tibet and Mongolia, the Emperor's actions solidified the Qing claim to sovereignty.

---

The actions of Ismail and the Kangxi Emperor illustrate many of the ways rulers and their peoples related to one another during the sixteenth and seventeenth centuries. Leaders made increasingly audacious claims to rule great expanses of territory and resources. To turn claims into action, they created laws and constructed rituals to stitch together diverse ethnic, religious, linguistic, and social groups into political bodies ultimately loyal to only one head. They deployed religious, military, and judicial enforcers and distributed material rewards and harsh punishments to reinforce their claims. In this chapter, we analyze the actions of different claimants to power and explain how and why some succeeded and others failed during this time. We will explain first how the era's new economic and technological landscape altered the way elites made war and built states. Then we will analyze the ways competing groups and individuals justified these new forms of power philosophically, religiously, and culturally. Our goal for this chapter is to show how material conditions, ideas, and individual agency influenced the practices of rulership, the relationships among rulers, and the tensions that could emerge between rulers and the peoples over whom they claimed sovereignty during this era of empire building.

## The Words and Deeds of Empire Building

During the sixteenth and seventeenth centuries, both the nature of war and the ability of rulers to use their power against populations changed dramatically. Rulers, and those who aspired to be, changed the way they prepared for and conducted war, driven by improved weaponry that altered strategies and tactics. State builders who wished to prosper in overseas realms built larger and more heavily armed ships to traverse the world's waterways. New features of warfare held the promise that those who mastered their techniques could take and hold more territory.

No technological innovation transformed warfare more than gunpowder, which originated in China in the ninth century. Weapons based on it spread through Afro-Eurasia over the subsequent centuries. The significant transformation of the sixteenth and seventeenth centuries was not gunpowder's invention but the changing scale of new weapons and the means to acquire and use them. Rulers across the supercontinent—Safavids, Mughals, French, Spanish, English, Ottomans, Qing, Asante, Dahomey, and others—turned revenues into firearms and soldiers. New weapons and ammunition, and their innovative use, could help determine victory and defeat, but not alone. Enduring factors like the economic resources available to supply or resupply a war effort, decisions made in the heat of battle, and the commitment of troops to their cause could still determine their outcomes.

In Chapter 4, we will examine the early modern global economy in detail. For now, just keep in mind that the resources to support larger, more expensive armed forces and military campaigns varied in their specific origins, but could all be traced to the processes of globalization we have already described. More material resources for state building were now available, as were larger and higher quality weapons for use on land and sea. Merchants and manufacturers filled government coffers in exchange for the right to bring goods to markets around the globe. Innovations in finance lubricated global commerce and also allowed states to wage larger wars on the promise that they would pay for them with the spoils of victory.

The changing stakes were not lost on those seeking power in the sixteenth century. Niccolò Machiavelli (1469–1527) was a keen observer of political and military affairs who served as an official of the city state of Florence on the Italian Peninsula. Machiavelli concluded that no overarching or universal set of religious or ethical rules guided or constrained political interactions, so understanding and using power was the essential component of political leadership. Machiavelli's advice on how to act on this insight is contained in his most famous work, *The Prince*; but Machiavelli produced other works that contain observations on both conceptual and practical matters, such as *The Art of War* and *A Discourse about the Provision of Money*.

Machiavelli was not alone in trying to understand what states were and how they worked during this time period, nor was this process limited to Europe. The historical sociologist Charles Tilly (1929–2008) described this process as the achievement of "stateness," a process that Linda Darling notes is one of the defining features of this "Early Modern" era across Afro-Eurasia. The emergence of stable, larger, centralized states was accompanied by the proliferation of political advice literature on how states work, which appeared not only in Christian Europe but in Islamic kingdoms as well, written in Arabic, Persian, and Turkish. For example, both *The Jalalian Ethics* by Jalal al-Din al-Dawani (1427–1503) and *The Conduct of Kings*, by his student Fazlullah ibn Ruzbihan, elaborate on the connection between power and action in ways similar to Machiavelli and others, analyzing both the conceptual foundations of the state and the practical applications of those concepts.[1]

Of course rulers, groups, or institutions exercising power—and elites writing and thinking about it—were not new in the 1500s. Armies, taxes, and courts of law did not originate in this period. However, from the end of the fifteenth century to the middle of the seventeenth century, we see a broad trend in which individuals and groups claimed greater control over more material resources and more aspects of more lives in greater expanses of territory, even across open ocean. Creating these ambitious states exposed a set of paradoxes. These new states often aspired to be highly centralized, with a single, strong leader. But, to organize the material and human resources needed to construct these larger states required cooperation among many groups, increasing the chances of conflict between the central leadership and potential rivals, often thousands of miles from their rulers' ancestral homelands but sometimes in the rulers' strongholds themselves. Finally, the construction of, and conflict among, empires during this era reminds us that every claim to sovereignty invites questions about legitimacy: is a claim to power recognized and accepted by people and institutions other than yourself? Can the claim be defended—logically and militarily—against challengers? For most people living at the time, the answers to such questions remained rooted in divine order. In the sections that follow, we examine these trends in a number of regional variations.

## Consolidation and Struggle in the Islamic World

Machiavelli is sometimes portrayed as a ruthless calculator who advised that any action was OK if it led to a positive outcome for the ruler. But what truly set Machiavelli's political philosophy apart from most of his contemporaries was that God was not at the center of his idea of rulership. Few people at the time shared this view; most assertions about rulership and sovereignty connected rulers with supernatural or divine powers beyond the scope of human comprehension. As a result, disputes over theology and religious practice linked the geographic spread of different religious traditions and empire building.

---

[1]   Charles Tilly developed his analysis over the course of a long career and many publications, including *Coercion, Capital, and European States: AD 990–1992*. (Cambridge, MA: Blackwell, 1990). See also Charles Tilly, "War Making and State Making as Organized Crime" in *Bringing the State Back In*, ed. Peter B. Evans et al. (Cambridge, England: Cambridge University Press, 1985), 169–191. This essay inspired our use of *The Godfather* reference earlier in this book. For discussions of the broader Afro-Eurasian context of state making and political philosophy during this era, see Linda Darling, *A History of Social Justice and Political Power in the Middle East: The Circle of Justice from Mesopotamia to Globalization* (London: Routledge Press, 2013); and Adeeb Khalid, *Islam after Communism: Religion and Politics in Central Asia* (Berkeley: University of California Press, 2014).

The full scope of religious transformation in this era is dizzying, so we will limit our discussion here primarily to the question of its relationship to state building. Through the sixteenth century, Islam spread far beyond the faith's geographic origins in the Arabian Peninsula. Along with an extensive commercial and political network based on the Arabic language, Islam linked believers to a larger world of commerce and learning. Muslim rulers could use this broader world to support themselves against challengers who claimed the right to rule based on other religious traditions. For example, as we saw in Chapter 2, the sultan of Aceh (in today's Indonesia) sent an ambassador to the Ottoman Empire during the reign of Suleiman I—a journey of more than five thousand miles—to negotiate an alliance with the great empire.

MAP OF THE MEDITERRANEAN COAST AND ALANYA FORTRESS (PRESENT-DAY TURKEY). From Piri Reis (1465–1555), *The Book of Navigation*, dedicated to Sultan Suleiman I (1495–1566). Piri Reis was an Ottoman naval officer and cartographer who produced the first world maps for Islamic rulers that attempted to incorporate the Western Hemisphere.

The sultan of Aceh (like many, but as we shall see not all Muslims) recognized the ruler of the Ottoman Empire as the Caliph, the successor to the prophet Muhammad and therefore leader of all of the Islamic faithful. The sultan also recognized that the Ottoman Empire was seeking allies in its multifront war against some of the world's other major military and economic powers.

In the Mediterranean region, the city of Constantinople, conquered by Sultan Mehmed II (1432–1481), had provided a strategic base for subsequent expansion. Mehmed and his successors continued to spread Ottoman influence from the outskirts of Vienna (Austria) in the west, south through Egypt, across the Red Sea to the holy Muslim cities of Medina and Mecca (in Arabia), and east to the Persian Gulf, reaching the lucrative Indian Ocean trading routes. As the empire grew, Ottoman sultans continued to tolerate communities of religious minorities within the empire under the millet system. Although comprised of many religions, languages, and ethnicities, the empire as a whole was held together by a Sunni Islamic legal and administrative system, with government funds supporting Islamic education and the training of the Sunni religious hierarchy.

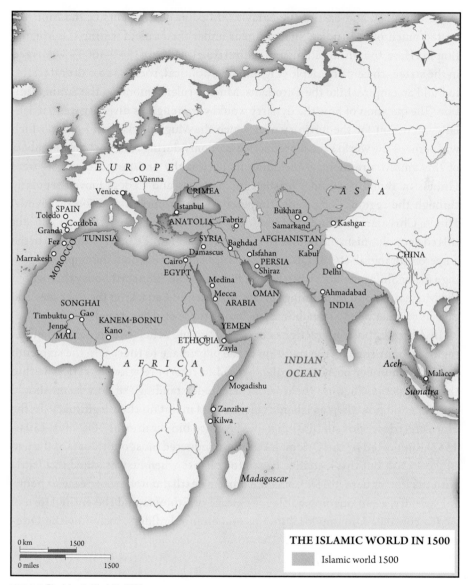

**THE ISLAMIC WORLD IN 1500**

Islamic world 1500

MAP 3.2  The Islamic World in 1500

Unlike the Ottomans, Shah Ismail I and his Safavid successors, based in Persia, were rooted in the Shiʿa tradition. The long-standing and important Sunni-Shiʿa split had roots in the seventh-century struggles over leadership of the faithful after the death of the Prophet Muhammad and had grown over time to include divergent interpretations of Islamic law and other matters. This Sunni and Shiʿa divide was one of several factors contributing to multiple battles between successive Ottoman and Safavid rulers.

To the south and east of the Safavids, Muslim descendants of the Mongols united much of the Indian subcontinent under their rule, forming the Mughal Empire. Here, too, an ambitious and skillful ruler—Akbar (1542–1605)—emerged in the sixteenth century, deploying military, political, social, and cultural tactics to build an empire. Like the Ottomans, Mughal rulers embraced the Sunni tradition. The question of how the dynasty would view religious diversity was particularly important for the territory over which the Mughals claimed to rule, which was perhaps the world's most productive economy during this era. Large numbers of this empire's residents—including many wealthy and powerful ones—were Hindus or Buddhists, and Christian missionaries and traders moved regularly through the region. For a time, Emperor Akbar promoted a fusion of Islamic, Hindu, Christian, and Buddhist traditions with himself as the unifying force, but this cosmopolitanism did not survive past Akbar's reign. A century after Akbar, the emperor Aurangzeb (1618–1707) provoked uprisings throughout the empire, including a major Shi`a rebellion, when he decided to impose Sunni orthodoxy throughout the Mughal Empire by banning certain practices and attacking the holy sites and objects of other religious traditions, including those of other strands of Islam.

In Africa, robust interactions continued among scholars and political elites, regularly nourished by the tradition of the pilgrimage to Mecca. In the sixteenth century, a number of African rulers vowed to reform religious practices within their kingdoms, aligning them with their understandings of how Islam should function and how they, as Islamic rulers, could maintain their legitimacy. In the Horn of Africa, a Somali Muslim named Ahmad bin Ibrahim al-Ghazi (ca. 1504–1543), supported by the Ottoman Empire, conquered most of Ethiopia at the end of the 1520s; but this initiative began to collapse when he was killed in a battle with the Portuguese in 1543. Imam Ahmad's death did not mean peace or political stability, as an ongoing battle for control of Ethiopia and the entire Horn of Africa continued among local groups and empire builders, including the Ottomans and the Portuguese.

## Christian Reformation

About the same time as Machiavelli was writing, a young Roman Catholic priest named Martin Luther (1483–1546) also offered some advice. A theology professor in the German city of Wittenberg, Luther wrote about how God's will was reflected in human practice. He concluded that the Christian institutions of his day were out of whack and reported his findings—ninety-five observations in all, usually called the Ninety-Five Theses—on Halloween, 1517. Luther's critique outraged his superiors, but Luther refused to back down. Instead, he expanded on his critiques in three pamphlets challenging the church's entire hierarchy, up to

THE MIRACLES OF THE ARCHANGEL MICHAEL, FROM A HOMILARY FROM GONDAR, ETHIOPIA. LATE SEVENTEENTH CENTURY. This book, a collection of inspirational stories of miracles performed by the Archangel Michael, was most likely commissioned by members of the Ethiopian imperial court for use during feast days in the capital. The Ethiopian royal court used such tools to reinforce the cultural connection between Christian traditions and its authority.

and including the papacy, as corrupt and immoral, and questioned its right to rule over Christians and interpret Holy Scripture.

From the perspective of Western Europe, Luther appeared to be challenging a monolithic Christendom dominated by the Roman Catholic Church, but Christianity was already—like Islam, Hinduism, or Buddhism—riven by differences among the faithful. Although the church based in Rome was the largest, distinct Christian hierarchies and practices existed in Russia, Ethiopia, and elsewhere. In these places, political leaders of the sixteenth and seventeenth centuries used Christian traditions as a fulcrum to move people and resources to their causes.

In Ethiopia, leaders invoked an Orthodox Christian tradition as the element of Ethiopian identity that could rally forces of resistance against Islamic warriors but to also expel missionaries who tried to bring the Ethiopian Church into line with the Roman hierarchy and tenets of the faith. In Russia, Ivan IV, the Grand Prince of Moscow (1530–1584) and first person to be called "Tsar of all the Russians," did many of the things the other empire builders we discuss in this chapter were doing. He armed the first permanent Russian military force with an early form of rifle, conceded monopoly trading rights to gain revenue from merchant groups, and developed a policy to secure an adequate labor supply for the empire's rural estates. He also commissioned elaborate Orthodox cathedrals to commemorate his victories over Islamic foes and supported the Orthodox Church in myriad other ways. The clerical hierarchy reciprocated by supporting Ivan's growing territorial claims of sovereignty.

So while Martin Luther's protests did not bring an end to a single universal Christian faith—he could not destroy something that did not exist—they did challenge religious and political authorities in Western Europe at an important moment. Luther's target, the clerical hierarchy, was in many ways the most powerful institution in this part of the world at the time. In addition to guiding the spiritual lives of Europe's population, which was overwhelmingly Christian, Church leaders controlled great wealth and often served as political advisers or even as de facto rulers themselves. In the region where Luther lived, to advocate or practice Christianity in ways that the Roman hierarchy did not sanction was subject to both religious and political punishment: public penance, excommunication, exile, imprisonment, and even execution. Luther and other "Protestants" (protesters against Church teachings or the clerical hierarchy) therefore challenged both religious and secular authority in Europe. Both the Pope and the Holy Roman Emperor, who claimed authority over the lands where Luther lived, leveled charges against him. In the spring of 1521, a special court condemned Luther as a heretic and criminal.

But Luther was never turned over to these authorities to face punishment. He was protected by the powerful Frederick III, Elector of Saxony (1463–1525), who had founded the university where Luther had worked. That Luther could be publicly condemned by leading political and religious authorities yet remain unpunished demonstrates the limits to the real power of both the Pope and the Holy Roman Emperor, and this is crucial to understanding this moment. Power in Europe—political, economic, and now religious—appeared to be up for grabs and a violent sorting-out process erupted.

The "Reformation" that Luther precipitated transcended religion. Over the coming months and years, supporters and interpreters of Luther's ideas launched rebellions from below against authorities throughout German-speaking lands and beyond. More than one hundred thousand people died in what became known as the German Peasants' War, a bloody conflict that illustrates the complex interactions of religion and politics at the time. In 1525, one group of rebels demanded the right to choose their own pastors and have more control over church funds, clearly reflecting the anticorruption rhetoric of Luther's protests. But the rebels went further, demanding that local elites respect their rights to hunt and gather wood and to limit their labor contributions to their landlords. Finally, they demanded fairness in the creation and enforcement of laws.

The rebels justified their demands with words: multiple and specific references to the Bible, based on Luther's insistence that the Bible was the ultimate source of all authority. But rather than being pleased by this interpretation of his call for reform, Luther condemned the rebels as "murdering, thieving hordes" and encouraged the rulers of Central Europe to simultaneously reform the practice of Christianity in their realms and put to death for their blasphemies those who challenged political authority.

## The Power of the Printed Word

In the ensuing war of words and deeds among Christians, all sides made use of a new and powerful weapon: the printing press. The importance of the printing press was appropriate given that the written word had been at the center of reform movements in Christianity for many decades. Like earlier reformers, including Englishman John Wycliffe (ca. 1328–1384) and Bohemian Jan Hus (1369–1415), Luther insisted that the Mass—the central ceremony in Christian religious life—and the Bible be presented in languages that most churchgoers could understand rather than Latin, the language of clergy and the educated. This was politically, socially, and religiously radical; it would place direct access to Holy Scripture into the hands of many more people—like the German-speaking rebels of the Peasants' War—threatening to diminish the power of the clergy, who were freer to interpret Scripture if it were available only in Latin.

For earlier generations, the cost of translating and reproducing new Bibles helped keep their protests largely theoretical. But by Luther's day, new technology made printing and distributing texts easier and less expensive. While in hiding after his trial, Luther set to work translating the Bible into German, arranging to publish his translation of the New Testament in 1522 and the Old Testament thirteen years later. This made the basic religious texts of Christianity accessible in new ways to millions of people and also shaped the modern German language. Translations of the Bible into English and other languages would have the same effect. Printing presses with moveable type dramatically lowered the costs of reproducing all types of information, not just the Bible. Written commentary on Luther's grievances spread quickly across Europe and beyond. Among the thousands of texts published during this era were cartoons and pamphlets—some lampooning the Pope, others demonizing Luther.

In ways like this, printing demonstrated the relationship between power and ideas in shaping the world. Printing, using carved wood blocks, had first developed in China, probably in the early centuries of the Common Era. In those first presses, an entire page would be carved (in reverse) into a piece of wood. Movable type, with individual characters that could be rearranged to print different content, did not develop until about 1300, using porcelain at first and then metal, in China and Korea. But printing did not become widespread, perhaps because the thousands of characters needed to print in classical Chinese—the elite language in both places—made a complete set of type expensive to produce and cumbersome to use.

European presses, though, needed multiple copies of just a few dozen characters—the letters of the alphabet—that could be rearranged to print each page. A Bible, printed in Latin by Johannes Gutenberg (ca. 1398–1468) in the 1450s was the first major printed work in Europe. Historians Lucien Febvre and Henri-Jean Martin documented how presses spread across Europe during the late fifteenth century, and their products flowed across the continent and beyond. In 1539, a press and printer arrived in New Spain (Mexico). More than one hundred titles were published in Mexico City in the sixteenth century. European colonizers and explorers from the sixteenth century carried books to help accomplish their goals of conversion and domination. Presses arrived in India (Goa, 1557), China (Macau, 1588), and Japan (Nagasaki, 1590). Jesuit missionaries first arrived in China around this time, and Matteo Ricci carried books with him as part of his attempt to convert the top layers of society to Christianity when he finally received permission to enter Beijing in 1601.

MATTHIAS GERUNG, "APOCALYPSE AND SATIRICAL ALLEGORIES ON THE CHURCH" (1546). This woodcut print was commissioned by a Protestant nobleman in Central Europe to illustrate an anti-Catholic pamphlet. The upper half of the image contrasts the rectitude of Protestant forms of worship with the corrupt practices of Roman Catholicism in the lower half.

In Europe, the circulation of books promoted the standardization of languages that served the needs both of rulers and printers who needed a large enough market place to sell their goods. More books began to be published in languages other than Latin—French and Italian especially. Reviews of printers' inventories and other records reveal that before 1500, three-quarters of the books published in Europe were in Latin (ten times more than any other language) and nearly half of them were on religious topics. During the sixteenth century, religious texts continued to dominate, but their share of all published works fell, as interest in the Greek and Roman classics grew. Books on history also became very popular, often printed both in Latin and other languages.[2]

---

[2]    Lucien Febvre and Henri-Jean Martin, *The Coming of the Book: The Impact of Printing, 1450–1800*, 3rd ed. (London: Verso, 2010).

Ruling groups saw the importance of this change in the way language was being used. As a result, languages that we sometimes assume today to be ancient and unchanging coalesced in this period. The first book of Spanish grammar, *Gramática de la lengua española*, was compiled by Antonio de Nebrija (1441–1522) and published in 1492. Nebrija asserted in the prologue that a written grammar for Spanish was important because history had proven that a proper language has always been the companion of empire. French was established as the official language of courts of justice in the Kingdom of France in 1539. Luther himself wrote his political pamphlet, "To the Christian Nobility of the German Nation" (1520), in German, not Latin, revealing both his confidence in the marketplace for publications in that language and his target audience: literate but not scholarly. Recognizing the political potential of the written word, rulers attempted to control it both by promoting languages, literatures, and histories that supported their claims to rule and by censoring and suppressing the printed word as if books contained state secrets. Politics, religion, and culture were clearly and closely entangled.

## Tangled Loyalties and the European Wars of Religion

Given these complex interconnections, you may not find it surprising that the bitter "Wars of Religion" that dominated the sixteenth century in Europe were about much more than religion. When Luther wrote his controversial theses, the Holy Roman Emperor Charles V—also at the time King of Spain and the most powerful ruler in Europe—held him accountable. Charles's grandparents, Ferdinand and Isabella, had supported Columbus's voyages and driven from the Iberian Peninsula Muslims and Jews who refused to convert to Christianity. The Spanish Inquisition, designed to enforce Christian thinking that supported royal power throughout the empire, reflected in its operations the roots of a modern state bureaucracy. Charles, then, controlled not only a large, land-based empire like those of central and eastern Eurasia, but also vast seaborne wealth and a fearsome crew of enforcers. Yet, he could not silence a German monk who dared challenge his authority.

### Fragmentation of the Empire of Charles V

Emperor Charles V claimed sovereignty over four million square miles of territory on three continents. When Charles abdicated in 1556, his titles and territories were divided between his brother and son. One got Austrian and German lands and became Holy Roman Emperor. The other inherited claims to the Netherlands, the Italian peninsula, Spain, and its New World territories. The son, Philip II (1527–1598), still ruled what was by many measures the strongest empire in Europe, but Philip overplayed his hand in efforts to tighten his control over the Netherlands. Consisting of seventeen distinct political entities covering today's Netherlands, Belgium, and Luxembourg, this was an economically and

MAP 3.3  Major Fortifications and Battles in Europe, 1450–1750

culturally diverse region, prosperous from commerce and manufacturing. Philip, seeking to finance the expansion of his empire and secure its unity, increased the tax burden on the Netherlands and worked to stamp out Protestantism. Resistance, including vandalism of churches, led Philip to send in ten thousand troops in 1567. Brutal suppression, including thousands of public executions, temporarily stalled the revolt, but ultimately the rulers of Spain could not control the Netherlands, which emerged independent in the 1580s.

Independence did not mean peace. Sporadic armed struggle continued between Spanish forces and those of the United Provinces of the Netherlands, coinciding with a continent-wide war in the early seventeenth century known as the Thirty Years' War (1618–1648). Viewed from one angle, this was a fight between the Roman Catholic south, led by Spain and the Holy Roman Empire, and the Protestant north, including many German states, led by the Empire of Sweden. But the war had as many political and economic aspects as religious ones. For example, France, under a Catholic sovereign, fought on the side of Protestant Sweden and the Netherlands, and the Muslim Ottoman Empire made an alliance with the (Protestant) Christian Prince of Transylvania. Strategic and economic interests guided the supercontinent's empire builders of the sixteenth and seventeenth centuries, complicating, and sometimes trumping, religious conflicts.

In 1648, the Peace of Westphalia ended the Thirty Years' War. The peace settlement attempted to address some of the root causes of conflict and establish some new grounds for relations between and among states. For example, the treaties established that religious difference alone could not justify war among Christian rulers and that religious practices within any state were the sole business of the ruler and not the rulers of other states. Reflecting new circumstances in international relations, the pope played virtually no role in the peace settlement. As the Thirty Years' War and its outcome help us to understand key components in the nature of relations among states during this era, analyzing examples of conflict within two very different Afro-Eurasian states and their outcomes will also aid our task of understanding the nature and evolution of states in general.

## Civil War in England

Within the vast expanse of Afro-Eurasia, tiny England seems an unlikely place for a fundamental shift of political organization to have global repercussions. It appeared a small theater of the "Wars of Religion" in the mid-sixteenth century, when the English throne passed to Protestant Elizabeth I (1533–1603) from her sister, Catholic Mary I (1516-1558). When Elizabeth sought to privilege the Church of England that her father, Henry VIII (1491–1547), had established, Mary's widower—Philip!—tried to resist. Militantly Catholic, Philip saw Elizabeth as a heretic and sought to replace her with her Catholic cousin (confusingly, also named Mary). Elizabeth in turn aided Protestant rebels in the Netherlands and even attacked Spanish shipping, demonstrating both England's naval power and the growing importance of maritime trade. When Elizabeth had her cousin Mary executed for plotting to take the throne in 1587, Philip launched his navy, known as the *Armada Invencible* (Invincible Fleet), to overthrow Elizabeth. The armada, though, was not invincible. Bad luck, bad strategy, and English tactics destroyed the Spanish fleet in 1588. Although Spain and England continued to fight for decades, the defeat of the armada opened the door for England's rise, with consequences across the globe.

In the sixteenth century, commercial revolution and religious reformation transformed— and destabilized—Europe. Both had important political implications, but the nature and direction of political change was not clear. Across Europe, owning land was usually the basis of political power, so merchants and other non-noble classes could become rich but remain politically impotent. And the most powerful landholder of all—the Roman Catholic Church—was fragmenting, leaving many of its resources to be redistributed and fought over. New political thought emerged in the struggle to make sense of this new era. As an island kingdom, England could not easily rely on overland expansion of wealth or sovereignty, but it was positioned to take advantage of the growing Atlantic maritime trade. Geography does not always determine the political development of states, but it is noteworthy that this kingdom whose borders were enforced by the sea would develop in theory and practice lasting and comprehensive limits on the powers of its monarchs.

During the first half of the seventeenth century, political tensions grew in England. The ruling Stuart Dynasty did not wish to be constrained in its ability to levy taxes and raise an army. Opponents of the monarchs' assertion of greater power argued that English tradition gave a consultative body—the Parliament— an important role in these decisions. To complicate matters, some influential members of Parliament were also interested in transforming religious practices in England and saw the King as an obstacle to that. In 1642, this increasingly intractable conflict erupted in civil wars that devastated England, Scotland, Wales, and Ireland (where as much as 40 percent of the population died as a result of the war). In 1649, Parliamentary forces executed King Charles I (1600–1649) for treason and abolished the monarchy. For more than a decade, the country had no king and struggled to establish a sovereign state with internal and external legitimacy. Under pressure from an army invading from Scotland, in 1660 a beleaguered Parliament restored the monarchy and invited the son of the beheaded king to take the throne.

In the shadow of the king's execution, Thomas Hobbes (1588–1679) published a book called *Leviathan*, subtitled *The Matter, Form and Power of a Commonwealth, Ecclesiastical and Civil.* Hobbes developed political theories that supported absolute government but argued that sovereign authority was based on the consent of *the people* and not on divine providence or natural order. Like Machiavelli, Hobbes wrote that a ruler was entitled to take extreme measures in defense of his power and his state but that these measures should serve the goal of a flourishing society—orderly and rich in culture—not the king's personal wealth. While acknowledging that people had to surrender many freedoms to a powerful sovereign—or suffer the "nasty, brutish, and short" life that plagued people in a state of nature without government—Hobbes also insisted that the legitimacy of the sovereign came from the consent of the governed in doing so, preserving for the people certain inalienable rights.

Hobbes was among the first to present a "Social Contract" theory of legitimacy. Later writers, especially John Locke (1632–1704) and Jean-Jacques Rousseau (1712–1778), would develop this idea in greater detail and draw some different conclusions, but the basic principles Hobbes suggested remained at the core: in the state of nature (i.e., the time before society and government), people were perfectly free but also absolutely vulnerable. Everyone could do as they pleased, but—because of this—there was no security, no safety. And so, the freedom of the state of nature was false; one was not even free to live in peace. In response, people could agree to give up some of their freedoms in exchange for security. Consider it this way: by giving up the right to take anything I want, I surrender some freedom; in exchange, my liberty is protected by the fact that others have also given up the right to take whatever *they* want. We make a contract to live as a society. We designate certain people to make rules—laws—by which everyone agrees to live, and others to enforce those laws, but only so long as they preserve the public peace and protect the public interest. Together these people—the government—preside over society in a way that benefits its members.

Hobbes's views troubled all sides in England's conflict and continued to vex future generations. He insisted that power to govern derived from the consent of the governed, angering those who argued that God, not the people, empower a ruler. On the other hand, he vested nearly limitless power in the state once it was formed, unsettling those wary of too powerful a sovereign. Nonetheless, his idea that a government's legitimacy comes from the people, and from its ability to protect the people's interests and well-being, ultimately emerged as the basis for many theories of the state in subsequent generations.

## Collapse and Restoration of Empire in China: From Ming to Qing

While Hobbes was contemplating Leviathan and war was brewing in England, war was also imminent on the eastern edge of the supercontinent where China's Ming dynasty, in power since 1368, faced financial and political crises on a scale that matched or exceeded those in Europe during the Wars of Religion. Indeed, it may be useful to think of China as akin to Europe because of its size and the diversity of languages, religions, and cultures found within territory claimed by China's imperial dynasties.

Like their counterparts around the world, Chinese rulers grappled with questions of legitimacy, authority, and sovereignty. Judaism, Christianity, and Islam all look to the God of the Hebrews as the Creator, so rulers across much of Afro-Eurasia had often used this idea of God (who was known to speak to his believers directly through earthly prophets and holy texts) as a source of legitimacy. In China, though, this was not an option for political elites. A key difference was the lack, throughout most of East Asian history, of any anthropomorphic idea of God, and certainly not one who spoke directly to people. As far back as 1000 BCE, rulers in China had appealed to the "Mandate of Heaven" (*tianming*) to justify their rule. Like the European idea of divine right, this notion of legitimacy derived from a supernatural source but in China, the well-being of the people indicated the holder of the Mandate. If the people didn't prosper, the Mandate could pass to another steward. This was not an idea like "the consent of the governed" constructed by Hobbes or other Social Contract theorists, but the suffering of the empire's subjects could indicate a ruler who had lost the Mandate, a prelude to being swept away. A ruler didn't need the people's consent to rule, but he (and it was almost always he) did need to rule over them well.

Within this framework, China developed a complex and sophisticated statecraft. The size and diversity of Chinese empires was a challenge even in good times, and natural or man-made disasters strained even the most capable of leaders. The Mongols, who had swept across most of Asia in the 1200s, established a sophisticated hierarchy and implemented some key financial innovations as part of their Yuan Dynasty in China yet could only maintain their dynasty for a century. That was when a peasant rebel named Zhu Yuanzhang (1328–1398) overthrew the Mongols and established the Ming Dynasty. Under Ming rule, China prospered politically, economically, and culturally, expanding its borders in all directions and knitting society together with an intensive commercial network. The early Ming emperors oversaw a state based on Confucian precepts of loyalty, benevolence, and propriety. As we saw in Chapter 1, Ming ships plied the waters of the Indian Ocean as far as the Middle East and East Africa, maintaining diplomatic and trade ties across the supercontinent.

By the late 1500s, however, the Ming state was in decline. Corruption at court and an inadequate tax structure undermined effective governance. Even the wars between Spain and England played a role: New World silver had been flowing into the Chinese economy, but English and Dutch raiders disrupted the supply. As the silver supply dwindled, its value increased. The government required that taxes be paid in silver but did not mint it into coins. As a result, Chinese peasants conducted most of their daily business in copper coins and had to buy silver to pay their taxes (the Chinese word for bank, *yinhang*, means literally "silver shop"). As silver became more valuable, more copper was needed to buy the same amount of silver, impoverishing the peasantry, dragging down the entire economy, and further reducing government revenues. Civil servants, including the military, were paid poorly and sometimes not at all. Public works projects, a traditional measure of a dynasty's effectiveness, were neglected. The Yellow River levees fell into disrepair; grain stored to ward off famine rotted. For a state with its legitimacy rooted in the well-being of its people, these were potent dangers. Several would-be rebels, including an unemployed post-station attendant named Li Zicheng (1606–1645), mobilized popular discontent against the Ming and initiated a rebellion in the 1630s.

Li and other rebellious peasants were not the only challenge facing the Ming. The Manchus—a confederation of tribes who were distinct linguistically and culturally from China's Han majority—had built their own empire starting in the 1500s to the northeast, in a region (Manchuria) that is a part of China today bounded by Russia and North Korea. Modeling their state largely on Chinese precedents, the Manchus expanded their territory until they were at the Ming's northern border. In many ways, in the early seventeenth century, the Manchu Empire appeared more stable and prosperous than China under the failing Ming. In the Spring of 1644 (the same era as the English Civil War, six thousand miles away), Manchu armies prepared to march on Beijing from the East, even as Li Zicheng's peasant army bore down on the capital from the West. The last Ming Emperor hanged himself upon hearing the news. With a rebel army occupying the capital and Manchu soldiers on the doorstep, the Mandate of Heaven seemed about to pass, but to whom?

The Ming's top general, Wu Sangui (1612–1678), remained in a position to play kingmaker between the two sides. The Manchu regent and Wu Sangui exchanged letters. Wu asked the Manchus' help to "destroy the roving bandits . . . and make manifest great righteousness in China." Manchu leaders argued for legitimacy using China's political logic: they would take up the Mandate of Heaven by restoring order to the Empire and its people. Maybe Wu believed this; maybe his calculus was more cynical. Perhaps he thought the Manchus simply had the resources to win and he would benefit if he backed the right side. Whatever his reasons, Wu Sangui backed the Manchu claim to the throne, although his actions were not universally admired. Many Ming generals, officials, and subjects rallied against the Manchu as illegitimate usurpers. The Manchu conquest of China became bitter and bloody, taking decades to complete. Some Ming princes attempted to maintain governments in exile, and many Chinese scholars remained loyal to the Ming dynasty, some choosing suicide or exile rather than aid the Qing.

## The New Qing History

Debates over the Qing conquest provide a good example of the way scholarship evolves based on new sources and new political contexts. For decades, scholars contended that the Manchus conquered China militarily; but then Chinese cultural superiority conquered the Manchus, and they became integrated into Chinese culture. Traditional Chinese historiography that tended to see "conquest dynasties" (i.e., dynasties led by non-Han rulers) as militarily capable but culturally weak shaped this view. Confucian scholars wrote history, and these men— actively or unconsciously—were biased in favor of classical Chinese practices and attitudes. It was impossible to deny that non-Chinese peoples had conquered China, but they could argue that the ongoing and more valuable elements of Chinese culture outlasted these "uncivilized" invaders.

Recent scholarship, based largely on new sources, has challenged this view of the Qing. The Manchus employed Han Chinese scholars and officials alongside Manchu ones, producing documents in both Chinese and Manchu (a language unrelated to Chinese and written in a completely different script). Few scholars, even in China, could read the Manchu documents, and many had assumed that the twin sets of correspondence were versions of the same information in different languages. Because few historians were reading Manchu (in part because few people believed it said anything new or interesting), this assumption went unchallenged.

Then, in the 1980s and 1990s, a movement called the "new Qing history" gathered momentum. More scholars began learning Manchu and looking at the records. What they found was that the Manchus retained many aspects of their culture and identity for much longer than people had supposed. The Manchus did employ many aspects of Chinese statecraft, but that did not mean that they simply became Chinese. Similar to the way Habsburg monarchs ruled Germans and Slavs, or Catholics and Muslims, differently, or as the Ottomans preserved religious autonomy through the millet system, Qing monarchs presented their rule differently to different parts of the empire. To the Han Chinese—who wrote imperial history as part of their own tradition—they adopted the air of Han Chinese emperors. But in Central Asia, or Tibet, or Manchuria, they presented themselves quite differently. And what of the "duplicate" correspondence written in Manchu and Chinese? Sometimes they were just translations for the use of non-Chinese speakers, but other times they were audits of Chinese officials or documents designed for direct use by the Emperor and kept secret from the Chinese bureaucrats.

Other scholars downplay the importance of the Manchus to understanding early modern China. In their view, even if the Manchu language can reveal nuances of policy debates and decisions, hundreds of millions of Chinese during this period lived their lives with little direct influence from the imperial government— regardless of their ethnicity. And even if the Qing emperors presented themselves differently in Tibet or Mongolia, the vast majority of the Qing Empire's population was Han Chinese. To this view, too much focus on the Manchus distorts the picture. The New Qing History is ongoing, a project involving thousands of scholars to move our knowledge of the primary sources forward.[3]

## How to Govern? "Seek Truth from Facts"

As they consolidated their rule, the Manchus, like other new governments, struggled to establish their legitimacy while they asserted their sovereignty. Although the Mandate of Heaven is an enduring foundational idea, many Chinese thinkers regularly revisited the foundations of legitimacy. One of them, Gu Yanwu (1613–1682), looked at the collapsing Ming dynasty and blamed its weakness on its unreflective adherence to ancient ways. According to Gu, scholarly obsession with the writings of Confucius, who lived two thousand years prior to the rise of the Qing dynasty, or even his later interpreters like Zhu Xi (1130–1200), had led to an inefficient and impractical state. Although Gu refused to serve the new Manchu rulers, remaining loyal to the fallen Ming dynasty, he did seek ways for China to strengthen itself. Gu traveled and observed widely and wrote about what he saw during his travels, on subjects ranging from geography to statecraft. Gu urged people to understand and act based on rigorous analysis, convincing evidence, and clear reasoning to "seek truth from facts." To promote these ends, he wrote practical studies of mining, banking, farming, and government, insisting on natural explanations for phenomena, rejecting the metaphysical speculation common in much Ming scholarship, which he blamed for the Ming's decay. Gu's methods exemplified *inductive reasoning*, which leads to generalizations about the world based on observation.

Gu's emphasis on observation had parallels across the supercontinent at this time, part of a stream of analysis changing the ways humans perceived and understood the natural world. Observations about the cosmos accumulated across Afro-Eurasia. The Indian astronomer Nilakantha Somayaji (1444–1544) determined that the planets Mercury, Venus, and Mars orbited the sun, observations confirmed by the Danish astronomer Tycho Brahe (1546–1601). At about the same time, Galileo Galilei (1564–1642) and Johannes Kepler (1571–1630) built on work by Nicolai Copernicus (1473–1543) to reimagine the earth's place in the solar system. All of these men, like Gu Yanwu, were practicing inductive reasoning, a key part of what the Englishman Francis Bacon (1561–1626) called the "Scientific Method."

---

[3]  Prominent examples of the New Qing History include Pamela K. Crossley, *A Translucent Mirror* (Berkeley: University of California Press, 1999); Mark C. Elliott, *The Manchu Way* (Stanford, CA: Stanford University Press, 2001); Laura Hostetler, *Qing Colonial Enterprise* (Chicago: University of Chicago Press, 2001); James P. Millward, *Beyond the Pass* (Stanford, CA: Stanford University Press, 1998); and Evelyn S. Rawski, *The Last Emperors* (Berkeley: University of California Press, 1998).

Induction relies on observation and building conclusions from observed phenomena. Like *deductive reasoning*, it attempts to prove its conclusions based on premises, but there are differences. Deductive reasoning relies on premises that would then be applied to the world, a process that, Bacon felt, limited understanding because it fitted observations into preexisting theories. Like Gu Yanwu, who praised observation and experimentation rather than abstract application of Confucian principles, Bacon suggested an understanding of the world that was based on what one perceived rather than on what one believed to be true.

Bacon's key work, *Novum Organum Scientiarum* (New Instrument of Science) depicted a vessel sailing out beyond the known waters to explore and understand the unknown. Symbolically, this represents his method, which he saw as enabling a more accurate and complete understanding of the world. His method was not entirely new—across Europe, China, India, and the Middle East, scholars were developing models based on experimentation—but Bacon's methods resonated strongly amid the upheaval in Europe at this time. Luther, remember, challenged received wisdom about the Bible and its interpretation by clergy alone. He advocated a "priesthood of all believers" who could read the Bible for themselves so that they could observe and draw conclusions. These ideas rippled through to the political order, suggesting that the legitimacy of government might be determined by observing its effects rather than deriving from abstract premises, and that political truths, as biblical truths, might be assessed by ordinary people.

## Conclusion

Studying the past forces us to examine carefully things we misunderstand or take for granted about our own times. This certainly holds true for states. Understanding states lies at the heart of this chapter. Over the course of the sixteenth and seventeenth centuries, different states gained, wielded, and lost sovereignty and legitimacy as they acquired new material resources. Conflicts broke out as rivals for power tried to supplant or suppress each other, leading to new ways of claiming

## TIMELINE

**1501**
Ismail establishes the Safavid Empire in present-day Iran

**1522**
Martin Luther publishes German translation of the New Testament

**1532**
First printing of Machiavelli's *The Prince*

**1556–1605**
Reign of Akbar the Great, Mughal Emperor

**1520–1566**
Reign of Suleiman the Magnificent, Ottoman sultan

**1524–1525**
German Peasants' War

**1539**
First printing press brought to Mexico City

and establishing legitimacy. The ferment of this period dislodged some long-standing relationships and understandings of the world, creating both new opportunities and constraints in the world of politics. Yet no one could have predicted that several centuries later, the idea and practice of the nation-state—where state sovereignty aligns with the construction of certain kinds of equality of identity and consent of the governed—would become dominant. In fact, in many ways, Afro-Eurasia's hereditary empires appeared stronger at the end of the seventeenth century than they did at the beginning of the sixteenth century. After the upheaval of the civil war, monarchy was restored in England in 1660. China under the Qing, after the civil war surrounding the fall of the Ming, was as stable, prosperous, and expansive as any ruling dynasty in China had ever been.

In many ways, in the late seventeenth century, empire building under the constraints of the biological old regime reached its apogee. States rose and fell, but the new global stakes created opportunities on a broader stage of action, changing the very idea of what a state and its rulers were and could be. Controlling evergreater resources came to be seen as imperative for the survival of political systems in this new global game of empire. So it is worth asking, how did the global economy work during this era? We turn to this subject in Chapter 4.

## A Few Good Books

Liam Matthew Brockey. *Journey to the East. The Jesuit Mission to China, 1579–1724.* Cambridge, MA: Harvard University Press, 2007.

Steven Ozment. *The Serpent and the Lamb. Cranach, Luther and the Making of the Reformation.* New Haven: Yale University Press, 2012.

Geoffrey Parker. *Phillip II.* 4th ed. Chicago: Open Court Publishing, 2002.

Douglas Streusand. *The Islamic Gunpowder Empires: Ottomans, Safavids, and Mughals.* Boulder, CO: Westview Press, 2010.

Sarah Schneewind. *A Tale of Two Melons: Emperor and Subject in Ming China.* Indianapolis: Hackett Publishing, 2006.

*For additional resources, including maps, primary sources, visuals, web links, and quizzes, please go to **www.oup.com/us/carter***

**1601**
Matteo Ricci receives permission to enter the Ming capital of Beijing

**1620**
*Novum Organum* by Francis Bacon

**1649**
Charles I executed for treason, England

**1661**
The Kangxi Emperor assumes throne of Qing Dynasty

**1613–1682**
Life of Gu Yanwu, Chinese scholar of political order

**1644**
Last Ming emperor commits suicide; Qing Dynasty begins reign over China

**1651**
Thomas Hobbes publishes *Leviathan*

(TOP) SILVER MINING AT POTOSÍ. This painting, ca. 1585 by an anonymous artist, provides one of the earliest visual records of the silver industry at Potosí. In the background, one can see miners and pack animals ascending the "Cerro Rico" to the mines. The refining works and counting house are in the foreground.

(RIGHT) INDIAN CALICO. Brightly colored cotton cloth imported from India, calico became popular in Europe in the seventeenth century. Trying to protect domestic textile manufacturers, the English parliament banned calico imports in the early eighteenth century. The fabrics take their name from the city of Calicut, where they were first manufactured (see page 60).

# Production and Consumption in the First Global Economy

## 1571–1701

More than twelve thousand feet high in the Peruvian Andes, the village of Huancavelica was a small agricultural community in the sixteenth century. Although the arrival of Spaniards in the Inca Empire in the 1530s disrupted many aspects of Andean life, decades later the few thousand indigenous inhabitants of Huancavelica and its surrounding areas still mostly farmed and herded in ways that would have been familiar to their ancestors. In the hills surrounding the village, though, a key to unlocking the tremendous mineral wealth of the Andes would soon help transform both the local and the global economies. As we saw in Chapter 3, silver became the biggest export from the Americas after the Spanish conquest in the early 1500s, but the ability to produce such huge quantities of silver relied on an extraction process that used mercury—also called quicksilver—a highly toxic metal that flowed as liquid through the veins of the earth outside Huancavelica.

Accounts of its discovery differ, but in 1571, Spanish colonizers already familiar with the use of mercury for silver production recognized its value and began exploiting the Huancavelica reserves. The fortuitous proximity of abundant mercury and silver ore, coupled with a Spanish imperial policy that focused on providing a steady labor supply to the mines, fueled a surge in production. Soon, Potosí produced much of the world's silver. The subsequent discovery of rich silver deposits elsewhere in Spanish America further increased the global silver supply.

In 1721, the British Parliament expanded the scope of the Calico Act, originally passed in 1701. The first law had banned or limited imports of cotton cloth, especially the brightly colored cloth from India known as calico. These fabrics were less expensive, higher quality, more comfortable, and considered more beautiful than anything produced in Britain. Imports of Indian textiles to Britain had surged in the

**GLOBAL TRADE IN THE SEVENTEENTH CENTURY**

MAP 4.1 Global Trade in the Seventeenth Century

seventeenth century, triggering a crisis for the British textile industry, pressed to compete with the higher quality, lower cost imports. Workers rioted and strikes broke out. Under pressure from wool producers, British legislators passed the first Calico Act, which banned the import and use of most Indian calicoes. The results were mixed, as a black market thrived. Prompted by further pressures, including a riot of four thousand weavers in London in 1719, the Second Calico Act of 1721 forbade the import and use of all cotton fabrics—even burial shrouds had to be made of wool. Despite these measures, Britain's textile industry still struggled to match that of India.

---

These two cases illustrate the unpredictable economic outcomes that accompanied globalization. In this chapter, we explain in greater detail how the global economy—the production, distribution, and consumption of material resources—worked. We will pay particular attention to both changes resulting from globalization and the enduring realities of a world where some key factors in economic life changed little despite increasing interconnectedness.

The global economy was not limited to precious metals like silver and manufactured goods like textiles. In the first section of this chapter, we survey the nature of the world's agricultural economy, where most human productive energy was directed. In examining agricultural production, we also provide an overview of different labor systems, including the growth of slavery in the Atlantic world. We then turn to the expanding production of manufactured goods, made in a wide variety of work settings. With mass production still in the future, most commodities (anything that can be exchanged in a marketplace, including food) were produced and distributed locally. In contrast, some manufactured goods like pottery, textiles, and firearms, as well as agricultural commodities like spices, tea, and sugar were consumed far from where they were produced. After discussing aspects of the global supply and demand for manufactured goods, we then explain how, where, and why the world's supply of precious metals increased, adding another important component to understanding the growth of long-distance trade and the expansion of markets.

Rulers, landowners, merchants, and other elites worked hard to understand the changing relationship between these global economic forces and their own wealth and power and to act to their advantage. Ongoing struggles over the world's resources and markets blurred lines between business, crime, and politics. At the same time, most common folk struggled to survive from day to day, an enterprise rendered even more difficult by climate change in the seventeenth century. The result was a global crisis, which will occupy our attention at this chapter's end.

## The World's Rural Economies

In the early 1500s, about 80 percent of the world's population tilled the soil or tended livestock to feed their families and passed some part of their production on as taxes to political, military, and religious authorities. If they grew enough, they could also exchange some of their surplus for metal tools, beasts of burden, and maybe even some luxuries produced on the other side of the globe. In the new global economy, some agricultural products were shipped to distant markets. Staple crops from around the world were transplanted to new locations, transforming the diets of millions of people. Meanwhile, enslaved people, primarily taken from Africa and destined for the tropical plantations of the Americas, constituted a growing sector of the global labor force.

Agriculture was (and is) practiced around the world, but rural, agrarian peoples produced and distributed their bounty in diverse ways. Even within a single empire, broad claims about how the agricultural sector worked unravel quickly. Local judicial and religious conventions, access to markets, community practices, and even the characteristics of the land itself make it nearly impossible to generalize. Allowing for this immense local variety, let us suggest some ideas about what life was like for most of the world's rural peoples in the sixteenth and seventeenth centuries. First, the idea of individual ownership of land would have made no sense to most agricultural laborers. People often had a close personal relationship to the land they lived on and worked, but that relationship was not about their right to do whatever they wished with a specific piece of the planet, whether to buy it, sell it, or change the way they used it. They would apply the same logic to the claims that any others had to land, even elites. A web of political, cultural, and religious relationships influenced decisions about how to use land. The term peasant usually refers to rural commoners who worked according to terms that granted them access to land for agricultural production and often other rights (e.g., hunting, gathering wood, grazing) but did not necessarily grant them the rights to sell the land, inherit it, or divide it among their heirs. Serfs were bound to the land they worked, and by law or tradition were unable to relocate or change jobs.

Rural elites—who controlled the land but did not work it directly—balanced prestige, political power, and religious obligation against risk, potential profit, and other economic calculations. The same was true for rural common folk, who produced staple foods not only for themselves and their political, religious, and ethnic overlords but also for a broader marketplace. Although they rarely owned land outright, agrarian peoples still made decisions about what they produced and participated in markets for both goods and labor. In the vast Chinese Empire, where ownership of land was widespread relative to other regions, approximately 80 percent of the population lived within one day's journey of a market town where they could sell their produce. Similar opportunities existed in many parts of the world. A robust market for rice existed throughout Southeast Asia, with thousands of tons of grain shipped through major port cities each year. In Spanish America, indigenous villagers' collective claims to agricultural land existed alongside—and conflicted with—agricultural enterprises focused on land rents and production for urban markets. Many rural people with access to communal lands still performed wage labor at least part of the year.

## Rural Responses to Globalization

It is tempting to think of explorers, merchants, generals, and kings as the agents who move history forward, while farmers and peasants resist it, preferring traditional ways of life. The diverse and dynamic patterns of agricultural life in the Early Modern world underscore that this is not true. The rural world, like every other place, was a site of contention where it would be impossible to draw a straight line leading from traditional forms of organization to modern ones. In the Russian Empire, for example, serfdom—legally binding rural workers to the land they tilled—actually expanded in the seventeenth century, as did resistance to the tsar's new agricultural labor laws. Most rural populations across Western and Central Europe had witnessed the demise of serfdom long before, but these regions also experienced repeated and violent confrontations between commoners and the authorities over their own changing rural relationships, like what land was available to them and how taxes were levied and paid. As we saw with the German Peasants' War in Chapter 3, rural peoples could use revolutionary ideas and methods to claim a restoration of tradition. Sometimes, even when popular rebels were claiming they wanted to restore tradition, they were actually pushing for innovations.

Over time, the new global interface did spur changes, not only for merchants and armies, but for farmers too. The influx of New World silver was one factor in permitting Asian rulers to increase their revenue by reforming their tax systems. In India, for instance, Akbar reformed the tax code in the 1580s so that rather than taking an annual percentage of agricultural production from a region, peasants would pay, in cash, a proportion of the prior ten years' average produce. China's Ming Dynasty accomplished something similar around the same time with its "Single Whip" reforms, making all taxes (previously collected throughout the year in a variety of forms, including produce and labor) payable once per year in silver. These reforms rationalized imperial accounting but also exposed agricultural populations to the global market in new ways. Silver was too valuable to be useful for most everyday transactions, where it would be like today trying to use a $100 bill to buy a pack of gum. Instead, peasants in China (and India as well) continued to use copper coins for most purposes, acquiring silver when they needed to pay taxes. As the silver supply fluctuated, determined largely by production levels in the mines of Spanish America and the economic networks that moved silver across the globe, tax burdens rose and fell relative to other costs.

The impact of global processes on rural life can also be seen in the Ottoman Empire. The central government would determine a tax quota for each region, and local landlords—feudal lords who controlled the land and the labor of those who worked it—would then be required to deliver this amount to the imperial government. Of course, they often collected more than what they owed so that they could profit from the arrangement. Ottoman rulers, expanding their empire through a series of expensive military campaigns during this time period, raised their tax demands. Rising demand produced a backlash. In Central Anatolia (the heart of what today is Turkey), a rebellion broke out in 1595, called the Celali Rebellion. Named for its leader, Celal—a preacher in a Muslim sect called Alevism—the rebellion brought tens of thousands of people to the regional capital, demanding relief from taxation and the corruption of local landlords. Although imperial troops soon captured and killed Celal, the rebellion continued for fifteen years. Periodic rebellions continued through the seventeenth century. Although none of these rebellions overthrew the empire, scholars have argued that they did weaken it.

Although the Ottoman case begins with similar strains to those in China and India, the results were different. Why do we see rebellion in one case and not in the others? As always, historians assess different kinds of evidence to debate an answer. One factor may have been religious and ethnic difference, but China and India were no less diverse than the Ottoman Empire. Of course, individual actions and decisions matter, so the charisma of Celal or the intransigence of local lords may have played a role. Historian Sam White offered an alternative explanation, pointing to climate change as the key factor.[1] The seventeenth century marked the height of a "Little Ice Age," when average temperatures in many parts of the world were markedly lower than immediately before or after. Global climate change does not affect all places in the same way, of course. The Little Ice Age hit Anatolia with severe drought, much more drastic than what occurred in India or China. The pressures of famine in one of the empire's most fertile regions may have driven peasants to desperation and revolt. If we add to this rising pressures on subsistence from fluctuations in the tax burden and the international silver market, we have a compelling illustration of how global processes interact with local conditions.

## Changing Foodways around the Globe

The Columbian Exchange affected every aspect of human life. Even more fundamental than changing tax burdens was the transformation of what people around

---

[1]    Sam White, *The Climate of Rebellion in the Early Modern Ottoman Empire* (New York: Cambridge University Press, 2011).

the world grew and ate. Indigenous peoples of the Americas faced challenges to their ways of life (including their foodways) from European settlers who brought competing notions of property, spatial organization, and agricultural production. European conquerors discouraged cultivation of some common staple foods, like amaranth, because of associations with pre-conquest religious practices. New domestic animals, including pigs, sheep, and cows, degraded the environment, simultaneously increasing the supply of animal protein and diminishing the overall supply of food directly available for human consumption. The introduction of wheat, rice, and other staple Afro-Eurasian food crops remade the diets of both immigrants and indigenous peoples of the Americas.

Conversely, Western Hemisphere crops that spread to other parts of the world became essential to the diet of Afro-Eurasian peoples. We've already mentioned tomatoes to Italy, but "Irish" potatoes and "Thai" chili peppers are also imports from the Americas. The potato, brought to Europe from South America, became the primary staple to allay hunger and enable population growth across northern Europe from Ireland to Russia. In China, American crops like sweet potatoes, maize, chili peppers, and others enhanced the diet, provided staple crops for regions where rice or wheat did not thrive, and helped the empire's population grow and spread.

Western Hemisphere transplants like maize and cassava also changed the food landscape of Africa. Maize was already established in West Africa by 1540, where in addition to meeting local demand, it was exported to feed transatlantic maritime traffic. Maize entered the African landscape from all directions. People in parts of East Africa associated it with Muslims who brought kernels back from the hajj, their pilgrimage to Mecca. In South Africa, Portuguese traders planted maize to provision their ships; residents of the southeast coast believed maize to have originated in India. African port cities cultivated the grain, along with chickpeas and other crops, to sell to vessels sailing the long-distance routes from East Asia across the Indian Ocean and around the Cape of Good Hope to Western Europe.

While staple crops were sometimes traded in long-distance commerce, most of the agricultural products that traversed the globe were luxury items that had higher value relative to their weight. Spices like pepper, cloves, nutmeg, and mace continued to be coveted rarities. Trade brought American crops like cacao (from which chocolate is made) and vanilla, African and Arabian coffee, and Asian tea to places where they could not be produced. Coffee, tea, and chocolate all first arrived in Europe around 1650, illustrating both increased global commerce and increased disposable income available to some portion of the world's population, mostly in urban commercial centers. By the end of the eighteenth century, hundreds of coffee and tea houses in cities like Amsterdam, London, and Paris became places to socialize and exchange information about business—ship arrivals, supply and demand for various commodities, who needed a loan, and who had money to lend.

This dynamic is a vital piece of global economic history but offers an incomplete perspective. Little that Europe produced could be traded profitably over the great distances that separated European ports from Asian markets. Cotton textiles from India, rather than woolen goods, were most coveted across Asia, while staple agricultural goods, spices, and other commodities traded in regional Asian markets. The Dutch East India Company (*Vereenigde Oost-Indische Compagnie*, or VOC), established in 1602, found one way to thrive in this environment, as most of its profits derived from transactions within Asia and not from trading Asian goods for European goods. A more revolutionary economic disruption in the "spice trade" can be seen in where, how, and by whom sugar was produced.

## The Sugar-Slave Plantation System

Sugarcane is picky. It requires lots of water and average daily temperatures around 80 degrees Fahrenheit to thrive. Planting, and especially harvesting, was labor and fuel intensive. Until 1500, much of the world's sugar was produced in the Arab world, where prisoners of war often worked the cane fields. Sovereigns and merchants regulated its supply to other parts of the world. As a result, we need to think of sugar prior to 1500 as a spice—perhaps of great abundance (at least to the wealthy) in one part of the world, but a costly thing and generally in short supply in others. A Muslim ruler might demand elaborate marzipan sculptures, whereas a European ruler might bestow small sugary gifts at Christmas on favorites of the court. The Columbian Exchange brought together this plant indigenous to New Guinea, American land, African labor, and European capital, transforming the relationship between humans and sugar. The new sugar marketplace made some men rich and many men slaves.

The Americas did not have the spices Columbus had been seeking, but they did have the climate needed to grow sugar. By 1600, Portuguese Brazil was the largest sugar producer in the world. At first, indigenous peoples did much of the work, but disease and harsh treatment depleted this labor force within decades. Over the course of the seventeenth century, the Brazilian sugar industry grew as a destination for enslaved Africans. Competing sugar complexes, particularly in the Spanish, French, and British possessions in the Caribbean, followed suit.

The forced migration and enslavement of Africans transformed economies, cultures, societies, and politics across the entire world, both directly and indirectly. As historians struggle to understand this overwhelming phenomenon, one of the major threads that ties recent investigations together is an increasing focus on the African perspective itself, from the role of African political elites in shaping the slave trade at its geographic origins to the important role played by strategies of resistance and self-manumission. None of these studies diminishes the horrible reality of the practice—the unnecessary deaths of millions caught up in

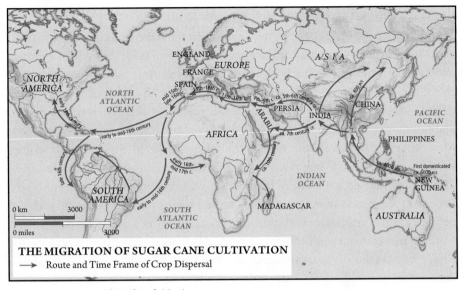

**THE MIGRATION OF SUGAR CANE CULTIVATION**
→  Route and Time Frame of Crop Dispersal

MAP 4.2 The Migration of Sugar Cane Cultivation

the slave trade, the daily cruelty inflicted on those who survived the passage from Africa, and the denial of the fundamental humanity of millions of people over the course of centuries.

What was it like to be enslaved on a sugar plantation in the seventeenth century? First, we have to dispose of the idea of a sugar plantation as just a big farm. Sugar was produced by an *engenho* (factory), an agro-industrial production facility, not a bucolic rural estate. Enslaved Africans did hard physical labor, without pay, for many hours a day. Sugar cane takes up to eighteen months to mature, but the same field can then yield a new crop in nine months without replanting. Harvesting a single crop could take six months of nonstop work. Working the sugar plantations was some of the most difficult work that a human could do, both because of the location—the low-lying, often marshy, plantations were hot and exposed—and nature of the field work, all done by hand. In addition to planting and fertilizing the cane with manure, enslaved Africans used machetes to hack the cane stalks, which are similar to bamboo in diameter (about two to three inches per stalk). Once they had cut the cane, laborers (mostly enslaved, but in some cases free) loaded it on carts and hauled it to the on-site refinery, where other workers crushed, cleaned, boiled, and cooled the final product. The most physically demanding work was assigned to adult males, while women, and those too young or too old to work the fields, were given other jobs like cleaning equipment or keeping pests from damaging the crops.

## Reconstructing the Lives of Enslaved Africans

Reconstructing the lives of enslaved Africans in the Americas challenges historians. Most of the documentation generated by the slave trade viewed the enslaved people as commodities to be bought and sold. As a result, detailed records exist about the transportation of enslaved Africans from the African coast—where African slave traders dealt with European ones—to their arrival and sale to plantation owners in the Americas. As for slave life on plantations, most records were generated by slave owners rather than those enslaved. Some records written by the enslaved exist, but many were not literate or not permitted to write. The diaries that do exist are rich sources; additional evidence helps to draw a fuller picture. Some researchers have studied the physical remains of enslaved peoples from Caribbean plantations. Physical anthropologist Kristrina Shuler, working in a cemetery in Barbados, found a high death rate from infectious diseases like measles, leprosy, tuberculosis, and dysentery. Skeletons showed evidence of injuries to limbs—apparently caused by machetes—and accompanying infections. The average life expectancy at birth for enslaved Africans in this sample was about eighteen years.[2] Other sources suggest that the average life expectancy for an enslaved laborer was about seven to nine years after arriving on a plantation.

Sugar production on the Caribbean islands grew after the mid-seventeenth century. In British Barbados, for example, the enslaved population increased almost seven times over between 1645 and 1680, by which time almost forty thousand slaves worked three hundred fifty sugar estates and produced eight thousand tons of sugar. Over time, as we will see in more detail in Chapter 5, competing empires attempted to incorporate sugar production, along with as many other activities as they could, within self-contained imperial economic circuits. Control of sugar producing areas and the slave trade therefore sometimes featured in war strategies and treaty negotiations, as in the Treaty of Ryswick (1697), which ceded control of the western part of the island of Hispaniola to the French. The French considered Saint-Domingue, as they called this part of the island, the economic jewel of their overseas empire. As such, it became one of the most productive, brutal slave regimes in the world. Over time, the use of enslaved Africans expanded in other sectors of the economy as well, including mining, crafts production, and domestic labor. The plantation-slave system is one illustration of the new global economy, but it is by no means the only one.

---

[2]    Kristrina A. Shuler, "Life and Death on a Barbadian Sugar Plantation: Historic and Bioarchaeological Views of Infection and Mortality at Newton Plantation," *International Journal of Osteoarchaeology* 21 (2011): 66–81.

SUGAR MILL, FRENCH WEST INDIES. This illustration, from a late seventeenth-century history of the Caribbean, identifies the various phases of sugar production. Fortunes were made and lost in the sugar business, as mass production on plantations like this transformed the global sugar supply. Plantation work was dangerous and difficult, built on the enslaved labor that sustained the sugar economy.

## Manufactured Goods and the Emerging Global Economy

On the second floor of the Philadelphia Museum of Art, a blue-and-white ceramic jar can tell us a lot about changing patterns of production, consumption, and exchange. At first glance, it reminds many people of a Chinese object, familiar for its design and color pattern. Ming ceramics were the most advanced and coveted in the Early Modern world, the reason that "china" became synonymous with fine ceramics in the English language. But the jar is not from China at all; it was produced in the city of Puebla (in present-day Mexico) around the year 1650. The potter, trained in a Spanish style of ceramic making, used local materials and added a variety of Iberian design motifs (including some from the Islamic tradition) to the obvious homage to Ming ceramics.

How can we explain this combination of Spanish technique, Mexican materials, and Chinese aesthetics produced in the middle of the seventeenth century? Puebla was one of Spanish America's largest centers of textile and ceramic production. Its prosperity was tied closely to the global economy. Although some precious metals were exported from Veracruz, on the east coast, to Spain, much was also exported from Acapulco, on the Pacific coast, to the Spanish port at Manila, in the Philippines. There it entered the thriving Asian trade network that included China, the largest market for American silver. The vase in the Philadelphia Museum of Art shows that this exchange was more than just silver flowing to China. Ideas, technology, and goods flowed in all directions in a network that encircled the globe: from the Philippines, to Acapulco, then down to South America, or across New Spain to Veracruz, then on to Seville in Spain, and perhaps elsewhere in Europe. European ships traveled down the African coast and into the Indian Ocean, where trade reached the Islamic world, India, Southeast Asia, and then China again. Ships flying the French, Dutch, and British flags challenged, and then supplanted, Spain and Portugal in oceanic trade.

Much of the global trade in manufactured goods from the sixteenth through the eighteenth centuries revolved around products made in Asia. Direct trade between Asia and Spanish America began in the 1570s, although the Spanish crown limited the number of trips and ships permitted on this route each year. This Manila Galleon system, named for the type of ship and its destination, moved a breathtaking volume of silks, porcelain, ivory, pearls, and furniture despite the limitations imposed by the Crown. Most of these goods remained in Spanish America, distributed throughout the region and paid for with shipments of silver and cochineal, a brilliant red dye made from an insect reliant on a specific variety of Mexican cactus.

JAR WITH HANDLES, PUEBLA (MEXICO), EARLY 17TH CENTURY. Attributed to the potter Damián Hernández. With Chinese, Italian, Spanish, and Islamic influences, this ceramic object, discussed in the text, shows the rich and complex commercial and cultural ties connecting Asia, Europe, and the Americas in the early modern world.

In the Portuguese Empire, the Brazilian cities of Salvador and Rio de Janeiro were ports of call on both ends of the commercial circuit that linked Lisbon to Goa, Malacca and Macau in trade networks that were less regulated than the Spanish galleon system. Millions of Chinese porcelain objects were sold in Brazil between the sixteenth and nineteenth centuries. In fact, all of the European empires coveted ceramics produced in China, Korea, and Japan because they achieved a quality that manu-facturers in other parts of the world could not yet match. In the seventeenth century, potters in other places tried to satisfy the market with Chinese-style ce-ramics, leading to distinctive cultural hybrids like the Puebla vase in the Philadel-phia Museum of Art.

Imitating Ming ceramics was a growing industry in the seventeenth century. In and around the city of Delft in the Netherlands, just as in New Spain, a robust industry developed to produce ceramics for Dutch consumers who desired, but could not afford, true Chinese porcelains. Like seventeenth-century Puebla pot-tery, Delftware of the same vintage is now coveted in its own right by museums and private collectors. However, although design and color were often imitated, European porcelain manufacturers could not compete with Chinese technical and aesthetic standards until the eighteenth century.

The story of ceramics helps us to understand the importance of maintaining a global perspective on economic developments in the era, rather than thinking about Europe as a trading hub and the rest of the world as spokes. Although European ships controlled trade between Asia and Latin America, and they increasingly

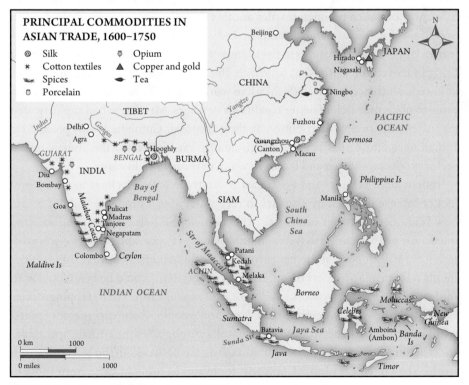

MAP 4.3 Principal Commodities in Asian Trade, 1600–1750

competed to move goods in South and East Asia, European states did not dominate the global trade in manufactured goods prior to the nineteenth century. There was no single state with the political, military, or economic power to dominate long-distance transactions. Nor was there consensus about how global commerce should be conducted. The growth of manufacturing in Puebla was not a sign of the general health of the Spanish imperial economy in the seventeenth century. Rather, it indicated that much of the economic dynamism of the empire remained outside of Spain itself, and much of the wealth generated by the empire eluded the imperial center. Textiles, the most important manufactured items traded in the Early Modern global marketplace, can tell us more about the relationships between trade, place, and power.

## Textiles and the Manufacturing Link between India and Europe

You are familiar by now with the idea that the search for spices motivated European sojourns into Asia, especially Southeast Asia. Pepper, cinnamon, and other spices unique to this part of the world were extraordinarily valuable and—like sugar— became precious additions to European tables. But, how exactly did Europeans get these spices? Europeans needed to bring to the Southeast Asian markets commodities that were in demand there and to which Europeans had competitive access. Silver was one such product, textiles another. Yet, the textiles most in demand in Southeast Asia were manufactured in India, not Europe. European merchants learned that to trade for spices in the islands of the South China Sea, they needed to bring Indian cotton cloth. Why was India able to produce such high quality textiles at lower cost than other societies? Indian workers had the flexibility to move from place to place in search of better conditions or wages. Merchants had sophisticated means of finance and distribution at their disposal. Combined with productive Indian agriculture that provided high-quality raw materials, the Indian textile sector produced cheaper and better goods than those from Europe.

Indian labor markets and Southeast Asian trade networks have been the subject of intense research by scholars in recent decades. Europeans did not create new trade networks out of thin air; they joined and helped to expand existing ones. European outposts in Asia—notably Goa, Malacca, and Batavia—were different from European settlements in most of the Americas in that these settlements were primarily ports through which negotiations could be conducted with indigenous merchant networks and political systems rather than stepping stones for vast claims of sovereignty over land and people. Robust trade continued within Islamic trade networks from Anatolia through Southeast Asia and across the religious divide between Islamic and Christian networks in the Mediterranean world. The Dutch East India Company, for example, brought cloth from India to Southeast Asia and rice from Siam to Taiwan, moving with other merchants along existing trade routes. Only when the timing was right, enabled by the twice-yearly shift in the monsoon winds, did ships even return to Europe, laden with spices and other luxuries for the European market. Over time, European merchants began to seek textiles from South Asia not only because they were trying to trade them for spices and other agricultural goods but to bring them back for sale in Europe.[3]

By the late seventeenth century, England, France, and the Dutch Republic were importing millions of yards of South Asian cloth, enough to alarm textile producers and governments in all three places. Local textile workers attacked elegant women clothed in high-quality cotton fabrics. Legislators in both France and England attempted to impose an outright ban on such imports. In Spanish America, textile manufacturers and other enterprises used free, slave, convict, indigenous, and mestizo laborers to supply their own markets, forming an economic system increasingly autonomous from Spain. As the seventeenth century progressed, the monarchy and elites in Spain joined their counterparts throughout Europe in the struggle to make sense of how their empires could profit from the global economy.

Most rulers, and aspiring rulers, recognized the need to develop a strategy to manage the relationship between the territory over which they claimed sovereignty and global commerce. Broadly speaking, approaches to this new commercial world lay along a continuum from embracing more global exchange to attempting ever tighter controls of production and distribution. On one end of the spectrum lay the Netherlands, which saw its prosperity, as articulated in the Dutch East India Company charter, as "principally a result of our mercantile trade and commerce . . . not only with neighbouring kingdoms and regions, but also with those located further away than these, in Europe, Asia and Africa." On the other extreme, Japan strictly limited external trade during the Edo period (ca. 1600–1868). The Dutch East India Company negotiated a monopoly from the Japanese government to bring goods from Europe to Japan (and vice versa) in 1641. In granting the monopoly, the Japanese government claimed control over the timing and quantity of the trade as well. Note that both the Netherlands and Japan were attempting to manage a relationship with the global economy. Despite the cliché that Japan "turned inward" and refused to deal with outsiders for several centuries, Japanese elites, like those in other countries, were attempting to adjust to globalization through regulation and custom, not withdrawing from the global interface entirely.

---

[3]   On this topic see, for example, numerous articles in Giorgio Riello and Tirthankar Roy, eds., *How India Clothed the World: The World of South Asian Textiles, 1500–1850* (Leiden, The Netherlands: Brill, 2009), especially contributions by Anthony Reid, Om Prakash, and Ian Wendt. Also, Robert Parthesius, *Dutch Ships in Tropical Waters: The Development of the Dutch East India Company (VOC) Shipping Network in Asia 1595–1660* (Amsterdam: University of Amsterdam Press, 2010).

# The Silver Supply and the Global Economy

The Spanish Conquest of the Americas did not affect the global marketplace immediately. Far from the front lines of the Spanish assault on the Aztec and Inca, Japanese silver production experienced a boom in the sixteenth century. Japan was the most important source of silver imports in China through the 1570s, when American silver began to arrive in China via Manila. But it did arrive in the following decades, in great quantities, so it is important to get a better understanding of this silver's impact on the global economy. Spanish conquistadors spent a lot of time looking for precious metals in the Americas, and what they ultimately found surpassed their wildest expectations. The transfer of mineral wealth from the Americas into the global economy was profoundly important to the history of the modern world, but we can only understand how if we view this new source of wealth in context.

Silver and gold had long been valued across the globe, and of course the mines of the Americas were not the world's only source of silver. In addition to the Japanese industry noted previously, European silver production had grown significantly prior to the discovery of the vast American reserves. This was the source of wealth for some of the most successful commercial enterprises in Europe, but the increased silver supply also led to inflation that caused popular unrest in parts of Europe in the early sixteenth century.

The American silver industry did not spring up immediately with the arrival of Europeans. At first, Europeans simply pillaged the silver stock of indigenous societies; over time this gave way to a more complex undertaking to extract the hemisphere's silver resources from the earth itself. This required a labor force as well as raw materials and other inputs—timber to build support beams for the underground mines, leather to make sacks for hauling ore, beasts of burden, tools, and food for the populations of the silver mining regions. The two most important silver mining sites in the Western Hemisphere—one in the southern region of the Inca Empire in the Andes and the other to the north of the Aztec Empire in Mexico—had different human and natural resource bases, but both followed the same general pattern of a dramatic increase in production during the first century of European control followed by a stagnation of production.

Potosí, the most famous and productive silver city in the Americas, lies high in the Andes Mountains, twice the altitude of Denver, Colorado. Soon after arriving in the region, Spaniards became aware that the indigenous peoples had been extracting precious metals from the area around Potosí and first tapped into its veins themselves in 1545. As the city's silver production skyrocketed, so did its population, exceeding one hundred fifty thousand by 1610 (for comparison, this was about the same size as the Dutch capital, Amsterdam). By the mid-seventeenth century, Potosí was one of the world's largest cities.

The high quality of its silver ore enabled Potosí's early productivity. Silver is rarely found in its pure form, usually existing as ore in combination with other metals that can be separated from each other only by smelting (heating the ore) or amalgamation (creating a chemical reaction to separate silver from other elements). In the first years of Spanish control, indigenous peoples controlled much of the mining in Potosí using their own smelting techniques. Furnaces located high in the mountains funneled the wind to create sufficient heat to extract silver from other elements in the Andean ore. However, by the end of the 1560s, both ore with high silver content and local fuel sources for the furnaces began to run out. Just twenty years after Europeans began exploiting Potosí's silver, it seemed poised to decline.

This is the point where the mercury deposits near the village of Huancavelica, mentioned at the start of this chapter, became important. As Potosí's productivity declined, mine operators, supported by the Spanish imperial government, initiated two major changes in the production process, with profound repercussions for the local population and for world history. The first was the introduction of a more effective technique, first developed in New Spain (Mexico) to extract silver by processing a toxic sludge of crushed ore, mercury, salt, copper sulfate, and water. Using the newly discovered mercury from Huancavelica, silver production in Peru grew to over three thousand tons per year in the 1590s. The new production process also left a legacy of poisonous mercury in the environment that survives to this day.

The second change involved the acquisition of labor to work the mines. Producing precious metals in the Americas was big business for Spain, which claimed a monopoly on many mines as well as the "Royal Fifth," a tax of 20 percent on the production of all precious metals in the empire. With enormous revenue at stake, imperial economic policy focused on securing labor for the mines. Wanting to maximize profits, mine operators did not pay wages sufficient to attract enough free laborers (they argued that they could not find enough laborers at any wage), so the colonial state helped them with the force of law. The colonial government imposed a labor tax, called the *mita*, on the indigenous villages of the Andes. Systems like this in which sovereigns demand payment of a tax, not in cash or goods, but in labor, were common in the Early Modern world and remain so in some societies.

## Following Silver From Mine to Mint to Market

Three historians—Peter Bakewell, Jeffrey Cole, and Enrique Tandeter—analyzed data from village censuses, tax collections, mortgage agreements, business inventories, and other materials to provide us with detailed analyses of Potosí under Spanish rule. Under the mita system, more than eleven thousand indigenous workers from the Andean highlands were forced into the mines and refineries. This coercion of indigenous communities to subsidize the accumulation of wealth by others skewed the allocation of resources throughout the colonial economy. Even as the costs of other factors of production increased and ore quality decreased, cheap labor enabled mine owners to still squeeze a profit from their enterprise. Some indigenous people chose to avoid the onerous—often deadly—labor obligations by migrating, making the painful decision to permanently leave their communities. Others made cash payments to mine operators who could use the money either to hire workers or simply keep the profit. Some mine operators referred to this cash as having "an Indian in the pocket."[4]

Other parts of Spanish America relied on different systems, using indigenous communal labor, enslaved Africans, indentured workers, and free labor. Between 1550 and 1650, these workers produced three hundred thousand tons of silver, dwarfing the production of the rest of the world. New Spain over the long run produced even more silver than Peru. From the beginning of the sixteenth century to the end of the eighteenth, American silver probably accounted for more than three-quarters of the world's supply.

What became of all that silver? Understanding where this new silver went helps illustrate the global trade networks and interconnections that are so vital to this period. Here again, researchers have used innovative methods to understand the past. Using the knowledge that silver from different sources carries a unique chemical signature, researchers can analyze objects made from silver to determine the original sources of the metal, even when silver from different sources is mixed together. The chemical signatures of coins tell us that English coins from 1550 to 1650 contain significant amounts of silver from Mexico and Europe but almost none from Potosí. And coins minted in Spain during the early seventeenth century contain virtually no American silver. This tells us a number of important things about silver generally and about American silver in particular. First, it tells us that one important use of silver was as coin. Second, it tells us that American silver at this time did not stay in Spain to be minted into coin by the Spanish crown (in the eighteenth century, because of changes in imperial policies, more American silver did make it into Spanish coins). Overall, approximately 20 percent of American silver wealth remained in the Western Hemisphere; 10 percent went directly to Asia; and perhaps 15 percent leaked to pirates and smugglers. Most of the rest moved through Spain quickly, often to pay off imperial loans or imperial armies fighting elsewhere in Europe. Chinese demand for silver drew much of the world's supply there. Japanese rulers in this era, in addition to asserting more direct government control over foreign trade as we have already described,

---

4    Peter Bakewell, *Miners of the Red Mountain: Indian Labor of Potosí, 1545–1650* (Albuquerque: University of New Mexico Press, 1984); Jeffrey A Cole, *The Potosí Mita, 1573–1700* (Stanford: Stanford University Press, 1985); and Enrique Tandeter, *Coercion and Market: Silver Mining in Colonial Potosí, 1692–1826* (Albuquerque: University of New Mexico Press, 1993).

implemented currency systems based on silver as a tactic designed to strengthen their regime.[5]

## The Expansion of Global Currencies

In our own time, we take for granted the existence of money issued by governments. Although the Early Modern period is not the first era in which currency was being used (government-issued paper money was first circulated in China in the 1100s), the extent to which the world's growing silver supply was being turned into currency—rather than decorative or religious objects and jewelry—is noteworthy. Currency is a search for liquidity. What does this mean? Consider a fundamental question in economics—how do you get things that you don't (or can't) make for yourself? One way is to barter. You and I can exchange things we produce with each other and figure out their value in direct exchange—how many of my tomatoes are you willing to take in exchange for your strawberries? The barter system is straightforward but presents problems for more complex transactions that involve things like delayed consumption (I don't want to eat strawberries today), a poor fit between producer and consumer (I want shoes but the shoemaker doesn't want tomatoes), long-distance exchange (I want tea but not strawberries), or large-scale transactions (I want to raise and equip an army to go to war with my enemies next month rather than eat my dinner tonight). Such dilemmas over the exchange of goods led societies around the world at different times to develop ways to make these transactions easier, using money (currency) and credit. Both practices enable a wider variety of transactions to take place, but also introduce additional complications to the world of production and consumption.

Currency is a tool for storing and transporting value. The challenge is convincing people that currency has real value in an economic exchange—if I give you cash for food, I can eat the food. Will you be able to exchange that cash for food when *you* need to eat? To solve this problem, some kinds of currencies actually consist of something seen to have high intrinsic value, like precious metals. One important role that rulers increasingly claimed in the global economy was as an issuer of currency in which buyers and sellers could have confidence. For example, if a coin were issued from a government mint with the ruler's seal on it, the state was claiming that users could be confident that the coin would really contain the amount of silver stamped on it. If the government collapsed, one would still have a valuable amount of precious metal.

---

[5]  Anne-Marie Desaulty and Francis Albarede, "Copper, Lead, and Silver Isotopes Solve a Major Economic Conundrum of Tudor and Early Stuart Europe" *Geology* 41, no. 2 (February 2013): 135–138; Dennis O. Flynn and Arturo Giráldez, "Cycles of Silver: Global Economic Unity through the Mid-Eighteenth Century," *Journal of World History* 13, no. 2 (Fall 2002): 391–427.

Other currency systems are based on a promise that sellers will be able to obtain things of value at a later date. These promises could be letters of credit or paper money. Open your wallet or purse: if you pull out cash from the United States, you have in your hand a "Federal Reserve Note" that the Treasury of the United States guarantees can be used to reduce or eliminate "all debts public or private." In the past, promissory notes were most often commitments that the issuer, whether an emperor or a merchant house, had a reserve of precious metal to make good on the promise being made. In fact, as recently as the 1970s, US currency (and most other currencies) entitled the bearer to redeem notes for gold. If you had a $20 bill, you could exchange it at the US Treasury for $20 worth of gold. But if participants in a marketplace no longer value the commodity in the same way (for example, if the world's silver supply changes) or they lose confidence in the issuers of the note of promise (for example, if a ruler is shown to not have as much wealth as claimed) this can damage a broad range of economic relationships. Just such a loss of confidence contributed to economic crises in both Spain and the Ottoman Empire in the seventeenth century.

The introduction of so much silver into the global economy had other unforeseen consequences. It increased opportunities for long-distance trade by bringing a much greater amount of a broadly accepted and easily transferred standard of value into the global marketplace. Thus, new opportunities for the expansion of relationships between producers and consumers, within and between states, empires, and regions, proliferated. Conversely, it also helped to throw off perceptions of how much things were worth (in relationship to silver and therefore in relationship to each other), contributing to a dramatic rise in the cost of living in some places over the sixteenth century and into the seventeenth. An extreme and infamous instance of fluctuating perceptions of an item's worth was the Dutch tulip craze of the 1630s.

## Tulipmania!

Native to Central Asia, tulips had long been cultivated and bred there, resulting in spectacular varieties. In Turkey, they attained great popularity, particularly at the Ottoman Court, as a favorite landscaping feature of many Sultans. Turkish tulip gardens earned great admiration from visiting dignitaries, and according to most accounts, tulips were first cultivated in Europe from bulbs obtained by the Austrian ambassador to the Ottoman Empire in the 1550s.

Within a few decades, tulips had been bred and adapted so that they could withstand the harsher climate of the Netherlands, which was becoming rich on global trade. Wealthy merchants, with fortunes earned in Southeast Asia, sought a way to display their new wealth and power. Tulips provided a riot of color against the gray Dutch skies, and were a perfect example of conspicuous consumption: a way to display one's wealth so that it would be noticed. "Broken" tulips—solid tulips of one color with the insurgence of a second color—were considered most valuable. The "Semper Augustus" (a blood-red and white variety) was the most desired and rare. A Semper Augustus bulb could cost thirty times more than the average Dutch worker earned in a year. At the height of Tulipmania, one tulip sold for as much as the grandest homes in Amsterdam: perhaps $10 million today!

Early in 1637, the number of paper promises invested in tulip deals was more than six times the total amount of actual currency in circulation. Moreover, very little of what was being bought and sold existed at the moment of the transaction. The Dutch were using an economic instrument called a futures contract. An investor could buy a contract for tulips to be delivered in the future at a certain price, hoping that the price in the marketplace would go up as the time came closer for the flowers to be delivered. The contract could then be sold to someone else for more than its original cost, making a profit. Sometimes, part or even all of the initial investment to purchase a contract was borrowed against the promise of future profits, to be repaid after the shipment of goods arrived and was sold.

Of course, there is a risk. You might buy a contract (i.e., make a promise) to receive tulips at $100 and be able to sell the tulips (or re-sell the contract) for $200, in which case you would make a tidy profit. But you might only be able to sell the tulips (or re-sell the contract) for $50, in which case you would lose half of your investment. In 1637, rumors of what the next deliveries of tulips to Amsterdam would be worth ran rampant, and robust re-selling of contracts drove contract prices to astronomical heights. Perhaps you have already guessed how the Tulipmania story ended. The first auctions of tulip bulbs in the winter of 1637 didn't get any bids at all, at a time when brokers were expecting huge profits. People who had invested vast sums, planning to get rich re-selling their bulbs, found that what they had bought was worthless. Prices are hard to verify, but it seems

INK ON PAPER DRAWING OF A TULIP, SEVEN-TEENTH CENTURY OTTOMAN EMPIRE. The model for this drawing, similar to artwork from the Mughal Empire as well, was most likely found in a Dutch book. Introduced from Western Asia, tulips were coveted throughout Eurasia. In the early seventeenth century, "Tulipmania," the frenzied commerce in tulip bulb futures centered in Amsterdam, was one of the first speculative financial bubbles to emerge in the Early Modern global economy.

that between early February and early May of 1637, the average prices of tulip bulbs fell 99.5 percent from their height. Imagine thinking you could sell a flower for more than $200 and being able to sell it for only $1. Now imagine that you had bought a nursery full of them with the same expectation, and the same result. Investors were ruined, including many common people seduced by the "guarantee" of easy money.

The Dutch tulip bubble was not typical, of course. Most people in the world remained far from that kind of speculative finance. However, this story points out that in this increasingly connected world, prosperity and poverty, economic growth and decline, became more closely linked to new economic factors, often far beyond the control of individuals or local authorities. These factors included the global supply and distribution of commodities, the ability of individuals and institutions to evaluate new kinds of risks and to make and keep longer-term promises about credit and debt. This new environment also challenged models for how rulers should make decisions about the relationship between their states and economic activity.

## Political Economy

In 1615, a Frenchman by the name of Antoine de Montchrestien (1575–1621) wrote *A Tract on Political Economy*, introducing a new term to Western European readers that reflected a growing sense among philosophers, financiers, and rulers that questions about the acquisition and distribution of wealth were intimately related to questions of what states were and how they worked. During this era, it was a common idea that the amount of wealth in the world was limited, and therefore economic activity was a zero-sum game: the global pie would never get any bigger, it could only be sliced up in different ways. Rulers, as a result, generally saw the role of the state in economic activity as granting and enforcing limits on how big the slices would be and who would get served. In many states, like the European and Ottoman empires, most products were manufactured by members of guilds, which were organizations sanctioned by the government that limited the number of producers, set prices, and trained the next generation of artisans. Merchant guilds existed as well. As Europeans expanded their participation in long-distance commerce and overseas colonization, guilds moved with them, as did other kinds of monopoly practices. For instance, in 1506, the Portuguese crown attempted to make the spice trade a crown monopoly, meaning all profits from the import and sale of spices in the Portuguese Empire would accrue to the monarchs themselves. In other cases, rulers sold monopolies to produce or distribute certain goods in certain places—brandy, ice, playing cards—to the highest bidder. In still other cases, rulers granted licenses to a group of investors, who formed a joint stock company, for a monopoly on trade or other economic activities in certain parts of the globe. The Dutch East India Company, mentioned earlier, and the British East India Company (founded in 1600) are two examples; but there are many others, including those that initiated some of the earliest attempts at English settlements in North America such as the Plymouth Company, in Massachusetts, and the Virginia Company. In nearly all cases, these companies—or individual merchants—paid fees to their rulers for economic privileges, ensuring that the state would accumulate wealth.

Mercantilism is a term describing economic systems that developed from this line of reasoning. In mercantilist thinking, one economic goal of a state is to accumulate wealth through a favorable balance of trade (exporting more goods than it imports). Tight restrictions on economic activity, especially across political boundaries, were therefore commonplace around the world. The Edo regime's policy of sakoku in Japan not only limited trade with Europeans; it was a general policy of strict control over economic interactions with all foreign entities, including China, Korea, and other regional states. The Chinese Empire organized an elaborate, tightly controlled, tribute system in which commerce was accompanied by ritual recognition of the Chinese emperor's power. Dozens of states conducted trade with China through this tribute system, including much of East and South Asia as well as European states. All claimants to sovereignty were trying to manage increasing global commerce and its unanticipated consequences.

## Conclusion

Despite all of the changes we have described in this book so far, agrarian concerns continued to dominate human activity across the globe through the seventeenth century. A compelling case can be made that a cooling trend over the course of this era reduced agricultural productivity in much of the world. Fears over scarcity—remember the zero-sum model—drove bellicose political decisions. War between nations was seen as the way to acquire more resources, and the apparent bounty of wealth flowing out the Americas or across the Indian Ocean was seen not as a way for all parties to benefit but as an opportunity to acquire more at the expense of rivals. Expensive imperial wars, designed to alleviate strains on resources, exacerbated suffering. Popular revolts spread. A loss of up to one-third of the world's population may have ensued. Not all regions and peoples were affected equally, but turmoil in some of the largest and most powerful of the Early Modern empires—including the Chinese, Ottoman, and Russian Empires as well as France, Spain, and England—must be placed in this material context.

Whereas most modern economic understandings reject the theories of wealth creation and preservation that prevailed during this era, there is no doubt that this was a world of strict limits, made clear by a convergence of multiple factors that contributed to a crisis across much of the globe in the seventeenth century. This was an understandable conclusion looking at a world dominated by the rules of the Biological Old Regime. It was, perhaps, a conclusion reinforced by scandals like Tulipmania in which fortunes appeared and disappeared as if by magic, leaving some to wonder if they ever really existed.

Most rulers certainly perceived power to be meted out in a zero-sum system. For any state to gain resources, another state would have to lose them. Sometimes the competitors erected legal or financial barriers, like the Calico Acts that banned Indian textile imports to Britain. In other cases, they sponsored violence, using privateers—essentially, state-approved pirates—to steal another state's wealth. Frequently, the answer was direct war. As the eighteenth century dawned, war, like trade and travel, became global in its reach.

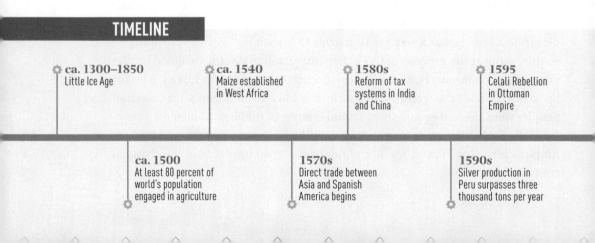

## TIMELINE

**ca. 1300–1850**
Little Ice Age

**ca. 1540**
Maize established
in West Africa

**1580s**
Reform of tax
systems in India
and China

**1595**
Celali Rebellion
in Ottoman
Empire

**ca. 1500**
At least 80 percent of
world's population
engaged in agriculture

**1570s**
Direct trade between
Asia and Spanish
America begins

**1590s**
Silver production in
Peru surpasses three
thousand tons per year

# A Few Good Books

Timothy Brook, *Vermeer's Hat: The Seventeenth Century and the Dawn of the Global World.* New York: Bloomsbury, 2008.

David Brion Davis. *Slavery and Human Progress.* New York: Oxford University Press, 1984.

Geoffrey Parker. *Global Crisis: War, Climate Change and Catastrophe in the Seventeenth Century.* New Haven, CT: Yale University Press, 2013.

Om Prakash. *Bullion for Goods: European and Indian Merchants in the Indian Ocean Trade, 1500–1800.* New Delhi: Manohar, 2004.

Alan K. Smith. *Creating a World Economy: Merchant Capital, Colonialism, and World Trade, 1400–1825.* Boulder, CO: Westview Press, 1991.

Jane Whittle and Elizabeth Griffiths. *Consumption and Gender in the Early Seventeenth-Century Household: The World of Alice Le Strange.* New York: Oxford University Press, 2012.

*For additional resources, including maps, primary sources, visuals, web links, and quizzes, please go to **www.oup.com/us/carter***

| ca. 1600 | 1615 | 1645–80 |
|---|---|---|
| Brazil is largest sugar producer in the world | Antoine de Montchrestien, *A Tract on Political Economy* | Enslaved population of Barbados increases by a factor of seven, to forty thousand |

| 1602 | 1636–37 | 1701 |
|---|---|---|
| Dutch East India Company established | Tulipmania in the Netherlands | First Calico Act limits imports of Indian cotton cloth to England |

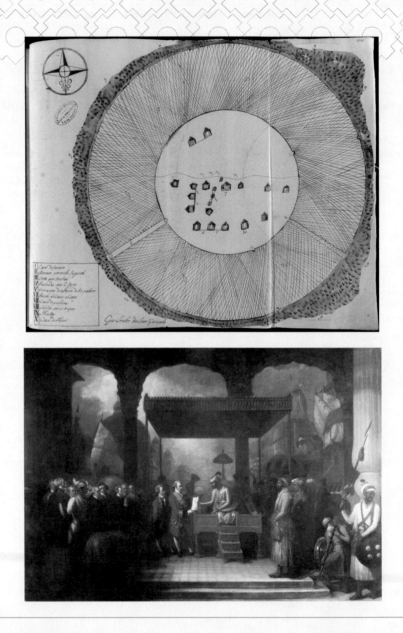

(TOP) MAP OF A QUILOMBO, ca. 1769. This sketch of the quilombo of Sao Gonçalo, Brazil , shows artisan workshops, including a blacksmith, gardens, and defense works surrounding the settlement. Over time, European settlers and imperial officials increasingly saw these independent Afro-Brazilian settlements as a threat to their plans for Brazil and worked to eliminate them.

(BOTTOM) SHAH ALAM, MUGHAL EMPEROR, CONVEYING THE GRANT OF THE DIWANI TO LORD CLIVE, AUGUST 1765. This is the second version of the same painting by Benjamin West (1738–1820), a well-known artist. The painting depicts the moment at which the Mughal Emperor granted the British East India Company the right to collect taxes and administer civil justice in his realm. The first version of this painting was commissioned by Lord Clive himself. This copy, ca. 1818, was created by West for Lord Clive's son, who donated it to the British East India Company. The image itself is a fantasy, as it portrays real people in the scene who were not present when these events took place.

# CHAPTER 5

# Global War and Imperial Reform

## 1655–1765

Zumbi dos Palmares—"Zumbi of Palmares" (1655–1695)—was born in north-eastern Brazil, in a settlement of free peoples of African descent. Palmares was ruled neither by the Portuguese, who dominated most of Brazil, nor by the Dutch, who were at war with the Portuguese across the globe, including in Brazil. It was a *quilombo*, an independent community under the leadership of Africans who had freed themselves from the sugar plantations on the coast. At its height, more than thirty thousand people—some born in Africa and some in Brazil—lived in Palmares, which some historians argue was governed along the lines of the African kingdoms from which many of its residents had been taken. Portuguese raiders captured Zumbi when he was six years old and gave him as a slave to a Catholic priest, who educated him in Latin and Portuguese. Escaping and returning to Palmares in 1670, he proved his military and political skill, and upon the death of his uncle, Zumbi became the quilombo's leader. Palmares's residents and leaders fought, negotiated treaties, and traded with indigenous peoples and the Portuguese until 1695, when the Portuguese captured Zumbi and beheaded him. Today, Brazil observes a national holiday on the date of Zumbi's death, which is known as "Black Consciousness Day," but in the late seventeenth century, the Portuguese crown granted the land Palmares had occupied to settlers who worked to ensure that the region's population would resist the encroachment of other European powers and return self-manumitted slaves to their owners.

A century later, in 1765, representatives of the Mughal Emperor Shah Alam II signed the Treaty of Allahabad with Lord Clive, an agent of the British East India Company. Britain had defeated France during the Seven Years' War, fought on land and sea across the globe between 1756 and 1763. In the years after the war, a tightening commercial embrace between Britain and South Asia became one of the important forces driving global change. The Treaty of Allahabad granted the company the right to collect and administer tax revenue across a large area of South Asia as

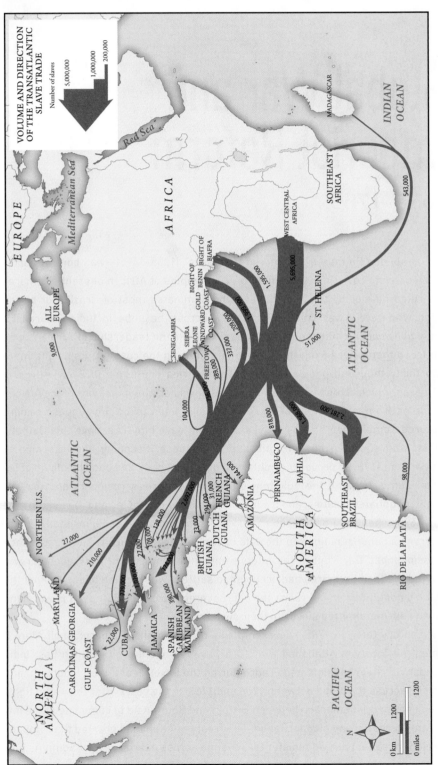

**MAP 5.1** Volume and Direction of the Transatlantic Slave Trade

well as the right to engage in duty-free commerce in the same region. This treaty culminated decades of unrest among indigenous rulers and their European merchant allies struggling to control parts of the Mughal Empire as it began to fragment after the death of Emperor Aurangzeb in 1707. With this treaty, the British East India Company asserted itself as an economic and military force in South Asia. In the coming decades, it served as a party to additional treaties and even placed some sovereign rulers on the company payroll, initiating a new and much more ambitious undertaking for British subjects in Asia.

---

These encounters in Brazil and South Asia bookend a multilayered global struggle over resources, commerce, labor, and territory that characterized much of the seventeenth and eighteenth centuries. During this era, many imperial rulers sought more direct control over their territorial claims so that they could extract greater value from their subjects and tributary zones and protect their interests against perceived internal and external threats. At the same time, the people and places from whom the early modern empires sought tribute developed according to their own political, economic, and social dynamics. In the 1750s, these two trends led to global war that altered the shapes of empires, political and economic policies, and the discourse of political belonging. This war has a number of names, the Seven Years' War (1756–63) being most common in European history books, although the French and Indian War may be a more familiar name to students of US history. In other parts of the world, it is called the Third Silesian War, the Third Carnatic War, or the Pomeranian War. In this book, we're calling it "World War Zero" and using it to illustrate the colossal scope and consequences of European conflict and expansion during this time.

The term World War Zero prepares readers to compare the Seven Years' War and the conflict of 1914–1918 that came to be known as World War I. Both were preceded by a global arms race and a series of limited regional wars that political leaders considered useful in the pursuit of their interests. In both cases, fear of (or desire for) changes in the balance of power in the Eastern Mediterranean and Central Europe fueled conflicts that preceded the larger conflagration, which played out on a global canvas with shifting alliances among European and non-European armies determining the outcome. After each war, the reallocation of territories and other concessions made to end the war led in short order to further violence, exposing the shortsightedness of the peace settlement. In the aftermath of war, leaders of the main protagonist empires, treasuries depleted, decreed changes within their realms that precipitated additional conflict.

In the first section of this chapter, we compare different practices of sovereignty across Eurasia from the mid-seventeenth to the mid-eighteenth centuries.

We then examine the growth of the slave economy and tensions between European and indigenous political and economic systems, two factors driving conflict in the Americas and the Atlantic world. Following this, we survey additional factors in the competition among rulers on the Afro-Eurasian supercontinent, as the pursuit of advantages over rivals became entangled in shifting diplomatic and military alliances. These different trajectories overlapped just after the mid-century in military confrontations in the Americas, Europe, Asia, and on the seas: World War Zero.

## Consolidating the Center: Modernizing Monarchies

Important ideas about the nature of political power that would continue to fuel debate and conflict through the coming centuries emerged from seventeenth-century experiences, although one would not have been able to predict which ones would become most influential and which would fade into obscurity. In 1688–1689, England experienced a "Glorious Revolution," in which the monarchy accepted clear limits on its power. The recognition in law of the limits of royal power did not inspire universal acclamation or immediate imitation elsewhere. Most Afro-Eurasian states remained autocratic hereditary imperial states (in theory, if not always in reality) into the nineteenth century. In many other empires, the concentration of royal power peaked in the decades *after* the Glorious Revolution in England. In this vein, the regimes of three other rulers—King Louis XIV of France (1638–1715), Tsar Peter the Great of Russia (1672–1725), and the Kangxi Emperor of Qing Dynasty China (1654–1722)—can be fruitfully compared to England and to each other. Each of these monarchs ruled for at least four decades, and although no ruler single-handedly manages an empire, the representation and exercise of royal power in these regimes helps us to understand the variety of ways sovereignty was constructed and sustained.

### Limiting the Power of the Monarch: England

John Locke (1632–1704) attended Oxford University in the 1650s. Locke found himself bored with the classical curriculum that had been in place for generations. Experimental and applied science, particularly chemistry and medicine—the practice of inductive reasoning—interested him in ways that memorizing ancient texts did not. After completing his degrees, Locke continued to pursue his eclectic interests with the help of powerful patrons who employed him in various ways, often as a secretary. These positions provided the opportunity for travel and also exposed Locke more directly to the political issues of his day, which inspired him to a deeper contemplation of philosophical principles and to change his thinking about some fundamental questions of political order still roiling England in the aftermath of the Civil War and restoration of the monarchy described in Chapter 3. At one point, Locke fled to the Netherlands out of fear he might be arrested as a conspirator against the crown. Locke returned to England in the entourage of Mary Henrietta Stuart (1631–1660), who, along with her husband William of Orange (1650–1702), was offered the English throne in 1688. Although Locke wrote many of his most important works on political philosophy in the 1670s and 1680s, they were not published until he returned to England.

Influenced by the recent history of his homeland—civil war, military rule, the abolition of monarchy, continued tensions between parliament and crown after the restoration of monarchy—Locke's most important writings search for principles to understand how states come into being, what their purposes are, the circumstances under which they can be altered, and to what end. The construction of political order that flowed from Locke's pen shared his countryman Thomas Hobbes's vision of life before government: human beings in a state of nature are free, and all individuals are sovereigns, that is, responsible for protecting their own lives and possessions. But what does that freedom mean? Consider squirrels, constantly gathering, hiding, digging up, moving, and fighting over acorns, all while hoping to avoid being devoured by a hawk or a fox. The absolute freedom of the state of nature can be a horrible freedom, a squirrel's freedom. States are formed when individuals try to move beyond this by creating a social contract for their mutual protection, which means giving up absolute freedom (and the idea of every individual as sovereign) for the enjoyment of greater security of person and property. However, unlike Hobbes, Locke asserted that those who rule—those to whom portions of individual sovereignty are entrusted—are bound by the same social contract. Rulers do not have absolute freedom of action either. If the holders of political authority (usually hereditary monarchs in Locke's day) impinge on the essential freedoms of their people embedded in the social contract, then there is tyranny, and that can be grounds for removing the officeholder from power. For Locke, any claim of *absolute* power violated the social contract that creates a state in the first place.

The agreement that King William and Queen Mary made with Parliament in 1689 reflects aspects of Locke's thinking on government. The English Bill of Rights, resulting from this agreement, confirmed that English monarchs could not arbitrarily suspend the enforcement of laws and that Parliament must participate in decisions about raising public revenues through taxation. As we have seen, such things are key components in the exercise of sovereignty and the maintenance of state power. The Bill of Rights also stipulated that the monarchy would not interfere with parliamentary deliberations or with judicial proceedings. Finally, it recognized that individuals had certain rights that must be safeguarded against state power, for example, protections against cruel and unusual punishment or excessive fines. In short, England's new king and queen agreed that the sovereign's power was neither absolute nor resident in the person(s) of the monarch(s). Sovereignty was a relationship of ruler and ruled that did not require the ruled to sacrifice all political power.

## Absolutism: France, Russia, China

When William and Mary came to power in England, the French Estates General, a consultative body with some similarities to the English parliament, had not met in decades. In contrast to England, in France the monarchy had defeated seventeenth-century revolts against increasing royal power. King Louis XIV strengthened the role of provincial officials called *intendants*, appointed by the monarchy. Intendants had administrative, judicial, fiscal, and military authority as the local base of a bureaucratic pyramid designed to enforce the will of the monarch. Ideologically, Louis's supporters reinforced the idea of royal absolutism. Bishop Jacques-Bénigne Bossuet (1627–1704), a renowned preacher and theologian in Louis's court, described royal authority as sacred, paternal, and absolute. In sharp contrast to the limited monarchy in England, Bossuet wrote in *Politics Drawn from the Very Words of Holy Scripture* that the French monarch "need render account to no one for what he orders."

King Louis's Russian contemporary Tsar Peter also claimed expansive personal powers, and as in France, his claims of greater authority were challenged. The Cossacks, a multiethnic group made up of peoples from across Eurasia (from Ukrainians to Turks to Buryats), remained hostile to the idea that a distant ruler could impose restrictions on them. Stenka Razin (1630–1671) led the largest uprising of the era in 1670, when thousands of troops, under the leadership of Cossack military veterans with experience in both land and naval warfare, took numerous towns and sought to establish an independent state along the Volga River. By no means universally popular or respected, Razin faced resistance from other Cossacks and was condemned by the Orthodox Christian hierarchy. Troops loyal to the tsar captured him in 1671 and brought him to Moscow, where he was tortured and put to death.

Peter, like Louis, attempted to consolidate military victories with administrative reforms. Peter terminated the Boyar Duma, an aristocratic consultative body, and replaced it with a Governing Senate. These reforms were couched within a claim of absolute power for the sovereign. The Senate, the highest organ of state, was appointed by the tsar to be his council of advisers and top administrators. Peter delegated administrative responsibility on a model largely borrowed from Sweden, but he still acted as an autocrat. Intending his new government to be more efficient and productive but not to diminish the tsar's personal power, Peter remained suspicious of the government institutions that he created. An imperial official called "the sovereign's eye" presided over the Senate, and other officials

**PETER THE GREAT INSPECTS A SHIP AT AMSTERDAM.** This painting, ca. 1700 by an unidentified artist, is another imaginary depiction of a real event that occurred during Tsar Peter I's 1697–98 diplomatic tour of Europe. Peter, who built up the Russian Navy, took a personal interest in naval engineering and military matters. While in Amsterdam, he was treated to a parade of ships and a mock sea battle, depicted here.

monitored and reported directly to Peter on the workings of various government ministries. The Russian Imperial Code stated that the sovereign's power was absolute. Peter himself sought—through imperial decrees—to govern even how people could dress and what kind of facial hair men could grow. Scholarly research from many cultures and time periods suggests that laws like these were impossible to enforce, but they are important indicators of a political system in which it is the sovereign's prerogative to make such rules in the first place.

A decree on hairstyle also played a role in the efforts of Qing rulers to establish their authority in China. In 1645, the chief advisor to the first Qing emperor—remember that the Qing were Manchu, not Chinese—issued a decree that Chinese men had to adopt the Manchu hairstyle called the queue. By shaving the fronts of their heads and braiding the hair in back in a long ponytail, Qing subjects would acknowledge the new regime's authority. The hairstyle symbolized a political transformation unacceptable to many Chinese; resistance to the Manchu conquest was fierce and persistent. Over time, however, the Qing Dynasty stabilized, real incomes increased for most people, and both commercial activity and

**MAP 5.2** China from the Ming to the Qing Dynasties

agricultural production expanded. A vast civil service, including over fifteen hundred county magistrates, selected (at least in theory) by examination rather than heredity, enforced the Qing Code, a compilation of laws for the entire empire adopted from the Ming and then revised and reissued several times in the seventeenth and eighteenth centuries. Under the Qing, three sets of examinations—local, regional, and imperial—were introduced. There were other ways to gain office, including buying titles and taking special exams, with quotas designated for particular ethnic, regional, or social groups, but government by meritocracy—based on merit and competency rather than social or familial privilege—remained a powerful ideal.

During a long and stable era that followed this early turbulence, Qing territorial control doubled that of its Ming predecessor. A growing population and economy appeared to signal that the dynasty was fulfilling the Mandate of Heaven to provide for the empire's prosperity, an impression the Kangxi Emperor showcased during the six grand inspection tours we described in chapter 3. These journeys were designed to impress the populace with the power and legitimacy of the emperor over a large, diverse, and at times rebellious population. The tours reinforced the association between central authority and public works, as when the entourage travelled along the Grand Canal through the commercial centers of the empire to the silk manufacturing city of Suzhou. The tradition continued under the Qianlong Emperor (1711–1799) who visited, among other sites, the flood prevention network that protected southern China's agricultural heartland. These emperors managed their images carefully, portraying themselves in the guise of Buddhist priests, shamans, Confucian officials, or powerful warriors, depending on their audience.

The economic expansion, rising affluence, population growth, and political stability of the Qing were no secrets to the broader world. China appeared to many a model of imperial rule worth emulating. Some, although by no means all, European political philosophers wrote admiringly of China's political and economic system, and the (often idealized) principles and practices of the Chinese civil service had real influence elsewhere. Over time, advocacy for merit-based systems to replace patronage appointments or hereditary government service attracted adherents in many countries. Indeed, managers of the British East India Company used the Chinese system to advocate modernization of their own company's training and appointment policies.

Of course, none of these rulers had truly absolute power. In comparison to the English monarchy, most Eurasian rulers made decisions with far fewer restrictions on them, but they all still relied on the advice of powerful individuals and groups within their empires. They also faced structural limits on the economic, military, and cultural resources available to carry out their programs. All of these leaders—Manchu, French, English, and Russian—incorporated in their decisions understandings of how the world was changing (or not changing), from economic activity to warfare, and all of them acted within constraints imposed by the availability of resources and the strength of other domestic or international actors and institutions.

## The Question of Control in the Atlantic Seaborne Empires

The sovereigns of seaborne empires could not travel their realms the way the Qing Emperors did—the distances and dangers of open ocean were too much—so they projected their power aggressively through symbols and subordinates. These monarchs claimed vast areas, yet no Spanish, English, or Portuguese ruler ever set foot in those territories. Viceroys and governors represented royal authority. Numerous and often overlapping political and ecclesiastical divisions further divided space and population, with religious and political officials sometimes cooperating and sometimes competing, all claiming to act on behalf of the sovereign.

## Resistance and Rebellion in the Americas

Complex and intertwined hierarchies of political, economic, and spiritual power evolved. Although in theory (and mostly in practice), European-origin peoples dominated all of these hierarchies, the indigenous, African, and mixed-race populations had some power of their own. The Spanish record contains many complaints against local officials, some manifesting themselves in public protests accompanied by cries of "Long Live the King, Death to Bad Government." These protests would yield investigations into the cause of upheaval (and the accompanying revenue shortfall) and in some cases the removal of officials. Indigenous and mestizo communities and individuals also used the imperial legal system to pursue their interests, often with success. Government officials, from local magistrates and judges to viceroys themselves, had great flexibility in implementing imperial policy, given the distance from Spain, the size of the empire, and the inability to communicate speedily. Officials in the Americas could issue formulaic rejections of directives from Spain—"I obey, but I do not comply"—that would suspend implementation of new laws and trigger an automatic review back in Spain. This reply acknowledged the crown's legitimacy (I obey my sovereign) while also asserting its ignorance of local matters (there's no way this law could work here).

In some places, Spanish authority was so limited that it could be totally reversed, at least temporarily. This happened in a region that today is part of the state of New Mexico in the United States. Spaniards first arrived there at the end of the sixteenth century, when Franciscan priests established a mission to convert to Christianity the urban-dwelling indigenous population, who came to be known as the Pueblo (Village) people to distinguish them from the nomadic groups that lived in the region as well. For decades, an uneasy relationship existed between the Pueblo people and the recent European arrivals, made even more complex by the threat posed to both of them from other indigenous groups. In the 1670s, a drought prompted Pueblo medicine men to perform indigenous religious rituals designed to bring back the water. When the Franciscans condemned the practice as sorcery, the Pueblo people revolted and in 1680 drove all of the Spaniards from the region for a decade.

Their abrupt absence transformed the region more dramatically than Spanish rule had. The horses and sheep that the Spaniards left behind in New Mexico in 1680 were quickly absorbed by the indigenous populations, transforming their societies. Horses, acquired through war and trade by indigenous peoples across

North America, enabled greater mobility and increased hunting efficiency. Firearms, another import from Iberia that Europeans did not wish indigenous peoples to acquire, also entered their possession through trade and confiscation. One indigenous group, the Comanches, made especially effective use of horses in building an empire across the southern plains, which the Spaniards called "Comancheria," that covered much of today's Texas, New Mexico, and Oklahoma. Across North America, from Hudson's Bay to northern Mexico, conflicting territorial claims between indigenous and European settlements endured through the nineteenth century. Some Spaniards on the northern frontiers of New Spain were so convinced of the superior numbers and firepower of hostile indigenous warriors that they warned repeatedly of the potential collapse of the entire European enterprise in that part of the world.

Demographic transformation and rivalries among indigenous and settler populations also caused recurring conflict between Europeans and indigenous peoples in eastern North America, from Virginia to Canada, where French, English, and Dutch settlers, with their rivalries, diseases, and economies, challenged indigenous populations. Indigenous governments adopted diverse strategies for dealing with the new arrivals. Alliances shifted; conflicts were common. The largest conflict in New England, known as "King Phillips' War," broke out in 1675 and lasted until 1678. The conviction in an English court of three Native Americans for the murder of another indigenous man who had converted to Christianity set off this clash between English settlers and the Algonquians, who attacked more than half of the towns in New England. Led by Metacomet (also known as King Phillip), the Algonquians found themselves fighting on multiple fronts—against the English and their indigenous allies on one; and against the Mohawks, long-standing rivals from the Iroquois Confederation, on the other. Disease, starvation, and bullets all took their toll. The Algonquians lost. King Phillip himself was killed, his head (like Zumbi's in Brazil) severed from his body and put on display, a sign of the hardening relationship between Europeans and North American indigenous peoples.

## Enslaved People and the Slave Trade

Conflict between indigenous and European-origin peoples was one factor shaping European endeavors in the Americas during this time. The growing importance of slave-based production, especially in the Caribbean and Brazil, was another. There are complex explanations for the rapid growth of Atlantic-world slavery during this era. The expansion of Europe into global trade routes had spurred European demand for tropical commodities, and this demand continued to rise. Unable to grow these products in Europe, or control these commodities at their sources in Afro-Eurasia, Europeans eyed those regions of the Americas that appeared to have suitable conditions, except for a steady labor supply.

The European demand for plantation labor in the Americas, the potential profits to be made, African political traditions and rivalries, and the individual decisions of countless people across the globe led to the enslavement of human beings on an unprecedented scale. In the century and a half between Columbus's landfall and 1650, an estimated three hundred thousand enslaved Africans were transported to the Americas. In the century that followed, the figure was ten times higher: almost three million people embarked. The number continued to grow over the subsequent decades, before declining in the nineteenth century. Europeans did not yet lay extensive claims to territorial sovereignty in Africa but negotiated instead with regional and local political leaders.

During this era, some African states paralleled developments in other parts of the world, replacing hereditary posts, reforming tax schemes and military organization, and fighting and negotiating with other states. The history of African slavery is intertwined with these transformations. For the most part, Europeans did not simply arrive and abduct tens of thousands of Africans. Enslavement was a common practice in Africa, as it was in many parts of the world, usually involving prisoners of war. Enslaving human beings is abhorrent, but the nature of slavery in Africa differed in important ways from what came to dominate the Americas. In Africa, servitude was often for a limited term, at the end of which people could expect to be free again and return to their homes. Further, children of the enslaved were usually considered free.

The growth of transatlantic slavery changed these terms, as the enslaved were transformed into commodities to be owned and traded. West Africa was the region most affected by these changes in the seventeenth and eighteenth centuries. This region was a crucial part of the early-modern Afro-Eurasian trade network, contributing gold and other products. This wealth drew the first Portuguese and Dutch traders, who named their ports of call after the riches they sought to acquire, for example, the Gold Coast (today's Ghana) or the Ivory Coast (Côte d'Ivoire). When Europeans arrived, different ethnic and political groups were already competing for power, much like the rest of the supercontinent. In this context, Europeans could be powerful allies in local conflicts, much as they had been in the Americas. Many African rulers at first did not trade in slaves with Europeans, instead trading local commodities for desired imports. European firearms—one area in which European technology was at the forefront of global manufacturing—were especially desired, as they could be key in defeating local rivals. Enslaving one's rivals could also change military and economic power relationships. The slave trade provides an interesting and paradoxical example of one of the *disadvantages* of stateness: African regions without effective centralized sovereign states appear to have been less subject to the depredations of the slave trade.

In the calculation of some smaller states, with fewer commodities or resources to trade, exchanging human beings for firearms appeared a sound strategy. These considerations combined with the burgeoning European demand for labor in their American colonies; the slave trade accelerated. Amid this emerging traffic in human beings, some African states, like Benin, refused to participate. Others gained and maintained control of greater territory and resources, in part as a result of participation in the slave trade (for example, Dahomey).

Slavery, and the long-distance trade in enslaved Africans, did not originate with Europeans, but Europeans transformed the practice. Once sold into bondage—usually at West African ports—enslaved people by the millions traveled across the Atlantic Ocean on ships flying the Portuguese, British, Spanish, Dutch, and even

**PLAN OF A SLAVE SHIP, SHOWING CONDITIONS OF THE MIDDLE PASSAGE BETWEEN AFRICA AND THE AMERICAS.** From the seventeenth to the nineteenth century, more than eleven million Africans were transported to the Americas under horrific conditions. This image depicts the way human beings were packed onto vessels to carry as many people as possible, maximizing potential profits for the traders. In the late eighteenth century, antislavery activists began to use illustrations like this in their literature to demonstrate the cruelty of the slave trade.

Polish flags. This "Middle Passage" of the Triangular Trade linking Africa, the Americas, and Europe was three to four months of hell for the newly enslaved Africans. No longer were slaves prisoners of war or temporary bondservants. European demand for labor led to "chattel slavery," a system in which slaveholders did not just control the rights to a person's labor (as in the encomienda system) or power over them for a fixed period of time (as with a prisoner). In chattel slavery, the enslaved person became property for life, a commodity that could be controlled, inherited, bought, sold, or otherwise disposed of as the owner saw fit. Children of the enslaved person also became the property of the parent's owner. The seemingly endless appetite for labor in the Americas transformed the scale at which the system operated.

## Sources for Studying the Slave Trade

Firsthand accounts of the Middle Passage are rare. By far the most widely circulated and well-known description of the experience comes from a memoir by Olaudah Equiano (1745–1797), who describes himself as having been born in what is now Nigeria before being enslaved and transported against his will across the Atlantic. Equiano's account provides another chance to see the challenges of historical inquiry. Scholar Vincent Carretta found evidence suggesting that Equiano may not have been born in Africa but in South Carolina. If this is the case, then Equiano may not have experienced firsthand the Middle Passage, which he describes in rich and horrible detail, but instead used information that he had read or heard from others. Historians disagree about this kind of evidence. If Equiano was not born in Africa (there is no consensus on this), does this render useless Equiano's description of the Middle Passage? Most historians would argue that all sources are flawed, incomplete, or compromised in some way, so we need to approach them all with care. If there is reason to question some details of Equiano's memoir, then what we need to do is examine it more closely rather than discard it. Carretta's research went on to show that other sources confirm most details in Equiano's book. The evidence also shows that Equiano's description of the Middle Passage is consistent with other narratives, even if it is not from firsthand experience. It may or may not be the case that Olaudah Equiano's account of the Middle Passage is a personal recollection, but we have every reason to think it is an accurate depiction of the experience.[1]

---

[1]   Vincent Carretta, *Equiano, the African: Biography of a Self-Made Man* (Athens: University of Georgia Press, 2005). A thorough, and critical, review of Carretta's book is Douglas Chambers, "Review of Carretta, Vincent, *Equiano the African: Biography of a Self-Made Man.*" *H-Atlantic, H-Net Reviews.* November, 2007. URL: http://www.h-net.org/reviews/showrev.php?id=13855. For a good overview of the debate, see "Olaudah Equiano: African or American?" in *1650–1850: Ideas, Æsthetics, and Inquiries in the Early Modern Era* 17 (2008): 229–248.

There are other sources for understanding the slave trade. Slave traders and shipping companies kept detailed records, reflecting the business of human trafficking. These records are spread around the world, principally in archives of the countries that dominated the movement of enslaved Africans across the Atlantic Ocean. Although scholars had been working with these records for years, in 1990 historians David Eltis and Steven Behrendt started to collect all available records into a single database. Combing collections from France, Britain, the United States, the Netherlands, Spain, Portugal, Brazil, and elsewhere, a comprehensive and detailed portrait of the slave trade became more accessible. Now hosted at Emory University, the Atlantic Slave Trade Database (www.slavevoyages.org) brings together records from more than thirty-five thousand voyages that carried more than twelve million Africans between 1514 and 1866. The database reveals both the vast scope of the slave trade and also the details of many individual lives, including the age, gender, and origin of millions of Africans; nearly one hundred thousand people are identified by name.

The Atlantic Slave Trade database also reveals the importance of resistance and shipboard revolts. Escapes, daily acts of defiance, and outright rebellions characterized slave societies. As we saw at the start of this chapter, enslaved Africans, brought to labor on sugar plantations, freed themselves and intermingled with indigenous populations, forming the *quilombos* of Brazil. Escaped slaves also formed communities, ruled by free Africans, in northern Colombia, Cuba, Jamaica, and Dominica, putting down roots alongside the autonomous indigenous states throughout the Americas that also survived well beyond the first century of the European invasion. In addition, conspiracies were endemic, for example, among the plantation slaves of the Virginia colony in the late seventeenth and early eighteenth centuries. Revolts also rocked the mining communities of New Spain and Peru. These actions, along with those of Europeans and indigenous peoples, shaped the flow of resources and the ways in which claims and exercises of sovereignty in the Western Hemisphere developed in this era.

## The Path to World War Zero

Over the course of decades the Eurasian Empires skirmished on a regular basis, building to a protracted war on three continents in the middle of the eighteenth century. The British and French Empires began the war in 1754; shifting alliances brought additional European powers into the conflict in 1756. Seven years later, the major European protagonists brokered a series of treaties. This sequence of events is the one from which the name "Seven Years' War" is derived, but these battles formed part of the larger, ongoing hostilities. This context provides a better foundation for understanding the importance of "World War Zero." Little European territory changed hands as a result of the Seven Years' War, but recent research on the war and its consequences has taken a broader perspective, showing the significant shifts it produced in global power relationships.

## Competition and Conflict among the Seaborne Empires

The transatlantic slave trade expanded rapidly in the seventeenth century. The morality of owning other human beings, or the concerns over the suffering slavery caused, remained for the most part in the background as empires tried to ensure revenues and compete with rivals in a rapidly changing global economy. Empires vied with one another to gain the economic upper hand, including the right to control the flow of slave labor. Rights over enslaved people were negotiated as lucrative contracts, or as pieces of international agreements, as when the British gained control of the slave trade to Spanish America in 1713. Valuable plantation territories also traded hands, as the Dutch-Portuguese rivalry in Brazil or the French seizure of Saint-Domingue in the second half of the seventeenth century demonstrated. In the period 1679–1700, in the early years of French control, around five thousand slaves disembarked in Saint-Domingue. In the next twenty-five years, the number passed forty thousand; and in the twenty-five years after that, it passed one hundred forty thousand. Saint-Domingue became the tropical economic gem of the French Empire, built on the expansion of human misery. In 1685, King Louis XIV issued an edict, commonly known as the "Black Code," regarding the French dominions in the Americas. Its provisions clarified crown policy regarding slave life, denying rights in court, rights in the marketplace, and rights to control the fate of their own progeny to enslaved people. The code also expelled Jews from the French Caribbean and suppressed the practice of any faith other than Roman Catholicism, even among slaves.

In its own territories in the Caribbean and North America, the British crown also asserted more direct control over colonial life and commerce. It established a Board of Trade and Plantations and pushed legislation both to raise the cost of commodities produced by rival empires and to require that goods shipped from Europe to British colonies had to pass through England. The Spanish and Portuguese followed similar practices. Events of the first half of the eighteenth century confirmed for all of these empires that they needed to defend their imperial interests even more aggressively.

War constantly accompanied the European maritime empires during this era. According to data compiled by Frank Tallett, in the century after 1610, Spain was at war with another European power on average three out of every four years. During this time, the size of armies and navies grew, weapons became more powerful, and the costs of preparing and conducting war grew with them. The main protagonists in the Thirty Years' War (1618–1648) had armies numbering approximately one hundred thousand each. By 1710, King Louis XIV could put over three hundred thousand French troops in the field and had the world's largest navy: about two hundred warships. England claimed approximately the same number as it emerged as the primary naval power in the world.[2]

The eighteenth century began with a dynastic crisis in Europe when the Spanish Empire passed into the hands of a member of the Bourbon family, which also controlled the French crown. Fearful of the potential for future unification of both empires, England led an alliance into a decade-long war over this issue. Significant concessions, including a commitment to maintain separate kingdoms in perpetuity, finally won the Spanish throne for the Bourbon family. These new Spanish royals launched a series of reforms in hopes of reviving the empire's fortunes after decades of stagnation. Borrowing from their French cousins, the Spanish Bourbons created a system of intendancies, with imperial officials reporting directly to the crown from throughout the empire. They also added new viceroyalties, courts, and military infrastructure to their Western Hemisphere enterprise and initiated sweeping economic and social reforms.

The Netherlands also had interests in the War of Spanish Succession. They were allies of the English because both were geopolitical rivals with France and Spain. However, the war also confirmed England's military and commercial primacy on the world's oceans, threatening the Netherlands, which relied on maritime commerce for its prosperity. In the 1680s, the Dutch East India Company (VOC) may have been the largest private employer on the planet, with almost twenty-two thousand employees. During the first half of the eighteenth century, however, the burdens of warfare, increasing encroachments on Dutch commerce from larger territorial empires, and a faltering domestic economy took their toll. The Netherlands remained prosperous by comparative global standards, but the Golden Age of Dutch commercial power came to an end during these decades.

## The Land-Based Empires of Central Eurasia

Important changes in the balance of power in Central and Eastern Europe, particularly the interventions of Russia and Prussia in regional affairs, also escalated armed conflict among these traditionally land-based empires during the middle of the eighteenth century. Russia was at war almost constantly during the reign of Peter the Great, who had set out not only to build a successful army but also a navy, taking a personal interest in nautical science and shipbuilding. With the help of British expertise, he built a navy of approximately thirty thousand sailors and almost fifty large ships, but it came at a high price: military expenditures

---

[2]   Frank Tallett, *War and Society in Early Modern Europe: 1495–1715* (New York: Routledge, 2010).

consumed up to 85 percent of government revenues. Peter's neighbors and rivals in Prussia (the state surrounding Berlin in what is now Germany) consolidated a powerful monarchy in the decades after the Thirty Years' War, introducing a system of permanent taxation to increase state revenue significantly. These revenues built a formidable army; by 1740, under the "Soldier-King" Frederick William I (1688–1740), Prussia had the fourth largest army in Europe, although it ranked only twelfth in population.

In the 1730s and 1740s, succession disputes in Poland and Austria precipitated more war. Prussia and Russia, having invested so heavily to develop their militaries, aggressively asserted their interests. They also engaged repeatedly in territorial disputes to the west, east, and south. Russia, for example, went to war with the Ottoman Empire in the 1670s, 1680s, 1710s, and 1730s. The reversal of Ottoman fortunes contributed to major changes in the Middle East and South Asia in the eighteenth century, but the Ottoman Empire managed to survive into the twentieth century. The same cannot be said for the Safavid Empire, which collapsed in the eighteenth century, or the Mughal Empire, which survived, but saw its power decline greatly over the same time period.

The Safavid Empire fought over territory and other resources with the Russian, Ottoman, and Mughal Empires. Its trading network—and the accompanying tax revenue—contracted at the hands of competition from European maritime commerce. Ongoing disputes over the alignment between political power and religious practice among different Islamic traditions also weakened Safavid claims of sovereignty. Sunni Afghans forced the Safavid ruler Shah Sultan Husayn (1668–1726) to abdicate in the 1720s. As the Safavid dynasty collapsed, Nadir Shah (1688–1747) proclaimed a new empire, the Afsharid, which lasted only a few decades. The son of Turkmen pastoralists from northwestern Iran, Nadir Shah attempted to resolve regional ethnic and sectarian disputes not only within the historical limits of the Safavid regime but also across the broader Islamic world. In 1736, he gathered religious, political, and military leaders from throughout the fractured empire and asked them to choose a new ruler who could unify them. Probably inspired and intimidated in equal measure, the group selected him. Fashioning himself in the tradition of Timur (Tamerlane), the famous unifier of the region from an earlier era, he used war and diplomacy to claim an empire stretching from the Indus River to the Caucasus. Economic development, religious initiatives, and strategic marriages cemented his relationships with local groups and other regional powerhouses, particularly the Ottomans, with whom he repeatedly attempted to reconcile by promoting an innovative solution to the Sunni-Shi'a rift in Islam. Nadir Shah was a brilliant military leader but not a diplomat, imam, or economist. He died at the hands of his own guards in 1747, leaving a legacy of increased vulnerability in the region rather than a shoring up of its resources around a central sovereign authority.

The Mughal Empire experienced similar pressures in the eighteenth century. The Mughal Emperor Aurangzeb may have been the wealthiest man in the world when he died in 1707, but after his demise regional power holders grew less willing than before to sacrifice sovereignty and material wealth to an imperial center returning uncertain benefits. European merchant groups, mostly French and English, established fortified trading posts and formed alliances with regional leaders that brought in resources, including weapons, which accelerated the ethnic, religious, and economic centripetal forces already in play. Like Europe, South Asia moved quickly from one war to the next through the first half of the eighteenth century.

## The Seven Years' War and its Aftermath

In 1754, British troops attacked French territorial claims in North America and seized French ships. Within two years, the other European Empires had entered the war: Prussia, Great Britain, and Portugal on one side; France, Spain, Russia, Austria, and Sweden on the other. Smaller principalities in Central Europe joined on both sides, as did indigenous states and peoples in North America and South Asia. Sea battles involved dozens of ships firing hundreds of cannons. Warfighting tactics included seizing ports, constructing forts, and disrupting trade. States entered and left the conflict at different times, and at least four different treaties ended hostilities The outcome of the war was significant for all of the protagonists: Among the European powers, Great Britain (England and Wales were now joined with Scotland as Great Britain, although England dominated political decision-making) appeared as the biggest winner—ever closer to a global power—and France the loser. Victories at Québec (1759) and Pondicherry (1760) left Britain dominant in North America and South Asia, respectively.

Both England and France doubled their public debt in pursuit of victory. Other European powers also accumulated significant financial burdens fighting the war. The war led Europe's political elites to conclude that a permanent war footing was essential. This combination of debt and constant preparation for the next war contributed to further changes in imperial policies, with many consequences, some by design and others a complete shock. These features of the context, conduct, and consequences of the war are why we like the term World War Zero.

For the British Empire, the Peace of 1763 carried great opportunity at a high cost. The size of British North America doubled; political elites in Britain debated how to make this vast territory best serve the empire's interests. Should the

**MAP 5.3** (a) The Seven Years' War; (b) The British Empire in 1763

To the Hon.ᵇˡᵉ George Picot Esq.ᴿ President of the Council & Governor of Fort St. George, this View of the Ruins of the Citadel in Pondichery is respectfully presented by

John M.ᶜLean
Sept. 8.º 1762.                                                  Practitioner Eng.ʳ

**RUINS OF THE CITADEL IN PONDICHERRY AFTER THE ATTACK BY THE BRITISH, 1762.** The British siege of the French fortress at Pondicherry, India, was the culmination of the East Indian campaigns of the global Seven Years' War. The destruction of the fortress after two years' siege in 1761 left Britain the dominant European power in the Indian Ocean and in control of an extensive maritime empire. The artist, John McClean (d. 1768), drew himself into the foreground of this sketch, which he dedicated to George Picot, then the Governor of Fort St. George, the oldest British fortress in India (established in 1644).

imperial center focus on managing commerce and tax revenues, or should more effort be expended to govern the territories themselves? Advocates of a more intensive approach to the overseas empire won the day, and Britain began to build what historians call its "New Imperial System." On the revenue side, parliament passed new taxes with the Sugar Act and the Stamp Act. In addition, the government increased efforts to curtail the flow of untaxed merchandise (contraband) through the empire and to stimulate trade between the Americas and Great Britain rather than simply within its Western Hemisphere territories. In the short term, the plan appeared to work, as revenue to the crown from its colonial enterprises increased significantly; but negative consequences also accompanied these policy changes, exacerbated by further decisions about how the empire was to be managed.

Emerging from the war, the British government decided to station imperial troops permanently in North America and also prohibit the movement of colonials west of the Allegheny Mountains, recognizing the potential threat posed by indigenous states in the region such as the Iroquois. These decisions affected some individuals and communities who had expected access to this territory. The changes in tax policies stirred even wider resentment. Some in the colonies also felt that the manner in which these decisions were made violated both the letter of the law and the implied social contract—think back to John Locke's writing presented at the start of this chapter—under which all Englishmen lived. However, disagreements over the course of action among the disaffected, coupled with regional social, political, and economic tensions, meant that collective action was neither universally supported nor easy to organize among those who agreed it was necessary.

One must be careful, therefore, not to assume that the seeds of an inevitable uprising were planted in British North America at this time. Most residents, although aggravated by certain imperial policies, did not advocate independence. They felt a deep and abiding connection with the empire, even if they had never set foot in England. The 1765 Stamp Act, which created a new tax on legal documents, provoked widespread protests, but most of these were self-contained, rarely spilling over into violence or extensive property damage. The repeal of the Stamp Act in 1766 did not heal a growing sentiment toward republicanism in certain sectors of British North American colonial society, but one should note that widespread organized violence against the empire did not erupt until well into the next decade, and significant portions of the colonial population remained loyal to the crown throughout the subsequent war for independence, which lasted more than seven years.

Spain neither gained nor lost significantly in World War Zero, but it responded to its lessons, accelerating a reform program under King Charles III (1716–1788). Spain imposed new taxes, new monopolies, and more colonial officials to enforce the royal will, creating a fourth viceroyalty (with its capital in Buenos Aires) and expanding military expenditures. As in British North America, imperial reforms sparked protests. In 1765, tax reforms designed to increase revenue flow to Spain triggered an unprecedented rebellion against Spanish imperial rule in the city of Quito (Ecuador) on the Pacific coast of northern South America. In this event, which came to be known as the Rebellion of the Barrios, elite petitions and meetings to devise bureaucratic maneuvers to overturn royal decrees gave way to popular rioting, culminating in attacks on the tax collector's office and the royal brandy distillery. As indigenous peoples from the surrounding countryside descended on the city to add their own grievances to the protests, rumors circulated that they were planning the mass murder of white people. Threatened, Quito's elite closed ranks to defeat the rebellion and retain their own place at the top of colonial society. In the years after the rebellion, across Spanish America, social and economic cleavages within colonial society continued to limit the depth and breadth of protest activities even in areas whose populations were the most aggrieved by royal interventions in American life.

## Conclusion

The bookends of this chapter—fighting among Africans, the Dutch, and the Portuguese in Brazil and a treaty between the British and Mughal empires—mark transitions of power, strategy, and structure that spanned the world during the period between 1655 and 1765. At the start of this era, a handful of large land-based empires dominated the Afro-Eurasian landmass. These included three large Islamic states (the Ottoman, Safavid, and Mughal empires) and two new dynasties governing established polities (Romanov Russia and Qing China). At the Western edge of the supercontinent, maritime empires competed over resources and power, especially France, Britain, the Netherlands, Spain, and Portugal. By 1765, the fortunes of these states had diverged. The Safavid Empire was gone. Spain, Portugal, the Netherlands, and the Mughal Empire remained, but their power was greatly diminished, leaving them to rely increasingly on the resources and goodwill of other states to maintain their places in the global order.

Some states, especially Britain, China, and Russia, appeared stronger at the end of this period than when it began. In England, a "glorious" revolution had retained the monarchy but limited its power, part of a broad reconception of sovereignty that made its government more responsible to the governed. This did not mean democracy in the sense of broad participation in the selection of government officials, but the principle that legitimacy derived from consent of the governed was an important innovation. The French, Russian, Chinese, and Ottoman empires, among others, retained the principle of absolutism, claiming that rule was ordained by a supernatural power, but even there competition from other stakeholders was increasing. In the Americas, indigenous peoples resisted the expansion of European-derived states, challenging the terms by which non-European, or mixed-race, people could exercise control over their own territories or have meaningful input into decisions about the imperial political, social, and economic order.

Increasing traffic in human bondage unified the world's great landmasses. Slavery was the essential piece in a triangular trade that brought labor from Africa to work in the Americas, mainly Brazil and the Caribbean. During this period, the slave trade engulfed and destroyed millions of lives and fundamentally transformed both Africa and the Americas. Most of the profits from this slave labor flowed into Europe, enriching the great maritime empires there and providing capital, in Britain particularly, for economic development. This, in turn, would fuel a new round of imperialism. The effects on Africa and the Americas cannot be overstated: although a few African polities thrived on the slave trade, most were depopulated, particularly of their most productive people, with demographic, economic, and political consequences that would last for centuries. During this period, African migration to the Americas—almost all of it forced—far exceeded European migration, contributing to a complex and often violent racial interaction that defined many aspects of American life.

At opposite ends of Afro-Eurasia, very different models of rulership emerged from this period. At one end, new ideas about sovereignty and legitimacy were taking hold. These ideas spread as Britain took the lead in overseas empire from rivals like France and Spain but they also challenged regimes across Europe (and European-founded states in the Americas) to find new sources for legitimacy, stability, and power. New ideas of rulership also developed in China, as Qing emperors appeared to grapple successfully with the cultural and political diversity of their empire. By 1765, the Qing Empire was at its height, expanding across what is now Mongolia and Tibet. Japan, too, was prosperous and stable. Given the upheaval in Europe and the Atlantic World that continued into the nineteenth century, one might have thought that the next hundred years would be "the East Asian Century," but it was not to be.

## TIMELINE

**1632–1704**
John Locke, English
political philosopher

**1645**
Manchu Qing rulers
require Chinese
men to wear the
*queue* hair style

**1661–1722**
Reign of the
Kangxi Emperor
of China

**1682–1725**
Reign of Peter
the Great, Russia

**1643–1715**
Reign of Louis XIV,
France

**1650–1750**
Nearly three million enslaved
Africans transported to the
Americas

**1675–78**
King Philips' War

**1685**
King Louis XIV
issues the
"Black Code"

# A Few Good Books

Daniel Baugh. *The Global Seven Years War, 1754–1763: Britain and France in a Great Power Contest.* London: Routledge, 2011.

Max Boot. *War Made New: Weapons, Warriors, and the Making of the Modern World.* New York: Penguin, 2006.

David Eltis. *The Rise of African Slavery in the Americas.* Cambridge: Cambridge University Press, 2000.

Jill Lepore. *The Name of War: King Philip's War and the Origins of American Identity.* New York: Vintage, 1999.

Jonathan D. Spence. *Emperor of China: Self-portrait of K'ang-hsi.* New York: Vintage, 1988.

*For additional resources, including maps, primary sources, visuals, web links, and quizzes, please go to* **www.oup.com/us/carter**

**1688**
"Glorious Revolution," England

**1701–1714**
War of Spanish Succession

**1745–97**
Life of Olaudah Equiano

**1765**
Treaty of Allahabad grants British East India Company right to collect taxes; Rebellion of the Barrios, Quito

**ca. 1690**
Height of Palmares *quilombo*, Brazil

**1736**
Nadir Shah assumes power in Iran

**1756–63**
"World War Zero" (Seven Years' War)

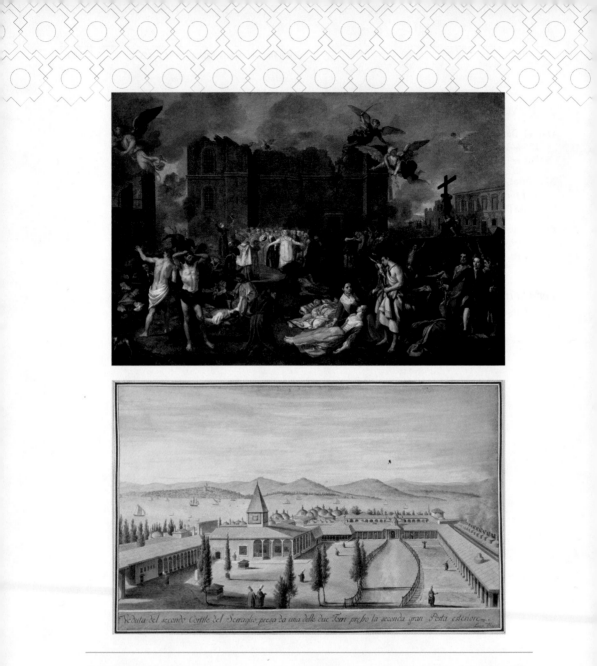

**(TOP) THE 1755 LISBON EARTHQUAKE.** The Lisbon earthquake of 1755 destroyed the Portuguese capital and killed as many as forty thousand people. This 1760 painting, by João Glama-Stroberle (1708–1792) depicts a scene in front of the Church of Santa Catarina. The painting conveys religious interpretations of the natural disaster. In contrast, the analysis and responses of many others, from scientists to government officials, leads many scholars to call this the first "modern" natural disaster.

**(BOTTOM) COURTYARD OF TOPKAPI PALACE, ISTANBUL.** The original structures of Topkapi Palace date to the mid-fifteenth century. At its height, the palace complex served as the sultan's residence and the seat of imperial governance, with several thousand people living and working within its walls. By the time the Gulhane Edict was signed there, it was no longer the royal residence but remained an important site for government offices and events. This watercolor, capturing the courtyards of the palace as they appeared in the 1780s, was painted by Luigi Mayer (1755–1803), an associate of Sir Robert Ainslie (ca. 1730–1812), for many years the British Ambassador to the Ottoman Emperor.

# A New Order for the Ages

## 1755–1839

O n November 1, 1755, a devastating earthquake flattened Lisbon, the capital of the Portuguese Empire. The quake, perhaps as powerful as 9.0 on the Richter Scale, caused damage across the Iberian Peninsula and generated a tsunami that struck islands in the Caribbean Sea, over three thousand miles away. Fires burned in the city for a week, destroying buildings that had survived the initial disaster. Tens of thousands of people were killed, injured, or displaced. Two-thirds of the city's housing stock collapsed; and most of its larger buildings, including churches, monasteries, convents, and government buildings, suffered significant, and in many cases irreparable, damage. The Lisbon earthquake is by some measures the largest natural disaster ever recorded in Europe.

Responses to the tragedy led some historians to describe this as the first "modern" European disaster. Some contemporaries called the event demonic or a punishment from God, but many others proposed natural and scientific explanations for the disaster and responded to it accordingly. Prime Minister Sebastião José de Carvalho e Melo (1699–1782) quickly centralized relief and rebuilding efforts, fighting the spread of disease in the short term and using the opportunity in the longer term to renovate central Lisbon, introducing a new architectural style and "earthquake-proof" construction. The Portuguese crown rewarded him with a noble title—Marquis of Pombal—and tremendous power over imperial affairs generally, which he used over the coming decades to impose the "Pombaline" reforms: broad changes in the Portuguese Empire designed to increase revenue for the royal coffers, subordinate clerical authority to the state, expand economic activity on the empire's periphery, centralize administration, and even raise the quality of Portuguese wines.

This style of problem solving, which many associate with "Enlightenment" thinking, was not limited to Western Europe or the Atlantic World during this era. In 1839,

MAP 6.1 Empires and Trade, ca. 1770

sixteen-year-old Ottoman Sultan Abdulmecid (1823–1861) presided over the announcement of the Gulhane (Rose Bower) Edict at the opulent Topkapi Palace before an audience of government officials, clerics, and foreign diplomats. Frequently attributed to the efforts of Foreign Minister Mustafa Reşid Pasha (1800–1858), who had been the Empire's ambassador to both Paris and London, the Edict announced a commitment to reform the administration of the Ottoman Empire and the relationship between the state and its peoples. Shaken by independence movements in Egypt, Serbia, and Greece; unrest in other parts of the empire; and shifting international power relationships, Ottoman rulers created new principles of taxation, military recruitment, and legal administration and applied them universally rather than distinguishing between Muslim and non-Muslim subjects. This edict initiated a half-century of sweeping changes known as the Tanzimat (Reorganization).

---

In this chapter, we analyze dramatic transformations in the global political order from the mid-eighteenth century to the mid-nineteenth century. We begin by surveying the philosophical ferment in the Atlantic World known as the Enlightenment, focusing on debates over the proper role of the state and its relationship to individuals. In the next sections of the chapter, we focus on the tensions in the British Empire between the imperial government and North American colonists that led to war and the Independence of the United States of America. On the heels of US Independence, the French Revolution and Napoleonic Wars shook the European continent and reverberated across the Atlantic Ocean as well. After explaining the nature and impact of these upheavals in Europe, we explain their relationship to the wars of independence in the Caribbean and Latin America.

By the 1820s, leaders in regions once controlled by the British, French, Spanish, and Portuguese began building independent regimes, writing constitutions, and fighting over the elusive formula to form and maintain nonhereditary, constitutional states. Decades of warfare replaced the formal European imperial presence with independent, liberal, republican constitutional nation-states. These new states struggled for political and economic stability and worked to define justice amid competing rights claims—liberal, national, popular—on both sides of the Atlantic.

In the next section of the chapter, we expand the discussion of nineteenth-century state reforms beyond the Atlantic World by turning to the Ottoman Empire during the Tanzimat. The proliferation of independent states in the early nineteenth century contributed to a burgeoning debate over definitions of nation and citizen and their relationship to territorial states. We describe the terms of these debates as they play out during this era, laying a foundation for subsequent analysis of the challenges to constructing a world of nation-states over the following two centuries.

## What Is Enlightenment?

Intellectual ferment and changing material circumstances converged in the Atlantic Empires during the eighteenth century, spurring changes on the peripheries of those empires but also in the imperial centers themselves. During this era, scholars, authors, activists, and provocateurs used metaphors of light and motion to describe their way of thinking about the world. In English, the term "Enlightenment" came to be associated with these thinkers, who did not agree with each other on all things but shared some assumptions about the world around them. These included a belief that the methods of natural science could be used to understand all aspects of life, including the principles that govern human behavior as well as interactions among peoples and societies. Enlightenment thinkers generally embraced the idea that the goal of inquiry was not only to discover these principles but to use this understanding to improve behaviors, structures, and interactions. Furthermore, many believed that properly applying these methods would lead to inevitable and continuous improvement: progress.

In the massive *Encylopédie*, an ambitious compendium of human knowledge edited by the Frenchman Denis Diderot (1713–1784), the entry on "Political Authority" asserted the foundational principle that "No man receives from nature the right to command others." Political power, the entry continues, must be the result of either coercion (fragile and illegitimate) or a social contract (enduring and just). Voltaire (1694–1778), another French Enlightenment thinker, praised the changes, reflective of John Locke's theories, written into England's political and social system at the time of the Glorious Revolution and the limits the English Bill of Rights placed on the monarchy. Voltaire turned this observation into a scathing critique of French absolutism.

The Prussian philosopher Immanuel Kant (1724–1804) tried to summarize the general approach of like-minded thinkers of the era in a magazine article entitled, "Answering the Question: What is Enlightenment?" In this essay, published in 1784, Kant asserted that the motto of the Enlightenment movement was *Sapere Aude!*—"Have the courage to use your own understanding," or more concisely, "Dare to know!" French writer Nicolas de Condorcet (1743–1794) expressed this faith in progress through reason most fully, writing that "the perfectibility of man is unlimited," dependent only on increasing education and its application. Foreshadowing the attempts to spread European interpretations of Enlightenment values and government across the globe, Condorcet believed these values to be universal and that all human beings—regardless of race, gender, nationality, or religion—would benefit from their implementation and that over time, the stewardship of self-defined modern countries over the earth's peoples and resources would deliver a better world for all.

Even as many, like Condorcet, celebrated the limitless potential of progress, others embraced another Enlightenment value: skepticism. Voltaire was famous for mocking religion—especially Christianity—but he also turned his caustic wit on those who believed that the use of reason would result in inevitable progress. Voltaire uses the character Pangloss in his 1759 novella *Candide* to stand in for overly optimistic thinkers like Condorcet. In the book, while the title character lies beneath the rubble of the 1755 Lisbon earthquake, his mentor and teacher Pangloss ignores Candide's pleas for help so that Pangloss can instead puzzle out the causes of the earthquake.

## New Ideas about the State

Enlightenment thinkers took on key questions about political structures and the distribution of resources. The Scotsman Adam Smith (1723–1790), one of the most influential thinkers in the area of political economy, trained as a moral philosopher. This background strongly influenced the analysis and prescriptions for the way states *should* create the conditions for prosperity that appear in his dense and lengthy book, *An Inquiry into the Nature and Causes of the Wealth of Nations* (1776). Smith challenged mercantilist views that states should hoard wealth, advocating instead a system of free trade through which individuals would generate wealth and contribute to the betterment of society. A subsequent generation of political economists, including Jean-Baptiste Say (1767–1832), Thomas Malthus (1766–1834), and David Ricardo (1772–1823), considered the role of individual choice in distributing resources, helping to shatter confidence in the received wisdom about the creation and maintenance of wealth but also raising questions about how social contracts could create a state that balanced the protection of property with competing claims to life and liberty.

Governments reformed structures and policies across Europe during this era, as many powerful elites accepted that the application of new ideas about "human nature" could improve society. Although Enlightenment ideals are often associated with aspirations toward democratic and republican forms of government, it was not necessarily so. Voltaire and Kant shared a belief that enlightened monarchs could effectively reform society. Kant wrote in "What is Enlightenment?" that a sovereign should see "no danger . . . in allowing his subjects to make public use of their reason and to publish their thoughts on a better formulation of his legislation and even their open-minded criticisms of the laws already made."

Based on ideas like this, Prussian King Frederick (1712–1786) and Russian Empress Catherine (1729–1796) practiced "Enlightened Absolutism," borrowing the Enlightenment ideal to make reforms autocratically.

Whether limited in power or absolutist, central governments were revising their views about the rights and powers of individuals within a state. This had an especially strong impact in the area of criminal justice. All across Europe, from Russia to England, attempts were made to discern the purposes of laws and the goals of punishment so that they might be used to improve society. As a result, many European regimes codified legal practices, standardized the operations of the courts, and abolished torture. In 1764, the Italian jurist Cesare Beccaria (1738–1794) laid the foundation, based on Enlightenment principles, for modern European opposition to both torture and capital punishment.

Ideas about the importance of compulsory education for children also circulated. In some parts of Europe, the idea that it was necessary for all children to have some education had roots in the Protestant Reformation of the sixteenth century—if one needed to read the Bible to be saved, one needed to be able to read. But it was only in the mid-eighteenth century that Frederick the Great of Prussia first established a state-mandated system of compulsory elementary education (1763) to develop future generations' social discipline and commitment to the state and its sovereign.

Historians debate the relationships between these ideas and the political changes that gripped the Atlantic World between 1750 and 1850. As we shall see in pages to come, some argue that the primary driving forces behind revolutionary upheaval were material circumstances—demographic and economic change. Others challenge the very idea of a coherent, chronologically bounded movement called the Enlightenment, arguing that it cherry-picks a small number of thinkers and texts from the many philosophical and political debates occurring over a longer period of time across a wider area. Nonetheless, as the political geography and operating instructions for sovereign states in the Atlantic World were reconfigured during this era, the main actors and groups debating and influencing these outcomes generally embraced the ideas and decision-making practices of the Enlightenment.

## The Breakup of British North America

The global conflict of the Seven Years' War left Britain the dominant imperial power across much of the globe, especially the Atlantic and Indian Ocean regions. North America, rich in resources and markets, was one large jewel in the British crown. After defeating the French at Québec in 1759, Britain dominated the eastern third of the continent, including the immensely profitable Caribbean Sea. Spain still claimed most of the rest of North America but the Spanish

Empire's centers of power were far from the population centers of British North America, and vast expanses of the continent were still controlled by sovereign indigenous groups. The thirteen colonies that would become the United States were an imperial economic engine. The northern colonies produced timber and some manufactured goods, while the southern colonies—as well as the British Caribbean—produced cotton, tobacco, and sugar, largely with enslaved labor. Colonial cities like Boston, Philadelphia, New York, and Charleston were markets for goods manufactured in England. After the Seven Years' War, Britain focused on enforcing policies to pay down the large war debt, control access to new territories from London, and receive greater benefits from the empire. As we noted in Chapter 5, these policies raised revenue for the imperial center but also provoked angry and violent colonial responses. Tensions between and among colonies—coupled with social, economic, and political differences within colonies—meant that collective action was slow to materialize. But the new laws had an adverse effect on all sorts of different regional and class interests, which helped to overcome internal divisions and create a stronger sense of unity within the colonies.

Economic and administrative changes led some colonists to question their ties to Great Britain. These kinds of questions were not new. Taxing the hinterlands to pay for central administration, and regional resistance to those taxes, had been an imperial standard for centuries. Some things were different in the eighteenth century Atlantic World, though. Both sides of the Atlantic buzzed with challenges to the foundational logic of political systems. Locke, Rousseau, Condorcet, and other Enlightenment thinkers argued that individuals had rights independent of their governments, that human society was moving toward perfection, and that government could only rule with the consent of the governed. Although nowhere near the speed of communication in our own day, these ideas nonetheless circulated back and forth across the Atlantic Ocean in books and pamphlets. Moreover, the people developing these ideas could themselves travel great distances more quickly and reliably than ever before.

The colonists' protest slogan, "No taxation without representation," was not a refusal to pay taxes; it was a demand to be included in the decision-making process. The few additional cents that colonists would pay for tea or newspapers was more an issue of principle than dire economic hardship, yet the idea that London could tax the colonists without consultation escalated into armed confrontation between local militia and British troops at Concord and Lexington, in Massachusetts, in 1775. A year later, the Declaration of Independence invoked Locke's Social Contract, asserting that humans have "inalienable" rights—rights that they have simply because they are human—and that governments are put in place to secure these rights, not to grant them, and certainly not to deny them.

Because the state (i.e., the British crown) had violated this contract, the colonists had the right to make a new state. Out of this conflict emerged the United States of America, but the rebellion's success was far from certain at the start.

By 1783, when a treaty signed in Paris ended the war, tens of thousands of people were dead, tens of thousands more headed into exile elsewhere in the British Empire, and leaders of the new United States of America were left to form a government. The first try—the Articles of Confederation—didn't last long; but the Articles' weaknesses point out some important features of modern states. The Articles strictly limited central authority and emphasized the power of the individual states that composed the union. When a rebellion broke out in 1786—again in Massachusetts, and again over economic grievances—the new government could not easily raise troops to put down the insurgency. Unable to levy taxes, regulate commerce, or maintain an army, the United States government had little power to exercise sovereignty. Many observers, including officials of the British Empire, expected the weak new state to fail entirely, which would open up new opportunities for European empires to return to the region.

The new state survived. Conceding the failure of the Articles of Confederation, a new document, drawn up in Philadelphia again, re-founded the nation-state, strengthening and more clearly defining the nature of its sovereignty and its relationship to its citizens. The Constitutional Convention that began in 1787 was originally convened to revise the Articles of Confederation, not to construct a completely new constitution as the basis for a national government, but the Massachusetts uprising, known as Shay's Rebellion, and other events prompted a more comprehensive effort to strengthen the central government so that it could enforce rules and maintain order while still protecting the prerogatives of state governments and safeguarding individuals from tyranny. Long debates and great compromise were at the core of the convention.

The US Constitution, finally adopted in 1789, was an early example of a literal social contract, containing both Enlightenment aspirations and the painful contradictions that reflected the social and economic realities of its day. It established the idea that the state guarantees and protects (but does not bestow) rights. This was a triumph of Enlightenment principles, but contradictions remained. For instance, if the state is guarantor of the rights of its citizens, what happens to people who are not included in that category? The new Constitution left many millions of people without a voice in politics, or even basic rights, as they were defined as "not citizens." Women, for instance, would not get the right to vote in national elections until the twentieth century. Even more egregiously, the new Constitution accepted slavery as a basic condition of the new nation.

## The Radicalism of the American Revolution?

The colonists protesting British imperial policy in North America in the 1760s and 1770s generally were not destitute. They were not enslaved. To the contrary, some of the men who played crucial roles in the American Revolution, such as Thomas Jefferson and George Washington, owned slaves themselves. Many lived on estates with servants. Subsequent upheavals in the Caribbean, Europe, and Spanish America would entail much larger numbers of poor, oppressed, and marginalized people. Many historians have even questioned whether the US War for Independence can really be called revolutionary. Revolution, after all, must be a radical step. By this logic, only extreme disruptions and extreme outcomes characterize true revolutions. Economically, the conditions in the American colonies weren't *too* different after Independence. Add to this the fact that those who held positions of power after Independence were often the same people who held power before it. An image emerges in some historical works that Independence was more a change of administration than a radical transformation.

Other historians challenge this point of view. In *The Radicalism of the American Revolution*, Gordon Wood argued that the revolution "created a society fundamentally different from the colonial society of the eighteenth century. It was in fact a new society unlike any that had ever existed anywhere in the world," overthrowing privilege and making a new category of independent men. Wood saw the revolutionary nature of American Independence not in immediate socioeconomic transformation but in ideological change. Doing away with hereditary privileges and social standing as the basis for political authority, the revolutionaries had fundamentally changed society and embraced Enlightenment values in a way no society had done before.

Wood's views were popular—his book won the Pulitzer Prize—but controversial. Some historians rejected Wood's narrow focus on elite sources. Many asked how a section of the book titled "Equality" could ignore the issue of slavery. Others wrote that Wood exaggerated the power of the British monarchy before the revolution and understated the importance of social class and privilege after it. How, some asked, could Wood claim that the revolution had made the United States the most egalitarian society in the world when he himself noted that income in the new country was more unequal after independence than before?

Wood argued, in response, that in the context of the 1770s, the revolution was radical and that the men who started the revolution—despite being wealthy and white—felt oppressed, drawing on the new Enlightenment doctrines that were redefining politics. They were not poor, but they were governed without their consent and stood on the principle that English rule over the colonies violated the social contract. Building alliances between wealthy gentlemen and the common farmers who comprised much of the colonial population might have seemed impossible, but the ideals of the Enlightenment provided common cause for New England farmers, Virginia plantation owners, and the small-scale merchants who all made a living in the colonies. A rich debate continues over the nature of the US War of Independence, enhanced by new research that focuses on previously neglected populations and issues. Tens of thousands of colonists remained loyal to the British crown and established their base in New York. Most left the new country after the war and dispersed throughout the British Empire, bringing ideas about the implications of their experiences with them. The royal governor of Virginia and other officials offered manumission to slaves who took up the crown's cause; approximately twenty thousand joined units such as the Ethiopian Regiment and the Black Pioneers. The war split the indigenous population as well. Some Native American nations formed alliances with the patriots and others with the loyalists, with repercussions for these communities long after the Treaty of Paris was signed. How would these populations assess the radicalism of the American Revolution?[1]

From the perspective of world history, in both conception and execution, the new United States was a bold experiment that sparked debate and action across the Atlantic World. In hindsight, the creation of a new nation that would become the world's dominant economic, military, and cultural power within two centuries was a watershed moment. At the time, however, the continuities of the new nation were as important as its differences. The same class of people—and sometimes the same individuals—held power. Many institutions and practices rooted in the Empire still governed and regulated the new nation, without a monarch atop them. Women remained disenfranchised. Slavery persisted. And the Revolution did not spread immediately: not even all of British North America revolted, as Canada remained part of the British Empire. The successful revolt of thirteen colonies against Europe's most powerful empire was impressive but was not perceived as a threat to the global order.

## Revolution in France and Haiti

A more comprehensive and violent revolution occurred in France. Radical and destructive, it overthrew one of Europe's most powerful monarchies and exported revolution to neighbors, as mass citizens' armies marched across Europe.

---

[1]    Gordon Wood, *The Radicalism of the American Revolution* (New York: Vintage, 1993). Many of the leading historians of the United States debated Wood's book in a forum, "How Revolutionary Was the Revolution? A Discussion of Gordon S. Wood's The Radicalism of the American Revolution," William and Mary Quarterly Third series 51, no. 4 (October, 1994): 677–716. Recent works that have examined the revolutionary era from new perspectives include Alan Taylor, *The Divided Ground: Indians, Settlers, and the Northern Borderland of the American Revolution* (New York: Alfred A. Knopf, 2006); and Maya Jasanoff, *Liberty's Exiles: American Loyalists in the Revolutionary World* (New York: Vintage, 2012).

French revolutionaries renamed the days of the week and months of the year, abolished noble titles, and turned churches into shrines to poets, authors, and scientists. Few of these changes lasted more than a decade, and the regime that followed was in many ways a reaction to the extremes of revolutionary fervor. However, both the enduring changes and failed transformations resulting from the French Revolution are important to understanding how revolution spread at the turn of the nineteenth century and also the limitations of Enlightenment notions of progress.

The French Revolution, like the American one, had mundane roots. France's eighteenth-century wars, coupled with aid to the American independence cause, had drained France's treasuries. A complex and antiquated tax system contributed to fiscal malaise; by 1788, the French government was spending 50 percent of its annual revenue on debt service. Population growth and rising prices squeezed peasants who by 1788 were spending half of their income just on bread. At the same time, a class of *nouveau riche* ("new rich") grew wealthy through trade and finance, fueling inequality and simultaneously challenging France's traditional socioeconomic order, still medieval in many aspects.

With fewer overseas colonies to generate revenue than Great Britain, the French crown looked within France itself to finance wars and other government ventures. In Britain, a new Central Bank helped to meet the nation's debt obligations by selling bonds, but the French royal debt was so vast that the government could not attract enough investors in such promises for future financial gain. Exasperated and desperate, King Louis XVI (1754–1793) convoked a traditional consultative body, the Estates General, which had not met since 1614. This institution was rooted in medieval notions of the distinct social classes (estates) of the political body: the clergy; the nobility; and commoners (the "Third Estate"). By custom, the Estates General organized the three estates into three voices of equal weight to offer advice and consent to the monarch on important state matters. But as Louis XVI and his advisers set into motion the revival of this cobwebbed institution, many observers, and then some delegates themselves, argued that this new meeting of the Estates General should be organized to better reflect the fact that each of the first two estates represented thousands of clergy and nobles, but the third estate represented *millions* of people.

Emmanuel Joseph Sieyès (1748–1836), a Roman Catholic priest who nevertheless represented the Third Estate, saw this one group as having "within itself all that is necessary for the formation of a complete nation." Production, consumption, distribution, regulation, administration: members of the Third Estate carried out all of these essential tasks. The nobility and clergy, Sieyès wrote, were feeding off the labor and ingenuity of the Third Estate. Leaders of the Third Estate called on the delegates assembling at the Versailles Palace to meet as one body, a National Assembly, and to take for themselves a mandate to consider fundamental changes in France far beyond the King's fiscal agenda.

## Revolution! Then, Reaction

Thus began a series of confrontations between delegates and the monarchy, with supporters on each side across France and beyond. In the summer of 1789, after winning the battle to meet as one body, the National Assembly crafted a Declaration of the Rights of Man and Citizen, with similarities in Enlightenment language and principles to the US Declaration of Independence and other revolutionary documents. A moderate Constitution issued in 1791, retaining the monarchy but limiting the king's powers, lasted only a year. More radical proposals emerged in the National Assembly, which created another new constitution (1792) embracing universal male suffrage and a republican government that stripped the King and all nobles of titles and privileges. The new state was to be based solely on reason: laws were passed to change religious practices and subordinate the clergy to the state because the Catholic Church and its practices were seen as irrational and undermining the goals of the revolution. Time itself was rationalized. At the height of the Revolution, the government declared that

**GEOGRAPHY GAME FOR THE FRENCH REPUBLIC PRESENTED TO THE NATIONAL CONVENTION.** A former professor of geography created this game in 1795 to help children learn the names and locations of the new Departments designated by the revolutionary regime. In the far upper left-hand corner of the game board, one sees Saint-Domingue (now Haiti), over which the revolutionary government in France still claimed sovereignty at the time this game was produced.

days would be ten hours long and that a new calendar would be adopted to elimi-nate all references to religion and royalty in the names of days and months. A new system of weights and measures was proposed. Although changes to the calendar did not survive, the metric system was one of the rational innovations that emerged from the revolutionary era.

Violence escalated along with debates over the future of France. Surrounded by hostile monarchies and beset by internal conspiracies against the revolution, lead-ers of the republic grew more extreme. In 1792, France declared war on Austria, ruled by Queen Marie Antoinette's brother. Prussia joined the fight against the revolutionary regime. That summer, amid popular unrest against the slow pace of political change, the King was stripped of his authority and a republic declared. Citizen Louis Capet, as King Louis XVI became known under the Republic, was executed as a traitor in January 1793. Summary justice was meted out against those accused of opposing the revolution, even as factions within the revolution-ary movement struggled to define their principles and establish a functioning government. An estimated fifty thousand people were killed and five hundred thousand imprisoned during a time of extreme violence and disorder that came to be known as "The Terror," which peaked in 1793–1794. One institution that appeared to be functioning well was the army. Mass conscription, a military draft, created a French army of hundreds of thousands marching off to defend the nation. They achieved success on the battlefield against the armies of surrounding monar-chies. Astute observers saw in this the future of warfare: the citizen soldier.

Weary of war and internal chaos, a new coalition formed to oppose the most radical leaders of the Revolution. Its members wrote another constitution and increasingly relied on a young military officer to assist them in reestablishing order. Napoleon Bonaparte, a dynamic general and charismatic leader, outma-neuvered his civilian mentors and took power in a coup d'état in 1799. By 1804, Napoleon was Emperor and France was again ruled by an autocrat.

## The Significance of the French Revolution

But if it was only this—a spasm of violence that resulted in the replacement of one autocrat for another and the metric system—why spend time and energy on it in a book about world history? To understand the importance of the French Revolution, one needs to look beneath Napoleon's title of Emperor and beyond the borders of France. The deployment of an army of citizen soldiers introduced new forms of organization and behavior into modern politics and warfare. The reorganization of the French legal and administrative system was wholesale and enduring, influencing discussion about the role of government and the practice of governance well beyond France.

The Revolution also sparked debates about how, when, and why political, social, and economic change can and should be implemented and at what cost. Women like Olympe de Gouges (1748–1793) and Sophie de Condorcet (1764–1822) greeted the early days of the revolution with great hope and then lambasted its hypocrisy when the revolutionary ethos of equality was denied to women. Olympe de Gouges advocated the application of Enlightenment principles across gender and racial lines, challenging laws denying women and blacks economic and political rights. She also protested social norms that restricted women to narrowly defined roles. When the *Declaration of the Rights of Man and Citizen* did not extend equality to women, she penned her own treatise, *Declaration of the Rights of Woman and Citizen*. An ardent opponent of the death penalty, who objected to the execution of the former King, she was herself guillotined during the Terror. The Revolution also inspired political thought that would coalesce into modern "conservative" thinking. Critics of the Revolution like Edmund Burke (1729–1797) saw it as a lesson in why political change should always be approached with caution, and calls to rewrite the social contract should be greeted with skepticism. Otherwise, argued Burke, the risk of chaos and the complete collapse of institutions built over generations was too great.

Adopting a global perspective, the events of the French Revolution and the Age of Napoleon transformed power relationships among the European Empires, as well as between these empires and their colonies. In particular, the turmoil contributed to the emergence of additional independent states in the Americas in the first decades of the nineteenth century, to which we turn now.

## Independence in Haiti

On the eve of the French Revolution, the western region of the island of Hispaniola—Saint-Domingue, later Haiti—was the most productive of France's sugar-slave colonies. The colony's half-million enslaved Africans produced more than one hundred thirty million pounds of sugar annually. It was also home to a much smaller but important population of free persons of color and a still smaller number of whites, some wealthy and some not. The emergence of the National Assembly in France linked local issues of rights and exclusions to empire-wide debates about citizenship. But while the colony's white population resisted any move to create equality for all free peoples, let alone abolish slavery, the National Assembly in France vacillated on both issues. Unwilling to await the outcome of debates in a distant and disintegrating imperial center, an uprising of people of color, both slave and free, began a war for Haitian independence in 1791.

As the French National Assembly moved slowly on abolition and racial equality, antirevolutionary Spain, seeking to undermine its French rivals, supplied arms to Haiti's people of color. When the revolutionary government in France finally agreed to abolition, internal dissent divided Haiti's people of color. In the ensuing civil war, François Toussaint L'Ouverture (1743–1803), a former slave, emerged as a political and military leader able to secure control over Saint-Domingue. Suspicious of Napoleon's intentions, Toussaint issued a new constitution in 1801 proclaiming autonomy from France and appointing himself governor-general for life. A subsequent French invasion captured Toussaint, who died in a French prison in 1803, but could not reconquer Haiti. Toussaint's successor, another former slave named Jean-Jacques Dessalines (1758–1806), defeated the French and declared Haiti an independent state. In sum, the second independent nation-state in the Western Hemisphere emerged from beneath the yoke of European colonialism only after a massive self-manumission movement of slaves and a long bloody war. The United States, the Western Hemisphere's first independent nation-state, did not establish diplomatic relations with Haiti until 1862, primarily due to their divergence on issues of race—one slave state and one at the vanguard of freedom for enslaved peoples.

## The Collapse of the Iberian Empire in the Americas

The parts of the Western Hemisphere under Spanish and Portuguese rule followed different paths through the end of the eighteenth century and into the nineteenth. Like other European empires, the Spanish and Portuguese monarchies implemented reforms designed to raise revenue and protect imperial interests overseas through rational government that adhered to Enlightenment principles. The Spanish monarchy instituted a series of policy changes, known as the Bourbon Reforms after the ruling family's dynastic name, in the second half of the eighteenth century. The Bourbons reorganized the empire's political and economic structures and changed appointment policies for imperial officials. New officials were sent from Spain rather than recruited from among Spanish Americans themselves. These new policies and officials aroused the resentment of local elites, as they attempted to enforce the will of the monarch more efficiently and rigorously than their predecessors. For many non-elites, the changed rules and enforcement policies led to greater poverty, as population increased but productivity did not, and the new rules took resources away from local communities.

The Rebellion of the Barrios in Quito, examined in Chapter 5, was an early example of a series of urban and rural rebellions across Spanish America during the second half of the eighteenth century. The archives document dozens of indigenous and slave rebellions in the eighteenth century in the Viceroyalty of Peru alone. The greatest threat to European rule in Spanish America during this time occurred in the Andean highlands where the leader of an indigenous community proclaimed the revival of Incan political and social order, took the name Tupac Amaru II (1738–1781) after the last Inca ruler from the time of the conquest, and called for the overthrow of the Spanish Empire. The Tupac Amaru Rebellion (1780–1782), and others like it in the Andes, frightened most nonindigenous people and split the indigenous elite. Both groups had complaints about the Bourbon Reforms, but fear of what would ensue if imperial order were overthrown outweighed those concerns. The rebels lost and were harshly punished.

## The Bourbon Reforms and the Napoleonic Wars

The Bourbon Reforms achieved many of their goals: silver production, agricultural output, imperial commerce, and tax collection all grew significantly. There were, though, high costs that varied by region and socioeconomic class. Intra-elite squabbles increased as crown policies favored those born in Spain (*peninsulares*) over those born in the Americas (*creoles*). Mounting tax burdens and the disruption of entrenched economic, political, and social relations fostered resentment between classes and among ethnic and racial groups. Their actions, and the responses to them, highlight an important contrast between British America and Spanish America. Indigenous peoples were largely seen and treated as an impediment to the policies of the British Empire and its legacy states, to be pushed to the margins. In Spanish America, indigenous peoples were the labor force, and the tax base, and their souls still were still perceived by many important actors in the empire as one of the primary treasures of imperialism.

The Napoleonic Wars hastened the collapse of the Spanish Empire in the Americas. Napoleon dreamed of building an empire to compete with England based on his Continental System, an enforced isolation of England from affairs on the European mainland. Attempting to implement this, Napoleon moved against the Iberian monarchs, arranging the abdication of the Bourbon monarch of Spain and deploying the French Army to the Iberian Peninsula. His decision to place his brother Joseph on the Spanish throne fanned the flames of a popular uprising in Spain.

Throughout Spanish America, populations had to decide quickly how to respond to this crisis. In some regions, elites moved swiftly towards autonomy from Spain. In others, elites vowed loyalty to the empire, meaning they wanted to see little change in daily life. Rebellions proliferated, with some claiming that imperial elites had allied with the French and others that the time had finally come to overturn an unjust social order. Violence spiked, much of it precipitated by simmering and long-standing local grievances. Forces loyal to the Spanish Empire were most successful in holding their ground where material, military, and cultural resources were most highly concentrated and where indigenous populations appeared to pose the greatest threat to power structures rooted in empire. Independence forces excelled in regions that had the shallowest political and cultural roots in empire and whose elites calculated they had the most to gain from greater autonomy. The regions around the cities of Buenos Aires (Argentina) and Santiago (Chile) achieved effective autonomy from the empire relatively quickly, while military forces loyal to the empire maintained control over the central regions of New Spain (today's Mexico) and Peru.

Over the next decade, loyalists in the Americas struggled to manage both rebels and the fragmenting Spanish Empire. In Spain, the resistance government meeting in the port city of Cádiz created a liberal constitution for the empire in 1812. When Napoleon was defeated and monarchy restored in 1814, this constitution was rescinded, but unrest inside Spain led to its implementation again in 1820. Even ardent monarchists tired of Spain's instability. In New Spain, the heart of the Spanish Empire in the Americas, military officers who had defended Spanish rule for years turned against the empire in 1820, helping win the independence of Mexico the following year. In 1826, a military unit loyal to Spain surrendered the Real Felipe fortress in Callao, Peru, leaving Cuba and Puerto Rico the only formal remnants of three centuries of Spanish colonialism in the Americas. More than a decade of warfare left much of the region depleted of resources and divided into regional military and political factions that would fight over the meaning of independence into the middle of the nineteenth century.

## Brazil's Path to Independence

Brazil's path to independence also culminated in the 1820s, but the road and the destination were different from Spanish America. The Pombaline Reforms, like the Bourbon Reforms, attempted to rationalize the relationship between colony and metropolis but did not have the same disruptive effect. One important reason for this was that distinctions between those born in Europe and those of European descent born in the Americas was never as important in determining political privilege in the Portuguese Empire as it became in the Bourbon-era Spanish Empire. Another key determinant in Brazil's path to independence was the Portuguese response to Napoleon's invasion of the Iberian Peninsula. Facing a French invasion, the Portuguese royal family, with more than ten thousand supporters and the royal treasury, was ushered to safety in Brazil by a British naval escort, becoming the first European royals to set foot in the Americas. There, they established Rio de Janeiro as the temporary new capital of the Portuguese Empire, leaving a governing assembly and an anti-French resistance movement back home. After the Napoleonic Wars, the Portuguese king returned to Europe, seeking to reassert his authority in Europe, but leaving his son Pedro in Brazil. Brazilian elites, unhappy with Portuguese legislators' efforts to subordinate Brazil to Portuguese imperial interests, persuaded Pedro to proclaim Brazil an independent constitutional monarchy. Some fighting ensued, but soon both Portugal and Great Britain signed treaties confirming Brazil's independence,

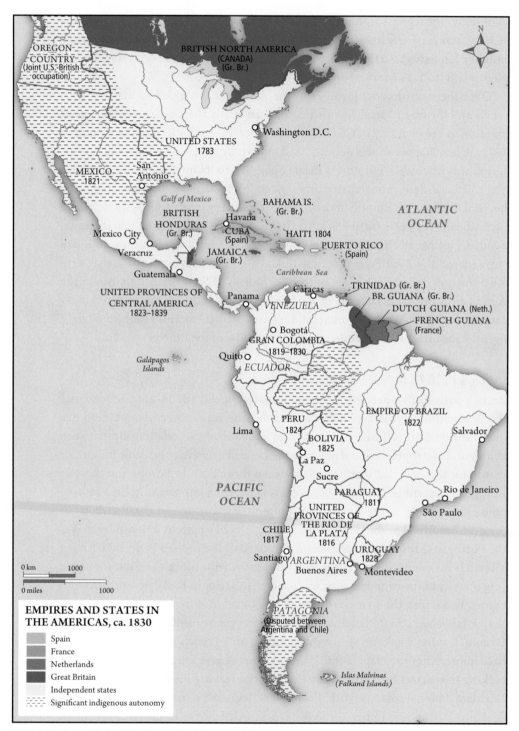

**MAP 6.2** Empires and States in the Western Hemisphere, ca. 1830

assuring the survival of a large, Portuguese-speaking, slave-dependent monarchy in South America. Both institutions—slavery and monarchy—remained intact together in Brazil until the end of the 1880s, longer than anywhere else in the Western Hemisphere.

## Making Nations in Post-Independence Spanish America

After independence, the Portuguese Empire in the Americas remained largely intact, and British America split in two. But the collapsing Spanish Empire splintered. Central America, the narrow land bridge between the former vice-royalties of New Spain and New Granada, first split off from New Spain and then fractured into five small, independent states. Armed disputes pitting the port cities of Buenos Aires and Montevideo against each other and both of them against the interior fragmented the former Viceroyalty of Río de la Plata. Simón Bolívar (1783–1830), a leader of the Independence movement in northern South America, envisioned a single republic, "Gran Colombia," stretching from the Atlantic Ocean across the Andes down to the Pacific, from Caracas to Quito

**MAP OF CENTRAL AMERICA AND THE ANTILLES.** This map, ca. 1845, was commissioned by the Belgian Colonization Company of Central America. If you look carefully at the point where eastern Guatemala meets the Bay of Honduras, you will see the short-lived Belgian Colonization Company concession in Central America, ceded to this private company by the Guatemalan government of Rafael Carrera. In the lower right corner of this map, the flag of the Belgian Colonization Company joins those of the region's independent countries, including the Texas Republic, as well as empires like Russia, which still had territorial claims in the Western Hemisphere at the time the map was made.

and beyond. Gran Colombia was established, with Bolívar as its first president, but the country was beset by conflict. Frustrated in his plans to build and lead a large, unified nation, Bolívar wrote shortly before his death that he was certain of only a few things in life, among them, "America is ungovernable," and "Those who serve a revolution plough the sea."

Historians have struggled to understand why Spanish America remained so unstable for so long. First, it is important to recognize that this vast area was geographically, ethnically, and economically diverse, encompassing tropical rain forest, glaciated mountain ranges, deserts, farm and ranchland, and cosmopolitan cities: generalizations are difficult. Spanish America had never been a single unified political entity, either before or after the Spanish conquest. After independence, this region became a living laboratory for experiments in constitutional nation-state formation. To understand why, let's do a thought exercise with some issues that actually faced the peoples of Spanish America after independence. Imagine that your job is to create a new political and economic system, to actually write a social contract. Familiar questions arise at first: How should the head of state be chosen? What should be the relationship between the legislature and the executive branch? How should power between the national, state, and local governments be balanced? What kind of economic development policies are you planning? Do you want a national bank or not? Will you protect your local artisans or allow imported goods to enter your country? There is a lot of room for dispute, as we saw in the United States when its first constitution, the Articles of Confederation, failed. Indeed, as we mentioned, many Europeans predicted that the United States would not survive as a unified country. (It almost did not, falling into Civil War that tore the country apart less than a century after it was founded.)

Now remember that you're not starting to build a new political or economic system from scratch—no state does. You're trying to reengineer an existing set of relationships in the former Spanish Empire after more than a decade of intense civil war and social upheaval. Do you think owning private property is the key to holding office or voting? Do you think that private property is an important principle at all? If you do, what are you going to do about a countryside that is filled with peasants who have access to land as members of a community rather than as individuals? What about former slaves who fought to help achieve independence: do they get to vote or not? If you decide to place restrictions on voting (based on literacy, income, property holding, etc.), how will you tell people who fought to have more control over their own destiny that they don't get a say in determining the country's future, including the selection of their own government? Are you ready to go to war with them? They still have their arms.

Then, there are other questions that are less apparent from our twenty-first-century vantage point. What if government revenue used to come primarily from special "Indian" taxes on indigenous peoples? Would you abolish them as unjust and watch the state collapse for lack of revenue? Or would you try to keep collecting that tax and alienate a population that won't see the difference between you and the former officials of the Spanish Empire, whom you condemned as tyrants?

These are precisely the kinds of questions that created roadblocks to the consolidation of stable nation-states in Spanish America until the middle of the nineteenth century, when constitutional republics began to emerge that more closely reflect the political geography and country names that are more familiar to us today.

## A New Order for the Ages?
## The Idea of the Nation-State

These attempts at creating new states in the Age of Revolution raised a fundamental question of stateness: how does one define the territorial and demographic limits of the social contract? To turn a phrase from the US Constitution into the compelling questioning of the day, one had to ask who and where are "We the People?" State builders and political philosophers of this era began to answer this question with the idea of nation. Defining this term is vital—it may be the single most important concept in the rest of this book—but it is a slippery idea. So, what is a nation? Most nineteenth-century nationalists sought to identify nations based on "common-sense" markers of communal identity: language, religion, physical features like skin and hair color; a population's relationship to iconic spaces like major cities or natural wonders. A collective experience of violence or trauma, especially in warfare, also became a touchstone for nationalists. Johann Gottlieb Fichte (1762–1814) argued that the nations to which people belonged manifest themselves throughout history and can therefore be readily identified. Writing his *Addresses to the German Nation* in 1807, Fichte described the struggle between Roman legions and the various tribes that lived north of the Alps as a nationalist struggle for German freedom almost two thousand years before any state known as "Germany" could be said to exist. For Fichte, the eternal spirit of nations transcended time and circumstance; modern states needed to be built to reflect and protect the nation. Ideally, these modern states should encompass all—and exclusively—the members of one nation: a nation-state. To use Fichte's example of Germany, all Germans should live in Germany, be governed by fellow Germans, and everyone living in Germany should be German.

Knowing that Fichte delivered this message while Napoleon sought to place all of Europe under French domination provides useful context. Even so, there are problems with Fichte's theory of nation. Defining what it means to be "German" (or any other nationality) turns out to be neither simple nor obvious. Even the German language, touted as a key component of German national identity, consisted of a variety of regional dialects—even distinct languages—within the territory that is now Germany. Fichte's idea of Germany would encounter numerous additional obstacles, like religious diversity among German speakers. Geographical barriers are sometimes useful borders for nations, or would-be nations, but not always. Imagine trying to apply Fichte's criteria to the disintegrating Atlantic World empires and you can see the complexities inherent in defining nations onto which states should be fitted.

If nations are neither natural nor unchanging, and the evidence overwhelmingly suggests that they are not, can historical inquiry help us to understand where nations come from? The scholar Ernest Gellner put it bluntly: "Nationalism is not the awakening of nations to self-consciousness: it invents them where they do not exist." Another influential scholar of the history of nationalism and the nation-state, Benedict Anderson, argues that nations are created when individuals join an "imagined community" based on notions of a history and culture shared with hundreds, thousands, or millions of other people, few of whom they will ever meet. These insights do not suggest that nations are not real or unimportant—they are both and shape human history in profound ways—but that they are malleable.[2]

A crucial, and controversial, idea of Anderson's is that the modern concept of nations, as described by people like Fichte, emerged from the particular historical context of Europe beginning in the mid-fifteenth century. He sees it as deriving from "print capitalism," that is, the circulation of printed materials in vernacular languages along commercial routes. These materials promoted nationalist visions because common identities could form through the shared experience of reading particular texts in the same language—books on religion and history as well as fiction and myth.

## The Dilemma of the Nation-State in Western Eurasia

Anderson recognized that print culture was not a sufficient explanation for the origins of nations and that the "imagined communities" of particular nation-states were constructed in myriad ways. As we have seen in the Western Hemisphere, there is no single model by which nation-states developed over the course of the nineteenth century. Nationalist uprisings also occurred across Western

---

[2]   Ernest Gellner, *Thought and Change* (Chicago: University of Chicago Press, 1964). Gellner elaborates on his theories of nationalism in *Nations and Nationalism* (Ithaca, NY: Cornell University Press, 1983). Benedict Anderson, *Imagined Communities*, rev. ed. (London: Verso, 2006).

**WESTERN EURASIA
AFTER NAPOLEON**

— Border of German Confederation

● Revolutionary activity with date

Foreign intervention to put down revolutions:

↑ Austrian
↑ British
↑ Egyptian
↑ French
↑ Russian

**MAP 6.3**  Western Eurasia after Napoleon

Eurasia in the 1820s and 1830s, but there the most important factor determining state formation tended to be the interaction of empires and not the claims of nationalists. In that context, most new nineteenth–century nation-states emerged at moments of political crisis in larger political structures. Belgium, a predominantly Catholic, French-speaking region that separated from the United Provinces of the Netherlands in 1830, and Greece, which separated from the Ottoman Empire in 1832, are two good examples. Nationalist movements worried the great empires of western Eurasia. The Russian, Austro-Hungarian, and Ottoman Empires all worked to suppress them within their own territories

*A TREATISE ON HOLY WAR.* Written by the Prime Minister of Persia in 1817, this book, printed with a Persian language printing press, analyzes the justifications for conducting jihad against Russia for its invasion of Persia during the Russo-Persian War of 1804–13.

and were even cautious about promoting such movements within rival territories for fear they would threaten the entire international system that they hoped to build after the Napoleonic Wars. The idea of nationalist movements among Serbs or Egyptians might appeal to the Russian Tsar and cause the Ottoman sultan to lose sleep; but in the case of Poles or Finns, the sleepless night would be reversed. Aware of this arrangement, most imperial rulers defended the status quo.

Rivalries among the European empires also played a role in shaping the nature and outcomes of nationalist movements. Western European empires worried about Russian imperial expansion in Asia if the Ottoman state were to collapse. In its interest to check tsarist ambitions, England aided the Ottoman Empire in its war with Russia in the mid-nineteenth century, repeating a pattern of Anglo-Ottoman cooperation during Napoleon's invasion of Egypt from earlier in the century. Conversely, Russia saw Great Britain as an expansionist threat, particularly as British interests in India and China grew. The Anglo-Russian rivalry led each of these empires to play a "Great Game" of intervention in central Asian affairs over the course of the nineteenth century. The tsarist regime attempted to spread the Russian language, culture, and loyalties across a broader empire; and the British used fear of a Russian invasion of India to pressure the rulers of Afghanistan, which the British saw as an important "buffer state" rather than a nation-state. In sum, the rulers of Eurasian empires cautiously viewed nationalist sentiment as a powerful force within their own realms, but at times fanned its flames when it served their self-interests. The solutions that Eurasia's major power brokers devised to manipulate or short-circuit nationalist movements often backfired, as nationalism continued to feed political upheaval through the nineteenth century and contributed to global warfare in the twentieth.

## Freedom and Equality

Enlightenment thought, the rise of nationalism, and the increasing incarnation of social contracts as constitutions raised basic questions about relationships among people and the role of the state in mediating them. Among the great international reform initiatives in this era was the movement to abolish the transatlantic slave trade, which connected conscience, international rivalries, and the agency of millions of African-origin peoples. The movement to abolish the transatlantic slave trade had its most effective early supporters among wealthy Quakers in England who pursued this goal relentlessly in the Parliament. While slavery pricked the consciences of these Christians, Enlightenment thought critiqued slavery on philosophical, political, and economic grounds. Opposition to the slave trade grew in England after the US War of Independence and then again during the Napoleonic Wars, although this often had more to do with the chance to damage the economic prospects of one's rivals rather than moral values. Be that as it may, people of conscience used those tactical political openings to expand their campaign for the much more difficult goal of general abolition—elimination of slavery itself, not just the slave trade. Great Britain abolished its slave trade in 1807, but the British Empire still included millions of enslaved laborers. It would take more than two decades to abolish slavery throughout the empire.

In most of the Western Hemisphere, abolition was intimately connected with the wars of independence and the creation of new nation-states. For Haiti, this is clear, as independence and abolition became virtually synonymous. In parts of Spanish America, many slaves freed themselves by fighting in wars of independence. Elsewhere, people of color also incorporated abolition as a key goal for their participation in independence struggles. Upon achieving independence, new states anxious to gain the recognition of Great Britain were asked to join the campaign to eliminate the slave trade and most did so rather quickly. Nonetheless, whereas Mexico and Central America abolished slavery by the end of the 1820s, the entrenched interests of slaveholders delayed abolition in most Spanish American republics until the middle of the century, as slaveocrats and resource-deprived governments contemplated and negotiated over the obligations that states had to compensate property owners (i.e., slave owners) if they were to confiscate their property (i.e., free their slaves). Slave regimes would survive in Brazil and the United States even longer, as we will see in a later chapter.

British abolitionist activities extended to Africa itself, not only in the establishment of Freetown but also in South Africa following the Napoleonic Wars when the British gained control of the Cape. The British not only asserted control over the colony but also guaranteed equal treatment before the law (including people of color). Residents of the long-term Dutch settlements (called Boers) felt both of these would be to their detriment, so they began to move in the "Great Trek" east and north of the British settlement, seeking new lands as well as cultural autonomy and political sovereignty. The movement of larger numbers of whites into the interior, and the ensuing conflicts over resources with indigenous groups, provided a preview of events to come on a larger scale later in the century.

## Reform in the Ottoman Empire

Emperors and their advisers faced a dilemma in the Age of Revolution: how to find a balance between accommodating concerns of the era and inadvertently damaging regime legitimacy. As we noted in earlier chapters, early modern empires functioned on the recognition and maintenance of difference among subject peoples for judicial, fiscal, and other reasons. One of the questions raised during this era for new states, as well as existing ones, was that of majority–minority relations. Equality before the law may strike a minority group as tyranny (after all, a majority can, by definition, have its way in a democracy). Nationalist efforts to promote greater identification with the state, its leaders, and cultural or political practices could threaten distinct cultures or undermine the logic by which an empire was constructed over generations. Majority populations, on the other hand, might resist reform efforts, fearing the diminution of their power and privilege in the pursuit of greater equality. The Ottoman Empire provides an excellent example of the variety of challenges that empires faced on this front. Having lost control of Greece completely, facing the growing autonomy of Egypt, and witnessing the disintegration of the Safavid and Mughal Empires, Ottoman rulers attempted to find a new balance in imperial administration. New legislation was designed to eliminate the millet system in which minority populations had managed internal affairs according to their own customs, with their own religious authorities supervising. However, many communities resisted the reforms, seeing them as encroaching on highly valued autonomy rather than an opportunity to be part of a broader, more efficient, more rational, modern political community. The Muslim majority was not always satisfied either: poor Muslims resented that they were now asked to pay taxes traditionally levied only on non-Muslims.

Despite resistance and obstacles, Ottoman rulers invested time and energy in the Tanzimat over the next decades. They established a new legislative body and a Ministry of Education, overhauled legal codes, abolished slavery, and adopted a new flag and national anthem. These actions resonate with broader trends that we have presented in this chapter, as the last surviving, early modern Islamic "gunpowder empire" attempted to create something like a national identity through an anthem and flag and to overhaul the relationship between the state and the residents of the territory over whom the sultans claimed sovereignty while not conceding that an entirely new social contract was necessary to survive in the new order.

## Conclusion

French revolutionaries marched to the cry of "Liberty, Equality, and Brotherhood." In the United States of America, it was "Life, Liberty, and the Pursuit of Happiness." These goals were imperfectly realized, but these ideals reshaped politics across the Atlantic World and beyond. Revolutionaries and reformers enacted versions of these goals with wide-ranging implications for society. In the 1750s, European monarchs ruled most of the Atlantic World and slavery was the foundation for the Atlantic economy. A century later, slavery was abolished, or soon would be, across the region, and just a fraction of the Americas remained governed by European powers.

Enlightenment principles undergirded much of the political and social change of this period. Equality—the idea that all human beings share rights based on their capacity to reason and not on their social status, wealth, or political power—was a foundation of those beliefs. Striving for equality sparked many of these revolutions, but it became quickly apparent that not everyone agreed on what equality meant. The American Declaration of Independence asserted that "all men are created equal," but this did not include enslaved peoples, who were treated as property. Many who argued against monarchy insisted at the same time that women were not fully rational human beings. The right to vote was seen as crucial to constructing a government that was responsive and representative, but most democracies reserved that right for men who owned property and, often, only of a particular skin color. In the first elections under the US Constitution, it seems that only about 5 percent of the population voted.

The new states that proliferated in the late eighteenth and early nineteenth centuries grappled with fundamental questions of political order in their constitutions. The meaning of equality was one, but equally important was the debate over difference. What kinds of difference were acceptable, or important, to the state? What kinds of difference mattered to political and social order, law, or economic activity? What was the proper relationship between the state and individuals and between citizenship and other identities that individuals might have, for example, as members of religious or ethnic groups?

Of course, these questions were important not only in Europe and the Americas. The nation-state, in idea and practice, would become the keystone of global political order in the following centuries. Ideas about equality, difference, and political power, often articulated with extraordinary passion and clarity

## TIMELINE

**1755**
Earthquake devastates
Lisbon

**1783**
Treaty of Paris ends war
between Britain and
Thirteen Colonies

**1793**
King Louis XVI of
France executed

**1776**
Adam Smith, *An Inquiry into the Nature and
Causes of the Wealth of Nations*; American
Declaration of Independence

**1789**
US Constitution adopted;
Declaration of the Rights of
Man and Citizen, France

during this period, set many of the parameters by which modernity would be defined and its achievements measured. In Chapter 7, we will examine a concomitant transformation—industrialization—which contributed additional dislocating tremors to the global order.

## A Few Good Books

Laurent Dubois. *Avengers of the New World: The Story of the Haitian Revolution.* Cambridge, MA: Harvard University Press, 2004.

Caroline Finkel. *Osman's Dream: The History of the Ottoman Empire.* New York: Basic Books, 2006.

Nicholas Shrady. *The Last Day: Wrath, Ruin, and Reason in the Great Lisbon Earthquake of 1755.* New York: Penguin, 2009.

Charles F. Walker. *The Tupac Amaru Rebellion.* Cambridge, MA: Harvard University Press, 2014.

Lynn Hunt. *The Family Romance of the French Revolution.* Berkeley and Los Angeles: University of California Press, 1993.

*For additional resources, including maps, primary sources, visuals, web links, and quizzes, please go to **www.oup.com/us/carter***

**1799**
Napoleon assumes power in France

**1807**
Johann Gottlieb Fichte, *Address to the German Nation*; United Kingdom outlaws slave trade

**1832**
Greece wins independence from Ottoman Empire

**1804**
Haiti gains independence

**1826**
Last Spanish Empire troops in South America surrender to independence forces in Callao, Peru

**1839**
Gulhane Edict, Ottoman Empire, initiates *Tanzimat* reforms

FITCH'S STEAMBOAT.
On the Delaware River, opposite Philadelphia.

ARRIVAL OF THE FIRST LOCOMOTIVE IN CHINA.

(TOP) FITCH'S STEAMBOAT *PERSEVERANCE* ON THE DELAWARE RIVER AT PHILADELPHIA, 1787. Although it would not be profitable for many years, a demonstration of the new technology of the steam engine was a perfect companion to discussions of how to build a new state at the Constitutional Convention in Philadelphia. Steam would power the expansion of the United States across North America over the century to come.

(BOTTOM) ARRIVAL OF THE FIRST LOCOMOTIVE IN CHINA. Eight years after the first steamship was launched at Shanghai, the first locomotive arrived in the city. Shanghai was the smallest of the five Chinese ports opened to foreign trade in 1842, after the first Opium War, but it soon became the most prosperous. Its central districts included a French concession and an "International Concession" run by British and American businessmen, but Shanghai maintained a mostly Chinese population. The city served as a key point for the exchange of ideas and technology between China and its overseas trading partners.

# The Engines of Industrialization

## 1787–1868

Suffering through the heat and humidity of a Philadelphia summer, delegates gathered in 1787 to work on a new Constitution for the United States of America. Now independent from Great Britain, the new nation was struggling to build a sovereign central state that respected regional autonomy and the competing rights claims of different individuals and groups, issues that had undermined the nation's first operating system, the Articles of Confederation. The delegates debated the new constitution with the doors and windows of the Old State House (today's Independence Hall) closed, to prevent the public from hearing—or jumping into—the deliberations. For many delegates, the afternoon of August 22 provided a break from the literal and figurative heat inside the State House, as they trekked about a mile down to the Delaware River to observe an exhibition that foreshadowed the global economic transformation that would move hand in hand with the political changes the delegates were pushing forward.

At the riverbank, inventor and entrepreneur John Fitch (1743–1798) met the delegates with a boat called *Perseverance*, an odd vessel, about forty-five feet long, with banks of paddles on either side. A steam engine ran the paddles, propelling the boat at a rate of about five miles per hour, not nearly as fast as a sailing ship with a stiff wind behind it, maybe not even as fast over a short distance as a rowboat with an experienced crew. The demonstration proved, however, that steam could propel a boat across the water, free from the vagaries of wind or the limits of human muscle. Fitch received a patent for his steam engine from the new US Government but never managed to create a profitable business based on the technology. Decades would pass before steam-powered engines would be broadly and profitably utilized in mining, manufacturing, and transportation.

In 1868, on the other side of the world, a much larger, more sophisticated steamship was launched on the Huangpu River near Shanghai. The *Tianqi* ("Auspicious")

**WORLD POPULATION GROWTH, 1700–1900**

— Boundary in 1900

Percentage population increase
1700–1900 of:

- 0–49%
- 50–99%
- 100–249%
- 250–999%
- over 1000%

City with population in 1800 of:

- ○ 100,000–500,000
- Cairo  100,000–500,000
- Paris  over 500,000

City with population 1900 of:

- ⊙ 250,000–500,000
- □ 500,000–1 million
- ⊠ over 1 million

**MAP 7.1**  World Population Growth, 1700–1900

was the first steamship to be built in China, with engines and other parts manufactured in the United States and Europe. It was the brainchild of Zeng Guofan
(1811–1872), a long-serving Governor-General in central China who had played an
important role in winning the Taiping War that devastated China in the middle of the
nineteenth century. In some ways, Zeng epitomized a traditional Chinese official,
loyal to the imperial dynasty and steeped in the ways of the Confucian scholar. However, challenged by the simultaneous threats of European armed aggression and
civil war, Zeng and his allies wagered the long-term survival of the Qing Dynasty on
factories to build munitions, steamships, and other industrial goods. He also sought
to reform the imperial bureaucracy. As part of his plan, Zeng advocated sending
Chinese youth abroad to study applied mathematics, science, and business. Not
everyone in the Qing imperial elite agreed with Zeng Guofan's proposals, and an
intense struggle over China's future ensued. Like people around the world, Chinese
elites recognized that industrialization was dramatically changing the world. There
was, however, little consensus in China, or anywhere else, about the best ways to
respond to these changes.

---

The events just described help us to identify key aspects of what industrialization was—and wasn't—about: technology, experimentation, risk-taking,
failure, war, and the whole world. It is difficult to pinpoint the exact start or direct
cause of political revolutions; this is even harder with a phenomenon like the
Industrial Revolution. Important changes in global economic organization began
before 1787, and the transformative effects of industrialization remain key components of our own time.

Industrialization will be part of the essential framework for understanding the
rest of this book. In this chapter, we focus on the first wave of industrialization
that occurred from the late eighteenth to the mid-nineteenth century—the key
events, decisions, interactions, and consequences. We begin with a fundamental
question: what is so revolutionary about industrialization? The answers to this
vital question are often taken for granted, but we think it's important to understand exactly why industrialization is so crucial to the modern world. Understanding the revolutionary nature of industrialization, though, does not tell us
much about how or why it happened the way it did; that's the question we turn to
next. By comparing the world of production, distribution, and consumption in
some of the world's most prosperous and productive regions in the late eighteenth
century, we can better understand the dramatic and unpredictable subsequent
changes in the relationships between peoples and resources. We then specify the
convergence of events that led to early industrialization and its impact. Finally,

we will offer a series of cases that show the shifting power relationships within and between states and empires that resulted from early industrialization.

## What Is Revolutionary about Industrialization?

"What is the industrial revolution?" appears at first to be a straightforward question, often answered with a string of dates and machines and inventors. We have found that it is actually quite hard to wrestle with this question, and the answer can be both more fundamental and more complex than this parade of information implies. Although all the inventions associated with the onset of the Industrial Revolution—the cotton gin, the spinning jenny, the steam engine, and so forth—are important and remarkable, they don't explain what industrialization really means or why it is important.

Industrialization is revolutionary because it enabled human societies to break free from "the Biological Old Regime." We used this term elsewhere to describe a set of constraints on human productivity that had been in place for thousands of years, but these conditions are worth reviewing. Beginning in the Middle East around ten thousand years ago—and in China, Africa, and the Americas around eight thousand years ago—some societies made the transition from hunting and gathering to sedentary agriculture. As people around the globe adopted techniques for farming and domesticating animals, they found the means to transform more potential energy into working energy than if they had remained as hunter-gatherers. The ability of individuals and groups to harness more energy for themselves and others allowed greater labor specialization, the growth of cities, and the accumulation of surplus. For thousands of years, societies around the world made little further progress in tapping into the potential energy available on the earth—they simply did not understand how or have the means to do it.

Under the Biological Old Regime, not all societies on earth had access to the same level or quality of resources (water, wind, sun, soil), nor did they all allocate resources in the same way. These differences contributed to the great variety of human political, economic, and social organization that we have analyzed to this point. Yet, under the Biological Old Regime, all civilizations—from those with the most resources to those with the fewest—operated under strict energy constraints that limited the ability of their populations to grow food or to change the ratio of agricultural laborers to the general population very much. Furthermore, we saw in the seventeenth-century crisis described in Chapter 4 that slight changes in a regional energy equation, like a small drop in average temperature over time, could contribute to serious declines in material conditions and population.

Industrialization is characterized by another great change in the relationship between people and the natural environment. Humans began to unleash the energy stored in fossil fuels, which had not been exploited on a large scale prior to the nineteenth century. This changed the material conditions for humans in truly revolutionary ways. Railroads, steamships, automobiles, and airplanes did not rely on favorable winds or currents to reach their destinations. New machines for planting and harvesting brought more land under cultivation, and fertilizers produced in factories raised the land's productivity. Electricity enabled refrigeration, keeping food fresh for longer periods. Combining these technologies, food could be brought from greater distances, preserved long after the harvest, and introduced in greater quantities and varieties in more places.

New technologies also made places once uninhabitable by large populations fit for dense urban settlement. New transportation infrastructure enabled easier movement from place to place, temporarily or permanently. Electric lights could create a perpetual, artificial daytime. The sheer variety and amount of goods— and the energy used to create them—are mind-boggling compared to preindustrial societies.

Industrialization altered human attitudes toward the natural environment. Floods, droughts, and storms continued to remind humans that they did not control nature; but fewer people organized their days or lives according to the constraints of local environments, thanks to massive amounts of energy unleashed from long-dead life forms compressed into coal, petroleum, or natural gas. But now that we know what is revolutionary about industrialization, how did it happen?

## Spinning the Industrial Revolution Story

Be forewarned that in the pages that follow, we'll undermine in many ways the story we're about to tell in this paragraph, so be prepared to rewrite your notes! The Industrial Revolution is often explained in terms of the machines themselves. For example, the rural work force in preindustrial India, makers of those fine and highly desired cotton textiles described in earlier chapters, took about fifty thousand worker hours to hand spin one hundred pounds of cotton yarn. In other words, it would take one worker fifty thousand hours, or fifty thousand workers one hour to produce one hundred pounds of yarn. To put this in the context of how most of us organize our lives, if a single spinner worked eighteen hours a day, every day—no days off—spinning yarn, it would take about *eight years* to produce the one hundred pounds of yarn. Advances in textile spinning technology began to change that in eighteenth-century Britain. By the 1760s, spinning mules enabled one person to operate eight spindles at once. This number would double in the 1770s when British workers using these mules could produce that same one hundred pounds of yarn in just two thousand hours. More innovations followed until in the 1820s, it would take only one hundred thirty-five hours to produce one hundred pounds of cotton yarn. To return to the context of an

**MAP 7.2** Industrialization in Britain to 1850

individual worker, with eighteen hours a day of work and no days off, what previously took eight years to accomplish would now take about a week. Steam-driven machinery soon led to even greater productivity. Unprecedented productivity growth of steam-powered, machine-guided labor yielded more goods, of more consistent quality, at a lower cost. In this way, England, the pioneering center of productivity growth, became the workshop of the world. Other countries hurried to emulate its success, as fast as they could, if they could.

This explanatory vein focuses on the search for increased labor productivity as the primary motivator for industrialization, but something's wrong, or at least incomplete, with this picture. Certainly, machines transformed how things were made, and in turn this helped to transform the world. The problem with this as an explanation of how the Industrial Revolution happened, though, is that this is only one small part of the equation. These labor-saving devices did not solve any particularly pressing economic problem in the eighteenth century. Labor, for one thing, was not in short supply in England, so saving it was unlikely to have revolutionary effects in and of itself. And as important as these machines were, they were only part of a system: Where did the cotton come from? It wasn't grown in England. Where did the textiles go? The domestic market could not absorb all of the new cloth being produced. How did other states respond to changes in the productive capacity of the British textile industry? We know that the Early Modern global economy operated under rules in which states tried to carefully restrict the flow of goods. These are the kinds of questions we need to answer to better understand the nature and impact of industrialization.

## Scholars Debate the Industrial Revolution

Until the middle of the twentieth century, most publications agreed that the Industrial Revolution was a sudden, sharp break with pre-modern economies, that it originated in Britain, and that it was caused largely by major technological breakthroughs. In the past half-century, all of these assumptions have been challenged. Although the global textile industry changed rapidly, and that change is most easily seen through the lens of British technological innovation, contributions to industrialization from other parts of the global economy were less obvious, or slower, or had little to do with machines. A new picture of industrialization emerged based on the understanding that it was the accumulation of many changes rather than a few crucial inventions.[1]

---

[1]   For a concise overview of this transformation, see Kenneth Pomeranz, "Is There an East Asian Development Path? Long-Term Comparisons, Constraints, and Continuities," *Journal of the Economic and Social History of the Orient* 44, no. 3 (2001): 322–362.

Understandings of industrialization have been reframed in part by comparing different parts of the world to see how they changed over time. Numerous scholars have compared China and Europe during the 1700s, for example, examining the relationship between culture and industrialization. Some have concluded that the industrial revolution started in Europe, and not in China, because of distinct values in European culture, including, in the words of historian David Landes, a "Judeo-Christian" ethic, "respect for manual labor," "the subordination of nature to man," and "a sense of linear time." Historians who are persuaded by this line of reasoning place great emphasis on the idea that conditions existed in Europe generally, or more likely in England specifically, under which innovation and risk-taking were rewarded. They see this as a key to explaining industrialization.[2]

Other historians disagree with this cultural explanation for how and where industrialization first occurred. William McNeill, a pioneer in the study of world history, argued in a number of works that explanations based on cultural advantage ignore medieval technological and economic leadership in China and the Islamic world, or dismiss achievements in non-European realms as aberrations, while telescoping European innovations in earlier eras as signs of an industrial revolution to come, when that outcome was in fact unpredictable.[3] Other historians note that more careful study provides a corrective to some claims of precocious or exceptional European economic institutions or structures. In the last two decades, a number of scholars have suggested that Early Modern Chinese markets—the mechanisms whereby economic outcomes are based on negotiations between producers and consumers—were larger, more open, and more globally integrated than those in Britain during the same era. Extensive review of primary sources also reveals Asian societies that valued rationality, innovation, and, as Peter Vries notes, "love of profit" in ways similar to European ones. In sum, a good case may be made that economic institutions and behavior—culture—in China and Europe were not so different on the eve of the industrial revolution.[4]

If it wasn't culture, what prompted the industrial revolution? Kenneth Pomeranz has written one of the most thorough answers to this question. Comparing the

---

[2]   David Landes, *The Wealth and Poverty of Nations: Why Some Are So Rich and Some So Poor* (New York: W.W. Norton, 1998).

[3]   William McNeill "How the West Won," *The New York Review of Books* 45 (April 23, 1998), provides an accessible overview of McNeill's perspective.

[4]   Peer Vries, *Via Peking Back to Manchester: Britain, the Industrial Revolution, and China* (Leiden, The Netherlands: CNWS Publications, Leiden University, 2003), 35; R. Bin Wong, *China Transformed: Historical Change and the Limits of the European Experience* (Ithaca, NY: Cornell University Press, 1997); and Andre Gunder Frank, *ReOrient: Global Economy in the Asian Age* (Berkeley: University of California Press, 1998).

English midlands with China's Yangzi River delta, Pomeranz found that the standard of living in China may have been higher in the 1700s than it was in Western Europe; he also found that China's markets were just as free as Europe's, its labor force just as skilled and diversified, and trading networks just as extensive. For Pomeranz, the key to the divergence between Britain and China hinged on the distinct relationships these societies had with key resources such as coal and labor. Some of the relationships were about policy, but some were also about luck.

First, let's consider coal, which had long been a fuel source known to societies around the world. Wood, peat, animal fats, and other fuels also provided energy for humans to light and heat their worlds. For any energy source to be cost effective, the energy it produced had to exceed the cost of obtaining it (both in energy and in labor). Wood is not a terribly robust fuel (it doesn't produce a lot of energy), but it is easy to get and easy to burn; it's also renewable (though not inexhaustible). Coal can produce a lot more energy, but it varies greatly in quality and can be costly to obtain. It is usually found deep underground and is hard to dig up. Because pre-modern societies did not see coal as an essential resource (and because it was hidden underground), they didn't build cities to be near coal deposits. If a population center was close to an underground coal deposit, it was just a historical accident. In England, such an accident led to manufacturing centers, port facilities, and sufficient water supplies being near high-quality coal deposits, and this in turn facilitated continued experimentation in practical applications of coal to provide steam power, first for drainage pumps in mines and then in manufacturing and transportation. China had lots of coal too, but it was of poor quality and far from population and manufacturing enterprises. This factor, not under any individuals' or groups' control, must be brought into the story of why and when and where industrialization began.

Pomeranz also notes that Europe's relationship to Africa and the Americas added human productivity and natural resources to the energy equation of the Early Modern Atlantic world, permitting parts of Western Europe to expand beyond the regional constraints of the Biological Old Regime through the subsidies of conquest and colonization. The Americas provided raw materials and markets for manufacturing enterprises, profits for risk-takers, and a destination for European populations displaced by economic changes and government policies. For Pomeranz and other members of what is now called the "California School" of world history, it was colonies and coal—not culture—that created the conditions for industrialization.[5] A robust debate continues on these questions.

---

[5]  Kenneth Pomeranz, *The Great Divergence* (Princeton, NJ: Princeton University Press, 2000). A good introduction to the ongoing debate may be found in Patrick O'Brien, "Ten Years of Debate on the Origins of the Great Divergence," *Reviews in History* (http://www.history.ac.uk/reviews/review/1008).

## Freedom and Industrialization

Scholars agree that understanding industrialization is not only about the availability of natural resources like coal but also about the institutions and practices that conditioned the way resources were turned into commodities. As the British industrial economy took off in the nineteenth century, government officials and economic elites became leading advocates for global free trade. Adam Smith and others had articulated the philosophical principles supporting free trade in the eighteenth century, so one might get the impression that free trade practices led to Britain's industrialization. On the contrary, however, Britain relied on protectionist policies to build up its manufacturing base in the lead-up to industrialization. The growth of the British textile industry, for instance, occurred only after Parliament had banned Indian textiles from the British marketplace to protect British manufacturers from competition. This growth accelerated after the British asserted increasingly direct sovereign control— including the ability to influence costs and prices—over India itself. The free trade often supposed to have fueled British industrialization was not so free, even *after* Britain started to industrialize and became a leading voice for a global free trade regime.

Slavery also played a role in early industrialization. In the Early Modern era, the British economy received a subsidy from enslaved labor working its colonial plantations. British interests also earned significant profits from the slave trade itself. Ships flying the British flag carried more than half of the enslaved Africans bound for the Americas during the eighteenth century. Historians debate just how profitable slavery was for individual slave owners or shipping interests, but the transatlantic system enabled a vast and systematic transfer of wealth from Africans and indigenous Americans to Europeans.

Britain outlawed the slave trade in the empire in 1807 but not slavery, and its markets did not reject resources produced with enslaved labor. The plantations that produced raw materials for Britain's factories and agriculture products for its population continued to rely on slave labor. One of the machines that had a great impact on inputs for the British textile industry was the cotton gin, invented in the United States in 1793.

Eli Whitney's machine made cotton grown in North America more profitable than ever before, which spurred a dramatic expansion in cotton production while the labor force in the cotton fields remained enslaved. Author Gene Dattel estimates that slave labor produced as much as 80 percent of the cotton spun for use in the English textile industry. Cotton textiles accounted for 40 percent of British export earnings, at a time when the British government was the world's leading enforcer of a ban on the transatlantic slave trade.[6]

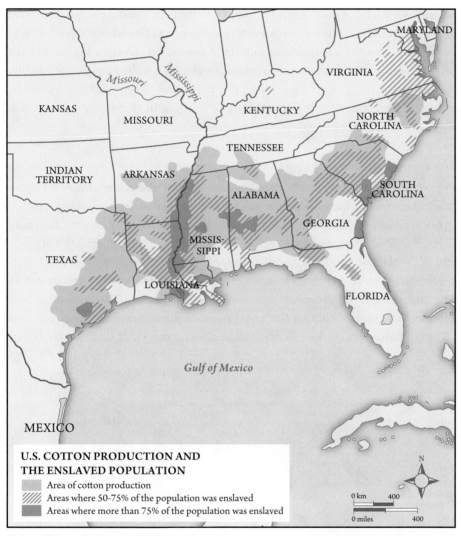

MAP 7.3  US Cotton Production and the Enslaved Population

As we can see, many factors contributed to determining where, when, and how industrialization began, reframing our understanding of the vanguard sector of the new economy—textiles. This approach does not negate the fact that, beginning in the late eighteenth century, new inventions produced textiles for just a fraction of what they had cost only decades before. These inexpensive goods, on a

---

[6]    Gene Dattel, *Cotton and Race in the Making of America: The Human Costs of Economic Power* (Chicago: Ivan R. Dee, 2009).

massive scale and of more uniform quality, came to dominate the world market and contributed to a tripling of global trade between 1820 and 1850. But focusing on machines as the cause of the industrial revolution misses a big part of the picture. New, more productive machines developed within a context of existing political and economic relationships. Over the course of the nineteenth century, industrialization itself would contribute to changes in those relationships that no one could have predicted.

## The Changing World of Work

For workers, early industrialization dramatically altered almost every aspect of life. Industrial production drew together raw materials, infrastructure, and labor in unprecedented quantities. Industry developed in population centers that could provide a labor force. Factories opened along existing transportation networks that delivered raw materials and distributed finished goods. The cities that industrialization created became the hallmark of the modern world. Manchester, in England, grew from about forty thousand people in the 1770s to six hundred thousand in 1900, becoming the world's most industrialized city and one of its most populous. Philadelphia's population grew in the years this chapter covers

**FACTORIES AT LE CREUSOT IN BURGUNDY, FRANCE, NINETEENTH CENTURY.** France did not industrialize as early or as rapidly as Britain or Germany, but this image shows the extent to which new factories could transform the environment, as smoke from the chimneys darkened the skies above the Loire River Valley. Le Creusot was one of France's first industrial centers, noted especially for its iron works.

from about twenty-eight thousand to more than five hundred thousand. As nations industrialized, they became more urban generally. In 1750, the population of Great Britain was 80 percent rural; by 1900, it was nearly 80 percent urban. The rest of Europe followed this trend, although more slowly. In 1800, 83 percent of the European population as a whole still lived in rural areas; a century later, only 40 percent did so.

Factories, the epitome of industrialization and the driving force of urbanization, changed the nature of work in fundamental ways. First, factory workers did not produce goods the way artisans did. Each person in a factory worked at a machine that most often contributed a small part to the manufacturing process, and they were paid either for how long they worked or for how many pieces of a larger product they contributed. Second, clearer boundaries emerged for most people between the home and the place of work. "Going to work" became common, replacing the integrated home and workplace that defined most preindustrial economies. Finally, factory employment crossed gender and age lines. Children and women were sometimes preferred as factory workers because most factory tasks required neither great physical strength nor lengthy apprenticeships, and women and children were often considered easier to control in the workplace. They were generally paid lower wages than men.

As the nature of work changed, family life changed alongside it, although historians who study the family find puzzles to analyze rather than a tidy narrative. For generations, historians assumed that the movement of many social and economic roles from the household economy to the workplace transformed family life, yet emerging scholarship challenges these assumptions. For example, research suggests that family size in France and England did not shrink dramatically after industrialization, defying expectations that industrializing economies yielded smaller, nuclear families, as wage labor replaced the rural farm family or the artisanal workshop multigenerational household economy. It appears now that the nuclear family was, in many places, prevalent even before industrialization. It is clear that industrialization transformed society, but it is less clear exactly how, and how much, family structures and relationships changed.

The modern, industrial city had new sorts of infrastructure. Sewers and power lines (gas and later electric) were installed. Trolleys, streetcars, and buses— horse-drawn at first in many cases—filled the streets. The world's first subway system, the London Underground, opened with steam-powered locomotives and gas lighting in 1863. By the end of the nineteenth century, underground or elevated rapid transit systems—now a defining feature of many modern cities—had opened in Berlin, Budapest, Chicago, Glasgow, Boston, Istanbul, Liverpool, Paris, New York, and Vienna. Economic output increased, and by many measures, so did the standard of living, although this is another difficult outcome to

CONSTRUCTION OF LONDON UNDERGROUND, 1898. Underground public transit, dependent on industrial technology, has become a standard feature of most large cities in the world, but London's Underground was the world's first. The initial lines, opened in the 1860s, were built using the "cut and cover" method where shallow trenches carrying rail lines were covered over with a roof. By the 1890s, deeper "tubes," enabling a more extensive network, were being dug using machines like this one.

measure precisely. It does appear that overall life expectancy in Europe rose markedly during the nineteenth century, while infant mortality dropped.

Yet, the accelerating pace and consequences of industrialization and urbanization ignited contentious debates about the quality of life in the nineteenth century and posed real challenges to the vast majority of the population living through the dislocations of rapid economic and social change. On one side of the debate were people like Andrew Ure (1778–1857), a Scottish professor who wrote *The Philosophy of Manufactures* (1835). Ure acknowledged—but applauded—that modern manufacturing deskilled workers to the point where human laborers might become "mere overlookers of machines"; men, women, and children might be interchangeable in the workplace. Ure responded to critics of the modern factory system by suggesting that the nature of modern work freed the minds of workers and often provided them with moments during the workday (entire minutes at a time!) to contemplate things other than their labor, which was difficult to do under preindustrial conditions. Ure also made the case that the productivity of British factories generated wealth for the benefit of the entire nation through trade and that industrialization promised an unpredictable but better future because machines "make it possible to fabricate some articles which, but for them, could not be fabricated at all." In other words, machines could make things that people could not.

## Critics of Industrial Capitalism

Others saw early industrialization less positively. German journalist Friedrich Engels (1820–1895) tried to shatter illusions of a modern utopia springing up through industrialization. Reporting from Manchester, Engels described filthy living conditions and a toxic, dangerous environment, with "heaps of *débris*, refuse, and offal; standing pools for gutters, and a stench which alone would make it impossible for a human being in any degree civilized to live." In his book, *The Condition of the English Working Class in 1844* (1845), Engels described similar scenes in cities throughout Britain and presented them as visions of a global industrial future. Engels would later collaborate with Karl Marx (1818–1883), another German speaker living in England, to produce a call to action among workers themselves to change these conditions.

Marx and Engels predicted that the industrial society emerging in the nineteenth century would collapse when workers rose up to overthrow this new system. This did not occur. Coupled with the collapse of Communist states in the late twentieth century—especially the Soviet Union and its European allies—that claimed the Marxist legacy, this might tempt one to skip over Marx's ideas, but they remain important for understanding the modern world in at least two ways. First, Marx's critiques of industrial capitalism and liberal democracy were crucial to debates about their failures and successes in the nineteenth century. Policy and practice changed in response to these criticisms. Second, Marxist ideas define key points of debate in political and economic thinking to this day.

What did Marx think? He wrote more than twenty books, so that's a big question, but here we will focus on just two of his ideas: his theory of human history and his critique of industrial capitalism. Marx's politics threatened the existing order, but his ideas were born of Enlightenment aspirations to explain human history in rational scientific terms. Marx's theories were rooted in materialism, the idea that economic production and distribution were the foundation of cultural value, political power, and the driving force of historical change. Building on the ideas of German philosopher Georg Hegel (1770–1831), Marx observed that, in all societies throughout history, one class held the economic upper hand by controlling the "means of production," that is, how wealth was produced. At different points in history, this could mean owning slaves, owning land, or—as in nineteenth-century Europe—controlling industry, which Marx related to having investment capital. The class in power tried to maintain wealth, prestige, and political power and would not yield it willingly; but in time, a new dominant class would always rise up in revolution to establish a new economic and political order. For Marx, the French and American revolutions happened because merchants and factory owners sought political power to match their growing economic power and wrote new laws to serve the interests of their class.

Marx admired the new system, industrial capitalism, as rational and efficient. It had led to the greatest material progress in human history but, he argued, the keys to industrial capitalism's success would also be its own undoing because the system was based on cutthroat competition and an endless search for new markets, continued profit margins, and greater efficiencies. Consider that the goal of any competition is—paradoxically—monopoly: as one factory or company competes with another, the goal is not to continue competing but eventually to win, driving competitors out of business or acquiring their assets. Over time, competition would concentrate wealth in the hands of fewer and fewer winners until society comprised a tiny number of very wealthy owners and an enormous mass of impoverished workers.

According to Marx, factory owners, bankers, landlords, and others like them—the "bourgeoisie" in the language of Marxists—controlled not only the means of economic production, but also political systems, which they used to create laws that would perpetuate their own power. Yet, inevitably, thought the Marxists, the motives that fueled the bourgeoisie would be its undoing. Factory owners would pay workers less and less for the increasingly unskilled labor of the factory. More efficient machines would require fewer workers, making jobs scarcer. With workers desperate for jobs, wages would go even lower. Eventually, wages would not pay enough for workers even to live on. Revolution would inevitably follow.

The communist revolution Marx predicted did not materialize in his lifetime. Violent conflict involving workers did break out periodically in Europe, and communism emerged to play an important role in defining many workers' organizations and the ideological orientations of workers themselves, but more often workers' movements struggled for marginal political and economic reforms rather than the overthrow of states. And they eventually achieved many of these goals, for example, expanding the right to vote to those who did not own property, establishing the right to form unions and bargain collectively for wages and benefits, and limiting the work day and week.

## The Transformation of Global Power Relations

Just as industrialization transformed the internal political and economic structures of those societies that industrialized, it also changed international relations, in part because it changed the nature of warfare. The machinery that made clothes, shoes, and housewares also made rifles, cannons, and warships. No major wars were fought in Europe for four decades following Napoleon's final defeat in 1815, but Europeans still fought. In the nineteenth century, especially during its second half, warfare was often tied to commerce, especially global commerce, and illustrated the emerging gap between industrial and nonindustrial powers.

## The Opium Wars

The Opium Wars (1839–1842 and 1856–1860) illustrate these trends. China remained the world's most productive economy into and perhaps throughout the eighteenth century. Its Manchu Qing Dynasty was at its height, expansive and stable, incorporating vast areas of central Asia, including the regions now known as Tibet, Mongolia, and Xinjiang, into its control. The expansion of the Qing Dynasty paralleled the growth of the British Empire following its victory in the Seven Years' War. Naturally, the world's most populous country was an inviting market, and Britain—like other European powers—persistently sought expanded trade with China.

For the Qing, though, the advantages of increased trade with Great Britain were not clear. China had a sophisticated regional economy and well-developed commerce, and Chinese merchants dominated trade in the South China Sea. The Qing state, though, was not active in overseas trade the way that European states were. In part this was because the Qing imperial economy was large and productive with few incentives built in for international trade and in part because private merchants conducted commerce without state sponsorship. Furthermore, the Qing state did not routinely participate in a diplomatic or commercial system familiar to Europeans. Foreign regimes, especially neighboring states like Japan, Korea, Vietnam, and Siam, organized periodic, formalized trade missions with China. China also interacted with other states, including Russia, with which the Qing had concluded treaties in the 1600s. But the Qing Empire did not have a single system for foreign relations into which nations like Great Britain could easily fit. Qing statecraft improvised a method for dealing with overseas European visitors, treating them as personal guests of the emperor through the Imperial Household Department.

This system was adequate for the missionaries who began arriving at the Qing court during the seventeenth century. By the middle of the eighteenth century, though, Great Britain was seeking to expand commerce into China and petitioned the court to normalize relations along European standards. The Qing refused, and in 1759 established the Canton System, restricting all overseas European trade to the southern city of Canton (Guangzhou) where European traders could reside while they did business with government-licensed Chinese merchants for a few months per year. The British, seeking to open additional markets for its goods, were frustrated by the Chinese refusal to accept their terms.

In 1793, Britain sent a mission to the Qing Emperor to ask for more open trade and also to establish a permanent trading base on or near Chinese territory. The Qianlong Emperor rebuked this mission, led by Lord George Macartney (1737–1806). In his reply to King George III, the Qianlong Emperor wrote, "Our Celestial Empire possesses all things in prolific abundance and lacks no product within its own borders. There was therefore no need to import the manufactures of outside barbarians in exchange for our own produce." The Canton System remained in place.

The sentiment expressed in this letter to King George was a blow to the British. Britain needed China to buy British goods because Great Britain wanted things that China—and often only China—produced. Silk and porcelain were important, but it was Chinese tea that had become a national obsession after being introduced to Britain in the seventeenth century. Because China purchased little in return, British traders had no choice but to pay in silver, leading to a trade deficit that British politicians and merchants were eager to erase if only they could find something they could sell in China.

While the British position appeared weak, the Qianlong Emperor was confident. The empire appeared prosperous and sound economically, militarily, and socially. Yet beneath the surface lay problems in all of these areas. A growing gap between rich and poor accompanied China's prosperity, which was built largely on interregional commerce and a trend toward urbanization: cities prospered as commercial centers, attracting job seekers from the countryside. This flow of labor into cities was not such a problem as long as the cities could absorb the additional people; but at the height of its prosperity, China was vulnerable in the event of an economic downturn.

Global events came together with unforeseen consequences. Victories over French forces (discussed in Chapter 5) left Britain the preeminent global trading empire. Britain in the late eighteenth century expanded "Company Rule" in India, which had not yet become a formal colony of the British. During this period, the British East India Company, a commercial monopoly that oversaw all British trade in Asia, began to take on many characteristics of a sovereign in the region. The British East India Company was granted the right to collect revenues and then established a capital at Calcutta. As a commercial enterprise, it was mainly concerned with increasing its profits. Controlling British trade with China and acting as its own government in India, the East India Company began to address its trade imbalance through the production and sale of opium. This narcotic had been used in China for centuries, often combined with other substances. Opium grown in China was not very strong, but even so, the imperial government was moving in the direction of outlawing the drug. As early as the 1780s, East India Company directives began moving in the other direction, promoting the sale of opium in China. By the 1830s, thousands of tons of opium were being illegally imported to China each year by British traders. As many as ten million Chinese, mainly in the coastal cities, struggled with opium addiction.

This was a major problem, but opium sales were not the most important economic factor affecting China at the time. The upheavals that led to independence in Spanish America in the first decades of the nineteenth century severely disrupted the world's supply of silver, diminishing the silver available in China, but also depressing European consumers' demand for Chinese goods. By the 1820s, the flow of silver had reversed. Silver was now leaving China, and the Chinese economy contracted. Unemployment, social unrest, and economic recession replaced the prosperity that the Qianlong Emperor had seen when considering Lord Macartney's request for increased trade in 1793.

British and Chinese interests were now completely at odds. Great Britain wanted to increase trade to China, and opium was its most profitable commodity. The Qing state, on the other hand, wanted to stanch the flow of silver out of the country and the flow of opium in. In 1839, the Qing Emperor reiterated the ban on all trade in opium and sent an official, Lin Zexu (1785–1850), to confiscate the opium stored (illegally) at Canton. Lin was partially successful, destroying several tons of opium by burning it and dumping it in the sea, but British traders objected to the seizure and refused to cooperate with the Qing Dynasty official. Lin then blockaded foreign merchants in Canton, holding them virtually hostage. The British crown intervened on behalf of its subjects, leading to war.

The war lasted three years and ended with a decisive British victory. This was largely due to one of the fruits of industrialization: HMS *Nemesis*, the first ocean-going ironclad steamship. *Nemesis* featured watertight compartments, six large guns and a rocket launcher, in addition to steam power and iron plating. The ship decimated the Qing navy, its crew navigating far upriver with its shallow draft, nearly impervious to opposing firepower. The supremacy of the Royal Navy forced China to accept harsh peace terms. The 1842 Treaty of Nanjing opened five Chinese ports to trade, permitted foreigners to reside permanently in China, and established Hong Kong as a British colony. The treaty said nothing about opium, but it permitted free trade. Disputes over interpretation of the treaty contributed to the Second Opium War, after which the trade in opium was explicitly legalized.

The Treaty of Nanjing also legalized Christianity, which had been outlawed since the 1720s. Merchants and missionaries from Europe and the United States flowed into China. Among the recipients of the new Christian message was a student named Hong Xiuquan (1814–1864), who received a Christian tract in Canton in the 1830s. Hong later interpreted the Christian tract he received to mean that he was the younger brother of Jesus Christ and that he had been sent by God to eliminate the evil (the Manchu Qing Dynasty) that had enslaved his homeland. In its place, Hong attempted to establish the Kingdom of "Great Peace"—Taiping.

The Taiping War lasted from 1850 to 1864, brought the Qing Dynasty to the brink of collapse, and caused the deaths of more than thirty million people. Many cities took decades to recover from the destruction; some never did. At their height, Taiping forces controlled nearly half of China. That the Qing did not fall was largely due to visionary regional leaders like Zeng Guofan, introduced at the start of this chapter, who raised a militia and allied with British and American generals whom the Qing had enlisted to fight the rebels. These regional leaders, championed by a faction at court that supported their policies, set out to modernize China. "Self-strengthening," as this movement was called, focused first on the military and education. From the 1860s to the 1880s, armories, shipyards, and military academies appeared in coastal cities.

## The Price of Industrialized War: Crimea

Industrialization changed military technology quickly and on a grand scale, bringing stronger steel, more reliable and more accurate breech-loading rifles, faster communications and transportation, and higher energy explosives seemingly overnight. The strategic, tactical, and ethical implications of these changes became clear much more slowly. In the mid-nineteenth century, an alliance of France, Britain, Sardinia, and the Ottoman Empire successfully deployed new weaponry to defeat Russia in the Crimean War (1853–56). The Crimean War was significant in numerous ways. It rebalanced power in Europe. France appeared to have the most powerful army on the continent, and Russia appeared in decline. But, more broadly, the conduct of the Crimean War forced a reconsideration of the battlefield. What we might now call "weapons of mass destruction" became a necessary part of any state's arsenal. Long-range, high-explosive artillery made it possible to inflict casualties miles away from the front lines. Whereas earlier muskets were only accurate at very close range, new rifles—"rifling" in the barrel of the gun spins the bullets as they are fired—had improved accuracy and range. In the past, war casualties on the battlefield were few and usually fatal, but the new technologies of explosives and rifles meant that more casualties were further from the front, perhaps not fatally injured, but permanently disabled or otherwise debilitated, and maybe condemned to a slow, excruciating death.

*"A HOT NIGHT IN THE BATTERIES." SOLDIERS LOADING AND FIRING CANNONS, DURING THE CRIMEAN WAR.* Fought between Russia and an alliance of France, Britain, and Ottoman armies, the Crimean War (1853–56) was one of the first to use industrial weaponry like machine guns and high-explosive artillery. This 1855 painting by William Simpson shows soldiers far from the front lines, loading artillery to be fired at an enemy miles away. Technology transformed warfare, making it more deadly, less personal, and with a much wider reach.

Four years after the end of the Crimean War, Swiss businessman Henry Dunant (1828–1910), traveling through Austria, stayed in the northern Italian town of Solferino. There, a battle between French and Sardinian armies—the largest battle in Europe since Waterloo in 1815—killed or wounded some thirty or forty thousand soldiers, with many of the casualties left on the battlefield. Touring the battlefield the next day, Dunant was so appalled by the extent of suffering, enhanced by the new industrial model of warfare, that he was moved to action. Dunant's experience at Solferino led directly to the creation of the International Red Cross—now the world's largest humanitarian organization—and the Geneva Conventions, an attempt to create more humane rules for modern warfare. Dunant was awarded the first Nobel Peace Prize for his work.

## Slavery, Industry, and the US Civil War

Images of men marching to battle with new types of weapons became familiar across several continents during the second half of the nineteenth century, both because it was happening with frequency but also because new technology, like still photography, provided viewers with these images. Some of the most famous early photographs of industrial warfare were produced by Matthew Brady, who documented the US Civil War in thousands of photographs. This war was fought over many things, including the power of states relative to the central government and each other, but at its heart was slavery. The US Constitution permitted slavery, but most Northern states had abolished it by 1800. Some historians contend that the US slave economy was on the verge of a crisis of sustainability in the late eighteenth century, as arguments about free labor and the morality of slavery gained momentum across the Atlantic World. After ending its slave trade, Great Britain made slavery in the empire itself illegal in 1833. Slavery was outlawed in most Spanish American republics in the early decades after Independence. But in the United States, industrial innovations—especially the cotton gin—gave the "peculiar institution" new viability. The cotton gin increased the profitability of the American cotton industry, as Southern plantations sold great quantities to the increasingly productive textile mills of both Britain and the Northern United States. Slavery boomed. Slaveholders from the United States expanded the cotton frontier into Texas, destabilizing a Mexican government that had already committed to abolition and contributing to the tensions that led to war between the United States and Mexico in the 1840s. By 1860, about 12 percent of the US population—four million of the total population of thirty-one million—remained enslaved, and in some southern states slaves comprised nearly half of the total population. In contrast, in Brazil, enslaved people comprised approximately 15 percent of the population, but slaveholding was more regionally diversified there.

The US Civil War cannot be separated from global industrialization and empire. Although the international slave trade had ended, much of the Atlantic economy still relied on slavery to subsidize the global expansion of industry and commerce. Bloodshed, rather than diplomacy, resolved the matter. When the war started with the secession of South Carolina following Abraham Lincoln's inauguration, it confirmed the pattern of industrial slaughter that Europeans had seen in the Crimea and Solferino. Many battles saw more than twenty thousand casualties and some twice that many. In four years of war—from April 1861 to May 1865—more than six hundred thousand soldiers were killed and almost as many wounded. The South's economy and infrastructure was destroyed; in contrast, the North ramped up its industrial capacity.

Emerging out of the Civil War, the United States faced the daunting political, social, and economic challenges of Reconstruction—the reintegration of the Southern states into the nation—but it was also poised for rapid economic growth. The New England states, especially, became world leaders in the manufacture of locomotives, steamships, clocks, and other industrial goods. Munitions companies that had armed the Union Army during the war—including Remington, Colt, Smith & Wesson, Sharps, and Winchester—became global leaders in the world firearms market.

## Arming the Nation

New industrial technology was used to expand, create, and defend states. One particularly consequential example of this process was the role played by Alfred Krupp (1812–1887) in the formation of a larger, unified Germany. Krupp had turned his father's steelworks to creating innovative weaponry, replacing bronze muzzle-loading cannons with steel breech-loaders, which he promoted as more accurate and faster than the standard he hoped they would replace. Few in the military shared his view, and Krupp gave his first steel cannon as a gift to the Prussian king, with no buyer to be found. In 1859, however, the King's brother—Wilhelm—ordered that the Prussian army purchase more than three hundred of Krupp's cannons. Krupp's weaponry became an instrument of Prussian state building. Within twelve years, Prussia had led the way in establishing a unified German Empire, with Wilhelm as its emperor. During the process, the German Army defeated France, the continent's largest military power. By the 1880s, Germany would also broker colonial competition in Africa and Asia, accelerating a new, even more destructive round of imperialism.

It was this same spirit of state building that led Zeng Guofan, in 1863, to send his protégé Yung Wing (1828–1912) to the United States seeking industrial technology and expertise. China's survival was largely due to the ability of Zeng and others to rally local militia to counter the Taiping cause and also the recognition by European states that dealing with a new state might be more difficult than enforcing current treaty structures against a weakened Qing Empire. Yung's mission to the United States succeeded: he returned with machinery and materiel to establish the arsenals, factories, and shipyards that were at the forefront of China's self-strengthening campaign. A subtext to his story sheds a different light on this era.

Born in China, Yung Wing became a naturalized American in 1852. He was the first Chinese-born graduate of an American university (Yale, 1854) and had two children with his American-born wife, Mary Kellogg. When he returned from China to the United States in 1863—in the midst of the Civil War—he offered to enlist in the Union Army. His offer was refused. Years later, in a feverish display of anti-Chinese xenophobia, his US citizenship was rescinded, and he was barred from returning to his adopted country.

## Conclusion

There's no question that industrialization changed the world. But many events—wars, plagues, assassinations—change the world without being called "revolutions." The industrial revolution was a revolution because it changed, directly or indirectly, everything: where people lived; how they worked; how they traveled;

how they communicated; how many people lived on the planet; how the globe's resources were distributed; and how states related to each other.

We cannot, in this chapter, catalog every single element of change, even in the narrow time frame of the mid-eighteenth to the mid-nineteenth centuries. We've tried instead to focus on some of the most important causes of the industrial revolution, including the importance of chance and the roles of colonialism and slavery. We documented some of the most fundamental changes that industrialization wrought in the first societies to industrialize. We've also tried to demonstrate the early connections between industrialization and warfare, as this theme recurs again and again as one of the more important in modern world history.

With industrialization, the global importance of the North Atlantic world—Europe and the Americas—became magnified. This is so because these states leveraged industrialization to expand far beyond their early nineteenth-century borders in pursuit of territory, markets, and labor. Industrialization adds another key to understanding modernity as we described it in the introduction to this book. In Chapter 8, we will explore how changing global economic relations fueled by industrialization dovetailed with the concept of an international political order based on a hierarchy of nations.

## TIMELINE

**1759**
Canton System restricts trade with Europe to one port in China

**1787**
Philadelphia: John Fitch's *Perseverance* demonstrates potential of steam power

**1820s**
British workers can produce one hundred pounds of cotton yarn in one hundred thirty-five worker hours

**1835**
Andrew Ure, *The Philosophy of Manufactures*

**1770s**
British workers can produce one hundred pounds of cotton yarn in two thousand worker hours

**1793**
Macartney mission to China; Eli Whitney invents the cotton gin

**1820–50**
Global trade triples

**1842**
Treaty of Nanjing ends First Opium War, opening China to European trade and establishing Hong Kong as a British colony

# A Few Good Books

T. S. Ashton. *The Industrial Revolution, 1760–1830.* Oxford: Oxford University Press, 1998.

Sven Beckert. *Empire of Cotton: A Global History.* New York: Knopf, 2014.

Mark Bostridge. *Florence Nightingale: The Making of an Icon.* New York: Farrar, Straus, and Giroux, 2008.

Peter Gran. *The Rise of the Rich. A New View of Modern World History.* Syracuse, NY: Syracuse University Press, 2009.

Tristram Hunt. *Marx's General: The Revolutionary Life of Friedrich Engels.* New York: Macmillan, 2011.

Julia Lovell. *The Opium War: Drugs, Dreams and the Making of China.* London: Picador, 2012.

Stephen R. Platt. *Autumn in the Heavenly Kingdom: China, the West, and the Epic Story of the Taiping Civil War.* New York: Knopf, 2012.

*For additional resources, including maps, primary sources, visuals, web links, and quizzes, please go to **www.oup.com/us/carter***

**1845**
Friedrich Engels, *The Condition of the English Working Class in 1844*

**1850–64**
Taiping War

**1854**
Yung Wing graduates from Yale University

**1861–65**
US Civil War

**1868**
*Tianqi*, first steamship built in China, launched

**ca. 1850**
80 percent of cotton spun by English textile industry produced by slave labor

**1853–56**
Crimean War

**1859**
Prussian army purchases cannons made by Alfred Krupp

**1863**
The world's first subway system opens in London

A FORCIBLE APPEAL for the ABOLITION of the SLAVE TRADE.

**(TOP)  A FORCIBLE APPEAL FOR THE ABOLITION OF THE SLAVE TRADE. RICHARD NEWTON, 1792.**  This satirical print, suggesting the undeniable cruelty of slavery if one would only consider its realities, was published in London on the eve of a parliamentary debate over a bill to ban the slave trade. A ban did not pass into law until 1807. Richard Newton (1777–1798) produced this print at the age of fifteen for the radical London publisher William Holland (1757–1815). The following year, Holland was jailed for publishing a work by Thomas Paine, who wrote *Common Sense*, the influential 1775 pamphlet that advocated independence for the British North American colonies.

**(BOTTOM)  FOUR YOUNG JAVANESE DANCERS, PARIS EXPOSITION, 1889.**  The creation of "living museums" was a popular feature of the world's fairs of the late nineteenth century. These dancers lived alongside other villagers, including artisans and musicians, who simulated life on the island of Java for fair-goers. The dancers performed with a live Javanese orchestra, drawing large crowds to the colonial pavilion.

# Modernity Organized
## 1840–1889

In the spring of 1840, Elizabeth Cady Stanton (1815–1902) took a seat at the first World Antislavery Conference in London. Stanton, an American, was in London on her honeymoon, attending the conference with her husband. Although Parliament passed legislation to abolish slavery in the Empire in 1833, the act called for a gradual transition to freedom for most enslaved persons. Slavery still remained in South America, the United States, and French and Dutch colonies around the world. This conference took as its goal, in part, "The universal extinction of slavery and the slave trade."

But the first day of the conference spent little time on abolition, as delegates instead focused on whether women would be permitted to participate. A majority decided that the several dozen women in attendance could remain only if they sat silently in a segregated area, out of view of the main proceedings. It was there that Stanton met and befriended Lucretia Mott (1793–1880), a Philadelphia Quaker. Stanton and Mott began to plan a different meeting, one that would focus on women's rights and equality. They convened a convention on women's rights eight years later, near Stanton's home in Seneca Falls, New York.

A much larger, and very different gathering, took place in 1889. In that year, Paris, just across the English Channel from where Mott and Stanton first met, hosted the *Exposition Universelle*, a world's fair, the crowning achievement of a generation of international exhibitions that began in the 1850s. Trade fairs and the competitive exhibition of goods had deep historical roots; but during this era, fueled by the industrial revolution and progressive ideology, these international gatherings combined commerce with arts, athletics, education, advertising, and propaganda, all on a grand scale. Today's readers, accustomed to wandering through retail stores piled high with merchandise from around the world, would find some aspects of the fair familiar. Other elements would seem bizarre and abhorrent: the most visited attraction in Paris was reputed to be the "Negro village," which housed four hundred Africans brought to Paris to live "as natives" in the French capital under the gaze of visitors to the exhibition—a human zoo.

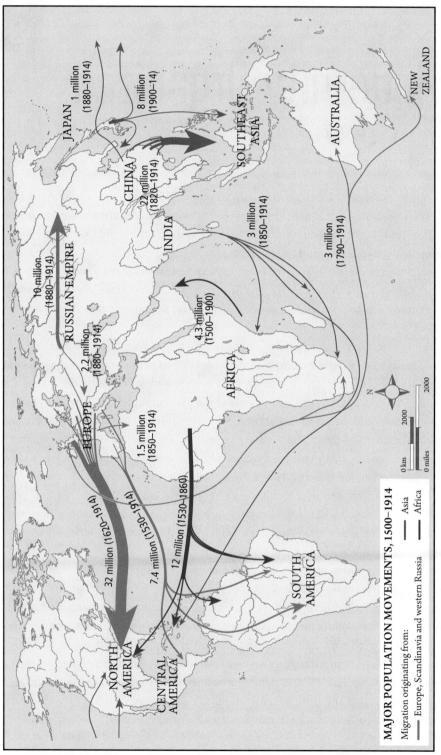

**MAJOR POPULATION MOVEMENTS, 1500–1914**

Migration originating from:

— Europe, Scandinavia and western Russia
— Asia
— Africa

JAPAN 1 million (1880–1914)

8 million (1900–14)

CHINA 22 million (1820–1914)

SOUTHEAST ASIA

AUSTRALIA

NEW ZEALAND

INDIA

3 million (1850–1914)

3 million (1790–1914)

RUSSIAN EMPIRE

10 million (1880–1914)

2.2 million (1880–1914)

EUROPE

4.3 million (1500–1900)

AFRICA

1.5 million (1850–1914)

32 million (1620–1914)

7.4 million (1530–1914)

12 million (1530–1860)

NORTH AMERICA

CENTRAL AMERICA

SOUTH AMERICA

N

0 km   2000
0 miles   2000

MAP 8.1  Major Population Movements, 1500–1914

The World's Fairs showcased the growing military and economic dominance of a small number of states but also held out a promise: all peoples could be organized into nations, and those nations were welcome to show the world what they had to offer. In places like London, Philadelphia, and Paris, nations and their peoples displayed technology, weapons, culture, and food. The central architectural feature of Paris's 1889 fair—coinciding with the centennial of the French Revolution—was the Eiffel Tower, still standing today as a symbol of modern France, as the fairs themselves embodied modernity for nineteenth-century audiences.

---

The antislavery conference, the Seneca Falls meeting, and the Paris World's Fair highlight major themes of the last two chapters to which we now return. In Chapter 6, we analyzed the search for new internal order in sovereign states, including the proper relationship between state and citizen. In Chapter 7, we focused on how industrialization disrupted and reconfigured economic relationships. Each of these chapters raised enduring questions: How can the number and size of nation-states be determined? How is citizenship defined, and what are the rights that citizens can demand? How would ever-increasing supplies of commodities be matched with markets for their consumption? What would be the long-term costs and benefits of industrialization, and how would they be distributed across the planet? In this chapter, we analyze "modern" answers to these questions that developed in the second half of the nineteenth century.

We begin the chapter with a review of the nation-state formation process in the second half of the nineteenth century, focusing on Eurasia and the Western Hemisphere where relationships between individuals and sovereign states changed significantly. In addition, we survey alterations in the relative size and power of states themselves. At the same time, industrialization and its effects spread and intensified. During the second half of the nineteenth century, these interrelated processes spurred debates about order, progress, liberty, efficiency, and prosperity, concepts increasingly defined in reference to the industrializing nation-states of the Atlantic world. Many of the world's elites, regardless of their religious, ethnic, social, or geographic locations, came to equate these definitions and policies with the idea of "modernity" and associated their embrace with survival. We conclude by exploring international exhibitions as staged events designed to both reflect and promote modernity.

## Reform versus Revolution

Karl Marx posited as a scientific fact that the internal contradictions of capitalism would cause communist revolutions in the most advanced industrial countries of the world. Marx thought nationalism—and religion, too—were designed to distract or deter workers from seeing the world as it really was. He argued that economic class was far more important to a person's identity than nationality: for instance, factory workers, whether in Germany, France, the United States, or England, shared more in common with workers in other countries than they did with factory owners (or the ruling classes) in their own. Once workers realized that imagined national identities and the very real states controlled by the bourgeoisie were both designed to oppress them, they would rise up and replace the existing political system with an egalitarian and transnational communist society. In the *Manifesto of the Communist Party,* Marx and his co-author Friedrich Engels concluded, "Let the ruling classes tremble at a Communist revolution. The proletarians have nothing to lose but their chains. They have a world to win. Working men of all countries unite!"

The year the *Manifesto* was published—1848—Europe was indeed ablaze with unrest. However, the nature of these movements challenged Marxist predictions. Industrial workers were in the streets, but rather than the dawn of a proletarian revolution, 1848 came to be called the "Springtime of the Nations," as wage workers joined others to demand universal (usually, universal male) suffrage or national independence. In Budapest, protesters called for Hungarian independence

UNIVERSAL, DEMOCRATIC, AND SOCIAL REPUBLIC. LITHOGRAPH. FRÉDÉRIC SORRIEU, 1848. Sorrieu (1807–1887), a French artist, was well known for his illustrations of the reform ideals of the mid-nineteenth century. During the "springtime of nations" in Europe, Sorrieu produced this print of the idealized triumph of nationalism as a pathway to brotherhood, greater equality, and progress.

and recited Sándor Petőfi's *National Song*: "The Magyar [Hungarian] name will be great again, Worthy of its old, great honor." In Prague, the Young Czech movement promoted their language against German domination. In dozens of other cities, all across Europe, revolutionary movements gained momentum, but they tended to be nationalist, not proletarian, in nature.

## Britain: The Exception That Proves the Rule

Great Britain in the first decades of the nineteenth century was Marx's model for understanding the link between economic and political power in industrializing societies. Yet, throughout all of the upheaval surrounding 1848, workers in Britain, the most advanced industrial economy in the world, played little role. Great Britain's proletariat was not leading the communist revolution as Marx and Engels predicted. Why not? It's difficult to explain why historical outcomes *don't* happen, but examining the history of English reform can help identify some of the resilience of the nation-state model in the face of crisis.

When the Napoleonic Wars ended in 1815, grain imports to Britain should have increased. Napoleon's anti-British Continental System attempted to exclude Britain from most trade with Europe, and the end of this embargo should have flooded the British market with grain, bringing down its price and providing consumers—especially the urban working class—with cheaper bread. But, declining grain prices would threaten domestic landowners' profits, and large landowners dominated Parliament. Recognizing what was happening, Parliament quickly passed the Corn Laws, virtually prohibiting the import of all grain ("corn" in British usage at the time referred to all grain, not just maize). British growers could maintain higher prices, which were then reflected in the price of bread.

Criticism mounted against not only the Corn Laws but also the restrictions on suffrage that enabled legislation like the Corn Laws to pass. At the time, voting in England was restricted to males owning at least £200 in property (equivalent to about $250,000 in 2014). This prevented most people from voting at all, but if you were fortunate to own property of this value in more than one district, you could vote in both of them! Besides that, no one in the House of Lords was elected at all: its seats were inherited by the landed nobility. The other house of Parliament—the House of Commons—was elected, but it didn't very accurately reflect the people's will either. In addition to the limited franchise, the geographical distribution of seats there had not changed since the 1600s. Since that time, industrialization had dramatically altered the size and distribution of the British population. Remember the growth of cities like Manchester? In 1819, all of Lancashire—including the cities of Bolton, Manchester, Blackburn, and others, and totaling close to a million people—shared just two representatives in the House of Commons.

With a government elected only by rich men, laws that protected the profits of wealthy landowners, and rising bread prices, violence seemed imminent, just as Marx predicted. Cavalry violently dispersed a rally for electoral reform at St. Peter's Field in Manchester in the summer of 1819. Fifteen people were killed and more than six hundred injured in what came to be known as the "Peterloo Massacre." Henry Hunt (1773–1835), the featured speaker and a leading reform advocate, was imprisoned for three years on charges of "disturbing the peace." Repression followed, as the government essentially outlawed public meetings and censored newspapers critical of the government.

Yet violence did not escalate to revolution. Instead, a wide array of actors— parliamentary delegates, factory workers, intellectuals—worked out a series of compromises. Beginning in the 1820s, social, political and economic reforms emerged from Parliament, culminating in the Reform Act of 1832, which redistributed electoral seats and doubled the number of eligible voters. Other parliamentary reforms of this era reduced some tariffs, reformed the criminal code, and placed limits on who could work and how long they could work.

Still, Britain seemed ripe for revolution. The 1832 Reform Act made Britain one of the most democratic societies in Europe, yet it still enfranchised just 5% of the population. Many deplorable labor practices continued, and the Corn Laws remained in effect. Proposals for additional reforms fizzled over the course of the 1830s, feeding political dissent. Threats overseas grew as well. In addition to the Opium War with China, rebellions against British rule roiled Ireland, Jamaica, Canada, and India. France, Germany, and the United States challenged British commercial and industrial superiority. But revolution never came. Political leaders repealed the Corn Laws in the mid-1840s, defying Marx's expectations by acting against their class interests. Many workers chose to focus their efforts on improving their ability to negotiate with their employers—commonly referred to as trade unionism—instead of trying to overthrow the state.

Established political leaders also discovered the value of nationalism during this era, using it to rally domestic populations in support of government policy as when the British government took direct administrative control over India in 1858. The move was precipitated by an 1857 uprising—the Great Rebellion or Sepoy Mutiny as the British press called it at the time—against the British East India Company. Reports, many of them fabricated, in the British press about atrocities carried out against English men, women, and girls rallied public support for the decision by the British crown to exercise direct rule in India.

## New European States

The formation of Germany and Italy, both established in 1871, also illustrates the power, promise, and limits of nationalism. The process that led directly to their formation took decades. Although many parts of Germany, and Italy, had been united under empires in the past, neither had ever existed as a nation-state, and cultural differences within the would-be nations were often profound. In both instances, over the course of several decades culminating in the 1870s, unification was a process whereby existing states (Prussia for Germany; Sardinia-Piedmont for Italy) expanded to create a larger state.

On the Italian peninsula in 1831, Giuseppe Mazzini created Young Italy, a secret society to promote "One, Independent, Free Republic." Young Italy sponsored a series of failed uprisings in the 1830s. Exiled to Switzerland and then England in the 1840s, Mazzini renewed the calls for a unified Italian state in 1848, as uprisings spread across Europe. Giuseppe Garibaldi (1807–1882), a Genoese who had served as a naval officer in the South American republic of Uruguay, took up Mazzini's patriotic call, leading military campaigns on the Italian peninsula and beyond through the 1850s and 1860s. Hailed as a hero, in Italy and abroad; as a man of the people; and a fighter for the cause of popular self-determination, Garibaldi did not see unified Italy become a republic, but he did serve in the parliament of the new Kingdom of Italy, proclaimed in 1871.

Also in 1871, Wilhelm of Prussia became Kaiser—Emperor—of Germany. German speakers had always lived in many different states across central Europe. The idea that a large and artificially divided German nation should be brought under one sovereign state gained traction during the Napoleonic era, from 1804 to 1815, when many German-speaking peoples lived under French control. It was in this period that Fichte and others spoke of their dream to "reunite" the German nation under one ruler.

The northeastern state of Prussia, long a formidable military power, became an industrial power as well in the nineteenth century, rivalling Austria as the dominant German-speaking state. When 1848 revolutionaries renewed the call for German unity, Prussian leaders responded, initiating diplomatic and military maneuvers to gain additional territory. Threatened by this growing power to the east, France was drawn into a war in 1870. The resulting Franco-Prussian War brought Prussian armies into the southern German-speaking states like Bavaria. After defeating France, the Treaty of Frankfurt proclaimed the Empire of Germany, with the Prussian king as its emperor, incorporating almost all of the European states with a majority of German speakers, except for Austria.

There was no "natural" reason for Austria to be excluded from the nation-state of Germany but Bavaria or Saxony—also mostly German speaking—to be included. And what about Bohemia, which had a mix of (mainly) Czech and German speakers? Or Alsace, where many spoke German, but many also spoke French or Alsatian? The same kinds of questions, with different details, applied to the Italian case. These questions were rooted in historical contingencies, reinforcing the point that nation-states

**THE GERMAN CONFEDERATION,
AUSTRIAN EMPIRE, PRUSSIA,
AND DENMARK, 1815**

Austrian Habsburg Empire
Prussia
Border of German Confederation
Denmark

**GERMANY: FROM CONFEDERATION TO EMPIRE**

Habsburg Empire    Border of German Customs Union (Zollverein) 1842
Prussia 1815    Southern border of North German Confederation 1867
Territory added to Prussia 1815–66    Border of German Empire 1871
Territory added to Prussia/German Empire 1871

A   Anhalt     **MS**   Mecklenburg-Strelitz
B   Brunswick     O   Oldenburg
**Ha**   Hamburg     P   Prussia
H   Hanover     **TS**   Thuringian States

MAP 8.2 Germany: From Confederation to Empire

aren't naturally occurring, self-evident political entities; they are constructed out of circumstances and limited by political possibilities.

In both the German and the Italian cases, nationalist ideologies undergirded the new states' proclamations of sovereignty; but modern technology and the use of force allowed court officers, police, military, and civil servants to make a state and define the terms of political belonging, subduing groups and individuals who had different ideas about what a social contract for a modern German or Italian nation should look like. In the two decades after unification, the German government passed laws creating public health insurance, retirement, and disability programs. German leaders, like political elites in other European industrial centers, argued that their political and economic system, based on private property and representative government, gradually improved the lives of their citizens and removed the need for the more radical actions advocated by Marxists. By the end of the nineteenth century, this dual expansion of the political role of non-elites and the rights of citizens contributed to the increased scrutiny of who was eligible to be a citizen in any given nation-state, a process that continues today.

## Challenges to the Ottoman and Russian Empires

The larger, more powerful German Empire profoundly affected states to the east. The Ottoman and Russian Empires were scrambling to outflank each other and to keep pace with their rivals at a time when both faced the dual challenges of nationalist ferment and global economic transformation. In response, both empires implemented internal reforms designed to quell potential fragmentation and meet growing external military and economic challenges.

In the Ottoman Empire, the Tanzimat (Reorganization), begun in 1839, continued. The government founded a Ministry of Health and Academy of Sciences. The first telegraph networks and railroad lines were laid out; steam-powered ferries began to carry commuters between home and work. A central bank and stock exchange contributed financial infrastructure for economic development. Over the next decades, the Ottoman political elite continued to transform military, fiscal, and administrative structures and the relationship between the state and residents of different faiths, all while fighting a series of international wars and separatist movements.

Tsarist Russia launched its own modernization effort, the Great Reforms, which peaked in the third quarter of the nineteenth century. The Peasant Reform of 1861 abolished the legal ties of serfs to the land. Reforms of the judicial system, municipal government, and military followed. The state used tax policies to protect new industries from competition and tax revenues to subsidize the growth of the railroad network. The state also attempted to manage more effectively the diverse territories and peoples over which it claimed sovereignty, from surveying

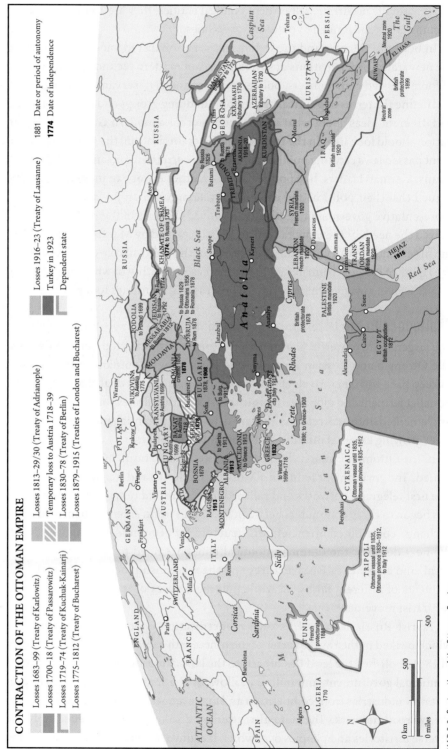

MAP 8.3  Contraction of the Ottoman Empire

expeditions to colonization schemes managed through government agencies with names such as the Ministry of State Domains and the Resettlement Authority. In these ways, both empires managed to survive through the end of the nineteenth century, although neither would make it past the second decade of the twentieth.

## Nation and Citizen in Spanish America

Many Western European states followed similar paths during the nineteenth century, as elites gave up some of their wealth and power to maintain order, yet held on to most private and public resources. In these countries, most of the working class chose reform over revolution. Suffrage expanded slowly (seldom including women until the twentieth century), and the relationship between states and citizens expanded to include claims of some social rights in addition to political and civil rights. In the Americas, several factors not present in Western Europe lent a distinct character to the consolidation of nation-states. These were states founded through anticolonial uprisings; their populations were characterized by high levels of ethnic and racial mixture; many had sizable and varied indigenous populations; and slavery persisted in much of the region through the middle of the century.

Throughout Spanish America, as we saw in Chapter 6, disputes over political and economic order and power drove regional wars in the first decades following the collapse of Spanish imperial rule. Emerging from this era, reformers like Guillermo Prieto (Mexico, 1818–1897) and Domingo Faustino Sarmiento (Argentina, 1811–1888) proclaimed liberalism as the key to progress in their countries. Believers in the transformative power of private property and commerce, Spanish American statesmen in the middle of the century presided over the abolition of slavery in the last of the Spanish American republics where it was practiced. They eliminated special privileges for the Catholic Church and wrote constitutions that emphasized the rights of individuals. Their successors—for example, the Generation of '80 in Argentina and the *científicos* (advocates of "scientific" politics) in Mexico—thought of themselves as adopting the most advanced ideas to bring positive changes to their countries. They encouraged, through additional legislation and their own actions, investment in infrastructure and private enterprise, often partnering with foreign investors.

But the success of these reforms was limited. The political systems that emerged throughout Latin America may be best thought of as oligarchic republics. They maintained periodic elections, separation of powers, equality before the law, freedom of assembly, and other features of liberal democracy; but corruption, fraud, and coercion undermined its practice, as small groups of very powerful men controlled inordinate amounts of political and economic power. In addition, many reformers continued to believe that their states faced "race problems" that could delay or derail progress. As a result, when nation-states were formed, many of the hemisphere's indigenous populations remained marginalized.

The Mexican government invited European immigrants to colonize northern Mexico and forced indigenous peoples off of their agricultural lands on one side of the country to work in export agriculture on the other. At the southern end of the continent, both Chile and Argentina subdued indigenous populations through military campaigns that inflicted tens of thousands of indigenous casualties in the 1870s and displaced many thousands more. As the Argentine general Julio Roca (1843–1914) put it, these campaigns were designed to "put down ... this handful of savages . . . in the name of law, progress, and our own security."

## Rebuilding the United States

In some ways, the United States fits the Italian and German models of national unification. US claims to wide swaths of North America from the Atlantic to the Pacific dramatically increased over the course of the nineteenth century. This expansion resulted from victory in a series of wars fought against other North American states that disputed US claims of sovereignty with their own counter-claims. The vast expansion of territorial claims against Mexico to the south and indigenous states and peoples to the west fueled an increasing debate in the centers of US political and economic power over the defining characteristics of its social contract and economy. As in Italy and Germany, the consolidation of a larger territorial state spurred reconsideration of political and economic relationships within it—a questioning of nation.

In the revolutionary year of 1848, Elizabeth Cady Stanton and Lucretia Mott organized the Seneca Falls Convention mentioned in the chapter's introduction. Conference participants pointed out that the Enlightenment rhetoric of equality and universal rights had been implemented in ways that conspicuously excluded women. The United States, founded on principles of equality and the rule of law, denied women the right to vote, to hold public office, to own property if married, and to serve on juries. Stanton's *Declaration of Sentiments* put the matter in familiar, and revolutionary, terms: "We hold these truths to be self-evident: that all men and women are created equal, and are endowed by their creator with certain inalienable rights."

In the years leading up to the Civil War, the movements to abolish slavery and enfranchise women tended to work together to expand the definition of equality. Frederick Douglass (1818–1895), a former slave, joined other activists like Stanton and Susan B. Anthony (1820–1906) to show the wide gap between the principles of equality that Rousseau, Kant, Condorcet, and others had articulated and their practical realization.

**ELIZABETH CADY STANTON APPEARS BEFORE THE US SENATE COMMITTEE ON PRIVILEGES AND ELECTIONS.** *NEW YORK DAILY* GRAPHIC ILLUSTRATION, JANUARY 16, 1878.  In the aftermath of the US Civil War, a schism opened between advocates for the enfranchisement of African American men and those, like Elizabeth Cady Stanton, who argued that the appropriate strategy to pursue in the 1860s was one that would gain all adults the right to vote. After the Fifteenth Amendment was ratified in 1870, Stanton turned her attention to advocating for another amendment specifying that women, too, enjoyed the suffrage, a change in law that did not occur until 1920.

After the Civil War, the federal government declared legal equality on the basis of race but would not pursue the same goal for women. The nation had determined that its founding phrase, "all men are created equal," included men of color but not women of any color. In 1869, the constitution was amended to prohibit denial of the right to vote based on race or color. Introduced to congress every year starting in 1878, a similar constitutional amendment giving women the right to vote in the United States was not enacted until 1920, 18 years after Elizabeth Cady Stanton died.

The Reconstruction era following the Civil War spurred a painful assessment of how the nation-state would fit together and how the government would relate to its population, including former slaves and an increasing number of immigrants from other parts of the world. Creating loyal and useful citizens drove the establishment and expansion of a public school system, as it did in Europe and elsewhere. Lessons designed for use in schools defined national character and the benefits of belonging. Unfortunately, the message sent by government actions suggested that some kinds of people still lacked the proper characteristics to have attained for themselves (yet or maybe ever) the right to full participation in the nation-state. Frequently, these were groups considered racially distinct like Mexicans, Chinese, African Americans ("Negros"), and Native Americans ("Indians"), and they included at the time groups eventually identified as "white," such as Jews, Irish, or Italians.

This attitude was reflected in territorial, immigration, and social policies. After the Civil War, the US government ratcheted up restrictions on the indigenous peoples of the Great Plains by instituting the "Indian reservation" system. Completion of the transcontinental railroad system escalated the conflict over resources as more white settlers moved west. Much of the work on the railroad was completed by immigrant laborers from China, yet in 1882 the US government passed a law prohibiting the entry of Chinese immigrants for ten years out of fear that they posed a threat to order. And, by the end of the century, racial segregation had been ratified as a constitutionally sound practice. In 1890, the state of Louisiana passed a law that required separate accommodations for blacks and whites traveling by rail. In 1896, the US Supreme Court reviewed the law (*Plessy v. Ferguson*) and ruled that the country could endure with its citizens being "separate but equal," a legal standard that survived until the mid-twentieth century.

## Abolition, Immigration, and the Meaning of Free Labor

In 1888, Brazil became the last state in the Western Hemisphere to outlaw slavery when Princess Isabel (1846–1921) signed a law of unconditional abolition. The "Golden Law" passed without the violent civil war that characterized the end of slavery in the United States, but abolition in Brazil did trigger the overthrow of the last monarchy in the Americas, as key sectors of the nation's elite questioned the ability of the imperial bureaucracy to cope with profound economic and social change.

On November 15, 1889, little more than a year after abolition, a coup d'état laid the groundwork for a constitutional republic. Brazil's new flag proclaimed the aspirations of the nascent regime. Across the center of the flag appeared the optimistic phrase "*Ordem e Progresso*"—"Order and Progress"—but Brazil's political elite was unprepared to entrust the direction of the republic to the masses, especially those recently emancipated. Voter eligibility rules for the non-slave population had actually grown more restrictive in the years prior to abolition, and elections remained tightly controlled afterward: less than 2 percent of the population was eligible to vote.

Concerns over citizenship were not limited to the formerly enslaved. Rising immigration of free people also intensified concern across the Americas over identifying, sorting, and preparing responsible citizens. Economic change and political reform in Europe and elsewhere displaced millions of people. Improved rail and steamship infrastructure moved people to where labor was needed, both within and between countries, including millions of people from throughout the world who came to the United States, Brazil, Argentina, Chile, and other parts of the Americas.

## The "Coolie" Trade and the Meaning of Slavery

The demand for labor combined with ongoing debates about what it meant to be free and to be a citizen. Even as slavery was being abolished, the demand for cheap labor continued to rise, leading to a market for indentured workers, many of whom moved from China, India, and Southeast Asia to work throughout the world. Chinese laborers were crucial not only to the completion of the transcontinental railroads in the United States and Canada but they also replaced enslaved labor across South America and the Caribbean. These laborers were generally provided through a contract between owners and agents in India or China. Sometimes paid nominal wages, and other times not at all, laborers were required to serve out the terms of a contact under conditions very similar to slavery.

The laborers—called "coolies"—existed in a gap between the enslaved and the fully free. Recent scholarship has clarified the relationship between the coolie trade in the Pacific and the Atlantic slave trade. British, and then Spanish, law banned the Atlantic slave trade during the first half of the nineteenth century, so even though slavery continued to be practiced, the labor needs of the sugar producing colonies in the Caribbean could no longer be met by importing enslaved Africans. The changes were immediate: in 1845, Spanish law forbade trade in slaves; the following year, a Spanish merchant contracted to import Chinese laborers to Cuba. More than one hundred twenty-five thousand Chinese "coolies" were transported through Cuba over the next twenty-seven years, laboring on sugar plantations alongside enslaved Africans in Cuba and other Spanish territories. In the British Empire, where slavery was illegal, the scale of Asian labor was even greater: eighteen thousand laborers from China and nearly five hundred thousand from India worked British plantations in the Caribbean during this same period. British authorities extolled their moral superiority to the Spanish by abolishing slavery, yet many contemporary observers suggested that conditions for "free" coolies and enslaved Africans were not noticeably different.

Historians have wrestled to make sense of the relationship between the coolie trade and the slave trade, and between Asian laborers and African laborers in the Americas. Although some argue that indentured Asian labor was in many ways equivalent to slavery, most see it as a third category, neither slave nor free.

Asian laborers saw themselves as deceived and mistreated but also saw their position as distinct from the condition of enslaved African laborers. Their employment continued to subsidize the plantation economy for many decades after the abolition of the slave trade.[1]

New flows of international labor migration like the coolie trade help to illustrate important changes in the interplay between global economic change and the way states categorized and evaluated individuals and groups in the hierarchy of the world's peoples. Events in East Asia in the second half of the nineteenth century challenged many of the assumptions that Europeans and Americans made about the nature of these hierarchies.

## Modernizing Japan

Many people in Europe and the United States saw the "opening" of China at the end of the First Opium War (Chapter 7) as part of an unstoppable march by Western powers through Asia. In July 1853, a decade after that war ended, Matthew Perry led a US squadron into Tokyo harbor. In the preceding four years, thousands of people had streamed to California, when gold was discovered in this territory ceded to the United States by Mexico after the war of 1846–1848. The Gold Rush announced the arrival of the United States as a Pacific nation. California joined the Union in 1850, and the United States was suddenly closer than any Western European power to the markets of Asia, made even more accessible by new developments in steam-powered shipping. Turning potential into power required a new type of infrastructure, though: coaling stations for refueling ships along the way. US steamships heading west from California soon connected a series of islands in the Pacific, including Hawai'i, Guam, and Midway Island. Japan appeared a logical link in the chain connecting the United States to China.

Perry was not the first American to enter Japanese waters. A handful of American traders—often flying the Dutch flag—had been trying to establish trade with Japan since around 1800, but none of them came with the orders—or the firepower—to open trade through military force if needed. Backed by some three hundred marines and some of the US Navy's most advanced guns, Perry refused the Japanese government's order to dock at Nagasaki, for centuries the only

---

[1]   Rebecca Scott, *Slave Emancipation in Cuba: The Transition to Free Labor, 1860–1899.* (Princeton, NJ: Princeton University Press, 1985); Evelyn Hu-Dehart, "Chinese Coolie Labor in Cuba in the Nineteenth Century: Free Labor of Neoslavery," *Contributions in Black Studies* 12, Article 5 (1994): 38–54; Lisa Yun, *The Coolie Speaks: Chinese Indentured Laborers and African Slaves in Cuba* (Philadelphia: Temple University Press, 2008); Moon-Ho Jung, *Coolies and Cane: Race, Labor, and Sugar in the Age of Emancipation* (Baltimore: Johns Hopkins University Press, 2006).

foreign point of access to the Japanese market. Defying Japanese protocols for foreign trade, Perry insisted that the Japanese government accept a letter from the US President (with a proposal to open additional ports) or suffer the consequences of war. When officials of the Tokugawa government refused, Perry and his ships conducted target practice in the harbor. The Japanese agreed to accept the letter, after which Perry withdrew from Japanese waters, returning months later with a larger force, including steam-powered frigates and several thousand marines. In March 1854, the Japanese assented to US requests. Within five years, the Japanese government signed similar agreements with European states, igniting conflict within Japan that would dramatically alter its internal political order and its relationship to the rest of the world over the next half-century and beyond.

Japan's response to the West is often presented as simple. Japan is supposed to have rationally and quickly perceived the advantages of modernization and transformed rapidly from a feudal to an industrial state. Some elements of this portrayal are indeed true: Japan did accept Perry's demands for open trade in 1853, and within a generation was well on its way to becoming an industrial, imperial power. Many of the conditions, however, that facilitated this transformation were already apparent before Perry's arrival. Japan's population was among the most urbanized in the world, with some of the world's largest cities and a thriving commercial class. Apparent ethnic and cultural homogeneity and natural geographic boundaries gave Japan advantages to state formation described (and sought) by Western nationalists.

In other ways, though, Japan was not modern: occupations were determined by birth, and law and custom restricted social mobility. Most of the country was feudal in its property relations. Although not as isolated as the seventeenth-century "closed-country" edicts (discussed in Chapter 2) would imply, Japan strictly regulated its relations with other countries. Within a generation of Perry's arrival, though, Japanese legislators wrote a constitution and did away with the feudal government system that had ruled the islands since 1600.

The new *Meiji* ("Enlightened Rule") government blended Western and Japanese institutions to modernize the country. The 1868 Charter Oath, although vague, pointed Japan toward Western models of modernization, echoing the US Declaration of Independence ("each be allowed to pursue his own calling so that there may be no discontent") and the Enlightenment ("everything based upon the just laws of Nature"). The Oath called for "knowledge to be sought throughout the world," prompting a series of overseas missions to the United States and Europe, gathering information about nearly every aspect of society as Japan tried to modernize. The findings of these missions led Japan to model Western institutions in many critical areas. A conscription law, to build a Japanese national army to replace the feudal samurai, went into effect in 1873. Tokyo University, the first Western-style university in Asia, opened in 1877.

Not everyone embraced change, though. Saigo Takamori (1828–1877) led an 1877 rebellion to retain a more traditional Japanese government, including a stronger role for the samurai. In a costly war in which both sides were armed with Western munitions, Japanese imperial forces defeated Saigo's samurai, effectively ending the samurai class in Japan and clearing the way for continued Westernization by the Meiji government. The Meiji Constitution, promulgated in 1889, modeled closely the German constitution.

## The Second Industrial Revolution

Tying together labor flows, the search for markets and resources, and questions of national identity are changing production and consumption patterns during this era, which some scholars suggest amounted to a second industrial revolution. The second half of the nineteenth century saw further change in unleashing the potential energy locked in fossil fuels. Bigger, more powerful engines and new fuels powered military, industrial, and consumer applications. The use of natural gas expanded, first for lighting, and then for cooking and heating. Drilling for gas and oil spread across North America and then Europe in the 1850s. By the 1870s, commercial production of internal combustion engines—the kind used in automobiles—had begun. In 1882, the first eighty-five customers lighting their homes through incandescent light bulbs hooked into a New York power station.

Engineering marvels (and spectacular failures) abounded. The Suez Canal linked the Mediterranean and Red Seas in 1869, shaving six thousand miles off a journey from England to India. By the end of the 1880s, both Mexico and Argentina had rail networks of over six thousand miles, in countries where almost no track existed in 1850. In the United States, the transcontinental railroad joined the Atlantic and Pacific coasts in 1869. In Europe, between 1850 and 1890, the German railroad network expanded by a factor of twenty and Russia's by more than sixty. In India, where no railroad existed in 1850, over fifteen thousand miles of track had been laid by 1890, and that number would double again in the following twenty years.

These rails not only facilitated imperial expansion. The global market for industrial consumer goods—bicycles, typewriters, sewing machines—exploded. Goods imported from Asia and Latin America inspired home decorating styles in the United States. Asian elements influenced new trends in art like Impressionism and Art Nouveau. Ordinary consumers had more access to greater quantities and varieties of durable goods and consumables. Entrepreneurs recognized the challenges of profiting from this changing equation and created new sales and marketing techniques to appeal to an ever broader audience including, for the first time in large numbers, women. New magazines and newspapers, such as *Ladies Home Journal*, first published in 1883, featured ads for typewriters and sewing machines that showed the convergence of technology and social change.

Along with his sewing machines, Isaac Singer (1811–1875) brought to the table consumer credit, which permitted large numbers of individuals to purchase a relatively expensive and sophisticated machine without having to scrape together the entire purchase price at one time. The retail revolution was also embodied by the rise of department stores, most prominently Harrods in London, which opened with the motto *Omnia Omnibus Ubique—All Things for All People, Everywhere—* in 1849. Like other early examples—Paris's Bon Marché (opened as a department store in 1850), Macy's in New York (1858), Wanamaker's in Philadelphia (1876), Eaton's in Toronto (1869), Mexico City's El Palacio de Hierro (1891), and Moscow's GUM (1893)—Harrods offered a wide variety of consumer goods in one store, at fixed prices, with money-back guarantees and other sales and marketing innovations that turned shopping into a leisure activity, complete with live in-store entertainment. Consumers far from cities could access a wider variety of goods through new mail-order catalogues that took advantage of expanded, faster, and cheaper shipping services in much of the world. Cash registers and adding machines tracked the exchange of money.

## Industrialization and the Food Revolution

Techniques for preserving food improved. New metal cans held foods more safely and conveniently for longer periods of time. In 1870, William Lyman (1821–1891) patented the first rotating wheel can opener. Pasteurization, a process that slowed spoilage, was soon applied to brewing beer around the globe. The growing British rail network made Bass Ale popular across the nation, and in 1876 its red-triangle logo became Great Britain's first registered trademark; soon it was visible across the continent. Anheuser-Busch developed a national distribution network out of its St. Louis headquarters, advertising that its Budweiser beer would "Keep in Any Climate." Heineken, shipped from its breweries in Amsterdam and Rotterdam, became the best-selling beer in Paris. A student of French chemist Louis Pasteur (1822–1895), who developed the Pasteurization process, cultivated the yeast strain that gave Heineken beer its unique taste; and a mechanical cooling system replaced the use of ice in the company's main brewery in 1881. The breweries that today produce Dos Equis (Mexico) and Sapporo (Japan) also opened during this period.

Other inventions changed the way people ate. Barbed-wire fencing transformed the livestock industry, simultaneously reinforcing new property rights claims over the vast grazing lands of the Western Hemisphere and allowing greater control over herds and breeding. Cattle and hogs began to move from ranch to slaughter-house to butcher shop on railroads; refrigerated boxcars carried all sorts of perishable goods. Frozen meat moved by ship from Australia and New Zealand to England. Russian wheat reached Western European markets. Argentina exported beef and other food products. Processes and applications to exploit natural resources found in limited places, like rubber (footwear and tires—Brazil) and henequen (binder twine—Mexico) brought investment, infrastructure, profit, and tax revenues to new locations or in larger quantities.

Financiers who risked their capital understood that the marketplace was littered with failures like Dent and Company, the British firm that grew rich on the Chinese opium trade and collapsed just as dramatically in an 1867 Hong Kong bank run. Yet these trends were not simply individual choice, circumstance, and luck interacting on a level playing field. Elites in the United States and Europe leveraged their power to develop global political and economic structures that yielded these spectacular advances but simultaneously constrained the choices available to many individuals and groups both within their borders and around the globe. The industrial economy enabled men like Cornelius Vanderbilt (1794–1877), Leland Stanford (1824–1893), J. P. Morgan (1837–1913), Andrew Carnegie (1835–1919), Cecil Rhodes (1853–1902), John D. Rockefeller (1839–1937) and other "robber barons" to accrue enormous personal fortunes and political influence around the world. Efforts to keep an ever more integrated global economic system moving forward in a world of distinct nations posed both grand and mundane challenges, however. In the final sections of this chapter, we will explore two distinct efforts to facilitate progress: the standardization of time and the staging of international exhibitions.

## Keeping Time in a Connected World

In 1884, the International Meridian Conference convened in Washington, DC. The conference brought together delegates from forty-one countries—the European powers, the United States, many South American states, as well as Japan—to establish a system for standardizing time across the globe. Time posed vexing problems for travelers. For one thing, keeping accurate time was essential to navigation at sea. When sailing near shore, landmarks could guide the mariner; but once out of sight of land, determining position and direction became more challenging. Chinese sailors had used the magnetic compass to determine direction as early as the eleventh century, and they were in widespread use. Determining one's position and course in open sea required additional aids, however.

In theory, by cross-referencing north–south and east–west positions on the globe, one could derive a precise location at sea even without landmarks. Determining latitude (north–south position) was relatively easy using a simple sighting of the sun at its highest point during the day. Longitude—the east–west position—was harder, a lot harder. The best way was to determine the altitude of the sun, at two different points, at the exact same time of day. Charts recorded the altitude of the sun at different places on different dates, and these could be used for comparison with a traveler's present location, giving longitude. On land, this was easy: just look at a clock. At sea, however, pendulum clocks were unreliable amid the rolling and swaying of a ship at sea. This problem was not resolved until the mid-eighteenth century when Englishman John Harrison (1693–1776) invented a timepiece that could accurately keep time aboard ship.

With this problem solved, navigators could more accurately keep track of their positions at sea, but it did not solve all problems. As one moves east or west across the globe, the time of day (based, roughly, on the height of the sun in the sky) changes. When the sun is at its highest point, we call that noon and build a cycle of twenty-four hours from one noon to the next. Telling time precisely—within a few minutes or even hours—was not important in the preindustrial world. Each town tended to keep its own time, and everything in the village or city was tied to that time. When traveling to a new place, the voyage was usually slow, and upon arrival, you could determine what time it was. Pocket watches, first developed in Europe in the fifteenth century, were expensive and rare.

Industrialization changed the need to tell time in numerous ways. To begin with, factories did not function by daylight like farms had. As workers began to earn hourly wages, or demand standard work shifts, keeping track of their hours became important. But the technology that globalized transportation and communication changed the need for keeping accurate track of time across long distances as well. Train travel required different stations to agree, precisely, on the time. Telegraphs and telegrams made it possible to communicate almost instantaneously over long distances. These new modes of transportation and communication revealed the discrepancies among different cities. In 1857, for instance, when it was noon in Washington, DC, it was—officially—12:12 in New York City, 12:24 in Boston, 12:02 in Baltimore, 12:18 in Hartford, and 12:08 in Philadelphia. *Dinsmore's Railroad and Steam Navigation Guide and Route-Book* observed, "The inconvenience of such a system, if system it can be called, must be apparent to all. . . . [M]any miscalculations and misconnections have resulted, which have not unfrequently been of serious consequence." The question, of course, was how to standardize time. There are North and South magnetic poles, which serve for setting compass points, but there is no "East" or "West" pole; some single line of longitude would have to be agreed on as a standard, from which other lines could be developed to synchronize time around the world. This was the goal of the 1884 Washington Conference.

The Royal Observatory in Greenwich, England, had sponsored the prize to find a reliable and practical method for determining longitude at sea; subsequently "Greenwich time" had become the standard in the eighteenth century for the development of shipboard navigation tables and, later, British railroad timetables. The dominance of British seafaring, and the extensive British Empire, made this the likely choice for the global time standard, a choice the Washington Conference confirmed. Within a few years, most of Europe and the Americas had adopted "Greenwich Mean Time" as the standard by which to set their clocks. Soon the whole world's day was measured in a standard, universally accepted way—synchronized with reference to a small town on the River Thames.

## Keeping Up: The World's Fair

England was also the site of the first modern world's fair, held in London in 1851. Similar events soon followed in Dublin, New York, Paris, and Vienna. In 1876 alone, the year in which Philadelphia hosted a US Centennial Exhibition and world's fair, similar international exhibitions were held in French Algeria, Uruguay, and Scotland. By the early twentieth century, these international exhibits became so frequent that another diplomatic conference was called to establish a Bureau of International Exhibitions. Exploring world's fairs in some detail provides an ideal canvas for understanding the many themes raised throughout this chapter, so we will end it with an exploration of two: Philadelphia (1876) and Paris (1889).

Philadelphia's world's fair was one component of the centennial celebrations of US independence in 1876. The original plan was for one large building divided into ten departments that would represent the stages of human progress. The complex and often conflicting goals of organizers, exhibitors, politicians, and investors rendered this idea unfeasible. Ultimately, two hundred fifty individual structures rose on almost three hundred acres of land several miles west of the city's center square. Between May and November of 1876, nearly ten million people wandered the grounds.

Almost fourteen thousand exhibitors from thirty-seven countries competed for both business and recognition; there were juried prizes in twenty-eight different categories. In exhibition spaces around the fairgrounds, small and large enterprises displayed pottery, porcelain, glassware, furniture, mechanical devices, woven goods, carpets, silks, clothing, jewelry, toys, stationery, firearms, ammunition, medicine, medical equipment, hardware, tools, cutlery, vehicles, fresh and preserved food, paintings, sculpture, and other items.

## Showcasing the New Order of Nations

Inventors and companies showcased new products for the marketplace at these international exhibitions—Alexander Graham Bell's telephone caused a sensation in Philadelphia. However, the fair was not ordered exclusively for private enterprises or consumers. The global economic and technological transformation, so much in evidence to visitors, went hand in hand with depictions of an emerging new order of nations at different levels of development. The main hall was ordered "by races," with clusters of displays from "Teutonic," "Anglo-Saxon," and "Latin" exhibitors. Eleven foreign countries constructed their own buildings. The British government built several structures to display its place as the globe's dominant political and economic power. Germany, just five years after unification, had its own building on the fairgrounds. Spain, Portugal, France, and Sweden also had separate buildings, while Brazil was the only independent Western Hemisphere nation to have its own building. Liberia was one of the few African states to exhibit. In all, almost forty independent countries participated in the fair. Some, like Belgium, Greece, and Italy, in addition to Germany, reflected the important changes in European political geography in the decades after the Napoleonic Wars. Others, like the Orange Free State in southern Africa and the Sandwich Islands (Hawai'i), would soon lose their political autonomy to a new wave of imperialism.

Latin American participation—twelve countries in total—drew attention to the changes in the Western Hemisphere. As more stable central authorities began to emerge, the nascent national elites of Mexico, Venezuela, Argentina, Nicaragua, and others saw the Philadelphia fair as an opportunity to rebrand their countries as stable participants in modernity, worthy partners in trade, and serious participants in international affairs.

While dazzling with the machines that epitomized the era, from machine guns to steam engines to telephones, the fair also reflected the connection between technology and agricultural production, a vital component of modernization and globalization. Agriculture and horticulture had entire buildings as well as demonstration grounds devoted to them, to show how technology had changed and would continue to change farming practices. Tins of Danish butter and refrigerated railcars demonstrated the promise of new food preservation techniques. Some of the displays of agricultural products from around the globe would have been inconceivable a generation before. Before the transportation revolution, very few kinds of food could be delivered over long distances inexpensively and/or without spoiling. At the Centennial Exhibition, wheat, corn, and rice displays from Australia and Chile, alongside the chemicals and machines that would lower the costs of their production and raise the productivity of farmland, marked the dawn of the global grain trade.

A new political economy of tropical agricultural commodities could also be glimpsed. Bananas and pineapples were still exotic commodities for Philadelphia consumers at the time of the Centennial Exhibition, where bananas were sold by the slice, wrapped in tin foil. The Sandwich Islands (today's state of Hawai'i), on the heels of an 1875 trade agreement with the United States, exhibited canned pineapple as well as sugar. Soon emerging transportation and preservation technologies would link multiple business interests in far-flung places, bringing tons of these products to more tables in the world's temperate zones.

The market for more familiar commodities—for example, sugar and coffee—was also transformed during this era. In fact, many countries at the centennial were there to sell one or both of these items. Both independent countries, like Liberia and Mexico, as well as the tropical outposts of the European empires brought their sugar and coffee. Roasters, often European, touted the magical transformation performed on the coffee bean by their special techniques and equipment. Many countries displaying coffee at the fair became increasingly

**LIBERIA SOAP AND COFFEE DISPLAY, AGRICULTURAL HALL, PHILADELPHIA CENTENNIAL EXHIBITION, 1876.** Liberia, a West African refuge for manumitted slaves since the 1820s, created a republican constitution in 1847. Official diplomatic relations between the United States and Liberia were not established until 1862, but Liberia participated in the Centennial Exhibition in the following decade. Like many other participants in the world's fairs, Liberians hoped to introduce the advantages of their products in a highly competitive global consumer culture. The sign in the middle of the display begins with the words, "Liberia offers. . . ."

dependent on it for export revenue in the subsequent decades, riding the volatile global coffee market like a roller coaster.

## The World Comes to Paris

In 1889, Paris hosted its own world's fair to coincide with another centennial, that of the French Revolution. One might have been forgiven for feeling as if time itself had accelerated since Philadelphia's US centennial exhibition little more than a decade earlier. Sixteen-thousand machines filled the Gallery of Machines in Paris, housed in the world's largest iron-framed building. The French reserved three-quarters of the exhibition space in the building for their own products, a reminder of the nationalist motivations driving counties to host these expensive undertakings. Visitors to Paris could see for themselves the first automobile using an internal combustion engine—the Benz *Motorwagen* patented in 1886—and also see the first public display of Thomas Edison's motion pictures. The fair's modern aesthetic did not please everyone, however. A group of artists and writers ridiculed the Eiffel Tower as "a gigantic black smokestack," but the majority's enthusiastic embrace of the ambitious iron structure drowned out the naysayers. Originally designed to stand for two decades, the tower remained the tallest structure in the world until it was surpassed by New York's Chrysler Building in 1930.

The notions of progress on view in Paris reveal as much (or more) about the values of the organizers and promoters of the fair as do the machinery and consumer goods. Fair-goers could observe the "natural" habits of "primitive" peoples at a "human zoo," as well as a "Palace of the Colonies," where they could see how less developed places on earth were learning how to be modern (or clinging to their "backward" ways). "Living" displays from Europe's new colonies brought the empire to Paris. A man from Senegal—one of France's African colonies—tended cows, sheep, and goats while crowds watched. The Dutch brought sixty men and women from Java to build a village. The villagers, who also performed (by living their lives!) at other international exhibitions, stayed on the fairgrounds for the duration of the exhibition. A small group of them staged a Javanese opera at regular intervals.

## Conclusion

Over the course of the nineteenth century, material conditions and a series of individual and collective decisions led elites in industrializing countries to surrender some of their wealth and power to maintain order. In turn, most members of the working classes chose reform over revolution. A slow, incremental expansion of suffrage occurred in most of these countries, accompanied by social rights legislation as well. Industrial production provided an ever-expanding cornucopia of goods to be enjoyed by the world's consumers. This was the world of progress on display at the world's fairs in Paris and Philadelphia, idealized versions of a well-ordered global marketplace of abundant, innovative goods and positive change over time.

Yet these displays were distorted snapshots. Some participating countries and groups were navigating the challenges of industrialization and globalization to emerge with more political, economic, and military power. Others were being undone by the challenges and swept away by change. Careful observers of this era made note of the high costs of "order and progress" to some peoples and in some places. It is to these concerns that we turn our attention in Chapter 9.

## TIMELINE

**1831**
Giuseppe Mazzini founds Young Italy

**1833**
British Parliament votes to abolish slavery in the British Empire

**1840**
World Antislavery Conference

**1848**
Seneca Falls Convention; publication of *Manifesto of the Communist Party* (Marx and Engels); revolutions throughout Europe

**1851**
First modern world's fair, London

**1857**
"Sepoy Mutiny": rebellion against British rule in India

**1832**
Reform Act doubles the number of eligible voters in Britain

**1839**
Tanzimat reforms begin in Ottoman Empire

**1846**
First coolies imported into Cuba

**1849**
California gold rush begins

**1853**
Matthew Perry leads US Naval mission to Japan

# A Few Good Books

Jean H. Baker. *Sisters: The Lives of America's Suffragists*. New York: Hill and Wang, 2006.

Christopher Benfey. *The Great Wave: Gilded Age Misfits, Japanese Eccentrics, and the Opening of Old Japan*. New York: Random House, 2004.

Seymour Drescher. *Abolition: A History of Slavery and Antislavery*. Cambridge, England: Cambridge University Press, 2009.

Joanne S. Liu. *Barbed Wire: The Fence that Changed the West*. Missoula, MT: Mountain Press Publishing, 2009.

Dava Sobel. *Longitude: The True Story of a Lone Genius Who Solved the Greatest Scientific Problem of His Time*. New York: Walker and Company, 2007.

Mike Rapport. *1848: Year of Revolution*. New York: Basic Books, 2004.

Robert W. Rydell. *All the World's a Fair: Visions of Empire at American International Expositions, 1876–1916*. Chicago: University of Chicago Press, 1987.

*For additional resources, including maps, primary sources, visuals, web links, and quizzes, please go to* **www.oup.com/us/carter**

| 1861 | 1869 | 1876 | 1877 | 1889 |
|------|------|------|------|------|
| Serfdom abolished in Russia | Suez Canal opens; transcontinental railroad completed in the United States | Bass Ale obtains Britain's first registered trademark | Opening of Tokyo University, Asia's first Western-style university | Paris world's fair |

| 1868 | 1871 | 1876–1910 | 1888–1889 | 1896 |
|------|------|-----------|-----------|------|
| Meiji government established in Japan | Unifications of Italy and Germany | *Científicos* influential in Mexico | Brazil abolishes slavery; monarchy falls the following year | *Plessy v. Ferguson* establishes principle of "separate but equal" in the United States |

(TOP) EDITORIAL CARTOON DEPICTING THE "SCRAMBLE FOR AFRICA" INAUGURATED AT THE BERLIN CONFERENCE (1884). The "New Imperialism" of the late nineteenth century saw Europe and the United States gain control over 80 percent of the earth's surface. The competition among European states for the resources of Africa is depicted in this cartoon, which shows the manner in which European nations like Germany (here represented by Bismarck, holding the knife) felt it their privilege to distribute African territory as they pleased.

(RIGHT) THE AMAZON THEATER, MANAUS, BRAZIL. Industrial commodities and global markets could bring sudden wealth to producers. In the late nineteenth century, a boom in rubber prices made Manaus, Brazil, deep in the Amazon rain forest, the richest city in South America for a time. To showcase its wealth, the city built a grand opera house—the Amazon Theater—with materials imported from France, Scotland, and Italy. The building was one of the first in the world to have electric lighting; but when the rubber market collapsed, the city's generators were too expensive to operate, and Manaus lost its electric lights for several decades.

# Globalization and Its Discontents

## 1878–1910

Two late nineteenth-century meetings in Berlin illustrate the ambitions of European powers to redraw the map of the world. That they were in Berlin showed the importance of Europe's newest power. Germany's capital had grown from four hundred thousand people in 1849 to nearly a million by the end of the 1870s, and its population would double again by 1900. In the first meeting (called the Congress of Berlin), in 1878, German Chancellor Otto von Bismarck (1815–1898) hosted diplomats from across Western Eurasia to sort out the aftermath of a war between the Russian and Ottoman Empires and redraw the map of Southeastern Europe. The results angered many participants. The Ottoman Empire lost territory in its western regions; Russian leaders were frustrated that victory on the battle-field did not translate into even greater territorial gains. Representatives of smaller states felt that the outcome privileged power over principle, and served neither the interests of their people nor those of long-term international stability.

In the mid-1880s, diplomats returned to Schulenburg Palace for another meet-ing, referred to now as the Berlin Conference, to redraw a different set of borders. This time, the great powers of Europe met to allocate "spheres of influence," for-malizing and giving order to the wave of European imperialism that was sweeping over Africa. Over the next three decades, the European states acted on these claims and attempted to exercise sovereignty over much of Africa.

In the same era, Brazilian elites focused on the tropical interior of their own country. Symbolizing their membership in the club of modern peoples, for three decades wealthy Brazilians had been lavishing the city of Manaus, the "Rubber Cap-ital," with the latest civic luxuries. Nine hundred miles up the Amazon River, Manaus rose to dizzying heights on income from the sap of the *hevea braziliensis* tree, the source of much of the world's rubber. A new industrial process that made rubber easier to shape, stronger, and more durable drove demand. Manaus, a city of

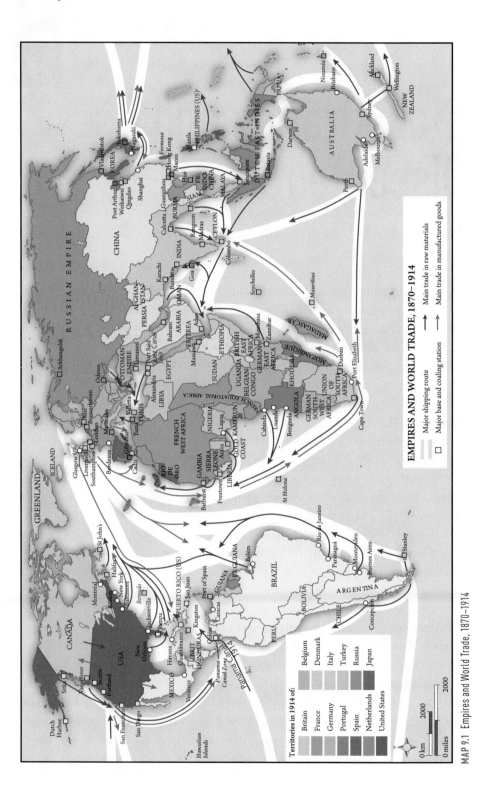

**MAP 9.1** Empires and World Trade, 1870–1914

several thousand people in the 1870s, opened its first bank only in the late 1880s but had one of the first electric trolley systems in Latin America a decade later. In 1897, the lavish Amazonas Theater—a multimillion dollar opera house designed by an Italian architect and built with materials imported from Italy, England, and France—opened its doors. The population of Manaus reached 100,000 as the price of rubber in international markets tripled between 1908 and 1910, when prices peaked.

Then, demand for Brazilian rubber stagnated and the price plummeted, as European firms, supported by their governments' imperialist practices, developed rubber plantations in British Ceylon (Sri Lanka), French Indochina (Vietnam), the Belgian Congo, and elsewhere. With their own colonies producing rubber, the Europeans no longer needed to buy from Brazil. Brazilian rubber production fell between 1910 and 1920, while global production increased by almost six hundred percent during the same period. The Amazonas Theater closed its doors and Manaus lost its luster, but life could not simply return to how it was before the rubber boom. The environment had changed. Patterns of production and distribution had changed. Relations between the wealthy and the poor had changed, and all were left struggling to adjust to the difficult political, economic, and social realities of the new century.

---

In this chapter, we analyze global political and economic interactions in the last decades of the nineteenth century and the first decade of the twentieth. We begin by defining the New Imperialism, as the Great Powers of Europe claimed vast territory in Africa and Asia as well as the right to set the terms by which the international political and economic order would be organized. We then examine some countercurrents that challenged the claims made by the architects of the new global order. Some states in Africa and Asia maintained territorial sovereignty during this era, and movements in both colonies and imperial centers rejected the principles of political and economic organization by which a handful of European states, along with the United States of America, dominated the globe. In the chapter's last section, we turn to the Western Hemisphere, exploring the environmental impact of a changing political economy and integrating the Latin American republics' experience of neocolonialism into our narrative.

## Redrawing the Map of the World

Radiating out from the two Berlin meetings, the New Imperialism cast a shadow across the globe over the ensuing decades. The Congress of Berlin (1878) remapped the Balkans—a religious, cultural, and political crossroads coveted by the Austro-Hungarian, Russian, and Ottoman Empires but whose residents were energized by the nationalist fervor and rhetoric of self-determination of the nineteenth century. As delegates in Berlin confirmed the independence of Serbia and Montenegro, the great powers determined the size and borders of these new states while denying sovereignty to other territories in the region—Bosnia, Herzegovina, and Bulgaria all remained parts of empires for the time being.

Although the congress focused on Europe and its immediate borders, the treaties that emerged from this meeting reveal ongoing concerns about the balance of power, which played out in ever more intense fashion on a global stage. The British Parliament declared Queen Victoria "Empress" in 1876, as the government took formal control of India away from the East India Company. Soon thereafter, troops moved into the Malay Peninsula and Burma. Russia continued to expand in Central and East Asia, facilitated by an ambitious railroad construction program. France went to war with China in the 1880s to gain territory in Southeast Asia.

Great power rivalries were even more plain to see in Africa, where events such as the completion of the Suez Canal and the discovery of diamonds in South Africa sparked further interest in controlling the region's resources. This strategic competition led to conflicting claims from France, Portugal, Britain, and Belgium in the Congo Basin, motivating the second Berlin Conference (1884). Bismarck noted his primary motivation for redrawing maps was Germany's place in European affairs, saying "My map of Africa lies in Europe. Here is Russia, and here . . . is France, and we're in the middle. That's my map of Africa."

The diplomats in Berlin defused the Congo crisis by sorting out the claims of European states in the territory, without regard to the indigenous populations. This outcome established the precedent by which European states had to physically enact claims on African territories to have other European states recognize their claims. With this understanding, Europeans accelerated the "scramble for Africa" using their existing settlements as launch pads to push their claims ever further. By 1910, European empires had transformed Africa into a quilt with patches named for European states stitched onto African territorial distinctions and compass directions—German East Africa, French West Africa, Anglo-Egyptian Sudan, Spanish Guinea, Italian Somaliland, the Belgian Congo, and on and on.

## Explaining the New Imperialism

We have defined and analyzed empires and imperialism repeatedly in this book, so what is "new" about the New Imperialism? Imperialism in this era, driven and facilitated by industrialization, was more extensive and intensive than the imperial dynamics we have described in earlier chapters. By *extensive*, we mean simply that imperial powers claimed more territory than ever before. Between 1878 and 1914, European empires claimed an additional 8.6 million square miles of territory (more than twice the entire area of Europe). At the height of the New Imperialism, Europe and the United States claimed more than 80 percent of the earth's land surface. In contrast, at the height of eighteenth-century imperialism, about 50 percent of the world—mostly in the Americas—was claimed by Europeans.

The New Imperialism was also more *intensive* than earlier imperial enterprises. Even the strongest or largest empires of the preindustrial world, by design or necessity, tolerated great variation in political and economic customs and practices. In the nineteenth century, imperialism attempted to penetrate more deeply into local society to enforce decisions made in the imperial center. This reflected the ideals of "order and progress" described in Chapter 8 in which hierarchical, professional bureaucracies were seen as the way to administer modern states, and the task of governments included improving people's behavior and economic practices. So, for example, imperial governments would rewrite property laws or ban certain cultural practices of an indigenous population in the territories they seized. Although these actions might sound familiar, during the age of the New Imperialism, improved technologies and logistics made these practices much more effective. New weapons, communications infrastructure, and transportation systems (including steam-powered navies and merchant ships) contributed to both the expansion and intensification of empire.

As we have seen, economic motivations have always been important to empire-building, but the New Imperialism more completely integrated colonies into an industrial network of extraction, manufacture, and distribution. By limiting how newly colonized regions could participate in the global economy, New Imperialist policies contributed to disparities in the distribution of the benefits of globalization. The colonized could neither autonomously develop their own internal economies nor participate freely in a global market as producers or consumers.

Debates have raged about the foundational and operational logics of the New Imperialism. Some historians maintain that outcomes during this era primarily resulted from colonizing powers and their social elites pursuing resources to further industrialize and maintain profit margins in the global economy while providing some surplus to industrial workers in the metropolis. Others argue that domestic political agendas drove imperialism, as European governments distracted or diverted potentially disruptive political movements or defeated their rivals by fueling nationalistic fervor for colonies and conquest. Another set of explanations sees the acquisition of colonies as an attempt to secure strategic positions—ports for trade and fueling stations for navies—as part of the geostrategic calculations of rival states in the nineteenth century. In this view, political changes in Europe, such as Germany's unification, drove the New Imperialism in the last quarter of the nineteenth century. Viewed in this light, European imperialism was primarily another venue for competition among European states.

These explanations tend to focus on imperial centers—Paris, London, Berlin, etc.—to understand the logic of the New Imperialism. Other historians focus on actions and ideas in the colonies themselves. Local agents of commercial enterprises, even diplomats, sometimes acted without the authorization or consent of superiors back home. In other cases, those seeking power, fortune, or glory acted to promote their personal goals rather than some preconceived imperial agenda. And it's also essential to consider the actions of African and Asian peoples. Some allied with European political and economic elites, but other individuals and groups turned to alternative forms of solidarity and power to resist imperialism. As we will see, understanding this era requires us to think about how a wide variety of historical actors—among them the advisers to emperors, civil servants in small colonial towns, and indigenous leaders—made choices and pursued interests in very different circumstances.

## Imperialism as Nature, Moral Uplift, or Oppression?

During the last decades of the nineteenth century, the growing control of European states and economies over the world's resources ignited debate about its logic and righteousness. To explain (and justify) this changing order, many political and cultural leaders, as well as ordinary people, latched onto ideas that can generally be called Social Darwinism, although these ideas often had very little to do with the actual theories of the British scientist Charles Darwin (1809–1882). For Darwin, the "survival of the fittest" did not refer to groups engaged in combat with each other for resources, with the winners demonstrating that they were most fit to control their environment. The Darwinian theory of evolution rested on the idea of natural selection at the level of individual organisms. In struggling to survive, animals cannot change fundamental features about themselves, for example, where their eyes or wings are located on their bodies. Rather, variations arising from random genetic mutation make some individuals better suited to a particular environment or task, so they are more likely to survive and reproduce, and pass on these characteristics to the next generation. Changes to the environment—climate, the arrival of new organisms—could undo those advantages, and variations that other individuals have might then prove more suited to survival. That is the motor of evolution. The finches of the Galapagos Islands that inspired Darwin certainly did not control the small variations on their beaks, yet those variations were the key to individual survival. Fitting a particular environmental niche led to the proliferation of birds with a particular adaptation.

Social Darwinism distorted this idea and applied it to conflicts and outcomes among entire human societies, insisting that the growing military and economic power of some states proved that they were the fittest, winners in a competition to dominate their rivals for the globe's space and resources. The European exploitation of Africa and Asia, particularly, was taken to be both proof of the superiority of European peoples and societies and justification for their actions. Social Darwinists expected the populations of "less fit" societies to decline over time and saw this as a necessary and appropriate result of natural processes.

A contrasting view of the New Imperialism presented it as the exercise of a moral duty to improve the lives of those not fortunate enough to be born in a place where "Western Civilization" had taken root. From this perspective, colonial institutions sought to transform and improve these parts of the world by imposing what were claimed to be Western values and methods. Alongside (or even within) rubber plantations, French colonizers in Indochina built schools to teach Catholicism, European history, and the French language. Vietnamese children learned from books that began "Nos ancêtres, les Gaulois" ("Our Ancestors, the Gauls") even though the students were born to Vietnamese parents and would likely spend their entire lives in Indochina. Advocates of this *mission civilisatrice* ("civilizing mission") brushed aside absurdities like this to emphasize the improvements—schools, hospitals, sewers, new ideas—that colonizers brought.

Rudyard Kipling (1865–1936) captured this sense of the costs and moral obligations borne by colonizers in his poem, "The White Man's Burden." One of the most popular writers in the English language in the late nineteenth century, Kipling portrayed imperialism as a difficult, thankless, but necessary job that included building "Ports ye shall not enter/Roads ye shall not tread" and waging "savage wars of peace" to end famine and sickness in the colonies. However well-meaning this may have been, Kipling's vision of a "White Man's Burden" was both racist and paternalist. The poem described the typical native of a colony as a "sullen" "half-devil and half-child" who preferred the ignorance of slavery to the responsibility that came from freedom. Only with the guidance of "civilized" (white) men could these societies hope to achieve maturity.

In Kipling's view, this duty had been shouldered by Europeans up to this point, but Kipling's poem also highlights another development of this period. Published in 1899, the poem bore the subtitle "The United States and the Philippine Islands," and suggested that the United States, which took control of the Philippines, Puerto Rico, and Cuba after a war with Spain, could now join the company of mature states if it would "Take up the White Man's burden" by exercising its imperialist obligations and "Have done with childish days." In a biting retort, the African American author and clergyman H. T. Johnson wrote *The Black Man's Burden* (1899), denouncing imperialism as a solution to the "problem" of the world's "red," "black," and "brown" peoples: "In vain ye seek to end it, with bullets, blood or death."

Debates over the causes and consequences of the New Imperialism occurred in the colonies themselves as well. Some admired the achievements of the imperial powers and welcomed the opportunities for development that were presented during this era. Sayyid Ahmad Khan (1817–1898), one of the foremost Muslim leaders of his day in India, declared boldly, "The British rule in India is the most wonderful phenomenon the world has seen." Writing on the eve of the Berlin Congress, Khan celebrated European institutions and sought to educate and elevate Indians through them, establishing a college for Indian Muslims who lacked access to British universities. Jamal al-Din al-Afghani (1838–1897), another Indian Muslim, could not have disagreed more strongly. While Khan created a Muslim college along British lines, Afghani saw Britain and other European states as plunderers: "Islamic states today are unfortunately pillaged and their property stolen; their territory is occupied by foreigners and their wealth is in the possession of others." Afghani, who spent time in Afghanistan, Iran, India, Egypt, Turkey, Germany, France, England, and Russia, attempted to bridge the ethnic and religious differences among Muslims and build a unified Islamic response to European expansionism.

## The Imperial Balance Sheet

The argument between Afghani and Khan captures the stark differences of opinion on the New Imperialism. Some viewed it as an actual, or at least potential, positive development. Others saw it as an unspeakable evil. Some, like Dadabhai Naoroji (1825–1917), tried to measure with some dispassion its costs and benefits. In his writings, and speeches as the first South Asian—and more generally, the first Asian—member of the British Parliament, Naoroji expressed his admiration of "English education, with its great, noble, elevating, and civilising literature and advanced science." He credited Britain with bringing "law and order" to India and introducing values like a free press, all of which made "a claim to gratitude upon the Indian people." But even in the praise he offered, there was a lament. Naoroji combined economic data, government documents, and personal observation to conclude that India provided enormous direct and indirect subsidies to England from profits and taxes and through the use of Indians to enforce British imperial rule around the world. Naoroji objected to British rule of India because it was "un-British"; he did not call for Indian independence but rather "true British citizenry" for its people. This view, which remained robust among many colonial leaders well into the twentieth century, held that European colonialism could be beneficial, but only if imperial rule included democracy, equality, and the rule of law.

**WOMEN CAPTIVES WITH GUARD, BELGIAN CONGO.** This early twentieth-century photograph, by Alice Seeley Harris, was used by the Congo Reform Association in its campaign against abuses of indigenous peoples in the Belgian Congo. Association records tell us that these two women were taken hostage because their husbands fled to the forest to escape the labor demands of the Anglo-Belgian Indian Rubber Company.

Nowhere can the gap between the rhetoric of European altruism and the reality of colonial exploitation be seen more clearly than in the Congo basin, the region that prompted the Berlin meetings of the mid-1880s. The conference delegates created an entity called the Congo Free State, an area of West-Central Africa as large as the United States east of the Mississippi River. The region was labeled "free" both because the European powers agreed to allow each other unrestrained travel through the region's river systems and also because they agreed to eliminate the international slave trade. In neither sense did the name fit.

The Belgian King Leopold II ruled the Congo Free State as a colony. King Leopold claimed that his goal was to promote trade and eliminate slavery once and for all. In correspondence with the former enslaved African American, George Washington Williams (1849–1891) in 1890, Leopold emphasized his efforts in the Congo as "a Christian duty to the poor African," for which he did "not wish to see one franc back." Williams was impressed at first, finding Leopold to be "one of the noblest sovereigns in the world … ruling in wisdom, mercy, and justice." Williams went to the Congo that year, evaluating the new colony as a

place where African Americans might seek relief from the legal and social oppression of the post-Reconstruction US South. What Williams found was not
Christian charity but what he called "crimes against humanity," employing perhaps for the first time a phrase that would be used, sadly, with great frequency
in the next century.

Edmund Morel (1873–1924), a clerk at a Liverpool shipping company, came to
conclusions similar to those of Williams. Forced from his job for calling out Belgian
abuses, Morel published numerous books and newspaper articles on the
Congo, became a leader of the Congo Reform Association in 1904, and travelled across Europe and the United States speaking out on the situation. His
slide show of imperialist atrocities presented shocking images that are often
used as primary sources to communicate what was done to African peoples
during this era. But, as scholars like Kevin Grant and Nancy Rose Hunt demonstrate, the contexts within which the photographs were captured, and the
ends to which they were used, provide us with a deeper, more nuanced understanding of this history, one that demands that we consider the burdens of
women as well as men.

The Baptist missionary Alice Seeley Harris (1870–1970), an influential activist in her own right who spoke at hundreds of public meetings on both sides of
the Atlantic Ocean, took the photographs that Morel used. Seeley's photographs,
taken with one of the world's first portable cameras, were used around the
world as damning evidence of Leopold's atrocities. These images shaped the
understanding—both in the Congo and outside of it—of Leopold's Congo
"rubber regime"; but Hunt and Grant remind us that using the photos runs the
risk of reducing real people's lives to two-dimensional artifacts, adding still
another indignity to what happened.

Importantly, other sources help us understand the people of the Congo as
historical actors rather than as photographic objects. Congolese men and
women gave more than two hundred fifty statements to a Belgian Commission of Inquiry in 1905–06. In addition, journalists, missionaries, and diplomats conducted extensive interviews, leading to a report on the Congo to the
British government in 1904. In the mid-twentieth century, an oral history
project collected more stories from the era's survivors. The detail, nuance,
and range of human experience and emotion conveyed in these testimonies
remind us of the power of primary sources. Boali, a Congolese woman who
was among Harris's photographic subjects, testified about her experiences on
a Belgian rubber plantation. One day, Boali resisted the sexual advances of a
plantation sentry (the guards were used to keep workers and their families *in*
the work camps rather than trespassers *out*). As Boali reports, the furious

guard, named Ikelonda, "fired a gun shot at me. . . . I fell on my back; Ikelonda thought I was dead, and to get hold of the brass bracelet that I wore at the base of my right leg, he cut off my right foot." The weight of evidence suggests that murder, starvation, amputation, and rape at the service of extracting African wealth for European benefit were commonplace.[1]

## Questioning Empire

In earlier chapters, we noted the relationship between sovereignty claims and the means to support those claims in understanding what states are and how they relate to each other and the people over whom they claim sovereignty. During this era, a wide variety of groups challenged the imperial claims of the Western powers. In some cases, resistance to those claims came from African and Asian sovereigns who used the tools of modern state-making themselves. In other cases, individuals and groups rejected the premises of modern state-making entirely.

### The Struggle to Maintain Sovereignty in Asia and Africa

For rulers in Asia and Africa, one of the keys to maintaining sovereign control of territory during this era was the ability to back up claims to rule with both skillful negotiation and military force. In Southeast Asia, successive rulers of Siam (Thailand) balanced their kingdom between the ambitions of France and Britain, conceding some territory and access to resources in return for the recognition of sovereignty. These rulers also adopted new fiscal policies, built railroads and telegraph networks, reformed the education system, negotiated commercial contracts with European investors, and transformed the military.

As in Siam, the Ethiopian ruler Menelik II (1844–1913), who ruled from 1889 to 1913, presided over political and economic reforms that reinforced his sovereignty and the efficacy of the state over an expanding territory, introducing new postal, telecommunications, banking, and electrical systems. He also made shrewd diplomatic maneuvers, building his empire through a strategic marriage and strengthening his relationship with Russia to counterbalance the ambitions of other European powers in the Horn of Africa. It was, however, his military victory against Italy in the mid-1890s, achieved with both nonconventional military

---

[1] Kevin Grant, "Christian Critics of Empire: Missionaries, Lantern Lectures, and the Congo Reform Campaign in Britain," *The Journal of Imperial and Commonwealth History* 29, no. 2 (2001): 27–58; Nancy Rose Hunt, "An Acoustic Register, Tenacious Images, and Congolese Scenes of Rape and Ruination," *Cultural Anthropology* 23, no. 2 (2008): 220–253. Boali's testimony is quoted on page 225.

**BATTLE OF ADWA.** On March 1, 1896, an Ethiopian army under Emperor Menelik II defeated invading Italian armies attempting to expand their empire in the region. By defeating the Europeans, Menelik consolidated his own power in Ethiopia and also fueled a variety of interpretations of the event. The Ethiopian victory was an important symbol of Africans' ability to resist and defeat invading armies. Some Europeans, however, dismissed the battle's importance by questioning Italian military skills or by arguing that Ethiopians were not "black."

tactics (guerrilla warfare) and superior artillery, that proved to be the key event in preserving Ethiopia's independence.

In both of these cases, indigenous claimants to sovereignty used changing international rivalries to defeat their local opponents; but this was a dangerous game that often backfired, as one sees in many other cases. For example, the competition between Nama and Herero peoples in what is today Namibia led the Nama leader Hendrik Witbooi (ca. 1830–1905) to form an alliance with Germany. Witbooi subsequently altered his position as German ambitions to control the entire region became clear to him. Witbooi died alongside his former Herero enemies in armed resistance to further German expansion.

## Comparing Japan and China

The cases of Japan and China further illustrate the complexities of maintaining sovereignty in the era of the New Imperialism. We saw in Chapter 8 Japanese debates over the appropriate response to Western expansion. An 1885 newspaper editorial titled "Goodbye Asia" urged Japan to emulate Western institutions and embrace Western technologies. Published anonymously, but subsequently attributed to author, entrepreneur, and journalist Fukuzawa Yukichi (1835–1901), "Goodbye Asia" argued that Japan's future hinged on its willingness to "leave the ranks of Asian nations and cast our lot with civilized nations of the West." The keys to Western success lay not only in its technology but also in its values, which he contrasted favorably to Japan's neighbors China, Korea, and Vietnam, described as weak. This was not the only view in Japan, of course. Diverse agendas and priorities competed, ranging from the ultratraditional to the completely new—some in Japan even advocated making English the new national language! In the end, Japanese elites undertook aggressive modernization, including the import and development of Western technologies, institutions, and structures. An industrial economy, linked to global markets, rapidly transformed society.

Debate among China's elites about the path forward in many ways mirrored the dispute between Sayyid Ahmad Khan and Jamal al Din al-Afghani. Were Western powers models to be emulated or predators that needed to be opposed? The Qing Dynasty's leaders decided on a program of "self-strengthening," a compromise solution embodied in the concept of *ti-yong*, a formulation adapted from ancient texts that called for embracing Western practical ideas (*yong*) while maintaining traditional Chinese values as the foundation for society (*ti*). This principle guided the Qing Dynasty's investment in modern military hardware and economic infrastructure.

Foreign aggression and internal rebellions continued to threaten the imperial government as the nineteenth century entered its last decades. The French invaded and occupied Indochina in the mid-1880s. Russia claimed territory in the north, pushing a railway across Manchuria. Germany claimed the city of Qingdao and its environs in the early 1890s (quickly planting hops and building a brewery that still produces Tsingtao beer). Many nations expanded the scope of their activities in ports like Shanghai, Tianjin, and Canton, where they were exempt from Chinese laws. Japan's Meiji government then joined the wave of New Imperialists searching for international prestige, strategic advantage, and economic resources at China's expense.

Japan's overseas expansion began first in Korea, just one hundred fifty miles across the Straits of Tsushima, which offered many of the resources and advantages that Japan sought in an empire. At first Japan competed for influence in the Korean royal court with China, as the Qing Dynasty still considered Korea a tributary state of its own empire. Political jostling broke into armed conflict between Chinese and Japanese forces. In September of 1894, armies of the two empires met at Pyongyang where Japan scored a decisive victory. The next day, Chinese and Japanese warships met at the mouth of the Yalu River, the border between China and Korea. The Chinese fleet was larger, with larger guns; and its two battleships—*Dingyuan* and *Zhenyuan*, both built in Germany—appeared more formidable than anything the Empire of Japan could put in the water.

The first barrages from the Chinese battleships had almost no effect—a combination of defective artillery shells and poor targeting—while Admiral Ito's first volley destroyed the flying deck of the Chinese flagship and gravely injured the

Chinese admiral. By the time the battle ended, nearly nine hundred Chinese sailors were dead, and five ships had been sunk. Another five hundred Chinese were injured. The Japanese suffered nearly three hundred killed and two hundred wounded, along with two vessels lost. The Sino-Japanese War ended just seven months later in a decisive Japanese victory.

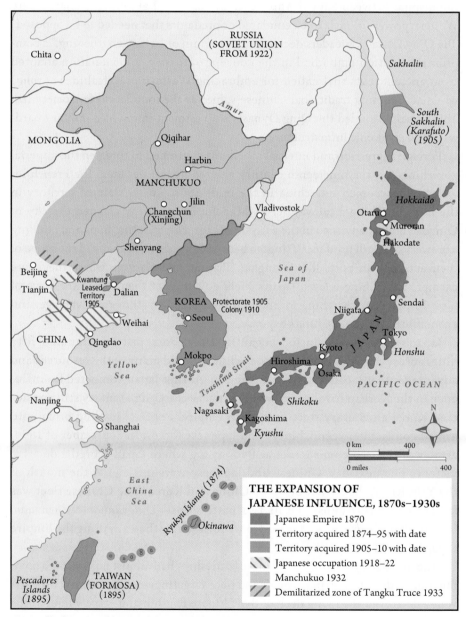

**MAP 9.2** The Expansion of Japanese Influence, 1870s–1930s

Explanations of the war's outcome often hinged on perceptions of the different Chinese and Japanese responses to modernity. Many observers at the time, and scholars for decades after, attributed the result to Japan's technological advantage, a result of its superior ability to modernize generally, and to China's failure to industrialize.[2] This explanation still dominates many popular references that characterize the war as a mismatch between modern Japan and tradition-bound China. Certainly, the outcome of the war illustrates that Japan was the superior military power, but recent scholarship challenges this interpretation of what made Japan superior. Benjamin Elman has argued that, overall, the failure of China to modernize its military technology and infrastructure has been exaggerated and that the Qing defeat owed less to a failure of science and technology than to political infighting that left the Chinese unable to respond effectively to Japan's attacks. Corruption and inefficiency were much greater problems than a lack of technological sophistication. Even where Chinese technology was clearly at fault—for instance, artillery shells that failed to explode when fired—Elman sees explanations in the political corruption that diverted funds from munitions and not from Chinese inability to build effective armaments. S. C. M. Paine has written carefully of the war itself, demonstrating the importance of training, logistics, and tactical decisions by leaders, rather than simply the number and type of ships and bullets, in determining outcomes. A recent reassessment of the war by Chinese military leaders draws similar conclusions, emphasizing failures of strategy, planning, and organization as keys to the Qing defeat. Paine also notes that this war, like all wars, was also about the decisions leaders of both states were making to manage not only their long-term position in the international order but also within their own countries. For both Paine and Elman, the narrative of China's failed modernization that emerged out of the war was perhaps the most important outcome of the war itself.[3]

Complex interactions, rather than a single overarching factor, produced the war's outcomes, which transformed East Asian geopolitics. China was vulnerable to further destabilization, as outside powers followed Japan's lead with even greater territorial aggression against China. Japan emerged as an imperial power, annexing Taiwan, formerly a Chinese province, as a colony in 1895. Korean

---

[2]  For example, the scholar Han Quansheng wrote several articles on the failure of Chinese industrialization during this time period, including "Qingmo Hanyang tiechang [The Late-Qing Hanyang Iron Works]," *shehui xuecong lunwen* 1 (1950): 1–33.

[3]  The narrative of failure is best described in Benjamin A. Elman, "Naval Warfare and the Refraction of China's Self-Strengthening Reforms into Scientific and Technological Failure, 1865–1895," *Modern Asian Studies* 38, no. 2 (May, 2004): 283–326. More general assessment of the war can be found in Benjamin Elman, *On Their Own Terms: Science in China, 1550–1900* (Cambridge, MA: Harvard University Press, 2005) and *A Cultural History of Modern Science in China* (Cambridge, MA: Harvard University Press, 2009); and S. C. M. Paine, *The Sino-Japanese War of 1894–1895: Perceptions, Power and Primacy* (New York: Cambridge University Press, 2002).

"independence" from China was just a brief euphemism, as Korea became a formal Japanese colony in 1910.

In the aftermath of defeat by Japan, Chinese leaders took bolder steps toward reform in the summer of 1898. The Guangxu Emperor (1871–1908) himself was among a group that enacted reforms drastically revising China's government, civil service, and educational system. The so-called Hundred Days' Reforms were without doubt a response to foreign encroachment but did not reject Chinese models wholesale. The scholar Kang Youwei (1858–1927) titled one of his works *Confucius as a Reformer*, recasting the ancient Chinese philosopher himself as one who could imagine changes of the scope being attempted at this time. In their efforts on so many fronts simultaneously, the movement's leaders misjudged others in the imperial government, even some who had supported the idea of self-strengthening. After 103 days, the Emperor's Aunt, Cixi (1835–1908), who had played an important role in China's government for decades, imprisoned her nephew and asserted her own control over the Qing court. Cixi ended the reform program—the reformers fled into exile—and reestablished the authority of Qing officials who had opposed reform.

## The Boxer Uprising

Intrigue over reform at the highest levels of the Chinese government occurred at the same time that a xenophobic, mystical movement that abhorred

**WOODBLOCK PRINT OF NAVAL BATTLE DURING SINO-JAPANESE WAR.** A traditional medium in Japanese art, woodblock prints like these conveyed the rapid modernization of the Japanese military. Scenes of the Sino-Japanese War (1894–95) encouraged patriotism and support of the war effort by illustrating the successes of "modern" Japan against "backward" China, but inspection of the scene reveals that both sides in the war attempted to muster the most modern military techologies available.

all things Western was percolating up from the peasantry. For many rural Chinese at the turn of the twentieth century, Western power was nothing to admire or imitate; it was to be feared and destroyed. The Boxer Uprising (1899–1901) emerged in poor, rural northeast China, where the new trade regime enforced by foreigners had wrecked local economies. In Shandong province, imports of foreign cotton (mostly on British ships from India) had undermined the local market, dropping the price farmers could earn from their crops below subsistence levels. Many farmers turned to growing opium poppies, which could be sold for cash. With less land given over to growing food, poor harvests produced devastating famine.

The Boxers claimed to channel the spirits of Chinese cultural heroes and deceased ancestors, practicing traditional Chinese martial arts rituals—called "Boxing" by foreign observers—that they claimed would resist foreigners' weapons, making them bulletproof or invisible. Economically dislocated and socially marginalized, tens of thousands of young Chinese joined the movement aimed at ridding China of Western influences. Boxers targeted, persecuted, and killed Christian missionaries and—especially—Chinese Christians and then besieged the Beijing neighborhood where most foreign legations were located, with many casualties on all sides. An expeditionary force of American, British, French, German, Japanese, Austrian, Russian, and Italian soldiers relieved the diplomats and civilians within the quarter. The Empress Dowager, who had announced the dynasty's support for the Boxers, fled but later returned and continued to rule, largely because external powers again preferred that a Qing figurehead remain in place rather than renegotiate existing treaties and relationships—with China and with each other—if the Qing regime were to be ousted. Loss of territory, coupled with unfavorable foreign concessions, demonstrated that although the Chinese imperial court had avoided a complete loss of sovereignty, it was still irreparably damaged by the New Imperialism.

## Rejecting the Modern State in North America and Africa

The Boxers were not alone in thinking that a radical indigenous cultural revival might counteract Western expansionism. In other parts of the world, where pressure from outside aggressors was unraveling indigenous economic, political, and cultural life, resistance movements emerged. Whereas expansionists believed in the magic of modernization—endless progress through industry and empire—the Maji-Maji rebels of East Africa and Ghost Dancers of Western North America countered this with their own magic formula: community solidarity and ritual held the promise for autonomous survival.

In the late 1880s, a Native American named Wovoka (also known as Jack Wilson, ca. 1856–1932) began practicing a ritual called the Ghost Dance, which called on the ancestors of the native people for assistance. After the US Civil War, the US Government turned its military attention to the indigenous peoples who still blocked the movement of goods and settlers through great swaths of the middle of the continent. Treaties signed in previous generations collapsed, and war escalated. By the end of the 1870s, indigenous control over the Great Plains was confined to the limited spaces and compromised sovereignty of the reservation system, which itself was altered in the 1880s by the Dawes Act to create private property allocations on reservations to individuals rather than granting collective control of resources to indigenous groups as a whole.

Wovoka prophesied that the dance, along with hard work and peaceful living, could unite Native Americans and return the natural abundance of their lands, which Native Americans would enjoy more fully again in the future. As the ideas and practices of the Ghost Dance spread, some came to believe that they could don special shirts, vested with powers to protect their wearers from harm. The movement spread across the high plains as tensions rose between the US Government and the Lakota Sioux over treaty violations. Rumors spread that leaders like the Lakota Chief Sitting Bull (d. 1890)—the architect of the indigenous military victory over US Cavalry at Little Big Horn in 1876—were using the Ghost Dance ritual to prepare for rebellion. Amid the confusion as a police contingent attempted to arrest Sitting Bull, shots were fired. Sitting Bull, as well as several other Native Americans and police officers, were killed.

Now connected to the death of Sitting Bull, the Ghost Dance grew as a powerful symbol. Local representatives of the US Government feared the indigenous response to Sitting Bull's death, while many Lakota worried about the US military's next moves. Three days after Christmas in 1890, US soldiers massacred one hundred fifty Lakota men, women, and children at a creek called Wounded Knee. The shirts that promised the Ghost Dancers protection from such violence did not save them. A week later, the bodies were buried *en masse* at Wounded Knee; and two weeks after that, on January 15, 1891, the last of four thousand Ghost Dancers surrendered to US Cavalry troops, effectively ending the movement.

The Maji-Maji Rebellion ("maji" means "water" in Swahili), which broke out in 1905, shared with the Ghost Dance movement a belief that indigenous practices could overcome the White Man's violence, but it bore even greater similarities to the Boxer Uprising. Both opposed foreign rule and changing patterns of land use linked to global trade networks: the economic depression that fueled the Boxers owed much to the collapse of domestic cotton prices in Shandong

MAP 9.3 Sovereignty Claims in Africa, Early Twentieth Century

because of British and American imports; in German East Africa, the colonial regime forced Africans to grow cotton and build roads to enter the same global economic system. In both cases, drought and famine, exacerbated by farmland taken out of food production and given over to cash crops, triggered the uprising. And like the Boxers, at the heart of the Maji-Maji movement was a mysticism that included claims that believers could protect themselves from the violent technologies of imperialists.

In the African case, Kinjikitile Ngwale (d. 1905) emerged to lead anti-German resistance, claiming he had contact with a deity who instructed him to unite the African people against the Germans. Emboldened by a special medicine that strengthened its users against German bullets, his followers rebelled. Kinjikitile Ngwale himself was captured and executed for treason in the summer of 1905, but the rebellion continued for two more years, leading to the deaths of more than ten thousand Africans but as few as fifteen Europeans. The Maji-Maji Rebellion was not the first or only revolt against European colonialism in Africa. Like the Wahehe Rebellion (1891–1898) that preceded it, and others before and after, the Maji-Maji Rebellion provoked brutal reprisals. German military officials encouraged crop destruction to promote famine as a means of subduing the population. Once the revolt was crushed, an even more rigid regime was implemented to monitor conditions more closely and quell potential revolt.

## Challenging the Modern Order at its Core

The Boxer, Maji-Maji, and Ghost Dance movements were based in non-Western cultures, but radical resistance to global political and economic changes could also be found in the West itself. Socialist political parties, anarchist movements, Marxist unions, general strikes, riots, and political assassinations showed that even in the wealthiest industrial centers, satisfaction with "the system" was not universal. The most enduring alternatives to global capitalism—a network of nation-states organized to protect private property—were Marxist movements. We will analyze the Marxist regimes that came to power in the twentieth century in subsequent chapters, but bear in mind that Marxism was already a powerful influence during this era.

Concurrent with political activism, other critiques challenged the idea that Western Civilization could bring endless progress. Some insisted that humans could not transcend nature; others observed that the seemingly irrational consequences of rational acts raised fundamental questions about what it meant to be human and civilized.

### Working-Class Agitation

Taking root among many movements that appealed to the working class with alternative conceptions of international organization was anarcho-syndicalism, which sought to merge the political ambitions of anarchists—the dissolution of any kind of formal state—with the economic goals of syndicalists: worker control of the industrial economy. Anarcho-syndicalism, which gained popularity in France, Italy, Great Britain, the United States, and many Latin American countries, represented just as radical a challenge as Boxers or Ghost Dancers, and a larger one in terms of number of participants and geographic spread.

One of the leading voices of the anarcho-syndicalist movement was Emma Goldman (1869–1940), who was born in the Russian Empire and immigrated to the United States in 1885. In 1892, one of Goldman's first major acts was to organize, with Alexander Berkman (1870–1936), the Homestead Strike against the Pittsburgh steel refineries of Andrew Carnegie. Plant managers attempted to use strikebreakers to put the plant back in production. A twelve-hour gun battle broke out between armed guards hired to protect the non-union workers and armed strikers. Sixteen people were killed. Berkman later snuck into the office of Henry Clay Frick (1849–1919), who managed the business for Carnegie, and shot him three times before stabbing and beating him (remarkably, Frick survived).

Berkman served fourteen years in prison for the attempted murder. Goldman was involved in the plot to kill Frick, which she hoped would "strike terror into the soul of his class"; but no evidence to arrest her was found, and so she remained free. Goldman was routinely arrested on other occasions, as she traveled the country addressing crowds of thousands and urging workers to take direct, even violent, action to advance their cause. Goldman was even implicated in the assassination of US President William McKinley (1843–1901). Although refusing to denounce the act, she was again cleared of any direct involvement in the murder.

## Darwin, Freud, and the Question of Human Nature

For some, the work of naturalist Charles Darwin and other scientific investigations of the natural world posed a challenge. They felt Darwin's theory used science to conclude that humans weren't particularly special because they were subject to the same rules of natural selection as all other living things. In reaction, some religious leaders and their followers revived arguments raised by their predecessors in the sixteenth and seventeenth centuries that modern science was not an ally, but an enemy of Western Civilization as it should be properly understood.

Darwin's *Origin of Species,* published in 1858, shaped the world in which another influential man of science, Sigmund Freud (1856–1939), grew up. Freud trained as a neurologist, but it was his theories and insights on human psychology that were most important. His first major work, *The Interpretation of Dreams* (1899), laid out many of his key principles about how humans operate. From the moment of their publication, Freud's ideas influenced debates about what it meant to live in the modern world. Freud's conclusions have been challenged; the charge that he looked for sexual symbols and motivations at every opportunity subjects him to caricature and ridicule. Yet, Freud's observations remain foundational to most modern understandings of human nature. Freud emphasized that important parts of the human mind function in ways that are not transparent, so individuals are often incapable of fully understanding themselves and the reasons for their own behaviors.

As different as their subject matters are, Freud's body of work resonates with that of Darwin. They are part of a wave of revisionist thinking to challenge the framing of the nineteenth century world as one of increasingly rational order and progress. Their ideas suggested that human beings—even civilized ones— needed to be understood as animals, and the world they inhabit (whether the world of the mind, of human society, or of the natural environment) is strongly influenced by events that might appear irrational or random and reside outside of human control. Whereas Newton suggested that with enough data and enough time he could predict every future action in the universe, Darwin and Freud insisted that the realm humans can rationally control, or even understand, is very limited. Darwin noted that humans cannot predict or control evolution. Freud argued that our forms of political, social, and economic organization extract a high toll that is paid out in conflict and suffering. The English title of one of Freud's later and most popular works is *Civilization and Its Discontents*.

Although many still shared the Enlightenment optimism articulated in the eighteenth century, celebrating and predicting the unlimited march of civilization and progress, Darwin, Freud, and others challenged the position that rationality would yield unlimited progress and increasing "civilization." The fate of two North American animal species demonstrates the ways in which certain forms of civilizing logic and rational behavior led to environmental devastation, revealing another challenge to the concept of endless progress.

## The Limits of Expansion: the Buffalo and the Passenger Pigeon

The railroad symbolizes both the industrial revolution and imperial expansion. Railroads, most of them designed by European and American engineers and built by laborers from across the world, knitted the globe together, transforming the surface of every continent. The expansion of the railroad both inspired and empowered efforts to further integrate much of the vast North American landmass into a single sovereign nation and economic system. As settlers pushed West, through the great disappearing Eastern forests to the plains, they encountered two species in enormous numbers: the passenger pigeon, and the American bison, or buffalo. Although quite different—one weighed just twelve ounces, the other, more than two thousand pounds—the two species defined the North American environment in the nineteenth century. One flock of passenger pigeons, one mile wide, three hundred miles long, took fourteen hours to pass an observation point in Southern Ontario in the 1880s. At one time, there may have been five billion passenger pigeons in North America. Now imagine as many as two hundred million bison grazing on the Great Plains, with smaller subspecies ranging East to the Atlantic Ocean and across the Rocky Mountains, from northern Canada all the way south into Mexico.

As new populations and systems of production, consumption, and distribution covered the eastern third of North America and then pushed westward, the consequences for both of these animals were quick and dire. Both had evolved to suit environmental niches that were disappearing in the nineteenth century: the Great Eastern Forest and the Great Plains. Buffalo had provided the native peoples of North America with food, shelter, clothing, and tools, but the introduction of the horse and firearms as part of the Columbian Exchange improved the ability of indigenous peoples to hunt the great herds. Bison numbers may have started to decline as early as the 1500s as humans hunted them more effectively. New European settlers prized these animals for their pelts and also found them an obstacle for the growth of railroads, farms, and ranches. Railroad managers and owners, eager to thin the herds, encouraged tourists to shoot buffalo from the windows of passing trains, even running special hunting trains. US military and political leaders made extinction a strategy, encouraging the slaughter of buffalo herds to eliminate them as a source of food for Native Americans. By 1884, the American bison was nearly extinct. It was no coincidence that Wovoka, the Paiute medicine man who developed the Ghost Dance, had linked the revival of indigenous peoples to the restoration of the buffalo to the Great Plains. This animal obstructed the expansion of one type of political economy in North America just as much as it sustained the indigenous ones, and its near destruction was not an accident. It was partly accepted consequence, partly explicit goal, of the transformation of the interior lands of North America.

The decline of the passenger pigeon was even more precipitous. Some environmental historians theorize that passenger pigeons were limited in number until the smallpox epidemics that accompanied European colonization limited demand for them as food; others disagree. What we do know is that by the eighteenth century, the passenger pigeon was the most abundant bird in North America, and perhaps the most abundant on earth. passenger pigeons were considered cheap food—including for slaves—and their immense flocks and communal nesting sites were easy targets. Hunting and deforestation began to decimate the enormous flocks. By 1900—just fifty years after John James Audubon (1785–1851) reported riding the entire fifty miles from Henderson, Kentucky, to Louisville under a single flock of passenger pigeons, it was rare to see the bird in the wild at all.

By 1907, just seven passenger pigeons remained in existence: four in a zoo in Milwaukee, and three in the Cincinnati Zoo. By 1910, a female named Martha was the last one. Martha became a celebrity for several years as the last of her species, and a bounty was offered to anyone who could find her a mate. No one was able to claim the $1,000 prize, however, and on September 1, 1914, Martha died. In less than a century, human beings had driven the most abundant bird species on earth to extinction.

## Neocolonialism

The formal colonialism of European states in much of Asia and Africa demonstrates one aspect of changing power relationships during this era. A more complete understanding of the late nineteenth century needs to include the financial and commercial networks that individuals and institutions in Europe, the United States, and Japan established beyond (or alongside) their own empires. Some scholars have used the term "neocolonialism" to describe this relationship. Others question the term's validity. Rather than review the debates over the merits of the label itself, we think it is important to consider the question behind the debate: to what extent during this era did formally independent states operate under a compromised sovereignty because they depended on external economic and/or military power to act like a state?

### Latin America in the Nineenth Century Global Order

The answer to this question varies from country to country, depending on the resource base, demographic characteristics, and geographic proximity to imperial centers. In Latin America, for example, systems of global finance, transportation, and resource management integrated with, and depended on, the centers of empire. While most of the region's states achieved political stability under liberal constitutional regimes controlled by small oligarchies that pursued integration into the global economy, we cannot make sweeping generalizations about a unitary Latin America. Although these countries received tremendous amounts of investment from the centers of empire and exported raw materials to the industrial economies, this does not mean that foreigners controlled domestic elites and decision-makers. Rather, domestic and foreign actors made alliances to pursue their interests. Foreign investors built railroads, mining and metallurgical facilities, utilities, and also made loans to governments, which built infrastructure and grew their militaries.

Where did the money come from to make these investments? Even with its vast empire in other parts of the world, British capital comprised 60 percent of all private foreign investment in Latin America at the turn of the twentieth century. German and French investors also participated in the Latin American economies. Until the early twentieth century, US investment was concentrated in Mexico, Central America, and the Caribbean rather than South America. What did the Latin American economies deliver to the global marketplace? The Central American republics focused almost exclusively on coffee exports, which made their economies quite vulnerable to fluctuations in the global coffee market. Mexico, Brazil, and Argentina had more diversified export bases. Overall economic growth under this model could be spectacular. For instance, Argentina, with an economy fifteen times larger in 1914 than in 1885, had one of the largest gross domestic products of any country in the world in the early twentieth century.

## The Boom-Bust Cycle

This system did not operate smoothly though. A series of booms and busts characterized the nineteenth century and economies careened from wild profits to collapse (remember the Brazilian rubber boom, described in the introduction to this chapter). Economic crises were sometimes the result of unforeseeable circumstances—crops still failed, competition was intense—but they could also be the result of mismanagement, speculative bubbles, or fraud. The Latin American economies were far from models of orderly growth and tranquility. Financial panics—wild fluctuations in the value of currency or debt—were frequent and often resulted in economic recessions: 1813, 1819, 1825, 1837, 1847, 1857, 1866, 1870, 1873, 1884, 1890, and 1893.

The transformation of Latin American economies, as elsewhere, was disruptive in many other ways as well. Like the United States, the southern cone of South America (Argentina, Brazil, Chile, and Uruguay) attracted European migrants displaced by industrialization and pressure on resources in their home countries. Many of these migrants traveled back and forth across the Atlantic Ocean in search of work. In addition, the wealthy classes in Latin America who had benefited from integration into the global industrial economy frequently fought with indigenous groups and peasant communities struggling to retain their economic, political, and cultural autonomy. Labor organizations seeking more benefits for workers met with bloody repression. The threat of invasion to secure the interests of foreigners, or the actual seizing of assets, were the quintessential acts of neocolonialism.

## Conclusion

In 1910, the governments of Chile, Colombia, and Mexico all organized lavish ceremonies to celebrate a century of independence from the Spanish Empire. Although none of these things were secrets, the speakers did not mention the decline of the passenger pigeon, the atrocities in the Congo, the tottering Qing Dynasty, or the seething resentments of Serbs and Bulgarians. Nor did they speak of the discontents of their own peoples—the strikes, rural rebellions, and food shortages. Instead, the men in morning coats and top hats spoke with great optimism about the future. Like their brethren around the world, they shared a belief that their future would resemble the recent past. The civilizing mission of Western culture would go on, the global economy would continue its bumpy but inexorable ride upward. The distress signals of a new century did not register as significant yet, but in the next generation, change came with a speed and intensity that upended the entire global order.

## A Few Good Books

Robert A. Bickers. *The Scramble for China: Foreign Devils in the Qing Empire, 1832–1914.* New York: Penguin, 2013.

Joel Greenberg. *A Feathered River across the Sky: The Passenger Pigeon's Flight to Extinction.* New York: Bloomsbury, 2014.

## TIMELINE

**1858**
*Origin of Species,* Charles Darwin

**1878**
Congress of Berlin mediates disputes over borders in Southeastern Europe

**1885**
Fukuzawa Yukichi publishes "Goodbye Asia"

**Late 1880s**
Wovoka begins practicing the Ghost Dance; American bison nearly extinct

**1875**
Sayyid Ahmad Khan founds Mohammedan Anglo-Oriental College in India

**1884–85**
Berlin Conference mediates competing European claims to African territory; Congo Free State ("the Belgian Congo") formed

**1889–1913**
Reign of Menelik II of Ethiopia

**1892**
Dadabhai Naoroji elected to Parliament; Homestead Strike, Pittsburgh

Adam Hochschild. *King Leopold's Ghost: A Story of Greed, Terror, and Heroism in Colonial Africa*. New York: Houghton Mifflin Harcourt, 1998.

Lynn Martin. *Commerce and Economic Change in West Africa*. Cambridge, England: Cambridge University Press, 2002.

Pankaj Mishra. *From the Ruins of Empire: The Revolt Against the West and the Remaking of Asia*. New York: Picador, 2014.

Gene Luen Yang. *Boxers and Saints*. New York: First Second Books, 2013.

*For additional resources, including maps, primary sources, visuals, web links, and quizzes, please go to* **www.oup.com/us/carter**

**1894–95**
Sino-Japanese War

**1898**
Hundred Days' Reform in China

**1904**
Edmund Morel becomes leader of the Congo Reform Association

**1910**
Korea becomes a colony of Japan; peak of Brazilian rubber production

**1897**
Amazonas Theater opens in Manaus, Brazil

**1899**
Rudyard Kipling, "The White Man's Burden"; H. T. Johnson, *The Black Man's Burden*; Sigmund Freud, *The Interpretation of Dreams*; Boxer Uprising begins in China

**1905**
Maji-Maji Rebellion, German East Africa

**1914**
80 percent of earth's land surface controlled by Europe and United States; Martha, last Passenger Pigeon, dies

(TOP) HIBIYA RIOTS ILLUSTRATION, *THE JAPANESE GRAPHIC* NO. 66, SEPTEMBER 18, 1905. Dissatisfied with the terms of a peace treaty between Russia and Japan, crowds in Tokyo rioted in 1905. The riots illustrated the perils of democracy and social protest as well as the dramatic changes that had taken place in Japan during the preceding decades. A special edition of the magazine *The Japanese Graphic*, entitled "The Tokyo Riot Graphic," appeared in mid-September. This illustration offers an image of Kono Hironaka (1849–1923), a Japanese politician and opponent of the Treaty of Portsmouth, stirring up the crowd at the "anti-peace mass meeting."

(BOTTOM) BENITO MUSSOLINI PRESIDES OVER THE FIRST ANNIVERSARY CELEBRATIONS OF FASCIST RULE IN ITALY, 1923. Mussolini denied fundamental principles of liberal democracy, dismissing majority rule and egalitarian principles as misguided and weak. Fascist movements in Europe emerged in the wake of the Great War, arguing that the failed political and economic systems of the past should be replaced with modern totalitarianism. Fascists often dressed in military garb to symbolize their commitment to physical struggle in support of their cause.

# CHAPTER 10

# Total War and Mass Society

## 1905–1928

Nearly thirty thousand demonstrators tried to gather in Tokyo's Hibiya Park in September 1905, angered by the outcome of Japan's recent war with Russia. They were not angered by defeat, however; they were protesting the terms of victory. During the summer, delegates from Russia and Japan had traveled to the US Navy Yards at Portsmouth, New Hampshire. There, they hammered out a deal, congratulating themselves and winning the Nobel Peace Prize for US President Theodore Roosevelt, who had brokered the negotiations. However, the treaty did not confirm territorial gains made by Japan during the war, nor was Russia made to pay an indemnity, historically the price of peace for the losing side. Many Japanese found these terms too concessionary. Informed about the war mainly from government propaganda, the people of Japan had no idea that their government had been unable to continue the bloody and expensive war for much longer.

To defuse the protest, the government kept the gates to the park locked, infuriating protesters like Yano Fumio (1850–1931), a writer and political activist who had founded *The Japanese Graphic*, a weekly magazine with illustrated news of the day. In a special issue titled "The Tokyo Riot Graphic," Yano described, in pictures and words, a broad array of people, from many walks of life—shopkeepers, rickshaw pullers, craftsmen, factory workers—taking part in the protest. When the police ordered everyone to disperse, the crowd instead marched on the imperial palace. Unable to enter the palace grounds, the protesters turned on any available symbols of authority, attacking firefighters, police officers, and even burning the home of a government minister. For more than two days, crowds marched in central Tokyo, setting fires and attacking public officials. More than three hundred fifty buildings were destroyed; seventeen people died, and more than five hundred were injured. Similar protests in other cities broke out as news of the Hibiya Riots spread. While foreign commentators and diplomats marveled that Japan's victory had been the first time in centuries that an Asian country had defeated a European power in war,

# MAJOR FIELDS OF BATTLE, 1914–45

- First World War 1914–18
- Second World War 1939–45
- Other major international war
- Major civil war

MAP 10.1  Major Fields of Battle, 1914–45

in Japan itself, the signing of the peace treaty was followed by a declaration of martial law to rein in popular unrest.

A quarter-century later, in the fall of 1928, a new law was passed in Italy handing the power of constitutional review, approval of legislative candidates, and the setting of government policy to something called the Grand Council of Fascism, a committee headed by Benito Mussolini (1883–1945), Italy's Prime Minister since 1922. Mussolini's aggressive supporters, called Black Shirts, used violence and intimidation to promote their cause. Whereas some Italians were coerced into supporting the Fascist leader, others enthusiastically embraced Mussolini's ideas and tactics, tired of domestic political disorder and economic stagnation and discontented with the international order of the early 1920s.

Mussolini, a former socialist and military veteran, came to reject not only socialism but also liberal democracy. He promoted a new ideology, called "fascism," as the politics of modernity, celebrating the interests of the pure nation-state's collective good over the debased and "possibly harmful freedom" of individuals. He wrote, "Fascism denies that the majority, through the mere fact of being a majority, can rule human societies" and challenged the idea of universal suffrage as an ill-conceived notion that was contrary to the survival of the national state. Instead, Mussolini subordinated individuals, and individual liberties, to the interests of the nation. In Italy, and elsewhere, the new political and social order that the fascists were building, designed to match the challenges of the twentieth century, required a new name—totalitarianism—used by both admirers and critics.

---

These two vignettes introduce the topic at the heart of this chapter: the changing connections among war, the modern industrial economy, ordinary people, and the global political order in the late nineteenth and early twentieth centuries. In this chapter, we cover the shortest chronological period of any chapter in the book, yet it is one of the most complex to understand, as so many events pivotal to the entire twentieth century occurred in this era and were related to each other.

Beginning with the arms and technology race that gripped the world in the late nineteenth century, we then describe three revolutionary movements—in China, Mexico, and Russia—in which growing tensions inherent in these countries' different paths through the nineteenth century erupted in the early twentieth century. This theme of increasing tensions born of nineteenth-century transformations and decisions is context for the Great War of 1914–1918. In the sections that follow, we offer an explanation of the changes in scale and nature of warfare that emerged during the Great War. At the end of the chapter, we explore the aftermath of the Great War, as leaders and common people struggled to make sense of the mass mobilizations for mass destruction that characterized this era.

# New Theories, Grand Strategy

As the nineteenth century waned, leaders across the globe invested heavily in the latest military equipment. European powers, the United States, and Japan acquired more than ten million square miles of land as colonial possessions during this time, populated by almost one hundred fifty million people. These imperial powers deemed naval power especially important, following the influential theories of Alfred Thayer Mahan (1840–1914), a captain and lecturer at the US Naval War College. In his 1890 book, *The Influence of Sea Power Upon History*, Mahan argued that navies determined the fortunes of European powers in the early modern period, an idea that resonated with contemporary political elites anxious to enhance their countries' positions in the new global hierarchy of wealth and power. Concerns about sea lanes, choke points, refueling stations, and safe harbors drove states to invest in ever larger, faster, and more heavily armed ships.

These military and strategic initiatives accompanied a dramatic reallocation of the globe's resources. By the early twentieth century, the North Atlantic world, led by Great Britain, Germany, the United States, and France, came to control approximately 80 percent of the world's manufacturing output, an almost complete reversal of the situation just one hundred years before when China and India combined were responsible for more than half. Small wars had been consistent features of the global reorganization. Warfare, however, was changing, as industrialization altered the arithmetic of confrontation. The newest battleships had a dozen or more guns that could hit targets more than ten miles away. A single machine gun could replace forty riflemen.

These new technologies, and anxiety over the consequences of failing to keep up with current or potential rivals, spurred an arms race. Military expenditures rose almost 200 percent for Europe as a whole, and over 400 percent for Germany, between 1883 and 1913. Beyond Western Europe, governments from the Ottomans to the Argentines commissioned ships, bought weapons, and arranged for European officers to visit their countries on training missions. Ships on both sides in the 1894–95 Sino-Japanese War had European officers aboard during battles. The Greek and Ottoman navies purchased experimental submarines. Latin American governments invited French and German officers to reorganize their militaries. Japanese officials offered Alfred Thayer Mahan a faculty position at their own Naval Staff College.

The industrialization of the military is one facet of the changing nature of warfare. Another emerged from the changing relationship between individuals and the state. In the late nineteenth century, warfare became entangled in the expansion of ties between states and their citizens, as universal male suffrage, public education and welfare systems, and compulsory male military service all became more common. By the end of the nineteenth century, most nations with aspirations to some share of global power, including Germany, Italy, and Japan, had adopted systems of compulsory male military service. In theory, the new citizen armies could mobilize millions of soldiers if necessary. But even in states that had yet to adopt universal military service, like the United States and Great Britain, going to war became key moments for building ties between states and their citizens. In 1898, US newspapers called on readers to "Remember the *Maine*," a US battleship sunk in Havana harbor, to rally opinion for war with Spain. Great Britain's *Daily Mail*, *The Times*, *The Guardian*, *The Morning Post*, and *The Morning Chronicle* all sent correspondents to South Africa to cover the Boer Wars (1880–81; 1899–1902). Their stories aimed to build patriotic sentiment for the empire and its wars.

Governments needed their citizens to invest, literally and figuratively, in the limited wars of the late nineteenth and early twentieth centuries. Residents of both the Ottoman Empire and France ran fundraising campaigns for the purchase of military hardware. Small tokens celebrated the military and its connection to the nation: Japanese postcards commemorating the war with Russia; and British trading cards found in cigarette and tea packets that featured the empire's flags, uniforms, and heroes. There were grand gestures, too, like military parades with processions of the latest weapons and technology during national holidays. These events were filmed so that audiences across the nation and around the world could witness the awesome spectacle of modern military power at ease but poised for action.

## Mass Unrest in Russia, China, and Mexico

Many of the world's political leaders maintained great confidence that they had mastered the balancing act of this new era, but mass uprisings in three distinct regions of the globe provide examples of the many ways states could unravel as the twentieth century dawned. Each revolution was different, and none can be considered typical, but events in Russia, China, and Mexico indicate the counterpoint to the talk of progress and grand strategy that dominated many European capitals.

### Russia

The Russian Empire appeared formidable in the early twentieth century. It was the world's largest state in terms of contiguous territory. In power since 1613, the Romanov Dynasty had overseen Russia's expansion across Central Asia and Siberia, reaching the Pacific in the mid-nineteenth century and even briefly claiming territory in North America (the state of Alaska today), which it sold to the United States in 1867. The Trans-Siberian Railway, completed in 1904, symbolized the empire's expanse and modernity as it traversed almost six thousand miles from Moscow to the Sea of Japan.

At the same time, however, internal dissent was growing across the enormous empire. Workers seeking labor reforms and better working conditions began striking with greater frequency. Some political dissidents increased their demands for a constitution and a transition away from absolutist rule. Others agitated for a radical break with the existing political order rather than gradual reform. Worsening economic conditions and bad news during the war with Japan fueled protests against the rule of Tsar Nicholas II (1868–1918). On January 22, 1905, a crowd of several thousand approached Nicholas's Winter Palace in Saint Petersburg to petition for improved working conditions and increased recognition of workers' rights. The protests began peacefully, exalting the tsar with patriotic hymns, but soldiers and police intent on dispersing the crowd moved aggressively, using swords and rifles against the protesters. The government acknowledged the deaths of around one hundred people; unofficial estimates exceeded one thousand killed. Strikes and protests spread around Russia in response to this "Bloody Sunday" massacre. Demands for reform intensified.

In October 1905, the tsar agreed. Unrest ebbed, although the "Fundamental Law" of 1906 still asserted that the tsar maintained "supreme sovereign power" mandated by God. In 1907, the tsar reconstituted the empire's legislature, the Duma. As the second decade of the twentieth century began, agitation for more radical political reform and additional labor unrest continued to challenge the empire's status quo. War in the nearby Balkans region in 1912 and 1913 drew the attention of both leaders and common people who cheered the aspirations of their fellow Slavs, seeing the promise of a better future for Russia if larger, independent Slavic-majority states were to emerge in the region. In 1914, events in the Balkans would spark a global war that fed a more dramatic social revolution in Russia from which the world's first communist regime would emerge.

## China

Revolutions do not occur according to anyone's schedule, not even those who plan them. The revolutionary end to two thousand years of imperial rule in China was no exception. In October 1911, Sun Yat-sen (1866–1925), the most important leader of China's nationalist republican movement, was traveling in the United States, building support and raising money for his planned revolution against the Qing Dynasty. On a train from Denver to Kansas City, he read that the revolution had started without him: the accidental detonation of a bomb exposed the conspiracy against the emperor, leading subversive military units to publicly declare against the dynasty. Sun returned to China as the Qing Dynasty collapsed and was sworn in as provisional President of a new Republic of China on January 1, 1912. Conceding defeat, the last Manchu emperor abdicated in February.

By starting the new republic on the Western New Year, rather than China's traditional lunar New Year, Sun made a statement about the future he envisioned. His "Three Principles of the People"—nationalism, democracy, and the welfare of the people—embodied the rhetoric of state formation that had come to define the modern world during the previous century. Sun proclaimed that his goal was "to place China in a respectable place in international society, to follow in the steps of the other powers of the world."

The quick revolution and abdication of the Qing Dynasty gave false hope to advocates of a smooth transition to a democratic republic. Sun Yat-sen had provided the ideological framework for the revolution, but he lacked the military resources to carry out his vision and quickly passed the presidency to Yuan Shikai (1859–1916), a former Qing general who controlled most of the military resources. When Sun's political party, the Chinese Nationalist Party (or KMT), won the republic's first elections and dominated the new National Assembly, Yuan Shikai betrayed a promise to observe democratic principles and instead proclaimed a new, authoritarian "Great Chinese Empire." The return to autocracy failed. Provinces began to secede from the central state amid calls for new revolution. Yuan renounced the new empire in March, but it was too late. By June, Yuan was dead (from kidney disease) and China was entering more than a decade of civil war—often called the Warlord Era—that divided the former empire among dozens of regional armies. There was no effective central government.

## Mexico

China and Mexico had little in common in the early twentieth century, yet both countries were plunged into civil war when their political systems collapsed and their militaries fragmented. In 1910, armed rebels called for an end to the regime of President Porfirio Díaz (1830–1915). Díaz had come to power in the 1870s promising a modern centralized state and liberal democracy. Instead, Díaz and his supporters ruled Mexico for four decades through a political machine rigged to guarantee his reelection. Foreign investment had transformed the Mexican economy, building infrastructure to integrate Mexico's exports and imports into an expanding global trading system. This economic strategy had high costs for peasants, displaced and impoverished, as well as workers in mining and manufacturing who were brutally suppressed when they tried to organize for better labor conditions. Some members of the middle-class and even certain elites grew increasingly disaffected from the Porfirian regime's principles and performance.

Francisco Madero (1873–1913) had challenged Díaz in the 1910 elections and been imprisoned for his troubles but was able to flee the country with the help of his influential family. From exile in the United States, Madero made a public announcement of the planned date and time for an uprising to begin. The call to overthrow Díaz resonated in many regions of the country, with exasperated common folk as well as aspiring elites and regional political operators. When armed insurgents defeated the federal army, the eighty-year-old Díaz chose to leave for Paris. He lived his final years in exile.

Madero served briefly as Mexico's new leader. His early actions enraged some insurgents who were fighting for broad economic and social reforms rather than just a change in national political leadership and institutions. Emiliano Zapata's (1879–1919) peasant army condemned Madero's "treason," while other revolutionaries remained loyal to the new regime. In 1913, reactionaries seized the opportunity created by this split to engineer a coup d'état, installing a military officer from the Díaz regime in the presidency. Mexico then, like China, plunged into a more than a decade of civil war, as insurgent forces, including the peasant armies of the south and more heterogeneous forces in the north, toppled the central government but then continued to fight among themselves over leadership and goals for the future.

## A Great War

In the summer of 1914, Mexico and China were both in the midst of bloody civil wars with no effective central sovereign authority or rule of law in either country. In contrast, the major powers of Europe had never been more confident in their stability and prosperity. When an act of political violence in Southeastern Europe threatened to spark war among the major European powers, few of the potential belligerents recognized that they too stood on a precipice, about to plunge themselves into bloodletting and political transformation. One who did was British First Lord of the Admiralty (and future Prime Minister) Winston Churchill, who wrote to his wife as the move to war accelerated: "My darling one and beautiful, everything tends towards catastrophe and collapse." Churchill's forecast was prescient.

### Nationalism at the Heart of It

On June 28, 1914, a man named Gavrilo Princip (1894–1918) assassinated the heir to the Austrian throne, the Habsburg Archduke Franz Ferdinand (1863–1914), and his wife in the city of Sarajevo. Princip had been active in a movement advocating the removal of Austro-Hungarian rule from the Balkans. The world's empires were full of diverse cultural, linguistic, and religious groups; yet, as we have seen, nationalism increasingly expressed itself in the nineteenth century in movements for self-determination, that is, claims that distinct peoples had the right to create and live within the borders of states over which they would exercise sovereignty. Southeastern Europe's Balkan Peninsula had long been the site of agitation by multiple groups that aspired to form their own nation-states rather than remain within the Austro-Hungarian or Ottoman Empires.

Serbs were one of many Slavic groups with national ambitions. A Serb kingdom had been a regular, although not constant, feature of southeastern Europe for many centuries. At the start of the twentieth century, Serbs lived in both the Ottoman Empire and Austria-Hungary, and also in an independent Serb principality recognized by other sovereign states at the 1878 Congress of Berlin. Many Serb nationalists considered territory still controlled by Austria-Hungary to be part of Serbia. Other national groups in the Balkans pushed for recognition of their own sovereignty, triggering war in 1912 and again in 1913.

Many predicted that a familiar pattern would repeat itself in 1914: a brief regional war, after which the Great Powers would restore peace and redraw the borders. These predictions were wrong, as the responses of Austria-Hungary, Russia, and their respective allies sprung a trap that had been set by changes in Europe's system of imperial alliances. Unified Germany had become an even more important economic and military power than any of its constituent territories—like Prussia—had been. Since the late 1880s, the German government under Kaiser Wilhelm II pursued a "New Course" of aggressive industrial and imperial expansion. Germany pushed to develop a navy that could challenge Great Britain and secure colonies in Africa and the Pacific. These new policies reshaped diplomatic relations among the European Empires. By antagonizing Russia, Great Britain, and Italy, Germany had only one reliable ally, Austria-Hungary, which had an aging leadership and contentious internal politics. In the summer of 1914, Germany and Austria-Hungary were pledged to defend one another if attacked, while Britain, Russia, and France formed a similar pact.

This shift in alliances added an additional factor that tipped the balance toward a broader war rather than a limited confrontation. Angered by the murder of the Crown Prince, and eager to send a message to the nationalists within its own borders, Austria-Hungary moved to punish the independent Serbian state. One month after the assassination, Austria-Hungary declared war on Serbia. Russia, which had the largest standing army in the world, mobilized for war, invoking their longstanding and self-proclaimed role as protector of the Serbs, their fellow Slavs and coreligionists. Almost universally, the other Great Powers interpreted this move in terms of Russia's strategic interests in the Balkans, which it was pursuing at the expense of the Ottomans and Austria-Hungary. Within days, Germany declared war on Russia. Soon, France and Germany declared war on one another and, after the German army invaded neutral Belgium on its way to France, Great Britain declared war on Germany. All of the major European powers were now at war.

Enthusiasms greeted the declarations of war as nationalism overwhelmed competing allegiances and ongoing tensions within the warring countries. Great Britain, which had not yet enacted a compulsory military service law, found eager volunteers. English poet Rupert Brooke (1887–1915), who volunteered and did not survive the war, captured the idealism of many who welcomed war as an opportunity to win glory for their nation, writing in his poem "1914": "Now, God be thanked Who has matched us with His hour, And caught our youth, and wakened us from sleeping." In a later stanza, Brooke celebrated the idea that dying for one's country would bring not only glory to the individual but would consecrate for the nation the earth on which one fell:

> If I should die, think only this of me
> That there's some corner of a foreign field
> That is forever England.[1]

In this chapter, as in one other in this book, we deliberately refer to poems, to demonstrate how historians sometimes turn to literary sources—poems, memoirs, or novels, for example—to try to convey the *zeitgeist,* or the spirit, of a time period. For reasons that still confound scholars, the Great War produced an impressive literature, expressed as both poetry and prose. Some of the most well-known novels of the twentieth century, like Ernest Hemingway's *A Farewell to Arms* (1929) and Erich Maria Remarque's *All Quiet on the Western Front* (1929), are set during the war. Hemingway worked as an ambulance driver in Italy, and Remarque served on the front in Belgium. Both were wounded, and their novels reflect their experiences of the battlefield and beyond. Vera Brittain's memoir *Testament of Youth* (1933) brings another perspective to the same era. Brittain (1893–1970) worked in a field hospital, tending to the wounded while coping with the deaths of her fiancé, brother, and two closest male friends in the war. Brittain's sadness, outrage, and pacifism contrasts poignantly with Brooke's excited patriotism and zeal: both illustrate aspects of that moment. As with all sources, though, one must be cautious in making any generalizations about history, even trying to illustrate the "spirit of the age," based on a single author's observations. As we will see following, Brooke's fellow English poet, Wilfred Owen (1893–1918), conveyed a very different spirit in his poetry. In addition, we must also remember that scholarly debates about how to interpret literary sources are just as contentious as they are for other kinds of sources.[2]

---

[1]  Rupert Brooke, *The Collected Poems*, ed. George E. Woodbury (New York: Lane, 1916).

[2]  Patrick J. Quinn and Steven Trout, eds., *Literature of the Great War Reconsidered: Beyond Modern Memory* (New York: Palgrave, 2001); Vincent Sherry, ed., *The Cambridge Companion to the Literature of the First World War* (Cambridge: Cambridge University Press, 2005). Vera Brittain, *Testament of Youth: An Autobiographical Study of the Years 1900–1925.* (New York: Macmillan Company, 1933).

## The Nature of the Great War

Volunteers exceeded British Parliament's call for five hundred thousand recruits. By late September of 1914, 750,000 men had volunteered to serve in the military in the United Kingdom of Great Britain and Ireland. By the end of the war, nearly one-quarter of the male population of the United Kingdom was in the military, with volunteers supplemented by conscripts beginning in 1916.

All of the other major combatants had conscription laws at the start of the war, but they also formed volunteer regiments. Tens of thousands of German university students left their studies to go off to war. Public celebrations feted the soldiers who marched to the front from Berlin, Vienna, Paris, and Moscow. Germany's Kaiser was so confident of his troops and their officers, he proclaimed that Germany would have, "Paris for lunch, St. Petersburg for dinner." Events of the summer of 1914 showed the tremendous power of the modern world's defining political institution—the nation-state—to organize and inspire.

The war celebrations in the summer of 1914 combined demonstrations of national pride and technological prowess in ways that could evoke the world's fairs discussed in Chapter 8, but the optimism of the summer of 1914 quickly collapsed under the weight of the war itself. Military leaders, trained in nineteenth century strategies and tactics, had little idea of how to use the massive numbers of often poorly trained troops and their new weapons, so they cobbled together an odd and lethal mix of the old and the new. Human runners, dogs, and pigeons still transmitted battlefield messages; soldiers carried pigeon lofts to the front. And although the futility of cavalry charges on horseback was obvious in the face of machine guns and barbed wire, horses still provided transportation and often were used to move artillery—millions of horses died during the war. Machine guns rendered traditional infantry charges ineffective. Although heavy and unreliable compared to later models, each German Maxim machine gun could fire between four hundred to six hundred rounds per minute, a barrage equivalent to between sixty and one hundred individual rifles. The new weapons were so efficient at firing that shortages of ammunition became a common problem.

British troops in Southern Africa and their Russian counterparts in Asia had recent experience of the important role that improvised fortifications like trenches could play in countering sheer firepower. On the opposing side, German strategists studied reports of these same campaigns; they trained and outfitted their troops accordingly. As a result, when Germany's original plan to quickly take Paris failed, the German army began to dig in, literally, as did their foes. Thousands of miles of trenches were dug across the Western Front over the following years. Barbed wire migrated from pastureland to battlefield, rolled out to render it impossible to overwhelm an opponent's trenches simply through sheer numbers.

**WORLD WAR I TRENCH MAP OF FRANCE AND BELGIUM.** This 1915 British Ordnance Survey map shows trenches in red. The new military technology of the twentieth century—machine guns, barbed wire, and artillery—turned nineteenth-century tactics of infantry charges into slaughter. In response, opposing armies dug extensive and elaborate trenches where soldiers lived, slept, and fought. By the war's end, more than twenty-five thousand miles of trenches stretched across the European landscape.

The Western Front was five hundred miles of artillery, machine guns, grenades, barbed wire, and trenches stretching across the French countryside from the North Sea to the Swiss border. The defining image of the Great War may be the trench itself. At the Battle of the Somme, the German army had three lines of trenches, reinforced by an additional seven thousand tons of barbed wire delivered to the front every week. As it became evident that there was no clear or easy way to take opposing trenches, both sides invested in their reinforcement. By the fall of 1916, some trenches on the Western Front were thirty feet deep, with timber beams, concrete reinforcements and steel doors.

The Great War turned into a nightmare. The poison gas both sides used resulted in only three percent of battlefield casualties, but its effect was much wider than these numbers suggest. The terror and anxiety caused by the ever-present threat of gas attack gnawed at troops on the frontline, and the gasmask became an icon of the new warfare. Wilfred Owen—who died in the last weeks of the war—described a gas attack in his poem, "Dulce Et Decorum Est":

> Gas! GAS! Quick, boys! – An ecstasy of fumbling,
> Fitting the clumsy helmets just in time;
> But someone still was yelling out and stumbling,

And flound'ring like a man in fire or lime . . .
Dim, through the misty panes and thick green light,
As under a green sea, I saw him drowning.
In all my dreams, before my helpless sight,
He plunges at me, guttering, choking, drowning.[3]

Owen's narrator sees—through the green-tinted lenses of a gasmask—a man drowning in his own blood as poison gas destroys his lungs. The poem evokes the psychological power of gas: although only one man dies in the attack, the ethereal killer terrorizes the entire platoon and haunts the narrator's dreams.

Chemical weapons showed how war twisted the promise of new technologies. The initial stockpile of chlorine gas, the most widely used chemical weapon at the start of the war, was generated as a byproduct of dye manufacturing. What began as a means for German manufacturers to produce cheaper, more brightly colored fabrics ended with a new form of devastation on the battlefield. In another perversion of prewar commerce and industry, British manufacturers continued to pay patent royalties to the German firm of Krupp for fuses used in grenades that British troops then lobbed at their German counterparts.

The increase in firepower, confusion over how to fight this new war, the growing complexity of battlefield injuries, the horrible conditions under which immediate treatment could be administered, and the transportation and communications challenges of wartime trumped improvements in the practice of medicine that had occurred over the course of the last century. Casualties were staggering on all sides. At the Somme, the British suffered sixty thousand casualties in one day, most of them to machine guns firing on troops attempting to advance on the German lines. The battle lasted five months—from July to mid-November, 1916—and total losses on all sides exceeded three hundred thousand killed and more than one million casualties total. Yet, no one won; the front line barely moved. The stalemate at the front led tactics to shift in several directions, including a greater reliance on heavy artillery to achieve complete annihilation of troops and infrastructure as well as a focus on the disruption of supplies to the enemy's entire population and economy. The key theaters of warfare shifted as the destruction mounted.

## Mobilizing the Population for Total War

From the first moments of the conflict, the "home front" was an important site of struggle. All sides employed propaganda to maintain morale among their own

---

3   Wilfred Owen, *Poems* (New York: Heubsch, 1921).

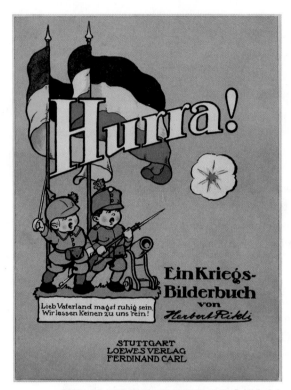

**COVER OF** *HURRAY! A WAR PICTURE-BOOK.* Published in Germany during the Great War, this book portrays one German and one Austrian boy—Willi and Franzl—on their way to war. The caption on the cover says, "Dear Fatherland, rest assured. We won't let anyone in!" Mobilizing for total war in the early twentieth century encompassed all strata of society, including the nation's future soldiers.

populations (and therefore productivity, the discipline of rationing, and the stability of governments) and to undermine that of the enemy. Newsreels, often produced directly by the armed forces, made their way into movie theaters, while posters appeared on the walls of buildings to remind all citizens of their important roles in the war effort (whether it was as a soldier, worker, mother, or investor) and to remind the people why the nation was at war, often by depicting the enemy as inhuman monsters. Radio, which would come into its own in both governmental and commercial manifestations only in the 1920s, was used on an experimental basis.

The idea of a "home front" is misleading, though. The case of poison gas illustrates the fading distinction between civilians and soldiers and the eroding concept of the "front" as a specific site where battle takes place. Development and production of chemical weapons on a large scale required the resources and cooperation of government planners, university researchers, and private companies. As the war dragged on, strategies to win increasingly focused on disrupting the economic and political engines that drove the war machines. The Great War did not introduce "strategic bombing"—the systematic bombing of targets away from the front lines to disrupt the war economy and demoralize an enemy's population—but it expanded the practice greatly.

Hundreds of German civilians were killed in bombing raids, primarily on munitions factories. About fifteen hundred Britons were killed, and another five thousand injured, in the aerial bombing campaigns carried out by zeppelins and airplanes against British cities. German U-boats sank more than six thousand commercial ships, taking almost fifteen thousand civilian sailors to the ocean floor. And as with poison gas, the number of casualties alone does not convey the full impact of these tactics, in which an unseen threat menaced everyone. Beyond the numbers, the fact that targets were increasingly far from the fields of military combat and often without direct military roles made clear that entire nations—not just opposing armies—were at war. These tactics also contributed to the transformation of this conflict into a truly world war.

## The Great War as World War

After the outbreak of hostilities, additional states joined the fray. Within months, the Ottoman Empire, which had military connections to Germany and was particularly concerned with its Black Sea rival Russia, was drawn into combat. By the summer of 1915, Italy, which had a historic alliance with Germany, was enticed instead to join the British by promises of territorial gains at war's end. Romania, Serbia, and Greece also lined up on that side, while Bulgaria joined the Germans. These maneuvers alone do not come close to capturing the extent to which the war grew into a global confrontation.

As imperial powers fighting an industrialized war, the antagonists set their sights on control of the globe's resources. The British, whose interests included not only the Suez Canal but also the vital Anglo-Persian oil pipeline, developed a strategy for what was now being called the "Middle East." As the Sultan of the Ottoman Empire declared a *jihad* against nonbelievers when entering the war, the British appealed to the nationalist aspirations of Arab Muslims, who revolted against the Ottomans.

The Europeans fighting from Egypt east through Persia made local alliances and implied promises about the future political geography of the region, but the secret Sykes–Picot agreement between England and France (1916) created a blueprint for a post-Ottoman Middle East without input from local leaders. After the war, many actors in the Middle East would feel betrayed by their ostensible allies.

The composition of their forces also revealed the reach of the European Empires. Over one million soldiers from the Dominions of the British Empire—Canada, Newfoundland, Australia, and New Zealand—crossed the seas to fight. More than one million volunteers from South Asia fought for the British Empire during the war, in Egypt, Persia, and Europe. Over one hundred thousand troops from West Africa joined the French lines. More than one hundred thousand Asian and African troops died in the European trenches alone.

The global stakes extended the conflict beyond just Europeans and their empires. Japan agreed to maintain sea lanes open for the British alliance and helped to suppress a rebellion of Indian troops stationed in Singapore. The Japanese government also used the war to gain control over the German colony of Qingdao in China and several islands in the Pacific. The Chinese Republican government, struggling to gain international recognition, sent one hundred forty thousand workers to support the European war effort. The US Government, concerned with maintaining access to the newly opened Panama Canal and its strong commercial

ياروپے۔بندوق اور
وردی کون لیگا
وہی
جو فوج میں موا بھرتی ہوگا

**BRITISH EMPIRE WORLD WAR I RECRUITMENT POSTER FOR INDIA.** The translation from Urdu reads, "Who will take this uniform, money and rifle? The one who will join the army." Approximately one and one-half million Indian volunteers took part in World War I. India's contribution to the war effort, including a high casualty rate, fueled nationalist demands for Indian autonomy and independence after the war.

and diplomatic ties to England, pre-empted the establishment of German fueling stations or safe harbors in the Western Hemisphere. Its relations with Germany deteriorated after US citizens died in the 1915 sinking of the ocean liner *Lusitania*, then broke in early 1917 when Germans resumed unrestricted submarine warfare in the Atlantic Ocean and made a clumsy bid to form an alliance with the newly formed revolutionary government in Mexico. The United States declared war on Germany in April 1917.

The direction of the war shifted after the United States entered. Fresh US troops and materiel bolstered their allies. In 1918, Germany's allies began to abandon the cause while Germany itself started a descent into domestic turmoil. The Kaiser abdicated on November 2, and the new German government signed an agreement to end the fighting on November 11. The fight over the peace began immediately thereafter.

## Negotiating the Future in the Shadow of the Great War

The statistics of death and destruction are overwhelming. In Europe alone, nearly ten million soldiers, and almost seven million civilians, died. Great Britain, France, Russia, Austria-Hungary, and Germany all lost more than 3 percent of their total populations. In the Ottoman Empire, more than 13 percent of the population died. This number includes Armenians who died as a result of policies designed and implemented by their own sovereign—a genocide that foreshadowed other great horrors to come. A global flu pandemic broke out in 1918, killing another fifty to one hundred million people.

## WESTERN EURASIA, 1914–23

— Boundary 1923
— Pre-war boundary
▓ Territory administered by League of Nations
▨ Demilitarized zone
1918 Date of independence

N

0 km 400
0 miles 400

FINLAND 1917/20
Petrograd
Helsinki
SWEDEN
Stockholm
NORWAY
Christiania (Oslo from 1925)
ESTONIA 1918/20
Tallinn
LATVIA 1918/20
Riga
LITHUANIA 1918/20
Kaunas
MEMEL TER.
Danzig
UNION OF SOVIET SOCIALIST REPUBLICS
Kiev
Petrograd
Brest-Litovsk
1920/23 from Russia
1921 from Russia
Lvov
1919/20 from Russia
Baltic Sea
Black Sea
GERMAN (EAST PRUSSIA)
1919 from Germany
POLAND 1916/18
Warsaw
Kraków
DENMARK
1920 from Germany
Copenhagen
Hamburg
Stettin
Bremen
Berlin
Hanover
Oder
GERMANY
Breslau
Dresden
Frankfurt
Prague
Brno
CZECHOSLOVAKIA
Bratislava
Vienna
Munich
Ulm
Rhine
SAAR 1919/20 from Germany
Bern
SWITZ.
AUSTRIA 1919/20 from Germany
HUNGARY 1918/44
Budapest
Zagreb
ROMANIA 1919/20 from Russia
Bucharest
BULGARIA
Sofia
YUGOSLAVIA 1918
Belgrade
1919 from Bulgaria
GREECE
Athens
ALBANIA 1918
Tirana
TURKEY
Constantinople
Aegean Sea
NETHER-LANDS
Amsterdam
BELGIUM 1920 from Germany
Brussels
LUXEMBOURG 1919/20 from Germany
FRANCE
Paris
Lyons
Bordeaux
Marseilles
Milan
Florence
Rome
ITALY
Corsica
Sardinia
Sicily
Tunis
Algiers
SPAIN
Madrid
PORTUGAL
Lisbon
North Sea
Mediterranean Sea
Adriatic Sea

## EUROPE IN 1914

☐ Russian Empire
▨ Austro-Hungarian Empire

NORWAY
Christiania
SWEDEN
Stockholm
FINLAND
Petrograd
RUSSIAN EMPIRE
POLAND
Baltic Sea
UNITED KINGDOM
NETHER-LANDS
Amsterdam
Brussels
BELGIUM
LUXEMBOURG
GERMANY
Hamburg
Berlin
Munich
SWITZ.
Bern
Milan
AUSTRO-HUNGARIAN EMPIRE
Vienna
ROMANIA
Bucharest
SERBIA
Belgrade
MONTE-NEGRO
BULGARIA
Sofia
OTTOMAN EMPIRE
ALBANIA
GREECE
Athens
Crete
Aegean Sea
FRANCE
Paris
Marseilles
ITALY
Rome
Corsica
Sardinia
Tunis
North Sea
Adriatic Sea

**MAP 10.2** (a) Europe in 1914; (b) Western Eurasia, 1914–23

Political regimes were casualties as well. Tsarist Russia, the Kaiser's Germany, Habsburg Austria-Hungary, and the Ottoman Empire all collapsed during the war or were in their death throes as it ended. The costs to the British monarchy and the French Republic were also great, although both survived the war with their basic political institutions, including their empires, intact. Of the world's industrial powers, the United States and Japan suffered the least damage from the war, marking a migration of the world's economic leadership away from Europe. Armed factions in China were still struggling to establish their sovereignty over the territory once ruled by the Qing Dynasty, as they had been before the war started.

The war's end presented a dramatic opportunity for reimagining the world. The United States, which had become the world's largest economy just prior to the war, was now an international power broker. Its leader, Woodrow Wilson (1856–1924), first articulated the principles of his vision for the postwar world in a speech before the US Congress in early 1918. Wilson advocated a postwar order of liberal, constitutional, sovereign, nation-states trading freely in a market-oriented global economy, with disputes resolved by a new "general association of nations." Implementing Wilson's ideas—summed up in "fourteen points"—bedeviled those who charged themselves with rebuilding global order from the rubble of the war. Wilson's lofty rhetoric was undermined by multiple factors, including the exclusion from the negotiations of representatives of many constituencies with stakes in their outcomes.

The case of a young Vietnamese nationalist illustrates both the hopes for change that Wilson's vision inspired and the undermining of those hopes. Vietnam had been brought under French control in three phases beginning in the 1880s; a movement against French rule had existed for just as long. Many, including a man called Nguyen Ai Quoc ("Nguyen the Patriot"; 1890–1969), saw the peace negotiations as a chance to change Vietnam's relationship to France. Nguyen, who was living in Paris when the war ended, petitioned the delegates at Versailles to support "equal rights for Vietnamese and French in Indochina, freedom of press and opinion, freedom of association and assembly, freedom to travel at home and abroad, and to substitute rule of law for government by decree." Nguyen's demands were rather moderate, seeking not independence but representation for Vietnamese in the French parliament and equality before the law. Despite this, a Vietnamese delegation was refused admission to the talks, and their demands were never considered. Rebuffed, Nguyen—who later took the name Ho Chi Minh— moved toward more radical anticolonial measures, eventually leading an armed movement in Vietnam against France.

Other cases illustrate further inconsistencies in the application of the fourteen points. Japanese and Chinese diplomats both sat at the victors' table. China's representatives expected to be recognized as equal partners in the settlement. China had come late to the Great War, entering the conflict on the Allied side a few months after the United States in the summer of 1917, but they had sent more than one hundred thousand men to work behind the lines in Belgium and France as laborers, orderlies, and in other capacities. At the very least, China expected to regain territory that Germany had colonized before the war, but the treaty's brokers ignored the Chinese position. German colonies in China were taken from Germany, but then given to Japan, seen as a greater military power and more important potential ally (or threat) to the victorious European powers.

When word of the treaty's provisions reached China, thousands of students from Beijing's universities protested, occupying the space that is now Tiananmen Square, chanting slogans and waving banners. In the following days, the protests spread across China, in a wave of Chinese nationalism directed against the actions of the very countries that Sun Yat-sen had claimed China would have as a partner when it had achieved modernity. The Chinese government refused to sign the treaty.

These treaties also established several mandates that provided tutelary roles for the victorious powers to move territories taken from the defeated powers toward eventual independence. The British took responsibility for Mesopotamia and Palestine; the French presided over Syria. Over the next three tortuous decades, the independent states of Iraq, Lebanon, Jordan, Syria, and Israel were carved from these mandated territories, inciting disputes that would continue through the end of the twentieth century over their borders, political organization, and even their reasons for existing while claims of other peoples to create their own sovereign nation-states were denied.

The future in Eastern Europe and the Balkans, the tripwire region for the Great War, involved other thorny challenges. New states like Czechoslovakia and Yugoslavia were created, and existing states had their territories reallocated, but few in the region were satisfied. The war's losers—Austria-Hungary, Germany, and the Ottoman Empire—were excluded completely from the decision-making processes about the future shape of the region. Furthermore, the Allies forced Germany to accept responsibility for the war, and imposed a punishing set of conditions, including loss of territory and colonies, compromised sovereignty, and reparations. Many Germans felt that the treaty denied their country the means to recover from the devastation of the war, leaving them humiliated and resentful.

Russia, too, was excluded from the postwar decision-making process, a result of the dramatic turn of events in the midst of the Great War that we introduced previously. At the start of the war, the Russian Empire fought Germany and Austria virtually alone on the Eastern front. The Russians scored some important victories, but Russia's industrial capacity and lengthy supply lines could never properly equip its military. Moreover, inflation and food shortages afflicted

Russian civilians. Amidst bread riots, strikes, and mutiny, the tsar abdicated in February, 1917, and was placed under arrest.

The collapse of an authoritarian regime was followed by civil war, as happened earlier in the decade in Mexico and China. In Russia, two main rival groups competed for military and political supremacy throughout the spring and summer of 1917, culminating in an October Revolution that installed revolutionary socialists—calling themselves "Bolsheviks"—led by Vladimir Lenin (1870–1924). Lenin had agitated for a Marxist revolution since the late nineteenth century and had been exiled by the tsarist government. Slipping back into Russia during the fall of 1917, Lenin's charisma, political acumen, and uncompromising tactics enabled his Bolshevik party to overthrow the provisional government in October and establish what would become the Union of Soviet Socialist Republics (USSR). The Bolshevik government withdrew from the Great War and signed a peace treaty with Germany. The new government also repudiated debts accumulated by the tsarist regime to Russia's old allies and released diplomatic correspondence that exposed the postwar colonial plans of these former partners. The Bolshevik government was not offered a seat at the table in Versailles.

## The United States and Japan as Global Powers

The war had shaken, but not destroyed, the nineteenth century global political order. The colonial empires of France and Britain remained in place, and the mandates of the new League of Nations confirmed their authority over the future of much of the world's territory and peoples. The League itself embodied liberal, progressive ideals that pledged to bring the world away from the darkness and devastation of the Great War. The United States and Japan had replaced the European empires as the world's economic engines, and they appeared poised to oversee a restoration of the prewar global order. The intellectual bridge between Europe as the old guarantor of civilization and the United States as the new one was made explicit in the movement to create "Western Civilization" courses at elite universities in the United States. These courses were designed to introduce US students to the idea that such a thing as Western Civilization existed and that these students had inherited it and needed to be custodians of it in the twentieth century.

The United States had in fact asserted its place as a guardian of a particular global order in the decades before entering the Great War, deploying troops and battleships repeatedly to the Caribbean, Central America, and Mexico and acquiring colonies around the globe, such as the Philippines, Hawai'i, and Puerto Rico. The opening of the Panama Canal and the outbreak of the Great War the same year led the United States to deploy significant military and economic resources to guard its strategic concerns, such as the sea lanes leading to the canal. In addition, concerns over protecting private investment and racist paternalism also contributed to decisions to occupy Haiti (1915–1934) and the Dominican

Republic (1916–1924) and to station marines intermittently in Cuba, Honduras, and Nicaragua. US troops invaded Mexico twice—in 1914 and again in 1916—during the Mexican Revolution.

The position of the United States in the global economy changed significantly during the course of the Great War. A net debtor in 1914, by 1917, the United States was a net creditor, buying up assets sold by Europeans to pay for the war. Unlike European fields, American farms had not become battlegrounds, and US agricultural output rapidly expanded. The United States made a significant contribution—militarily and economically—to the outcome of the Great War. Its leaders expected to play an important role in shaping the postwar world, but the nature and direction of US global engagement remained uncertain, symbolized by the fate of the Treaty of Versailles. Although US public opinion and many political leaders favored the treaty, including the President who helped inspire it, the US Senate never ratified it, and the United States never joined the League of Nations.

Similar questions could be asked about Japan's future role. Japan had been tasked with maintaining order in the Pacific for the Allied Powers during the Great War and had been rewarded for it. From the mid-nineteenth century on, Japan had rapidly industrialized and become an imperial power with overseas colonies (Korea, Taiwan) and a military force that had defeated China (1895) and Russia (1905). The 1889 Meiji Constitution had created Asia's largest democracy (although only about 1 percent of the population could vote), but the Meiji emperor's death in June 1912 had been followed by a political crisis, as rival constituencies vied for power. The military, angered by proposed spending cuts, used its constitutional veto power in the cabinet to prevent the formation of any government whose policies appeared not to suit it. Populist and progressive groups, feeling that the military had too much power over the government and its budget, staged protests, burning pro-government newspapers and occupying public spaces.

The so-called Taisho crisis, named for the new Emperor's reign, initiated a period of fitful growth of political parties and public participation but also instability. Prime Ministers changed fifteen times during the era of "Taisho Democracy," including one who was assassinated and two more who died in office. Progressive measures, such as the General Election Law (giving all men over age twenty-five the right to vote) were enacted alongside reactionary acts like the Peace Preservation Law (effectively banning public expressions of political dissent). When Taisho's successor, Hirohito (1901–1989), took the throne on Christmas Day in 1926, Japan's democracy was functional, although strong authoritarian factions continued to agitate.

While domestic forces in Japan wrestled with how to best implement and define democracy, the Great War presented Japan with an opportunity to grow its economy—the country's exports began to outpace imports during the war—and to expand its international influence. Japan supplanted Germany in East Asia, occupying the German colony of Qingdao in China and taking control of other German outposts in the Pacific. Pressing its advantage, Japan made "Twenty-one Demands" on China in 1915, insisting on special economic and military rights there. Japan had taken the opportunity presented by World War I to confirm its place among the world's great powers; but like the United States, the ends to which this power would be asserted remained unclear.

## Which Way Forward?

On the political level, troubling signs coexisted with efforts to move past the crisis. After the war, a broader electoral franchise, including women, continued its spread. Only a handful of states gave women the right to vote prior to the Great War, but many of the new states constructed after the war joined existing polities in extending the vote to all adults. Austria, the Baltic States, Czechoslovakia, Germany, Great Britain, Hungary, the Netherlands, Poland, Scandinavia, and the United States all expanded the suffrage in the ten years between 1913 and 1923. Women had earned the right to vote in Belgium, the United Kingdom, and the United States right around the end of the war after long and sometimes violent struggles, including the incarceration of suffragist leaders.

### The Enlightenment Model?

This expansion of the right to vote might seem to affirm an earlier generation's faith in progress, despite the catastrophe of the War, but in many places, laws still made voting difficult for the poor, less well-educated, and minority groups. Votes for women were still decades away in France and most of Latin America. Much of the world's population, both women and men, had no meaningful formal political representation.

The new European states were institutionally weak, and key groups did not appear fully invested in the maintenance of the new states' integrity or efficacy. The new Chinese state had a severely limited franchise, and voting had little impact in determining who held power. During the "Red Summer" of 1919, three dozen US cities experienced riots triggered by acts of discrimination against African American veterans coupled with postwar social and economic dislocations. That same year, at the southern tip of the Western Hemisphere, a police unit opened fire on striking workers in Buenos Aires, beginning the "Tragic Week" during which a general strike shut down the Argentine economy while violent clashes between civilians, the police, and military continued. President Hipólito Yrigoyen (1852–1933), who had been elected under the most inclusive electoral laws in the Western Hemisphere at the time, declared martial law.

In Mexico, revolutionaries attempted to consolidate their control over the country and navigate the complex challenges of forming a stable state by adopting a new constitution in 1917. This constitution had a specificity lacking in the social contracts of earlier generations—it was four times the length of the US Constitution. Dozens of references to the working class mark it as a document of the industrial age. It was also the first constitution to explicitly guarantee extensive social rights to citizens—such as rights to land, education, and social welfare—beginning a trend that would continue in the formation of new constitutions just after the Great War. The Mexican constitution defined the state as the protector of the interests of the Mexican nation, limiting the terms under which non-Mexicans could own property and empowering the state to redistribute land and seize other economic assets from private owners if these actions were perceived to be in the national interest.

Passage of the constitution did not end civil war in Mexico. Mexico's revolutionary military leaders finally resolved their disputes over power and policy off the battlefield by the end of the 1920s, but at a cost to pluralism. Revolutionary leaders built a political system that privileged a single party to allocate resources, reward loyalty, and punish dissent. This single political party, eventually known as the Party of the Institutionalized Revolution (PRI), would dominate Mexican politics for seven decades.

## Italy and Russia Follow New Models

The Mexican Constitution modified the model of the nineteenth century liberal state to embrace more mechanisms by which the state could mediate economic relationships for the benefit of the nation. The Bolshevik state emerging from the ashes of the Russian Empire rejected liberal models of the state-economy-individual relationship entirely. The most important leader of the Bolsheviks, Lenin, was grounded in the Marxist tradition and believed that the liberal state and the capitalist economic system that determined its nature could not be modified but had to be destroyed on a global scale for the world's peoples to enjoy the full benefits of modern life.

Lenin analyzed the global crisis that resulted in the Great War, and his prescription for the future, in a pamphlet, "Imperialism, the Highest Stage of Capitalism." In this document, Lenin incorporated assertions that had already been made by other radicals that Marx's analysis of the path to revolution required some revision. To explain why the socialist revolution predicted by Marx had not occurred in the nineteenth century, Lenin borrowed from the theories of English economist John Hobson (1858–1940). Hobson held that imperialism enabled the production of capitalist economies to outstrip demand if they could conquer—militarily or economically—territories that had not industrialized. By creating modern empires to extract such "superprofits" from the globe's natural and human resources, elites in the world's industrial centers had coopted political leaders

**MAP 10.3** Revolution and Civil War in Russia

who might otherwise lead revolutions, and even for a time marginally improve the lives of workers in the industrialized states without fundamentally changing the political or economic power structures of their countries. Workers who supported the regimes that provided small victories—reductions in hours of the workday or small wage increases—became complicit in both imperialism and their own oppression.

Lenin's description of global capitalism bore little resemblance to Adam Smith's idea that individual actors pursuing their own interests would result in greater efficiency for the benefit of all. Instead, Lenin argued that this image of a global capitalist economic order enforced by the world's great political and military powers was vital propaganda in the effort to blind the world's population to what was really going on: "the financial strangulation of the overwhelming majority of the population of the world" by "two or three powerful world marauders armed to the teeth (America, Great Britain, Japan), who involve the whole world in *their* war over the sharing of *their* booty."

According to Lenin, the means to break free from this required a highly disciplined organization to cultivate and execute the revolution. This idea led Lenin to carefully organize and develop the Communist Party structure, which gave him and his followers a tactical and strategic advantage once the Russian Revolution began. The Communist Party then became the key institution of the post-tsarist state.

The idea of a tightly organized vanguard with a special claim on political insight and power became a centerpiece of movements across the political spectrum in the twentieth century. In Italy, Mussolini employed this idea in building the Fascist Party (formed in 1921) from the Fascio di Combattimento ("Combat League") he had founded in 1919. Mussolini's hardcore followers adopted a uniform, styled after an elite corps of the Italian military, and became known as "Blackshirts." They also gained a reputation for violent attacks on other political groups, union headquarters, and newspaper offices. Mussolini leveraged this reputation in October 1922, calling for a march on Rome from across Italy, promising that the Fascists would not stand down until the current government handed over the reins of power. Rather than test the Fascist threat and potentially plunge Italy into civil war, King Victor Emmanuel met with Mussolini and invited him to form a government as the new prime minister. The Fascists did march into Rome at the end of the month, in celebration of Mussolini's triumph.

## Conclusion

The reorganization of global power in the nineteenth century was violent—in places, such as the Belgian Congo, obscenely so—but underpinning it was the myth of order and progress that we have analyzed in earlier chapters. As the twentieth century began, the myth was buried under wave after wave of violence, accompanied by massive political and economic dislocation. New technologies, including the continual development of more powerful, more accurate, long-distance firepower, aerial bombing, and chemical weapons, transformed the nature of warfare and further dissolved the barriers between military and civilian life. Although atrocities in war were not new, earlier armies had clearer physical limits on the damage they could inflict. Now, artillery shells could hit targets many miles away, aircraft could drop bombs on civilians far from the front, and mustard gas's insidious, mysterious toll on the human body could build over the course of days.

Technology was not the only factor undermining the separation between soldier and civilian. Nationalism encouraged the idea that entire societies, not just armies, went to war, that national solidarity could overflow social and class barriers. The Japanese state, for instance, had worked hard to generate nationalist sentiments among its people so that the victories over China in 1895 and Russia in 1905 would seem like victories not just of the military but of the entire nation. The Hibiya riots showed both how successful the government had been but also how nationalism might turn people against their own governments.

The experiences of the Great War led to questions about fundamental principles of political, social, and economic organization. Billions of dollars had been expended on the latest technology in pursuit of geostrategic interests. Millions of soldiers, workers, and citizens mobilized for their nations' causes. Then, the most advanced industrial economies, the most modern sovereign states, descended into an orgy of destruction. The question that haunted the subsequent generation and helped to set the stage for further conflict was, what was the point?

Wilfred Owen, one of the English poets quoted earlier in this chapter, worried about twentieth-century nationalism's power to mobilize people to fight and die in the ways that the Great War had revealed. He concluded his poem about chemical warfare, "Dulce Et Decorum Est" by addressing the reader directly:

> If in some smothering dreams you too could pace
> Behind the wagon that we flung him in,
> And watch the white eyes writhing in his face,
> His hanging face, like a devil's sick of sin;

> If you could hear, at every jolt, the blood
> Come gargling from the froth-corrupted lungs,
> Obscene as cancer, bitter as the cud
> Of vile, incurable sores on innocent tongues,

## TIMELINE

| **1883–1913** | **ca. 1900** | **1904–05** | **1910** | **1912–13** |
|---|---|---|---|---|
| European military expenditures increase 200 percent | North Atlantic countries control 80 percent of the world's manufacturing output | War between Japan and Russia | Beginning of the Mexican Revolution | Balkan Wars |

| **1890** | **1904** | **1905** | **1911–12** | **1914** |
|---|---|---|---|---|
| Alfred Thayer Mahan, *The Influence of Sea Power Upon History* | Completion of Trans-Siberian Railway | Bloody Sunday Massacre and Revolution of 1905, Russia; Hibiya Riots, Japan | Chinese Revolution; end of Qing dynasty | Beginning of Great War |

My friend, you would not tell with such high zest
To children ardent for some desperate glory, The old Lie;
Dulce et Decorum est
Pro patria mori.

Owen's concluding line quotes the Roman poet Horace: "It is sweet and fitting to die for one's country." Owen, after seeing the effects of the war that had been rushed into so enthusiastically, decried such sentiment as an "old lie."

Mussolini disagreed. He exhorted his followers to believe, "All in the state, nothing outside the state, nothing against the state." After the Great War, both communist and fascist movements in many countries challenged the liberal conception of the state, the relationship between state and nation, and between state and individual. In Chapter 11, we will follow these conflicts through the ongoing crisis of global order, the economic meltdown of the Great Depression, and renewed global warfare at the end of the 1930s.

## A Few Good Books

Sheila Fitzpatrick. *The Russian Revolution.* New York: Oxford University Press, 2008.

Friedrich Katz. *The Secret War in Mexico.* Chicago: University of Chicago Press, 1981.

John Keegan. *The Face of Battle: A Study of Agincourt, Waterloo, and the Somme.* New York: The Viking Press, 1976.

Alan Kramer. *Dynamic of Destruction: Culture and Mass Killing in the First World War.* New York: Oxford University Press, 2009.

Margaret MacMillan. *Paris 1919: Six Months that Changed the World.* New York: Random House, 2003.

William Manchester. *The Arms of Krupp: The Rise and Fall of the Industrial Dynasty that Armed Germany at War.* Boston: Back Bay Books, 2003.

*For additional resources, including maps, primary sources, visuals, web links, and quizzes, please go to **www.oup.com/us/carter***

| 1915 | 1917 | 1918–20 | 1922 | 1928 |
|---|---|---|---|---|
| Japan presents China with "Twenty-one Demands" | October Revolution in Russia; Mexico adopts a new constitution | Flu pandemic kills fifty to one hundred million people worldwide | Mussolini marches on Rome | Grand Council of Fascism established in Italy |

| 1916 | 1918 | 1919 | 1925 | 1929 |
|---|---|---|---|---|
| Lenin writes "Imperialism, the Highest Stage of Capitalism" | Woodrow Wilson issues fourteen points; armistice ends Great War | Peace negotiations after the Great War conducted in France | Death of Sun Yat-sen | Publication of Ernest Hemingway's *A Farewell to Arms* and Erich Maria Remarque's *All Quiet on the Western Front* |

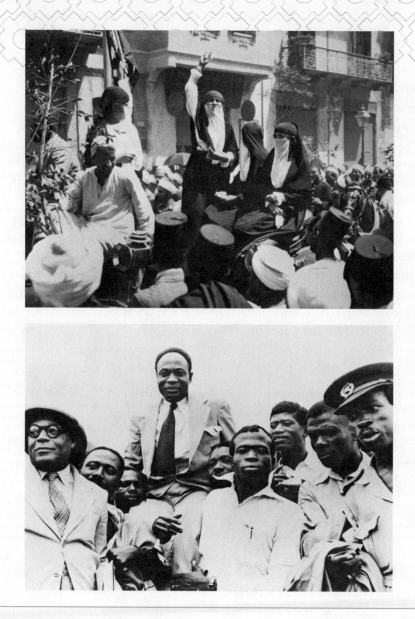

(TOP) CAIRO PROTESTS, 1919. Women constituted an important group among the thousands of protesters who filled the streets of Cairo after the Great War, expressing Egyptian nationalism and advocating for independence. The Cairo Protests resembled similar anti-imperialist and nationalist protests that took place this same year around the world, including Turkey, China, Germany, and Korea.

(BOTTOM) KWAME NKRUMAH, GHANA'S FIRST PRESIDENT, BEING CARRIED BY SUPPORTERS, APRIL 14, 1957. Born in the Gold Coast (now Ghana) and then educated in Britain and the United States, Kwame Nkrumah returned to Ghana in 1947. He was arrested in 1948 during riots in Accra when Ghanaian soldiers protested the colonial government's failure to deliver promised benefits. Nkrumah was not involved in planning the riots and was soon released, but he used the incident to launch a campaign that led to Ghana's independence within a decade, and he became the nation's first president.

# The Ongoing Crisis of Global Order

## 1919–1948

In the spring of 1919, massive protests gripped Egypt, a part of the Ottoman Empire since the sixteenth century. British forces had occupied Egypt early in the Great War and made it a protectorate, deploying Egypt's population and resources to serve the Empire's wartime goals. At the end of the war, an Egyptian delegation, like many other groups seeking self-determination, was denied access to treaty deliberations. When leaders of the Wafd (Delegation) Party pursued diplomatic and legal maneuvers to end the protectorate, British officers arrested several prominent Wafdist leaders. A cross section of Egyptian society then took to the streets in protest. Huda Sha`rawi (1879–1947), founder of the Intellectual Association of Egyptian Women, emerged as a key figure in the protests, organizing women of means to join the movement. Sha`rawi became head of the Wafdist Women's Central Committee as pressure on the British government mounted, including strikes and acts of civil disobedience. In 1922, the British conceded limited independence and a new constitution for Egypt was promulgated in 1923.

Huda Sha`rawi's subsequent career illustrates the enduring complexities of defining sovereignty, democracy, and justice in the modern world. As Egypt transitioned to independence, women were not granted the suffrage. Sha`rawi resigned her position with the Wafdists in protest and focused her energies on the work of the Egyptian Feminist Union and, later, the Arab Feminist Union. Sha`rawi, who publicly removed her veil as an act of protest in 1923, argued that Egypt, and the Arab world more generally, could only prosper when women's equality became a defining characteristic of independent, sovereign states.

Three decades later, in early 1948, veterans of another world war gathered in the city of Accra, in the British colony of the Gold Coast (today's Ghana). These African soldiers had fought alongside other British troops, and had been promised an array of veterans' benefits, but returned home to find these promises ignored. The veterans' concerns dovetailed with a broader protest movement developing in Ghana,

**COLONIES AND MANDATES, 1939**

Colonies belonging to:

| | |
|---|---|
| Belgium | Netherlands |
| Britain | Portugal |
| Denmark | Spain |
| France | United States |
| Italy | Japan |

Mandates or protectorates of:

| | |
|---|---|
| Australia | France |
| Britain | Japan |
| South Africa | Belgium |

MAP 11.1 Colonies and Mandates, 1939

fueled by high unemployment and rampant inflation. In 1947 protest leaders organized an economic boycott as their primary tool. When businesses agreed to lower
their profit margins in response to the boycott, the movement announced a date
for the boycott's end. On the very last day of the boycott, Ghanaian veterans approached the colonial Governor's offices to demand their promised benefits. The
police blocked their way and eventually fired into the crowd, killing at least one
veteran and wounding dozens. Five days of riots followed.

In the aftermath of the disturbances, imperial authorities arrested six political
leaders, including Kwame Nkrumah (1909–1972), as masterminding the protests.
He was not one of the veterans but a leading decolonization advocate and organizer.
This action exacerbated the situation in Ghana, and the men were soon released.
Afterward, Nkrumah organized a political party, the Convention People's Party, in
1949. The party became the dominant institution negotiating the transition of Ghana
from colony to member of the British Commonwealth (1957) to independent republic
(1960). Kwame Nkrumah served as the first Prime Minister of the self-governing
commonwealth country and later first president of the republic, proving to be both
a staunch advocate for African independence and unity and an increasingly authoritarian ruler.

---

These events offer an intriguing introduction to the goals of this chapter.
During these three decades, political revolutions, economic catastrophes,
and global wars obliterated nineteenth-century promises of order and progress.
When the Great War ended in 1918, optimists labeled it a "war to end war," hopeful that lessons learned from its causes and conduct would prove a deterrent to
future conflict. Yet, the Great War was only a prelude to further destruction; new
political and economic experiments proliferated in the 1920s, and enduring
resentments festered. A decade after the Great War ended, the global system of
production and consumption—what many had come to see as the symbol of
modernity itself—collapsed. Economic hardship followed by another bloodletting characterized the 1930s and early 1940s. At the end of the Second World
War, individuals and groups vowed not to repeat the perceived errors that precipitated and perpetuated the "Three Decades' Crisis," yet the similarities between
events in Cairo in 1919 and Accra in 1948 demonstrate the challenges that accompanied this commitment.

In the first section of the chapter, we analyze the struggles over territorial reorganization in the Middle East and Asia after the Great War. In the next section,
we survey the consolidation of the USSR and emergence of other communist
movements, followed by an explanation of the economic events in the 1920s that

culminated in the Great Depression. We then examine the political and economic fallout of the 1930s, focusing on the spread of fascism and the outbreak of global war. In the last sections of the chapter, we examine the nature of the Second World War and the challenges facing the global community in its aftermath, as the victorious allies in the war attempted to reconcile competing ideas about property, equality, democracy, and citizenship while much of the world's population clamored for a seat at the negotiating table over the world's future.

## Struggles over Political Order in the Middle East and Asia

The theoretical commitment to self-determination of sovereign nation-states embodied in the League of Nations clashed with the perceived self-interests of the victorious powers at the end of the Great War. These states decided to redraw the map of the postwar world according to their own interests. Nowhere could this be seen more clearly than in the Middle East, where the former Allies worked to squash or marginalize other ideals or organizations. The League of Nations determined that the former German colonies in Africa would be transferred to the administrative authority of the British and French governments for the foreseeable future. In contrast, the political reorganization of the former Ottoman Empire had many regional variations. Much of the Middle East and North Africa traveled on a path toward independence for which the French and British claimed to serve as navigators. The League of Nations also determined that Great Britain would facilitate a "national home for the Jewish people" in Palestine while simultaneously protecting the rights of the territory's Arab population. Popular unrest, like that in Egypt, greeted the new rules and rulers, as the contemporary forms of the states of Iran, Iraq, Jordan, Syria, Lebanon, Cyprus, Saudi Arabia, Armenia, Egypt, Palestine, and Israel began to evolve at this time.

### The Republic of Turkey

In the short term, the most prominent internationally recognized, fully sovereign independent state to emerge from the former Ottoman lands was the Republic of Turkey. Mustafa Kemal Ataturk (1881–1938), the first President of the Republic, enshrined secularism in the country's 1924 constitution and introduced both profound and mundane reforms to distinguish Turkey from the Ottoman Empire. Ataturk liquidated the connection between political rule and religious authority, doing away with the positions of Sultan and Caliph. The government established a new alphabet for the Turkish language based on Latin letters rather than Arabic script. Laws required government officials to wear Western suits rather than Islamic religious robes, turbans, or veils. The education system was secularized; classroom instruction in Arabic and Persian was stopped.

**APPEAL FOR RELIEF.** Established in 1915 with the aid of the US State Department, the American Committee for Armenian and Syrian Relief provided humanitarian aid to Armenians forcibly deported from Turkey to other parts of the Ottoman Empire during World War I. This poster solicited private contributions to the fund, which were distributed by the US Embassy in Istanbul. The term "genocide" was later coined to describe the forced dislocation and murder of Armenians during this era: one and one-half million people were killed.

Non-Turks living under the Ottoman Empire paid a high price for the construction of modern Turkey. A pattern of aggression against Armenians that began in the nineteenth century turned into a systematic policy during the Great War, organized by leaders intent on creating a more ethnically pure population. Scholars estimate that between 1915 and 1923, more than one million five hundred thousand Armenians perished either from direct assault or the deprivation of the means to survive. Although the treaties ending the Great War called for the prosecution of those responsible for these crimes against humanity, the Great Powers ultimately opted to accept the expediency of stable government in the region. A small, independent Armenia emerged, and the new regime in Turkey was not held responsible for prior acts committed against Armenians. No individuals or institutions were ever held accountable for the Armenian genocide.

Although the Great Powers espoused principles of self-determination and national sovereignty, they failed to implement them in their own empires and spheres of influence. Great Britain remained by far the leading imperial power on the planet at the end of the war, ruling over one-fifth of the world's population and one-quarter of its territory. British leaders expressed little doubt that they were acting with justice and rectitude throughout the empire. Government documents still described British actions throughout the empire as being for the uplift of subject peoples. Challengers to the imperial order in places like Egypt consistently exposed the contradictions between the victors' high principles and their questionable practices. These challenges can perhaps be best seen in the so-called "Jewel in the Crown" of the British Empire: India.

## Challenges to British Rule in India

Opposition to British rule in India continued to build after the Great War, in the context of events in other places, especially the Middle East. One million Indian soldiers served in the Great War, and more than seventy-five thousand died. Nationalists in South Asia argued that these sacrifices had earned India greater autonomy. British politicians proposed some reforms, but supreme power remained with the Viceroy (the top British official in India), including the unilateral authority to define sedition and suppress dissent. Brigadier General Reginald Dyer (1864–1927) horrifically demonstrated the extent of these powers in April 1919 when he gave the order to fire on an unarmed crowd in a public square gathered in defiance of his ban on public meetings. Dyer's troops fired for some ten minutes, focusing their fusillade on the plaza's exits. Estimates of those killed range from slightly less than four hundred to almost fifteen hundred. The Amritsar (or Jallianwala Bagh) Massacre widened the rift between Indian activists and British officials. At the end of 1919, Parliament passed the "Government of India Act," introducing more shared governance between elected Indian officials and appointed British ones; but in the shadow of the massacre, this attempt at compromise found little favor among Indian nationalists.

In this atmosphere, Mohandas K. Gandhi (1869–1948) rose to the leadership of the Indian National Congress, a leading nationalist organization. Born in Gujarat, Gandhi had been educated in London and worked for years as a lawyer and activist in South Africa, another outpost of British imperialism. In his 1909 pamphlet "Indian Home Rule," Gandhi invoked the social contract tradition of sovereignty, writing, "I have no objection to your remaining in my country, but although you are the rulers; you will have to remain as servants of the people. It is not we who have to do as you wish, but it is you who have to do as we wish." Increasingly, the wish of South Asians appeared to be the formation of a new social contract.

Gandhi played a key role in turning the political consciousness raised through Indian participation in World War I and the 1919 massacre into action. His tactical position on how to mobilize was clear: he opposed violence in the pursuit of Indian independence. At times, Gandhi's uncompromising commitment to his own vision frustrated both allies and opponents, as opinions among South Asians hardened after the war between supporters of a single independent Indian nation-state and those who believed that multiple independent states would better serve the interests of the region's peoples. These divergent perspectives defined the following two decades in South Asia. British officials argued that policies like advisory councils and expanded suffrage laid the groundwork for eventual autonomy. South Asian nationalists saw these modest reforms as delaying tactics by an empire desperate to maintain its hold over the region, but the nationalists continued to struggle over their own goals for the long term and tactics for the near term.

## Nationalism Frustrated in China

Disappointed expectations over postwar political outcomes also rattled China in 1919. As we saw in chapter 10, news that the Great Powers, meeting in Versailles, had given Germany's former colonial holdings in China to Japan sparked protests in several major Chinese cities, especially Beijing. Taking its name from the date of these protests, the May Fourth Movement signaled a fundamental change in China's attitude to the West. For generations, modernizers in China tended to reject traditional Chinese culture as "backward" and advocated reform using Western political and cultural models. "Modern" was generally taken to mean "Western." Revolutionaries had overthrown China's monarchy, enthusiastic to emulate a Western model of modernity; the new republic had sent one hundred forty thousand men to Europe in support of the allies' war effort. The May Fourth Movement expressed a new sentiment: that the Great Powers had betrayed China as it struggled to constitute itself into a functioning state. Furthermore, the horrors of World War I called Western liberal democracy sharply into question. Was a civilization that culminated in imperial treachery and trench warfare one that China should emulate?

Communism—neither traditionally Chinese nor liberal—offered an alternative to some Chinese eager for new models of modernization. Founded in 1921, the Chinese Communist Party reflected Marxist-Leninist thinking with strong Soviet influence, including an emphasis on China's need to industrialize first before it could proceed to communism. Alternatively, Sun Yat-sen's Nationalist Party still remained an important force in China, increasingly divided between one branch sympathetic to socialist ideas and another branch that hewed at first toward liberal democracy and a market economy and later tilted toward fascism. When Sun Yat-sen died of cancer in 1925, disagreement raged over the leader's political agenda and legacy. Even within Sun's family, there was no consensus.

When Japanese-trained, staunchly anti-communist Chiang Kai-shek (1887–1975) succeeded Sun as head of the KMT, he moved to unify China and rid the country of communism. In a brutal purge, Chiang massacred most members of the Communist Party in Shanghai in the spring of 1927 as part of the Northern Expedition to reunify China under Nationalist rule. The leaders of China's "new" republic, while maintaining many of the formal structures of the state inaugurated in 1912, concentrated power in the office of the President and moved toward fascism, suspicious of multiparty politics and political debate. The surviving members of the Communist Party eventually coalesced around Mao Zedong (1893–1976) who articulated a revision of communist revolutionary doctrine, suggesting that peasant societies like China could stage a successful revolution without having to industrialize first.

## A Communist Future?

Marxists around the world debated various political strategies and tactics after the Great War. In the 1920s, in the transition from Bolshevik Russia to the Soviet Union, communist leaders constructed a new internal order and sought allies to share their vision of the future. Lenin's hopes for global revolution against capitalism had been high. A handful of communist uprisings followed the Great War. The new USSR, with Russia as its core, tipped the balance in power struggles of bordering countries, incorporating Ukraine and Belarus. Mongolia became a Soviet client state, the Mongolian People's Republic, in 1924. The proliferation of new communist states was limited and short-lived, however. Uprisings in Hungary and Germany were put down harshly, and no additional communist states emerged in the immediate postwar years, although the Soviet Union continued to provide a different model of political economy around which an international order might emerge. Beginning in 1919, a new Communist International (Comintern) became an arm of Russian (after 1922, Soviet) foreign policy that advised communist groups around the world on the correct path to global revolution. Marxists, either in association with the Comintern or independent of it, attempted to organize Communist parties and mobilize politically. At least fifteen countries in the Western Hemisphere alone had Communist political parties by 1929.

### From Lenin to Stalin in the Soviet Union

When Lenin died in 1924, Josef Stalin (1878–1953) emerged from a group of would-be successors to gain control of the Communist Party and the future of the USSR. Stalin guided the country through rapid industrialization, centralizing control over production and distribution of resources. The USSR became for a time the world's largest producer of many industrial commodities, including oil, coal, iron ore, and natural gas. Politically, Stalin's Soviet Union denigrated Western liberalism as a tool of the wealthy designed to bamboozle the proletariat. The Soviet Union rejected representative democracy in favor of "democratic centralism," which held that the Communist Party represented the will of the people and therefore party actions were by definition democratic. Anyone who opposed the Party's actions could be imprisoned as an enemy of the people. Millions of criminals so defined (including political dissidents but also common criminals and others whose crimes were never fully explained) were deported to a state-administered system of labor camps, known by the acronym "Gulag." In addition, to achieve rapid industrialization, Stalin implemented a campaign to collectivize agricultural production, taking decisions about production and consumption away from local producers and consumers. Famine gripped some of the Soviet Union's most fertile grain-producing regions. Five to eight million people starved to death in Russia and Ukraine in 1932–33, and as many as one in four Kazakhs died in this same period in the name of rapid economic transformation.

## Debating Famine in the Soviet Union

Understanding and interpreting these events challenge researchers. How do we assess the extent of the famine and its toll, its root causes, and their implications for the Soviet political and economic system and its subject peoples in the 1920s and 1930s? Demographic data during periods of trauma are difficult to interpret even when records are detailed and accessible. Many victims do not literally starve to death but succumb to disease or injury because they are already weakened by malnutrition. In addition, birth rates drop in a famine, so some researchers also factor these "missing people" into the toll of the catastrophe.

Record-keeping on these Soviet famines was anything but thorough or transparent. Soviet authorities at the time worked to hide the cause and extent of the famine, going so far as to publish deliberate misinformation about harvests and other local conditions. Then, when reports were published suggesting widespread famine had occurred, the Soviet government insisted it was propaganda circulated by its ideological enemies. Access to sources that might aid researchers trying to understand what happened was systematically denied.

Further considerations add to the difficulties of historical research on a topic like this. Many Ukrainians, descendants of those affected by the famine, perceive these deaths to be the goal of a Soviet policy they call *Holodomor*, or "Extermination by Hunger." Historians, each shaped by an overall view of the Soviet Union and global affairs at the time, can be drawn to minimize, maximize, or even avoid discussion of these events. Robert Conquest, a prominent biographer of Stalin, concluded in his book *Harvest of Sorrow* that the Ukrainian famine amounted to genocide, although he later revised some of his original claims. Scholars Dana

Dalrymple, Norman Naimark, and Timothy Snyder also support the view that the famines were the intended result of Soviet policies. Other researchers, such as Mark Tauger and Stephen Devereux, attribute the disastrous outcome more to incompetence and generally bad economic policies than to intentional genocide, defined as policy designed to exterminate an entire people. The debate, hampered by incomplete or inaccessible sources, goes on. The overall evidence, however, indicates that Stalinism was an extraordinarily repressive system that delivered industrialization at a very high cost to the people of the USSR.[1]

## The Global Economy in the 1920s

The Great War challenged the global liberal economic and political order. Communist leaders posited that a command economy, in which the state controls decisions about the production and distribution of resources, would provide the best means to manage a modern economy. Even some non-communist leaders, like the new revolutionary government in Mexico, believed that the national state should play a larger role in managing a modern economy for the benefit of the nation. In contrast, most elites in the world's largest economies—Western Europe, Japan, and the United States—advocated a limited role for government in economic planning and social welfare activities, encouraging individuals and businesses in the private sector to allocate resources and drive growth and prosperity. They tried to put together a system to do that.

Before the system could be reformed, though, it had first to be repaired. The war had disrupted the global economic order, and although some economies had surged during the war years, the 1920s began with economic recessions in much of the industrialized world, including Europe, the United States, and Japan. Recovery soon followed in some places, but Germany and its allies remained crippled after the war. Monthly inflation rates reached 100 percent in Austria and Hungary and 200 percent in Germany—prices were doubling every few days. Germany defaulted on its foreign debts. World leaders struggled to adjust to the myriad economic consequences of the Great War: ten billion dollars in military expenditures, devastated infrastructure, denuded agricultural land, nine million dead and twenty million wounded.

---

[1] Some of the important contributions on this question are Robert Conquest, *Harvest of Sorrow* (Oxford: Oxford University Press, 1987); Norman Naimark, *Stalin's Genocides* (Princeton, NJ: Princeton University Press, 2011); Timothy Snyder, *Bloodlands* (New York: Basic Books, 2012); Sheila Fitzpatrick, *Stalin's Peasants* (Oxford: Oxford University Press, 1996); R. W. Davies and Stephen Wheatcroft, *The Year of Hunger* (New York: Palgrave MacMillan, 2004); Mark B. Tauger, "Arguing from Errors: On Certain Issues in Robert Davies' and Stephen Wheatcroft's Analysis of the 1932 Soviet Grain Harvest and the Great Soviet Famine of 1931–1933," *Europe-Asia Studies* 58, no. 6 (September, 2006): 973–984.

## Rebuilding Global Commerce

The biggest economic change since 1914 may have been the shift of wealth and productive capacity. By the end of the war, the United States was responsible for nearly half of the entire globe's economic output and financial wherewithal. US agriculture and manufacturing had expanded to fill the gap left as the other major industrial powers turned their economies into war machines. US financiers supplanted Europeans as the world's bankers. When the war was over, the European economies were wrecked, and their currencies were of questionable worth. European states owed private investors and the United States government about ten billion dollars. The treaties ending the war punished Germany by forcing it to pay the victorious countries over thirty billion dollars in reparations.

These conditions meant that the United States was the only engine that could drive the postwar global economy, and both the League of Nations and the US Government emphasized international commerce as the key to a peaceful and prosperous future. With this in mind, political and business leaders concluded that it was essential to address the monetary systems of the war's belligerent powers. Who would get paid first? On what terms? Would repaying debts and reparations stifle economic recovery? Or would readjusting their terms trigger financial chaos, political upheaval, or military intervention? Should the amount of cash available in any given national economy be limited to the amount of gold reserves in its national treasury, or would that limit the availability of credit, which was crucial for future growth?

## Repairing the Global Financial System

Two attempts to answer these questions and address financial uncertainties emerged in the mid-1920s. First, the victorious allies, led by the United States, brokered the Dawes Plan with Germany, reorganizing the German financial and tax system. This plan also revised the war reparations process and encouraged investment in Germany. Second, more than twenty countries returned to the "gold standard," tying the value of their currency to that of gold. Advocates of this system asserted that fixing the value of national currencies in relation to gold would boost global economic confidence by reducing uncertainties about how individual currencies related to each other.

The postwar economic overhaul was not limited to Europe. The leaders of Latin American and Caribbean countries who hoped to partake in renewed economic growth powered by a return to robust agricultural and raw materials exports recognized that their primary economic partner now would have to be the United States. Many of them contracted the "money doctor," Princeton University's Edwin W. Kemmerer (1875–1945), who brought evangelical fervor for the gold standard and balanced government budgets to his prescriptions for re-forming the financial systems of Mexico, Guatemala, Colombia, Chile, Ecuador, Bolivia, and Peru. Kemmerer also worked in Poland, China, and South Africa. US bank loans and private direct investment also helped to fuel the economies of Asia and the Middle East.

The "money doctor" and his policies seemed to do the trick. Confidence in a global economic recovery, fueled by American optimism and cash, soared, along with stock prices. The United States experienced the "Roaring Twenties" and France "Les Années Folles" (The Crazy Years). But as the champagne flowed, struc-tural weaknesses remained in the global economy. In the agricultural sector, global demand for food had changed during the Great War. The farms of Europe had become killing fields, while hungry soldiers and civilian populations still needed to be fed. Commodities prices climbed, and producers in other areas of the globe—North and South America, Africa, and Australia—had responded by converting acreage into food crops, with the expectation of greater profits. The rapid return to productivity of European agriculture, aided by new industrially produced fertilizers and the dynamic output of newly independent states in East Central Europe, overwhelmed the agricultural market in the 1920s. Prices fell as supply increased. Income stagnated for farmers across the world, yet some re-gions still suffered food shortages, as populations could neither produce enough food locally nor afford imported staples.

Besides the glutted commodities market, the other hidden weakness in the global economy was the accelerating use of credit in economic transactions, which maintained an appearance of prosperity with little real wealth to support it. A belief in future economic growth made retailers willing to sell goods on installment plans and consumers willing to buy them. Both buyers and sellers believed that it wasn't important whether you had the money to buy something now because next year you were sure to have more than enough! This attitude was at its most extreme in the US stock market, where investors borrowed money from stockbrokers for the purchase of stocks, expecting to repay the loan from future profits.

## The Collapse of the Post-War Order

These transactions depended on both economic growth and also the belief that this growth would continue indefinitely. When perceptions about the potential for continued growth changed, the value of stocks began to fall. As stock prices fell, the profits that investors were counting on to pay for the stocks they had al-ready bought shrank, then disappeared. Brokers demanded the money they had loaned out, and investors began selling their stocks, even at prices lower than the original purchase price. Instead of getting rich, investors were losing money.

As more people lost more money and more people demanded to be paid, investors sold stocks at whatever price they could, driving down the market. "The Crash" came on October 28 and 29, 1929, two days in which the New York Stock Exchange lost more than thirty billion dollars in value. The Dow Jones Industrial Average—an indicator that measures the market value of large corporations in the United States—declined 89 percent between 1929 and 1932; it would not reach the levels of early 1929 again until 1954.

## The Great Depression

The great stock market crash of 1929 was itself an effect of larger problems in the global economy, but it made clear that the system was in crisis. Panic spread across the globe. "Bank runs" proliferated, as many financial institutions lacked the cash reserves to meet the demands of customers who wanted to withdraw their money. One-third of the banks in the United States closed. The largest commercial bank in Austria closed its doors in 1931, followed by important banks in Germany and Britain. As credit dried up, industrial output fell, and jobs disappeared. Unemployment rose to 20 percent in England, 25 percent in the United States, and 30 percent in Germany.

Economic cycles of growth and contraction have always characterized the global economy, but this contraction was particularly severe and long-lasting. For the world's economic elites, the great strength of the global economic system that they were trying to rebuild in the 1920s was its interconnectedness, which allowed goods and services to flow easily across borders. This same interconnectedness meant that the economic crisis in the United States and Western Europe spread quickly around the world. General financial chaos erupted, as buyers, sellers, and lenders lost confidence in the economic future. Frightened business people and government officials scrambled to respond. Governments began to abandon the gold standard for their currencies so that they could increase the amount of money in circulation without having to sock away more gold reserves. Countries also raised tariffs in the hopes of protecting domestic industry and domestic employment at the expense of global integration. The effect was further economic slowing, not recovery. Desperate for solutions, fascists, socialists, communists, and liberals traded accusations and proposals in the world's legislative assemblies and the media—and often traded blows on the streets—as the economic crisis continued.

## Political Repercussions of the Economic Collapse

The effect and duration of the Great Depression varied by country and region. In the United States, over fifteen million people—about 30 percent of the labor

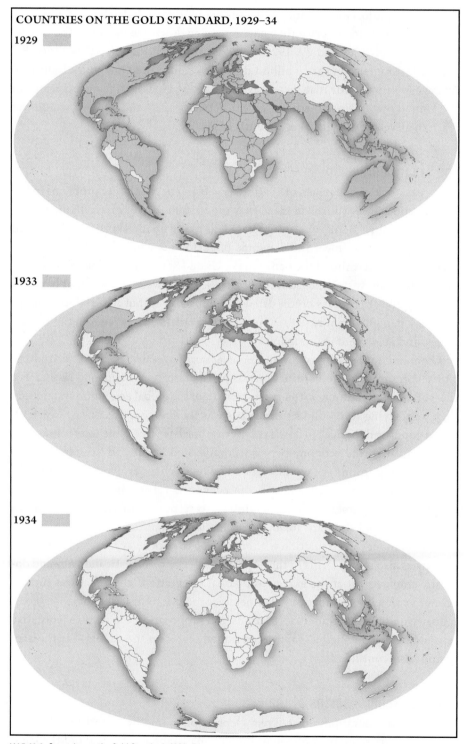

**MAP 11.2** Countries on the Gold Standard, 1929–34

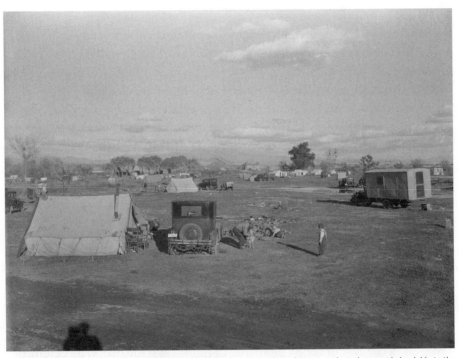

**A HOOVERVILLE IN BAKERSFIELD, CALIFORNIA.** The Great Depression brought unprecedented economic hardship to the world's industrial economies and called into question the principles that were at the core of the global financial system. "Hoovervilles"—named for US President Herbert Hoover—were communities of homeless, often unemployed, people across the United States, where unemployment rates approached 25 percent during the early 1930s.

force—were unemployed in March 1933, the month President Franklin D. Roosevelt (1882–1945) took office and initiated a series of experiments to address the crisis.

Known collectively as the "New Deal," these policies changed the relationship between the US economy and the state, based on the premise that the modern state had an obligation to manage the economy and address the social welfare needs of the population. A flood of initiatives and laws followed. Some, like the Social Security Act of 1935, which established support for senior citizens and aid for children living in poverty, became cornerstones of a new American social contract. Others, like an attempt to directly control wages and prices, were challenged in court and overturned. Economic recovery was uneven—by the mid-1930s the economy was again in recession, and unemployment, even in 1939, was at ten million (around 18 percent)—but the US political system survived the ordeal. The same could not be said everywhere.

In Latin America, responses to the global economic collapse varied. Six major military coups occurred between March and December of 1930 alone. More would come in the following years. Chile, described by the League of Nations as the country most devastated by the global economic collapse, moved in the opposite direction, as a military regime—incapable of managing the crisis—yielded to an intensely partisan, diverse, democratic political system. In all these cases, new governments wondered how to rebuild political and economic order while the region's traditional economic partners in Western Europe were floundering and geostrategic alliances were highly volatile. This established a pattern for the future, as the region's militaries took the power to determine acceptable political behavior and economic policy away from civilian political systems and reserved ultimate authority for themselves.

Around the world, the Great Depression triggered economic experimentation and reassessment of assumptions about how modern economies work. Several trends predominated in efforts to pull countries out of the malaise. Many, like the reforms in the United States, included an expanded role for the state in managing modern economies. Fiscal and monetary policies were adjusted, with higher tariffs and abandonment of the gold standard common practices. Some countries used deficit spending to initiate public works programs, creating employment opportunities. Many countries nationalized foreign-owned businesses, as in the case of the oil industries of Bolivia and Mexico. Other countries also saw some growth in domestic industry as traditional supplies of industrial goods were cut off. Social welfare programs were created or expanded to address basic needs.

Many countries looked to strengthen their regional spheres of influence or colonial economic relations—the shadow of mercantilism. For example, in 1932, the British Empire established a system of lower tariffs for goods traded within the empire than for those entering from outside. The United States pursued new trade agreements within the Western Hemisphere, becoming the major trading partner with most Latin American countries by 1938. Germany also pursued trade in Latin America but built its most important international economic relationships through special agreements with Austria, Hungary, Poland, and Yugoslavia. In Asia, Japan strengthened its privileged trading ties with colonies in Korea and Taiwan, as well as the puppet state of Manchukuo, created when Japan invaded Manchuria in 1931.

## Fascism Spreads

As the 1920s wore on, economies recovered, currencies stabilized, and investment flowed; it appeared that fragile political systems might resist the pull toward fascism that had enveloped Italy. However, the dislocations of the global economic collapse, lingering resentments of the victorious powers' postwar actions, and a growing collaboration among fascist groups reversed the trend in the 1930s. In Germany, Adolf Hitler (1889–1945), took over the small National Socialist German Workers' (Nazi) Party, which attempted to topple the German government by force. Sent to prison in 1924 for his role in a failed coup, Hitler wrote a manifesto entitled *Mein Kampf* (*My Struggle*), published after his release. *Mein Kampf* promised a future when a *Führer* (this word is rarely translated, but means "leader") would oversee the creation of a new German empire. Beginning in the mid-1920s, a reorganized Nazi party produced an ultranationalist message, opposing both communism (because it emphasized class over nation) and liberalism (because it emphasized individual over nation). The Nazis also institutionalized Hitler's scapegoating of Jews, blaming a fictional international Jewish conspiracy for German economic woes. Like other totalitarian groups, the Nazis emphasized military-style organization and mass events to demonstrate that their movement went well beyond that of a political party. Hitler led the Nazis into the 1928 elections, where they attracted only 2.8 percent of the German vote, but Nazi poll numbers grew consistently after the collapse of the global economy. By 1932, the Nazis had become the most popular party in Germany, although still not a majority in the legislature.

Disagreements among Hitler's opponents prevented them from pooling their votes to form a successful coalition against the Nazis. Instead, Hitler convinced nationalist and conservative politicians outside the Nazi party to support his bid to be appointed Chancellor. Within the first month of his term in office in 1933, Hitler blamed a suspicious fire at the German parliament building (*Reichstag*) on the German Communist Party, which held the second largest delegation in the parliament. An emergency edict banned the Communists, leaving their seats in the legislature empty and giving the Nazis a majority.

## The Invasion of Ethiopia

In the mid-1930s, fascism appeared to be ascendant, and not just in Germany. The fascist idea of a world of warring nations contrasted with the vision—expressed in the dream of a League of Nations—of a world free from conflict and dedicated to human progress. Conflicts between fascist states and others became increasingly common. Italian fascists invaded Ethiopia to realize their vision of a new Roman empire, using chemical weapons—banned by international treaty—to achieve their objectives. Ethiopian Emperor Haile Selassie (1892–1975) appealed to the League of Nations for help, imploring the League's delegates to action, asserting, "In a word, it is international morality that is at stake. Have the signatures appended to a Treaty value only in so far as the signatory Powers have a personal, direct and immediate interest involved?" Yet, no coordinated effort to counteract Mussolini materialized, in part because other European states could scarcely object to Italian imperialism in Africa when they—the Belgians, British, French, Portuguese, and Spanish—had their own African colonies. Besides, the addition of independent Ethiopia to Italy's African empire, which also included Libya, Eritrea, and Somaliland, did not appear threatening to any of Europe's great powers.

## The Spanish Civil War and Aerial Bombing

Not everyone agreed that the invasion of Ethiopia was unimportant. A young English journalist named George L. Steer (1909–1944) reported on the downfall of independent Ethiopia as part of a worrisome trend, both in terms of fascist aggression and the unconventional methods employed. The next battleground Steer covered, the Spanish civil war between fascists within the military (Nationalists) and defenders of the civilian government (Republicans), seemed to confirm his fears. In April 1937, Steer reported on a raid against Guernica, a Republican town in the Basque region of Spain, in which aircraft dropped forty tons of explosives in an unprecedented use of modern military technology to attack a civilian population. Film footage of the bombed-out city fueled widespread outrage that civilians had been deliberately targeted. Pablo Picasso (1881–1973) depicted the carnage in an abstract painting that showed the suffering of the town. The painting briefly toured the world, bringing attention to the raid and to the war.

Steer reported that German flyers and aircraft had carried out the raid on behalf of the Nationalists. Illustrating just how far this attack on nonmilitary targets strayed from accepted morality, Hitler's German government denied participation in the raid, claiming this was propaganda used by its enemies. Fascist General Francisco Franco (1892–1975), who came to power when the Nationalists won the war in 1939—and who presided as Spain's authoritarian ruler over three decades—asserted that the damage at Guernica had been self-inflicted by the Republicans to deny resources to the Nationalists and to rally international sympathy to a losing cause. (Picasso's painting of Guernica was not shown in Spain until 1981, after Franco's death.) Although supporters of Franco's view presented their own films and photographs as evidence of their assertions, the weight of historical evidence clearly demonstrates that the German military was supporting its allies in the Spanish army, turning Spain into a living laboratory for experiments in new military tactics like carpet-bombing. Support from their allies helped the Nationalists secure another victory for a fascist movement. The research also suggests that the bombing was part of a broader strategy, not primarily an attack on the civilian population. It is likely that the actual death toll was lower than the first published reports, like those of Steer, suggested. Still, the bombing of Guernica remains an important entry point for consideration of an increasingly common question in modern, industrial warfare: what are the moral and ethical implications of aerial bombing?[2]

## Japan Seeks a New Order in Asia

In Japan, the depression hit the industrial economy hard and the agricultural sector even harder, as demand for exports and prices for farm goods fell. Although no single leader emerged as in Germany, Italy, or Spain, the Japanese military claimed the authority to act directly on behalf of the nation and its people, arguing that pluralism, with its mess of party politics, electoral conflicts, and rights claims, had failed the nation and betrayed the Emperor. Although the army and navy had frequent internal disputes, military officers increasingly controlled public policy and even sanctioned political assassination. By 1936, Japan was in effect a dictatorship, led by a faction within the military that espoused industrialization via a partnership between the state and private cartels that would bring domestic prosperity and place Japan in its appropriate position in a new international order.

Informally at first, then with an official pronouncement in 1940, Japan promoted a "Greater East Asia Co-Prosperity Sphere," promising to end Western colonial domination of Asia. Under this policy, Asian resources would be marshaled under the leadership of Japan, which had already demonstrated its ability to resist, and defeat, Western powers in war. As part of this movement, the Japanese government promoted totalitarianism as efficient, necessary, and moral. In 1941, the Japanese Ministry of Education produced a pamphlet called "The Way of Subjects," which emphasized devotion to the Emperor and the Japanese state and rejected key liberal tenets, expressing a belief that individual freedoms were not keys to progress or goals to be realized; they were evils to be fought against.

Even cloaked in the language of benevolence, Japan's imperial rule in East Asia resembled, and even exceeded, the colonial regimes imposed from Europe and America. During the 1920s and 1930s, Japanese rule directed Korean industry and agriculture to serve Japanese expansion elsewhere. Japan invaded Chinese territory in 1931, 1932, and again in 1937. Echoing the gas attacks in Ethiopia and the civilian bombings in Spain, Japanese bombers attacked residential neighborhoods in Shanghai; and Japan's advancing armies carried out mass rape and biological warfare.

---

[2]   Peter Monteath, "Guernica Reconsidered: Fifty Years of Evidence," *War and Society* 5, no. 1 (1987): 79–100; James S. Corum, "The Spanish Civil War: The Persistent Myths of Guernica," *MHQ: The Quarterly Journal of Military History* 22, no. 4 (Summer 2010): 16–22; Ian Patterson, *Guernica and Total War* (Cambridge, MA: Harvard University Press, 2007).

JAPANESE AERIAL BOMBING OF CHONGQING, CHINA, 1937. For Europeans, World War II began in 1939, but war had started in Asia two years earlier. Driven from their capital of Nanjing—near Shanghai—by Japanese armies, the Chinese government relocated to the city of Chongqing, nearly one thousand miles to the west, where Japanese bombers conducted regular raids on the city's civilian neighborhoods. Aerial bombardment of civilian targets—practiced by the Japanese against Shanghai and Chongqing, or the Germans against London, was widely condemned; but by the end of the World War II, all sides employed strategic aerial bombing of cities.

While the Chinese government resisted Japanese aggression, the collapse of the global economy had confounded Chiang Kai-Shek's plans for a unified non-communist state. As both industrial and agricultural production declined in the early 1930s, Chiang increasingly embraced elements of fascism, styling himself "Generalissimo," and promoted a state-centered ideology—the New Life Movement—designed to subordinate the individual to the nation and public life to the service of the state. Chiang even pursued a military alliance with Hitler's Germany.

## War Without Limits

By the mid-1930s, Germany's government under the Nazis was implementing its program to create a new *Reich* (Empire), expanding Nazi sovereignty over territory based on extreme forms of nationalism and cultural solidarity. First bending, and then shattering, the restrictions imposed on it at Versailles, the German government rearmed and redeployed its military and then absorbed Austria and part of Czechoslovakia into a "Greater Germany." Some objected to German actions, but most leaders in Western Europe saw greater threats from the potential outbreak of another global war or communism's spread. Germany's anti-communist treaty alliance with Japan (1936) and then Italy (1937) therefore appeared not as

MAP 11.3  Japan in China, 1931–45

a threat but as a buffer zone surrounding the USSR. Imagine the surprise among those leaders when, in 1939, Hitler signed an agreement of nonaggression with Stalin, stating that if Germany went to war, the Soviet Union would remain neutral, and vice versa. Other world leaders would have been less surprised by this strange alliance had they known—as documents uncovered after the war revealed—that Hitler and Stalin had formed a secret side agreement to allow each to take control of parts of East-Central Europe.

## The Path through the Second World War

On September 1, 1939, soon after signing the Hitler–Stalin pact, Germany invaded Poland, leading Great Britain and France to declare war. German military forces, employing the modern technology of planes, tanks, and other motorized vehicles in a *blitzkrieg* ("lightning war"), subdued Poland, Denmark, Norway, the Netherlands, Belgium, and France within ten months. By the spring of 1941, Greece and Yugoslavia were also occupied, and the Hungarian, Bulgarian, and Romanian governments acceded to Nazi demands. Great Britain remained the only sovereign European state with its full capacities devoted to war against Germany. The British lobbied furiously for US aid, but the United States would not take on a combat role in the European war through the fall of 1941.

In Asia, Japan, already engaged in an undeclared war against China, signed another treaty in 1940 confirming its commitment to a global anti-communist "Axis" with Germany and Italy. The Japanese occupied French Indochina in July 1941. The United States grew increasingly wary of the turn of events in the Pacific and curtailed shipments to Japan of vital resources like rubber, scrap iron, and fuel. In addition, the United States and other countries froze Japanese assets deposited in their financial institutions. In the spring of 1941, the United States began supplying China, Great Britain, and other combatants fighting the Axis.

Demonstrating the contingent, unpredictable nature of history, two decisions made by Axis leaders changed the course of the war during the second half of 1941. That summer, Germany reneged on its pact with Stalin and invaded the USSR. Then, in December, the Japanese launched a preemptive strike against the US Naval base at Pearl Harbor, Hawai'i. Neither action delivered a decisive blow to the target country, but they did turn the Soviet Union and the United States into military allies against the fascist states. This would prove to be decisive in turning the war against the Axis. Although both the United States and the Soviet Union were reeling from these attacks, the two states recovered quickly, ramping up industrial production and pouring troops and materiel into the war.

In the Pacific, Japanese successes continued for several months after Pearl Harbor, defeating British and American forces in the Philippines, Burma, Malaya, Singapore, the Dutch East Indies, and islands across the Pacific. Forced to rely on aircraft carriers after many of its battleships were sunk at Pearl Harbor, the United States (aided by breaking the main Japanese communications code) defeated the Japanese decisively at the Battle of Midway, in the central Pacific, in June 1942. Although many lives would be lost in three more years of fighting, Midway marked the end of Japanese expansion in the Pacific.

In Europe, the war turned in a similar time frame. The Soviet Union seemed on the brink of collapse for many months, and at many moments, after the initial German invasion. The German armies advanced across the Soviet Union, eventually being stopped at Stalingrad in a five-month battle that began in August 1942. This was one of the bloodiest in human history: as many as two million casualties were inflicted on the two sides during the campaign. Defeated at great cost to both sides, German armies never again achieved success on the "Eastern Front" and were slowly driven back by the Soviet Red Army.

American and British forces opened a second front against the Nazis. Following victories in North Africa, US and British armies landed in Italy in the autumn of 1943, and in June 1944 launched the largest amphibious invasion ever mounted, on the coast of France. In both the East and the West, supported by the enormous industrial capacity of the USSR and the United States, the Allies began to turn back German forces.

Although in retrospect we can see that the war turned in the summer of 1942, the outcome remained in doubt and the blood continued to flow. The brutal Second World War dragged on into 1945. Ultimately, the Allied forces achieved victory, first over the Nazis, and then over the Japanese, but these came at mind-boggling material and human cost. More than sixty million people—2.5 percent of the world's population—were killed in the war, including unprecedented numbers of civilians. This war encompassed even more territory and combatants, more battlefield and civilian deaths, and more industrial technologies applied to inflicting pain and suffering than the "war to end war" had done only two decades earlier. The war's scale and conduct cast a long shadow over the following decades.

## Mass Killing and the Modern State

During this Second World War, air power continued to erode the importance of physical distance between combatants. Continuing the grisly trend seen in Shanghai and Guernica, military strategists, political leaders, and ordinary people blurred the line between acceptable military targets and tactics and morally indefensible abominations. Aerial bombing of population centers became a standard feature of modern warfare. Germany's "blitz" of English cities from September 1940 to May 1941 killed forty thousand civilians, half of them in London. Allied governments protested the deliberate targeting of civilians, but soon all sides employed strategic bombing. Japanese bombs killed more than ten thousand civilians in China's wartime capital, Chongqing. Allied firebombing included the German cities of Hamburg (forty-two thousand killed) and Dresden (twenty-five thousand in a single night). The systematic firebombing of Japanese cities was even more extensive: one hundred thousand people died in one night's raids on Tokyo, and in total more than three hundred thousand people died in dozens of raids.

The war also accelerated a race to develop a new generation of superweapons using scientific innovations. The new and shocking power of nuclear weapons was introduced on August 6, 1945, when a single atomic bomb, dropped on the city of Hiroshima, killed tens of thousands instantly, and more than one hundred fifty thousand in total. A second bomb was dropped on Nagasaki three days later. The United States did not monopolize this technology for long, as the Soviet Union, through research and espionage, developed its own nuclear weapons program shortly after the war ended. Other countries would follow.

In the First World War, the experience of chemical weapons like mustard gas had been so horrible that international conventions banned their use in combat. However, although chemical weapons were removed from the battlefield, they remained one of the deadliest weapons of the Second World War, but their victims now were civilians targeted for genocide rather than soldiers. Adolf Hitler, himself wounded in a gas attack in the First World War, forbade German armies from using chemical weapons in combat, but he oversaw the industrial slaughter that came to be known as the Holocaust—"the Final Solution"—a government policy of genocide. Blaming Jews for Germany's defeat in World War I and its economic struggles afterward, the Nazis targeted the entire Jewish population of Europe. Other groups deemed unfit for living under the new Reich were also identified for extermination, including Romani (Gypsies), Slavs, homosexuals, communists, and those with disabilities. With macabre efficiency, the German state murdered millions of Jews in gas chambers after methods like mass execution by firing squad were deemed too time-consuming and demoralizing to the soldiers. Estimates of the number of civilians killed across Europe and the Soviet Union by the Nazis range as high as seventeen million; at least six million were Jews.

The Holocaust hideously distorted the technologies that had fueled dreams of progress since the dawn of industrialization; it also demonstrated the failings of modern political ideals and structures. Hitler rose to power through democratic processes, although once in power he dismantled them. The civil and military bureaucracies of the German state linked with the industrial infrastructure to support the political system, with catastrophic results. Millions of ordinary people played roles in delivering victims to concentration camps across Central Europe.

The grim realities of the Final Solution, embedded in the broader context of several decades of global crisis, raised challenging questions for the future. Could this war's victors do a better job at ensuring peace than those who tried at the end of World War I? What, if any, limits might be placed on state sovereignty in the interests of protecting individuals and groups living within any given state? Could a system of international security respect the principle of self-determination while still safeguarding some broad, enduring global balance of political, economic, and military power? Under what circumstances, if any, could the development or use of weapons of mass destruction, like nuclear or chemical weapons, be controlled and/or general rules of warfare be enforced?

## Unraveling Empire as a Key to the Future

As the Second World War came to an end in 1945, questions about empire came to the forefront. How would the map of the globe be redrawn this time? Which principles, institutions, and actors would be privileged in the decision-making process? For most of the tens of millions of people resident in the colonies of Afro-Eurasia, the Second World War simply confirmed disillusion with the good intentions of imperialists. This was not only because of the devastation in the belligerent nations but also because the destruction was once again visited on peoples across the globe. In India, beyond the two and one-half million soldiers who fought on behalf of the British, the additional political and economic costs of imperial rule achieved further clarity. Some nationalists in the Empire argued that support for the war effort should be the most important short-term priority, but Gandhi's Indian National Congress argued that independence should be paid up front as the price of Indian support. As a result, Congress leaders were imprisoned for the duration of the war.

The wartime economy certainly laid bare, as it had during the First World War, the relationship between colony and colonizer. Production, distribution, and consumption priorities were determined by policy decisions about what was best for the war effort, but these decisions were often experienced in colonies as privileging the metropolis. In India, for example, wartime economic decisions contributed to a major famine that killed approximately three million people in Bengal province in 1942–1943. Some of the blame for the famine may be attributed to the Japanese conquest of Burma, which had previously provided significant amounts of rice to the rest of British India. Imperial policies also bore much of the responsibility, however, as Britain continued to export rice from Bengal to support the war effort even when local officials asked that it be kept back to aid in famine relief.

The situation in Burma provides another striking example of the dilemma for colonized peoples across Afro-Eurasia during the war. Many in Burma had celebrated when Japan, promising Burmese independence as part of its "Asia for the Asiatics" program, moved against British rule there in 1942. Anticolonial forces in Burma, which had been organizing for years, were armed and trained by the Japanese as the Burmese Independence Army. Fighting against them were hundreds of thousands of soldiers from British India, Burma, and West and East Africa. On both sides, the relationship of soldiers to imperial armies was tenuous. The Burmese leader Aung San (1915–1947) came to realize that the Japanese promise of independence was at least as hollow as that of the British. Burmese units fighting for national independence rebelled against both the Japanese and the British. Meanwhile, many of the soldiers who fought for the British in Burma came from other regions of the Empire. They fought with the expectation that their service would earn economic opportunities and greater autonomy in their homelands after the war. Such was the case of the Gold Coast veterans, whose 1948 protests in Accra introduced this chapter.

## Conclusion

At the end of the Second World War, much of the world smoldered in ruins. Many perceived the crisis of the preceding three decades to have been a product of the global political and economic order that had emerged in the nineteenth century. Imperialist and nationalist rivalries had led to war; global capitalism had fueled depression; science and technology had killed, on an unprecedented scale, soldiers and civilians alike. The survival of an increasingly interconnected, and bellicose, global population depended on reordering fundamental global political and economic relationships. The victorious allies agreed that, with fascism's defeat, such a project was essential. The problem, clear even before the end of the war, was that these allies did not agree on what those new relationships should look like. In Chapter 12, we explore the debates over a new global political and economic order, the conflicts that emerged between the world's major powers after the Second World War, and the increasing role of claims made against all power holders on behalf of the world's people.

**TIMELINE**

**1909**
Mohandas K. Gandhi publishes "Indian Home Rule"

**1919**
Comintern founded; Amritsar Massacre, India; May Fourth Movement, China

**1922**
Egypt achieves limited independence from Britain

**1924**
Dawes Plan reorganizes German financial and tax system

**1929**
Stock market crash, New York; beginning of Great Depression

**1915–23**
Armenian genocide

**1921**
Chinese Communist Party founded

**1923**
Republic of Turkey declared; Huda Sha'rawi founds Egyptian Feminist Union

**1925**
Chiang Kai-shek assumes control of Nationalist Party in China; Adolf Hitler publishes first volume of *Mein Kampf*

# A Few Good Books

Lizzie Collingham. *The Taste of War: World War II and the Battle for Food*. New York: Penguin, 2012.

Lawrence James. *The Rise and Fall of the British Empire*. London: St Martin Griffins, 1997.

Laure Marchand and Guillaume Perrier. *Turkey and the Armenian Ghost: On the Trail of the Genocide*. Trans. Debbie Blythe. Montreal: , McGill-Queen's University Press, 2015.

Rana Mitter. *Forgotten Ally: China's World War II, 1937–1945*. New York: Houghton Mifflin Harcourt, 2014.

Aviel Roshwald. *Ethnic Nationalism and the Fall of Empires: Central Europe, the Middle East and Russia, 1914–23*. New York: Routledge, 2000.

Robert Service. *Comrades. A World History of Communism*. London: Macmillan, 2007.

*For additional resources, including maps, primary sources, visuals, web links, and quizzes, please go to* **www.oup.com/us/carter**

**1932–33**
Massive starvation in Russia and Ukraine

**1935**
Italy invades Ethiopia

**1937**
Beginning of Second Sino-Japanese War

**1940**
Japan pronounces "Greater East Asia Co-Prosperity Sphere"

**1945**
Allied victory over Axis; US drops atomic bombs on Japan; evidence emerges of millions killed in Holocaust

**1933**
US unemployment peaks at over fifteen million; Hitler becomes German Chancellor

**1936–39**
Spanish Civil War

**1939**
German-Soviet nonaggression pact; Germany invades Poland

**1941**
Germany invades USSR; US enters war

**1949**
Kwame Nkrumah founds the Convention People's Party, Ghana

**(TOP) GERMAN SS OFFICER PREPARES TO SHOOT A POLISH JEW.** In this photo, most likely taken in 1942, a member of the German SS Einsatz Gruppen D prepares to shoot a Polish Jew who is kneeling on the edge of a mass grave almost filled with other victims. Nazi leaders soon thereafter decided a system of industrial death camps should be implemented. At least six million Jews were murdered in the Holocaust between 1941 and 1945. Overall, as many as seventeen million civilians were killed by the Nazis during the war.

**(BOTTOM) MPLA POSTER, ANGOLA, 1975.** The People's Movement for the Liberation of Angola (MPLA) was one of several armed factions, with roots in the 1950s, struggling against Portuguese colonialism. When a new government in Portugal declared its intention in 1974 to withdraw from its African colonies, the MPLA seized the initiative and declared itself in charge of an independent Angola in 1975. Other armed factions disputed this assertion, plunging Angola into years of bloody civil war fueled by Cold War rivalries.

15 ANOS DE LUTA ANTI-IMPERIALISTA

# CHAPTER 12

# Hot Wars, Cold Wars, and Decolonization

## 1942–1975

Feigele Peltel (1921–2012) was in her early twenties in the summer of 1942 when the Nazis began a campaign that killed over three hundred thousand Jews from her home in Warsaw in a matter of months. For three years, the Germans had occupied the Polish capital as they waged war to expand their *Reich* across Europe. As part of their plan to purify the *Reich's* population, the Nazis had begun to concentrate Jews into a ghetto, building a wall around it to control entry and exit. The Warsaw Ghetto's four hundred thousand residents, nearly 30 percent of the city's population, made it the largest of all the Jewish ghettos in Nazi-occupied Europe. In 1941, the Nazis put into operation a plan of mass murder in Poland, at extermination camps like Auschwitz-Birkenau, Treblinka, and several others. These camps would serve no other purpose than to efficiently gather and slaughter human beings, and the Jews of the Warsaw Ghetto became a primary target.

Because Feigele Peltel "passed" for a non-Jew in the eyes of the Nazi authorities, she lived outside the ghetto, taking the name Vladka. When Jews in the ghetto organized an armed resistance to the Nazis in response to mass deportations, she smuggled weapons, helped Jewish children to escape, and communicated with groups outside Warsaw. The resistance shocked, then enraged the Nazis, who leveled the entire ghetto in the spring of 1943, killing more than seven thousand and rounding up fifty-five thousand others for deportation to work and extermination camps. Years later, from a prison cell, the operation's Nazi commanding officer, Jürgen Stroop (1895–1952), expressed pride in a final act of desecration, demolishing Warsaw's Great Synagogue.

Vladka/Feigele, who published a memoir of her experiences, survived to see the Germans defeated, although she lost her father to pneumonia in the ghetto and her mother and two siblings to the extermination camps. After the war, she heard commitments from the victorious Allies that the world could not allow such atrocities to be committed again. However, hostilities within the victorious anti-fascist coalition presented an obstacle to turning this, and other commitments to a better world, into consistent practice. Her place of birth became an early focus of the deep-seated disagreements between the anti-fascist allies, as the United States, Great Britain, and the Soviet Union fought over the type of government and territorial limits that

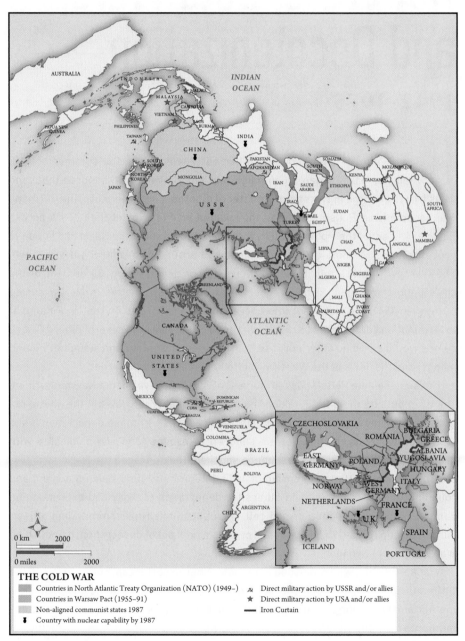

**MAP 12.1** The Cold War

independent Poland would have after the war. Such disputes, played out in a series of meetings between the leaders of these countries, nurtured the seeds of suspicions that would dominate global relations in the coming decades.

Both the United States and the USSR claimed an interest in allowing the world's peoples to enjoy self-determination and popular sovereignty. However, in the decades after the Second World War, alongside important advances in material life and conceptual commitments to human well-being, disputes over power based on ethnicity, religion, and other factors, exacerbated by the interventions of these ideologically polarized superpowers, often resulted in civil war, authoritarian government, and the skewed distribution of material, political, and social resources.

The agonizing history of postwar Angola, in Southwest Africa, highlights the challenges of the era. In January 1975, leaders of three armed factions signed an agreement with the Portuguese government to work together toward a peaceful transition to independence for Angola. Portugal, like Europe's other imperial powers, had moved aggressively to establish and enforce claims of sovereignty over Angola after the Conference of Berlin in 1888. During the first half of the twentieth century, Angola, rich in natural resources, became an important source of wealth for Portugal, whose government encouraged Portuguese colonists to settle there.

After the Second World War, as movements for the self-determination of African peoples accelerated, the Portuguese refused to consider the issue of Angolan independence. In the 1960s, armed guerillas forming around regional, ethnic, and ideological affinities, created civil unrest. A coup d'état in Portugal in 1974 proved to be a turning point for the relationship with Angola. Leaders of the new regime committed to a transition to independence in Angola and signed an accord with three major rebel groups. Rather than peace, civil war and a refugee crisis ensued.

In the months after the transition agreement was signed, the apartheid regime in South Africa moved troops into Angola, supporting its own interests as well as anticommunist armed factions in Angola. The US Central Intelligence Agency ran operations out of neighboring Zaire. China and the USSR provided support to competing Marxist groups. In late 1975, Cuban President Fidel Castro (1926– ), acting independently of the Soviet government, committed thirty thousand Cuban ground troops to support the communist MPLA (People's Movement for the Liberation of Angola). Factional strife, financed by external aid and the export of diamonds and oil, tore Angola apart for three decades.

---

The Warsaw Ghetto Uprising and the Civil War in Angola, different as they are, reflect important aspects of the dilemmas encountered in rebuilding global relationships in the twentieth century. Extreme nationalism and racialist theories hitched to technologies of destruction produced the Holocaust: mass murder presented as rational progress. Fascist governments in Japan, Germany, Italy, and elsewhere distorted some modern ideals and rejected others, denying political rights to millions of people and glorifying militarism.

The Allies who fought the Second World War to end fascism disagreed on major tenets for the construction of a postwar order. Warsaw had become capital of an independent Poland under the principle of "self-determination of peoples," after World War I, and Britain entered the Second World War to protect Polish sovereignty. But after the war, Poland became embroiled in the emerging conflict between the United States and the Soviet Union. This face-off recurred frequently as new nation-states, formed through post-war decolonization processes, became embroiled in the superpowers' fundamental disagreements about political and economic organization.

In the first section of this chapter, we explore how the Second World War Allies began to plan the contours of a postwar world in the midst of the war itself. Determining how the lessons of the first four decades of the twentieth century would be turned into institutions and policies depended to a large degree, but not entirely, on the actions of the dominant military powers that emerged from the war—the United States and the Soviet Union. In the next section of the chapter, we show how an emerging universal language of human rights, self-determination, democracy, and economic development manifested real actions and outcomes within a global context of persistent inequality in the distribution of material resources, competing interpretations of the lessons from the past, and clashing programs for humankind's future.

In the sections that follow, we map out regional variations of how the global superpowers traded arms and economic aid for expressions of loyalty from leaders of other nation-states—or aspiring nation-states—in a "Cold War," simultaneously attempting to undermine rivals through diplomacy, violence, espionage, and even cultural combat. As we have seen throughout this book, though, at times individuals and groups around the globe have used a variety of tools at their disposal to influence events, sometimes out of any proportion to their material resources. In the final section of the chapter, we examine attempts to establish political and economic movements that transcended the bipolar confines of the Cold War.

## Uncomfortable Allies Plan a New Order

The closing days of the Second World War in Europe revealed the scale of fascist atrocities. At Nazi death camps like Treblinka and others, Allied soldiers discovered piles of corpses, crematoria, and other evidence of mass murder on an unprecedented scale. These discoveries confirmed for the "Big Five" allies—the United States, Soviet Union, Great Britain, France, and China—the justice of their war. Even before these discoveries, the Allies began planning for a postwar global order that would oppose fascism and be based on "common principles in the national policies of their respective countries on which they base their hopes for a better future for the world." These words became the core of a "Declaration of United Nations," approved in January of 1942 by twenty-six countries, including the major Allies. In addition to reiterating a commitment to the destruction of "Nazi tyranny," the signatories agreed to seek no "aggrandizement, territorial, or other" from the current conflict and that both "victor and vanquished" would be given equal access to economic opportunity after the war. In other words, the Allies were repudiating the victors' justice that shaped the treaties ending the First World War. In the long shadow of the Great Depression, they agreed to bring about global cooperation to secure "improved labor standards, economic advancement and social security." Acting on this commitment, in July 1944, delegates from forty-four countries met at a resort in the White Mountains of New Hampshire to lay the groundwork for the economic future. The Bretton Woods Accords, named for the town where the meeting took place, established a blueprint by which the international financial system would be managed in the coming decades through organizations like the International Monetary Fund, the World Bank, and the World Trade Organization.

Despite the veneer of unity, deep tensions divided the Allies, especially the United States and the Soviet Union. The two countries agreed that they were fighting *against* fascism, but they had very different ideas of what they were fighting *for*. The US vision of a limited state, free trade, and a consumer society was at odds with the Soviets' faith in a centrally directed economy, with state planners determining production quotas and the distribution of resources. Both countries trumpeted democracy as their foundation, but their definitions and implementation of this ideal varied greatly. The differences among the Allies became clear in a series of meetings among the leaders of the United States, Great Britain, and the Soviet Union. In Tehran (1943), Yalta (February 1945), and Potsdam (July–August 1945), the three countries disputed over tactics in the last stages of the war but also over the occupation and future of defeated territories, especially Germany and Eastern Europe. Despite these attempts to plan, the war ended much more suddenly than anyone expected, following the two atomic bombs dropped on Japan. Illustrating the emerging conflict between the United States and the USSR, the American bomb dropped on Hiroshima caught the Soviets completely by surprise. It happened just four days after the end of the Potsdam Conference, but the atomic bomb's existence was not shared with the Soviet delegates. With the war suddenly ending, the former allies rushed to secure their interests around the world.

Institutions and individuals escalated tensions between the Soviet Union and the United States. Winston Churchill asserted that communist movements around the world "are established and work in complete unity and absolute obedience to the directions they receive from the Communist center": Moscow. He saw in the postwar world "a growing challenge and peril to Christian civilization" and used the phrase "Iron Curtain" to describe how Soviet machinations were isolating Poland and the rest of Eastern Europe from the broader world. To prevent Soviet expansion, the North Atlantic Treaty Organization (NATO) was formed, establishing alliances between the states of Western Europe, the United States, and Canada.

Stalin responded that the Soviet Union lost many more people in the Second World War than the British and Americans combined, and asserted that the communist resistance had been the staunchest anti-fascist fighting force in Nazi-occupied Europe, conveniently ignoring the secret nonaggression pact he had signed with Hitler at the war's beginning. He concluded that it was therefore in the interest of both the Soviet Union and the peoples of Eastern and East-Central Europe to establish communist governments that would be reliable allies of the USSR. These allies would later be formalized as the Warsaw Pact, a political and military organization established as a Soviet counterpart to NATO.

In response, US President Harry Truman (1884–1972) committed the United States to a policy of containment that would prevent communists from coming to power in additional countries. Thus, Allied unity in the face of fascist aggression had become a bipolar power struggle, embodied most vividly in the ongoing conflicts over Germany. Because the occupiers could not agree on the defeated enemy's future, two separate countries were established in 1949, a communist German Democratic Republic ("East Germany"), allied with the Soviet Union, and the German Federal Republic ("West Germany"), supported by the United States and Western Europe. The situation was novel and tense—neither state was admitted to the United Nations until 1973—especially in Berlin, where Soviet, American, French, and British forces divided the city itself. Churchill's "Iron Curtain" eventually took concrete form in 1961 when the East German government erected the Berlin Wall, a militarized boundary nearly one hundred miles long separating the communist from the non-communist sectors of Berlin and the city's residents from each other.

## The Search for Common Ground

When the "Big Five" sat together to figure out how to reorder the world as the fighting drew to a close, they were vastly different in terms of material assets, ideological frameworks, and visions of the future. The two most powerful states—the United States and the Soviet Union—differed fundamentally on economic and political goals. Great Britain and France were struggling to regain stature in a world where Western European military and economic might no longer dominated. Within months, Chiang Kai-shek's battered Chinese republic was embroiled in a civil war Chiang would lose. All of these countries, except the United States, were physically devastated by the war and struggling to rebuild infrastructure and institutions. The United States, by contrast, had suffered many casualties, but its economy was now fully recovered from the Great Depression and embarking on the longest period of sustained economic growth the world had yet known.

Given these vastly different circumstances, even those structures designed to serve common interests were in some ways contradictory. The representatives of fifty countries who came together to form the United Nations just two months after the Japanese surrender ended the war claimed multiple goals in the organization's charter, including saving succeeding generations from war, reaffirming the existence of fundamental human rights, the dignity of the human person, and the basic equality of all nations regardless of size or resources. The signatories agreed to work to create a framework of international law that would support these principles, as well as create better standards of living and "social progress" for all the world's peoples.

Early successes bolstered the international community that had committed to these goals. Acting without precedent—some contended illegally—special tribunals held in Germany and Japan established new rules for conduct in war and convicted perpetrators of the Holocaust and other crimes against humanity. As further evidence emerged of what had happened in the Nazi death camps, widespread condemnation fueled hopes that such crimes would be impossible to perpetrate in the future. World War I had not turned out to be "the war to end wars"; but perhaps World War II, which brought the globe to the brink of annihilation, could inspire a new era of international harmony through the United Nations.

## United Nations

Three issues—involving power, participation, and principle—demonstrate both the enormous potential and the inherent limitations of forming an international community committed to realizing such utopian ideals. First, power: although the UN Charter asserted that "the Organization is based on the principle of the sovereign equality of all its Members," the five wartime allies received permanent seats on the UN's most powerful body, the Security Council, and each had veto power over key initiatives. Some have argued that this created an organization that merely served the interests of these most powerful nations; others contend that this created a more durable institution than the League of Nations by reducing the odds that the key actors on the global stage might exit the institution and doom it, as had happened to the League.

Second, participation: although the organization aspired to universality, most of the world's subject peoples were not fully represented when the UN was formed. This was denounced as a concession to the postwar Western European powers who wanted to retain their empires, yet others have pointed out that the Atlantic Charter (on whose tenets the UN was built) and the broader public debates opened by the formation of the United Nations created a space where demands for self-determination could be aired and, in some cases, resolved by the international community.

Third, principles: as we have seen previously, the victorious allies in World War II defined basic political and economic concepts differently. Critics of the United Nations argued that, depending on the interpretation, the meaning of the concepts expressed by the institution skewed to one side or the other in the growing Cold War confrontation. Supporters of the institution responded that the highest aspirations of the international community were expressed in documents like the 1948 Universal Declaration of Human Rights. Some features of this document harkened back to John Locke and later Enlightenment philosophers, but others responded to the realities of an era more intertwined and more unequal than any in human history. The United Nations proved to be more durable, its scope of activity much broader, and its accomplishments more tangible than its predecessor. And its membership grew rapidly, as the political geography of the postwar world was transformed by the anguished construction of dozens of new nation-states.

## The Cold War Era in East and Southeast Asia

As we have seen, a mixture of cynical politics, philanthropy, racism, and greed drove imperialism. Western companies and Western products spread alongside Western power in the nineteenth century. Colonies provided raw materials, markets, and cheap labor. At the end the Second World War, imperialist countries, like France, Britain, the Netherlands, and Portugal, were still in no rush to give up their colonial enterprises, even though the imperial system was interwoven with decades of global crisis. Now, however, nationalist and anti-imperialist movements found renewed ideological (if not always practical) support from the Soviets, the United States, and the founding principles of the United Nations. The UN charter reaffirmed "equal rights and self-determination of peoples" as universal organizing principles for the postwar world. Postwar realities made explicit colonialism ideologically unsustainable, but attempting to turn principle into practice often resulted in bloodshed and displacement.

The Cold War complicated the process. In East Asia, after the withdrawal of Japanese troops, war resumed between communist and non-communist factions throughout the region, even as European powers returned to their colonial possessions. Chiang Kai-shek's Republic of China was a founding member of the

United Nations and held one of five permanent seats on the Security Council, but in 1949, its wartime ally, the Chinese Communist Party led by Mao Zedong, forced Chiang's government to flee to the island province of Taiwan. In the spring of 1950, it was widely expected that an invasion from the mainland would complete the communist victory. The United States, which had supported Chiang's government throughout the war, indicated publicly and privately that it would not intervene against the anticipated invasion from the newly founded People's Republic of China.

All this changed in the autumn of 1950 when attempts to peacefully reunify the Korean peninsula failed. Korea, like Germany, had been divided into "temporary" administrative zones of communist and non-communist influence at the end of the war. North Korean communist troops invaded the south to reunify the country by force, leading the United Nations to condemn the action and form the first multinational armed force (from sixteen countries) to operate under its auspices. China's new communist government also entered the conflict, seeing the UN army as a tool of the United States, which provided the largest number of troops. The war resulted in a standoff and an uneasy settlement that divided the peninsula into a communist North Korea and a non-communist South Korea.

The war in Korea was significant in its own right, claiming more than one million lives, but it also reinforced Cold War frames of reference. The containment policy that guided US foreign policy in Europe—driving American aid to anti-communist forces in Greece and Turkey, for instance—was applied more broadly in East Asia. The United States redefined its defensive strategy to stop the spread of communism, reversing its policy on Taiwan and bringing the island within the American defensive perimeter, where it remained a focal point of the Cold War for decades. In addition to basing thousands of troops in South Korea, the United States also restored formal sovereignty to Japan (after years of US occupation). The new Japanese government allowed the United States to develop military bases and station troops on its territory as part of a bulwark against communist expansion.

Throughout Asia, the legacies of colonialism promoted unlikely alliances. National independence movements had grown up against the French in Indochina (today's Vietnam, Laos, and Cambodia); the Dutch in what is today Indonesia; and the British in today's Malaysia, Myanmar, and Singapore. The same factors that spurred Europe's New Imperialism motivated the Japanese advance into Southeast Asia, including the search for industrial raw materials (especially oil, rubber, and metals). The Japanese, though, presented themselves as *anti*-imperialists who would ally against the European colonial powers to create, as their official slogan proclaimed, "Asia for the Asiatics." In Burma, Indonesia, and elsewhere, many rebels in Southeast Asia allied with the Japanese, perhaps taking the Japanese at their word or perhaps simply seeing an opportunity to be rid of their European overlords. Others remained loyal to European colonial governments, hoping to be rewarded with autonomy or independence at war's end. Still others operated in the gaps between the warring powers, hoping to establish themselves as an independent force.

In this context, individuals and groups had overlapping and sometimes contradictory identities and affiliations. Vietnamese nationalist Nguyen Ai Quoc, whom the Allies had rejected at Versailles in 1919 (as we saw in chapter 10), traveled afterward to Moscow, where he trained with the Comintern before finding his way back to Indochina during the 1930s. Despite his time in Moscow, Nguyen—now called Ho Chi Minh—was ideologically pragmatic, working with American military intelligence and helping to rescue American pilots shot down over Vietnam during the Second World War while still maintaining his connections with the Comintern. Ho seized the opportunity of the sudden Japanese surrender to declare Vietnamese independence. Always aware that to succeed, his movement would need support from at least one of the world's superpowers—but not caring too much which it would be—he drafted a declaration of Vietnamese independence designed to

**SAIGON UNDER SIEGE, MAY 1968.** During the first half of 1968, North Vietnamese forces and Viet Cong (South Vietnamese communists) launched a major attack on strategic positions across South Vietnam, including Saigon, the capital city. Cholon, the Chinese section of Saigon shown in this photograph, was badly damaged by both the original attacks and the South Vietnamese/US counterattack. The Vietnam War, which grew out of the Vietnamese anticolonial struggle against France, became one of the longest and bloodiest confrontations of the global Cold War. More than a million Vietnamese, and fifty-eight thousand Americans, died in the conflict.

appeal to both the Soviets and the Americans. In it, he quoted extensively from the US Declaration of Independence (a copy of which had been provided by American intelligence agents) while also citing orthodox Marxist theory.

Ho's statement depicts both the long influence of Enlightenment ideals and the extent to which colonialism had exposed their hypocrisy. The Vietnamese Declaration of Independence notes that, "for more than eighty years, the French imperialists, abusing the standard of Liberty, Equality, and Fraternity, have violated our Fatherland and oppressed our fellow citizens. They have acted contrary to the ideals of humanity and justice."

## Decolonization

Ho Chi Minh's observation reflected an important contradiction of the era. The French Revolution promised equal rights to "all men," and France took great pride in its history of "liberty, equality, and brotherhood," yet France aggressively opposed nationalist movements in its colonies that tried to implement those principles. Eager to reclaim its empire (an empire that explicitly denied equal rights to colonial subjects), France sent armies across Asia and Africa, including Vietnam, Algeria, Cameroon, Madagascar, and elsewhere.

Other European powers clung to their empires as well. Violent wars of independence, infused with Cold War stakes, ensued. One hundred thousand people died in the Dutch East Indies (1945–49) and Congo (1960–66), and one million perished in Algeria (1954–62). There were dozens of other smaller wars as well. Achieving independence in Africa and Asia also drained human and material resources, heightened factionalism among forces fighting for independence, and cast suspicion on the motives of international organizations in which the former imperial powers played important roles.

### Gandhi and the Indian Subcontinent

Great Britain, like France, took great pride in its tradition of democracy and civil rights. It also, like France, feared that the demise of its empire indicated a changed global order. But the British Empire's postwar path was different, in large part due to events in South Asia, most vividly illustrated in the actions of Mohandas Gandhi, the foremost advocate for Indian independence.

Gandhi was much more than just an Indian nationalist. His role in the Indian home rule movement fundamentally altered the ways that people address power relations. In fact, his tactics and teachings have become an essential part of understanding the modern world. Gandhi's 1909 book *Hind Swaraj* (Indian Home Rule) articulated two crucial concepts: true civilization and civil resistance. Both of these ideas rejected common understandings of what the world should look like and how it should work.

MAP 12.2  The Partition of India

Gandhi challenged those who continued to speak reverently of "order and progress" (as emblazoned on the Brazilian flag) that resulted from industrial regimentation. Gandhi rejected the idea that more, better, or faster machines held the promise of progress. Quite the opposite, he asserted: "Formerly, men worked in the open air only so much as they liked. Now, thousands of workmen meet together and for the sake of maintenance work in factories or mines. Their condition is worse than that of beasts." And to those who held up Europe as the apex of civilization, Gandhi responded that material obsessions had "taken such a hold on the people in Europe that those who are in it appear to be half mad. . . . This civilization is such that one has only to be patient and it will be self-destroyed."

This belief that Western civilization was morally flawed and unsustainable led Gandhi to reject violence—which he saw as the instrument of imperialism—as a means of achieving independence. This was a radical split from many anticolonial nationalists in India and elsewhere. Gandhi believed that nonviolent resistance required more courage and moral strength than armed resistance. Even in the wake of atrocities like the Amritsar Massacre, Gandhi was steadfast in his commitment to nonviolence. Rather than military campaigns or violent insurrection, Gandhi opposed British rule by calling on his followers to make their own salt (to undermine a British monopoly on salt production) and spin their own cloth (rather than buy cheap, ubiquitous British textiles). When he wished to emphasize his resolute disapproval—of either his supporters or opponents—he would go on a hunger strike: but he never resorted to violence. This strategy strengthened his stature, and frustrated his opponents, who had no effective means of response to someone who, as Gandhi wrote, "will not obey a law that is against his conscience, even though he may be blown to pieces at the mouth of a cannon." Winston Churchill dismissed Gandhi as a "half-naked fakir," but Gandhi's prediction that his strategy and tactics would bring victory proved correct. On January 1, 1947, India became an independent state.

It would be a happy ending to learn that Gandhi's doctrine of nonviolence had changed politics forever. Perhaps, after decades of war and genocide, civil resistance had shown the way to a peaceful future. Such was not the reality, however. Even as India was born, it splintered. Over Gandhi's strenuous objections, communal divisions, based on religion, destroyed his dream of a unified, independent India before it could be realized. Promoting such divisions had for decades been a policy of the British in India, who thought these would help prevent nationalists from unifying. Majority Muslim parts of India—the northwestern and eastern border regions—became the independent state of Pakistan. East Pakistan would later secede from Pakistan, becoming Bangladesh in 1971. The partition of India was bloody. Many Muslims in Indian territory and Hindus in Pakistani territory began to relocate voluntarily or out of fear. The mass migration led to instability and then violence. More than ten million people moved during 1947, and between five hundred thousand and one million people died. One of those casualties might be said to be Gandhi himself. He was shot at close range by a Hindu extremist who felt Gandhi had been too accommodating of Muslims.

## The Case of Kenya
Postwar Africa presented the greatest challenge to the integrity of the global commitment to self-determination. Kenya illustrates several important themes for understanding why. For one, it shows that the rhetoric of "self-determination" accompanying the end of World War I had little impact on European policies outside of Europe. Although significant numbers of Europeans arrived in Kenya in

the 1850s, and Britain declared it a "protectorate" in 1895, it did not become a formal colony until 1920, after the peace treaty endorsing national autonomy.

From the beginning, indigenous people resisted the European presence, which provoked major rebellions in the 1880s, 1910s, and 1940s. British policy in the region was, from the start, extraordinarily violent; one Member of Parliament remarked in the 1890s that the main beneficiary of Britain's colonization of Kenya seemed to be Hiram Maxim (1840–1916), the inventor of the machine gun. What formerly had been a prosperous, fertile region became increasingly violent and dispossessed of resources, with profits and people—first slaves and later soldiers—extracted from Africa for the benefit of Europeans. During the Second World War, while Kenyan soldiers fought for the British Empire, wartime austerity and inflation reinforced poverty at home.

At war's end, violence in East Africa mounted. Winston Churchill worried to aides that the slaughter in Kenya, if widely known, would hamper British policies around the globe. In 1952, a movement called Mau Mau responded by embracing

**BRITISH POLICE GUARDING MAU-MAU SUSPECTS, APRIL 28, 1953.** Most decolonization struggles were bloody and destructive on all sides. The Mau Mau Rebellion (1952–60) in Kenya illustrated this. Both the British colonial state and the Mau Mau fighters massacred civilians, including children. British officials implemented a system of concentration camps, designed to isolate the rebels from the population, and used torture to gather intelligence about the movement.

violence of its own. Mau Mau mobilized people from the Kikuyu region of northwest Kenya against policies that took land from Africans and then forced many of them to work this same land—now owned by Europeans—for low wages. The origins of the movement are unclear; even the meaning of the term "Mau Mau" is disputed.

Colonial rulers portrayed the Mau Mau as a terrorist organization, using words like "hooligans," and "savages." Although attacks on Europeans were brutal and highly publicized, most Mau Mau violence was directed at other Africans. The many divisions within African society—some encouraged or even created by the colonial authorities—belie neat categories of "resistance fighters" or "collaborators." Pursuing a strategy to separate loyalists from rebels, the colonial government collected Kenyans into villages surrounded by barricades and booby-traps, similar to the "strategic hamlets" that the United States would establish in Vietnam a decade later. The colonial state also brought overwhelming firepower to bear against the Mau Mau. By the time the war ended, the Mau Mau had killed about two thousand people (only about thirty of them Europeans). The number of Mau Mau killed is difficult to estimate, but twenty thousand or more seems plausible.

Among those apprehended as part of the Mau Mau movement was Jomo Kenyatta (ca. 1891–1978). Jailed as a "leader and manager" of the uprising, Kenyatta had studied in London and Moscow during the 1920s and 1930s, becoming committed to an end to British rule in Kenya. Along with Kwame Nkrumah and others, he was a prominent leader in the pan-African movement and was first president of the Kenyan African Union party, which advocated for Kenyan independence. He was not involved directly in the Mau Mau movement but was still sentenced to a lengthy prison term. In 1961, after mass demonstrations in the capital of Nairobi, Kenyatta was released from detention. He resumed his position of leadership and was the principal Kenyan negotiator at the talks leading to Kenyan independence in 1963.

The Mau Mau wars offer another chance to view how interpretations and analyses of history change over time and also how questions of politics, perspectives, and sources shape historical debate. Supporters of British imperialism depicted it as more beneficent and humane than other what European powers practiced. In many early historical accounts, the British process of decolonization was presented in similar fashion. Recent scholarship responds with the Kenyan case, offering evidence suggesting the British were just as cruel as the Mau Mau and much more systematic. Historian Caroline Elkins has argued that colonial officials used a system of labor and detention camps, along with strategic hamlets, to carry out "a murderous campaign to eliminate Kikuyu people" that she compares to the Nazi Holocaust. Other scholars reject the comparisons with Nazism and the implications that the Mau Mau and the colonial government were in any way equivalent. Recently, Niall Ferguson published a sweeping assessment of British imperialism in its entirety. Ferguson, who does not discuss the Mau Mau war, acknowledges that violence was a regular component of the imperial enterprise but concludes that British imperialism overall was beneficial to the world generally, and to the subject peoples of the British Empire specifically.[1]

## Superpowers and Decolonization

The European empires—France and Britain especially—were forced to accept a new world in which their international leverage was greatly reduced. In one case, the British and French combined forces to roll back decolonization, invading Egypt in 1956 to reverse Egyptian president Gamal Abdel Nasser's (1918–1970) nationalization of the Suez Canal. Although the British and French forces, aided by Israel, achieved their military objectives, pressure from the United States and the Soviet Union forced them to withdraw. The failure of France and Britain to enforce their interests illustrated the extent to which both had lost power. The new superpowers—the United States and the Soviet Union—considered decolonization important but filtered their understandings of the process through their own confrontation. The United States agreed to formal independence for the Philippines at the end of the war and reiterated its commitment to self-determination, although it did not enforce this principle consistently: Hawai'i was incorporated formally into statehood in 1959, and territories like Puerto Rico remained under US control without full political representation.

In Asia, events in Korea reinforced the commitment to the "containment" policy, which prioritized anti-communism over respect for rights and elections. South Korea and Taiwan developed into anti-communist, single-party police states. Under the umbrella of containment, the United States became deeply involved in the internal affairs of countries in the Western Hemisphere and the Middle East as well. In 1953, the United States and Great Britain provided covert funding and operational support for a coup d'état in Iran, after the elected government had nationalized its oil industry and jeopardized assets of British Petroleum. The following year, using similar techniques, the United States supported a coup d'état against the Guatemalan government, which had enacted an

---

[1]    Judicious historical overviews of the end of the British Empire, which help to situate the debates among scholars, are found in Judith M. Brown and William Roger Louis, eds., *The Oxford History of the British Empire: Vol. 4. The Twentieth Century* (New York: Oxford University Press, 2001); David Anderson, *Histories of the Hanged: Britain's Dirty War in Kenya and the End of Empire* (New York: W.W. Norton, 2005); Caroline Elkins, *Imperial Reckoning: The Untold Story of Britain's Gulag in Kenya* (New York: Holt, 2005); and Niall Ferguson, *Empire: How Britain Made the Modern World* (New York: Penguin, 2012).

**MAP 12.3**  Decolonization in Africa and Asia, 1945–75

DECOLONIZATION IN AFRICA AND ASIA, 1945–75

Independent before 1945
French
British
Dutch
Belgian
Portugal

Spanish
Italian
Japanese
American
Dependent territories, 1975

*Dates Indicate Year of Independence*

KOREA (Divided 1945)
TAIWAN (to China) 1945
PHILIPPINES 1946
VIETNAM (Divided 1954)
BRUNEI
CAMBODIA 1954
LAOS 1954
MALAYSIA 1963
INDONESIA 1949
SINGAPORE (from Malaysia 1965)
BANGLADESH (from Pakistan, 1971)
BURMA 1948
CEYLON 1948
PAKISTAN 1947
INDIA 1947

INDIAN OCEAN

KUWAIT 1961
SYRIA 1946
IRAQ
JORDAN 1946
SAUDI ARABIA
YEMEN
SOUTH YEMEN 1967
SOMALIA 1960
MADAGASCAR 1960
SWAZILAND 1968
LEBANON 1945
CYPRUS 1959
ISRAEL 1947
EGYPT
ERITREA 1967
ETHIOPIA
SUDAN 1956
UGANDA 1962
KENYA 1963
TANZANIA 1964
MALAWI 1964
MOZAMBIQUE 1975
RHODESIA
LESOTHO 1965
LIBYA 1951
TUNISIA 1956
CHAD 1960
CENTRAL AFR. REP. 1960
RWANDA 1962
BURUNDI 1962
ZAIRE 1960
ZAMBIA 1964
ANGOLA 1975
NAMIBIA
BOTSWANA 1966
SOUTH AFRICA
ALGERIA 1962
NIGER 1960
NIGERIA 1960
CAMEROON 1960
GABON 1960
CONGO 1960
EQUATORIAL GUINEA 1968
MOROCCO 1956
MALI 1959
MAURITANIA 1960
SENEGAL 1959
GAMBIA 1965
GUINEA 1958
SIERRA LEONE 1958
IVORY COAST 1960
LIBERIA
UPPER VOLTA 1960
GHANA 1957
TOGO 1960
DAHOMEY 1960

ATLANTIC OCEAN

N

0 km    2000
0 miles    2000

agrarian reform that promised to disrupt the operations of the Boston-based United Fruit Company. The new regimes in Iran and Guatemala supported the United States for much of the Cold War, but the memories of these actions inflamed subsequent generations of anti-American activists. The coup in Guatemala convinced a visiting Argentine doctor named Ernesto "Che" Guevara (1928–1967) that his life's work lay in fomenting revolution against the US imperialists. Che Guevara would go on to lead the Cuban revolution with Fidel Castro, and he stated in his 1967 address to the Tricontinental Congress in Havana that he would work to "create two, three . . . many Vietnams throughout the world."

While Guevara and others railed against US imperialism, Soviet forces brutally suppressed dissent in Hungary (1956) and Czechoslovakia (1968). Although the Gulag system was drastically reduced after Stalin's death in 1953, the Soviet government continued to stifle political debate by defining Communist Party decisions as the people's will. As they sought new allies, the two superpowers found themselves in direct military and economic "aid wars" and indirect conflict through "proxy wars," sponsoring overt and covert military operations around the globe, as in 1974, when Soviet-backed military faction took control of an increasingly chaotic Ethiopia. They deposed Emperor Haile Selassie (returned to power with British assistance during World War II), abolished the monarchy, and declared a Marxist-Leninist future. Over the next decade, tens of thousands of regime opponents were executed, imprisoned without trial, or driven to exile.

## Economic Development and Nonalignment: Three Worlds?

At the end of World War II, there were several indisputable facts about how global economic power had changed since the start of the Great War in 1914. First, the United States held three-quarters of the world's gold reserves. Second, the Soviet Union had managed a remarkable feat of industrialization since the collapse of the tsarist regime. Third, the European economies were in ruins; the same could be said of Japan.

To these facts, we need to add an assumption shared by most of the world's elites across the ideological spectrum: industrialization was the key to future prosperity. This included not only building factories to make goods but also improving agriculture through mechanization and chemical fertilizers. Beyond these facts and this shared assumption lay fierce debates about how to achieve sustained economic growth, how to avoid the regular and devastating booms and busts of the previous century, how to fairly distribute the world's resources

**DELEGATES TO THE NON-ALIGNED MOVEMENT CONFERENCE, BELGRADE YUGOSLAVIA, 1961.** In the late 1950s, the leaders of India, Egypt, Ghana, Indonesia, and several other countries attempted to create a space for international political and economic relations to grow outside the boundaries of the Cold War rivalry between the United States and the Soviet Union. This photo depicts leaders of the Non-Aligned Movement at its inaugural conference.

(both within countries and across political boundaries), and how the Cold War would shape responses to these questions.

## Rebuilding the World, Again

The policymakers who met at Bretton Woods during the Second World War sought to build a postwar global capitalist economy on predictable transnational financial exchanges and (relatively) free trade. The productive power of the US economy and its stockpile of gold—much of the world's known reserves—would form the bedrock of this new economic order. For the quarter-century after the war's end, most of the world's currencies were fixed in relationship to the US dollar, and the value of the dollar itself was pegged to a precise amount of gold. Over forty countries subscribed to an International Monetary Fund (IMF), setting aside government assets to maintain monetary stability. Funds were contributed in proportion to the size of a country's economy, and decision-making was apportioned in the same way so that wealthier countries had a greater say in how and when the funds of the IMF would be accessed.

A second institution to emerge from Bretton Woods was the International Bank for Reconstruction and Development: the "World Bank." Whereas the IMF was designed to smooth out hiccups in global currency transactions, the World Bank, through direct loans and guarantees of private loans, would "help in the restoration of economies destroyed or disrupted by war, the reconversion of productive facilities to peacetime needs, and the development of productive facilities and resources in less developed countries."

A third item on the minds of negotiators at Bretton Woods was global trade, but key decisions on trade agreements and tariffs were postponed until after the war. Ultimately, negotiations to establish an International Trade Organization (ITO) failed. The United States, unhappy with some of the treaty provisions, never ratified the organization's charter. A different treaty, the General Agreement on Tariffs and Trade (GATT), which the United States did champion, was signed by only twenty-three countries, as many developing countries saw the treaty provisions as blocking their industrialization prospects. In addition to the GATT, regional trade agreements and bilateral treaties, including two in Europe, were designed to facilitate international commerce.

One of the largest factors in shaping the postwar global economy was the European Recovery Plan, commonly referred to as the "Marshall Plan" after the 1947 Harvard University commencement speech by US Secretary of State George Marshall announcing the policy. Stalin's Soviet Union forbade its Eastern European allies from accepting Marshall Plan funds, but billions of dollars from the United States helped to rebuild sixteen Western European countries between 1948 and 1952. The funds were used to purchase food, fuel, and machines (mostly imported from the United States) as well as to create a pool of money for loans to private businesses.

The United States, which occupied Japan from 1945 to 1952, also played a large role in creating the circumstances under which the Japanese economy would recover. The Japanese postwar constitution (written in English by American lawyers before being translated into Japanese) included a clause forbidding Japan from maintaining a military. With the United States providing security, Japan was freed to invest in infrastructure and industrialization. Through well-coordinated public–private partnerships to manage its postwar recovery, the Japanese economy grew rapidly.

These strategies produced remarkable results. Global economic growth between 1950 and 1973 averaged 5 percent per year. The value of international trade rose even faster, growing at almost 10 percent per year between 1948 and 1973. The marketplaces of Western Europe and the United States filled with consumer goods. These numbers hide some underlying problems, however. First, the vast increase in global trade was driven primarily by increases in the value of manufactured goods and less by an increase in the volume of goods traded. Second, the long-term trend in the global economy appeared to favor the economic fortunes of those countries exporting mostly industrial goods rather than primary products like agricultural staples. In this environment, the world's leaders committed their countries to industrialization as the key to future prosperity.

## Models for Development

There is no simple formula for industrialization. Two major models emerged. One, most popular in Latin America, was Import Substitution Industrialization, which focused on developing a manufacturing base to meet domestic demand. Tariffs and other government policies allowed local industries to grow without being undermined by imported goods. Often, the state controlled privileged industries. The other model, Export-Led Industrialization, required countries to hold down wages and domestic consumption to develop industries that could compete quickly in the international marketplace. The so-called "Asian Tiger" economies—Hong Kong, Singapore, South Korea, and Taiwan—employed this strategy. Both seemed to work in their own way. The growing population of Mexico purchased shirts and shoes produced in domestic factories built with cement produced domestically, with machines fueled by a state-owned petroleum company. Economic growth averaged 6 percent for decades. In South Korea, annual growth rates exceeded the projections of government planners, averaging more than 10 percent per year in the late 1960s. In both countries, government policy actively influenced economic planning and resource allocation.

Eastern Europe, China, North Korea, and North Vietnam implemented communist models of political economy. Organizing production and consumption in a centralized manner appeared viable to many, and perhaps even superior or more appropriate in many contexts than the capitalist alternative. Even Western textbooks reported the Soviet "economic miracle" of continuous 6 percent annual economic growth and full employment from the 1930s to the 1960s. In addition to competing with the United States in promising and delivering military aid to client states, the Soviets also provided technical assistance and development aid, a conspicuous example being the Aswan High Dam project in Egypt in the late 1950s.

Examining the period from the Great Depression to the end of the 1970s as a whole, in places where direct comparison is possible, the results are inconclusive. In Germany, after struggling with postwar reconstruction, non-communist West Germany grew robustly; and by the early 1960s, its citizens enjoyed a standard of living far higher than their counterparts in Communist East Germany. In Korea, however, the story was at first reversed: the Communist North in the 1950s and early 1960s was Asia's second-most industrialized economy, with rapid growth in production and higher standards of living. Many ethnic Koreans living in Japan returned to North Korea in the early 1960s, believing it had better economic prospects than capitalist South Korea. It was not until the end of the 1960s that the South took the lead.

Beyond these countries, Marxist-Leninist guerrilla groups and communist political parties struggled to gain control of additional countries. Some, like Cuba, relied on Soviet commitments for their economic survival, but it would be misguided to think that the communist world marched in lockstep to the beat of a Soviet drum. For example, Cuba's policy of supporting socialist movements in Africa defied Soviet grand strategy. A clearer example of the split among communist states was the growing tensions between China and the Soviet Union, which saw themselves as rivals with divergent visions of Marxism as a global movement.

## Trying to Reject the Cold War: Non-alignment

Despite the internal variation within their camps, both the Soviet Union and the United States portrayed the world as a choice between one side or the other, but not everyone accepted that every country had to choose sides in the Cold War. Some powerful voices on the world stage argued that the rivalry was distracting attention and resources from important issues confronting many former colonial states. In April 1955, the leaders of Burma (Myanmar), India, Indonesia, Pakistan, and Sri Lanka (formerly known as Ceylon) organized a conference in Bandung, Indonesia. Delegates from twenty-nine countries, representing half the world's population, emerged from the meeting with a document calling for peaceful coexistence, an end to racism, and economic cooperation. The delegates expressed concern that the Cold War atmosphere had quickly diminished the principles of respect for sovereignty, self-determination, and human rights that guided the foundation of the United Nations. Two years later, India's first prime minister, Jawaharlal Nehru (1889–1964), summarized the goals of what came to be called the "non-aligned movement," asserting that most of the world's leaders and peoples would prefer to "maintain friendly relations with all countries, even though we may disagree with them in their policies or structure of government."

The leaders of the nonaligned movement embraced the idea that most of the world's rapidly growing, increasingly urban, population lived in the countries of the "third world," a place that was part of neither the "first world" of the United States and its military allies in Western Europe nor the "second world" of the Soviet Union and Eastern Europe. Leaders of the nonaligned movement believed that the elusive common ground of the postwar era could be found in serving the interests of the world's majority. Similar sentiments were expressed in 1958 at the All-African People's Conference held in Accra, Ghana, where delegates expressed frustration at the slow pace at which European powers, now organized into Cold War defense agreements with the United States, were decolonizing. The conference fueled agitation for independence across the continent, and a wave of independent states were established over the next decade. At the Accra Conference, the prominent African American scholar W. E. B. Dubois (1868–1963), who would spend the last days of his life as a Ghanaian citizen, admonished the delegates to transcend local or regional interests to achieve a greater good. Dubois echoed the aims of the nonaligned movement, yet this vision proved difficult to realize. In the two decades following World War II, dozens of newly independent states in Africa, like Angola, and Asia, like Vietnam, collided head-on with Cold War schemes and arms. Coupled with conflicts among rival elite and popular factions, and fueled by divisive ethnic and religious rhetoric, this drained the political, social, and economic capital of the Third World.

## Conclusion

Between the early 1940s and the mid-1970s, the organization of the world changed profoundly. The principle of national self-determination was implemented at an unprecedented pace, as nearly one hundred countries achieved independence during this era. A decades-long economic boom produced extraordinary global wealth and accelerating technological, demographic, and social change. An international organization of nation-states embraced the premise that slaughter like the Holocaust must never again be tolerated and that every human being had rights based solely on his or her humanity and not on membership in a particular national, economic, religious, racial, or ethnic group.

Yet this era was also one of great tensions and enduring conflict. Violent repression of dissent continued to characterize many political regimes, both new and old. Shocking inequalities within countries and among them undermined confidence that growth meant prosperity—or even basic material security—for most of the world's population. Principles such as democracy, self-determination, and human rights too often appeared less as ideals toward which the global community was striving and more as rhetorical cudgels with which opposing sides beat each other. The ever-present threat of nuclear war and the global gamesmanship between the world's superpowers overshadowed every issue of global consequence.

It would have been hard, then, for any of the actors in the Angolan wars to guess that in the next generation, the Soviet Union would disappear and the Communist regime in China would embrace the global market economy. Nor, we bet, would they have predicted that their own civil war would outlast the Cold War—which it did—and that, in its aftermath, their country would become one of the world's largest oil producers, yet provide most Angolans with average earnings of only one dollar per day. In Chapter 13, we analyze the surprising path through the end of the twentieth century that yielded these kinds of outcomes.

## A Few Good Books

Andrei Cherny. *The Candy Bombers: The Untold Story of the Berlin Airlift and America's Finest Hour.* New York: Berkley Trade, 2009.

Frederick Cooper. *Africa since 1940: The Past of the Present.* Cambridge: Cambridge University Press, 2002.

Ian Buruma. *Year Zero: A History of 1945.* New York: Penguin, 2013.

Piero Gleijeses. *Conflicting Missions: Havana, Washington, and Africa, 1959–1976.* Chapel Hill: University of North Carolina Press, 2003.

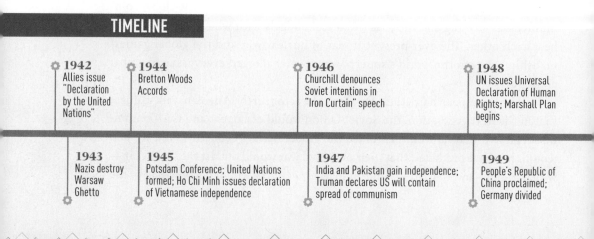

## TIMELINE

**1942**
Allies issue "Declaration by the United Nations"

**1943**
Nazis destroy Warsaw Ghetto

**1944**
Bretton Woods Accords

**1945**
Potsdam Conference; United Nations formed; Ho Chi Minh issues declaration of Vietnamese independence

**1946**
Churchill denounces Soviet intentions in "Iron Curtain" speech

**1947**
India and Pakistan gain independence; Truman declares US will contain spread of communism

**1948**
UN issues Universal Declaration of Human Rights; Marshall Plan begins

**1949**
People's Republic of China proclaimed; Germany divided

Christopher Koch. *The Year of Living Dangerously.* New York: Penguin, 1983.

Vladka Meed. *On Both Sides of the Wall: Memoirs from the Warsaw Ghetto.* New York: Holocaust Library, 1979.

Kushwant Singh. *Train to Pakistan: A Novel.* New York: Grove Press, 1994.

Vazira Fazila-Yacoobali Zamindar. *The Long Partition and the Making of Modern South Asia: Refugees, Boundaries, Histories.* New York: Columbia University Press, 2010.

*For additional resources, including maps, primary sources, visuals, web links, and quizzes, please go to* **www.oup.com/us/carter**

| 1950–53 | 1953 | 1955 | 1958 | 1963 | 1975 |
|---|---|---|---|---|---|
| Korean War | Stalin dies; US backs coup in Iran | Bandung Conference sets groundwork for Non-Aligned Movement | All-Africa People's Conference, Ghana | Kenya achieves independence | Angola achieves independence; fall of South Vietnam to communist North Vietnamese forces |

| 1952–60 | 1954–62 | 1956 | 1961 | 1968 |
|---|---|---|---|---|
| Mau Mau Rebellion, Kenya | Algerian War of Independence | Suez Crisis; Soviet invasion of Hungary | Berlin Wall erected | Soviet army suppresses "Prague Spring" in Czechoslovakia |

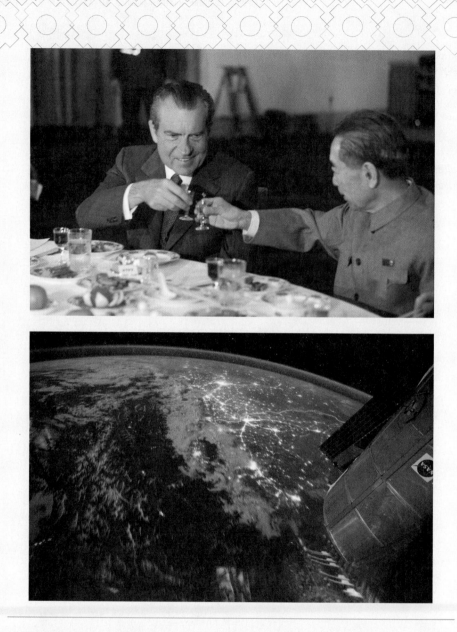

(TOP) US PRESIDENT RICHARD NIXON AND CHINESE PREMIER ZHOU ENLAI SHARE A TOAST, FEBRUARY 25, 1972. Nixon's anti-communist reputation made his overtures to the People's Republic of China, in the midst of the Cold War, surprising to many. The new US-China relationship was part of a Chinese reform policy that helped shape the end of the Cold War and also laid the foundation for China's reemergence as a major world power.

(BOTTOM) SOUTH ASIA FROM SPACE ON A CLEAR NIGHT. The orange line results from the intense lights that form part of the security corridor on the border between India and Pakistan. India is now the world's fourth largest consumer of energy. In 2012, the country's power grid experienced a massive failure: almost the entire top portion of this image would have gone dark.

# CHAPTER 13

# The Many Worlds of the Twenty-first Century

## 1972–2012

In February 1972, US President Richard Nixon (1913–1994) became the first American president to visit China while in office when he stepped off an airplane in Beijing. At the time, in the depths of the Cold War, the United States still did not have official diplomatic relations with the People's Republic of China (PRC), founded by the Chinese Communist Party in 1949. Few foreigners lived in China; travel there from most other countries was so restricted as to be almost impossible. Over the course of a week, Nixon and his wife visited Beijing, Shanghai, and Hangzhou; met with numerous Chinese officials; and toured schools, factories, and the Great Wall. They saw a ballet entitled "The Red Detachment of Women," depicting the transformation of a peasant girl into a model member of the Chinese Communist Party. At the end of the visit, the two countries issued a joint document—the Shanghai Communiqué—committing to the "progressive development of trade between the two countries," which at the time was virtually nonexistent. By 2013, China–US trade totaled more than five hundred sixty billion dollars.

In July 2012, more than six hundred million people in India—almost twice the population of the United States—lost their electricity as the country's power grid failed. In the early twenty-first century, India was forecast to surpass China as the world's most populous country and also to become one of the most productive regions of the global economy again, as it was in the Early Modern era. Its technology sector and contentious but resilient democratic government put it at the forefront of global forecasts of countries to watch. Lasting several days, the blackout exposed technical and logistical flaws in India's power grid that were also present in other areas of Indian life. Like many parts of India's infrastructure, the growth of the power grid had not kept pace with skyrocketing demand. Experts estimated that up

## THE WORLD IN 2015

*There are currently 193 member states of the United Nations. How many could you place on this map?*

**MAP 13.1** The World in 2015

to 30 percent of the power generated was lost to theft and outdated distribution systems. Advocates of alternative methods of generating power, as well as public and private sector interests, fought over different economic plans, delaying needed planning and development. The blackout also highlighted the dramatic disparities in the distribution of wealth and resources in our world: one-third of the households in India did not lose power during the blackout because they did not have electricity in the first place.

---

These brief overviews of Richard Nixon's visit to China and the energy challenges facing India help us understand shifts in economic, political, and cultural power in the waning decades of the twentieth century and into the new millennium. In this chapter, we begin with the changing alliances and ideologies that broke down Cold War identities and affiliations and altered the globe's political geography, including the US–China relationship and upheaval in the Middle East, Latin America, and Southeast Asia. In the next sections of the chapter, we explain the factors that contributed to the collapse of the Warsaw Pact nations and the breakup of the Soviet Union.

Then, we present the numerous factors that changed global economic interactions and fueled the growth of economic powerhouses like India and China, along with the major conflicts that emerged in the multipolar, post-Cold War international environment, including ethnic, religious, and other forms of sectarian violence. As the chapter's narrative moves closer to the present day, we sketch the emergent tensions between economic globalization and the enduring model of the nation-state as the primary form of political sovereignty. Finally, we include in the chapter a brief assessment of the costs and benefits of the "biological new regime" under which all of the earth's inhabitants lived in the early years of the twenty-first century.

## The Cold War and 1970s Political Realism

The establishment of relations between the United States and the PRC highlights the complex interplay of strategic interests, economic development strategies, and ideology in the decades following the Second World War. As noted in Chapter 12, neither side in the 1945–49 Chinese Civil War conceded defeat, and both continued to claim sovereignty over China, even after the defeated Nationalists fled to the island of Taiwan. There were two Chinas—although neither side admitted as much. One was the size of the United States and the other the size of Maryland. Using its global clout, the United States protected Taiwan from its much larger enemy and even managed to preserve the Taiwanese delegation as the official representative of China in the United Nations.

This position was increasingly hard to maintain. In 1970, the government in Taiwan ruled over some fourteen million people and fourteen thousand square miles, whereas the Beijing government ruled over some seven hundred million people and almost four million square miles. In the mid-1960s, the PRC developed and tested nuclear and hydrogen weapons, an expression of power that needed to be acknowledged by the international community if it was to be managed. In 1971, a majority of United Nations members defied US objections and recognized the PRC. Reassessing its position, the United States began to pursue "Ping-Pong Diplomacy," which involved US Ping-Pong players visiting China in 1971. Alongside this public cultural gesture, serious negotiations between US and Chinese politicians occurred in secret, establishing the parameters for the American President's visit to China.

This public recognition that the communist world was not a single entity came at a time when the United States was still at war in Southeast Asia to stop the spread of communism. However, both the US and Chinese governments understood that the bomb shelters China constructed in the 1960s were designed primarily to defend against Soviet nuclear missiles, not American ones. China and the Soviet Union had fallen out over border disputes, ideological differences, and personal conflicts between their leaders in the late 1950s. By the 1960s, Chinese propaganda was just as likely to depict anti-Soviet as anti-American slogans. Even while the PRC pitched and yawed through its radical Cultural Revolution, some in the Chinese leadership began proposing a strategy to reach out to the United States as an ally against the Soviets. The rapprochement between the United States and China showed how political realism could trump ideology in international affairs.

## The Cold War Endures in Latin America and Asia

Nixon's visit to China did not mark the end of the Cold War. Its rhythms were determined not only by the actions of superpowers but by constituencies within nation-states and in regional alliances and confrontations. In Latin America, for example, a brief flourishing of intense, multiparty democracy in the mid-1940s gave way to a bitter clampdown in the 1950s and 1960s. Military coups proliferated, justified in terms of the global Cold War but carrying the distinctive marks of different countries' ethnic, racial, and regional conflicts and histories. In the 1970s, almost every country in the region had anti-communist, authoritarian governments. In response, residents of many of these countries created both peaceful protest organizations and armed guerilla movements in both urban and rural areas to attempt regime change. These home-grown, ideologically diverse

movements and their demands were often denigrated, and their repression justified, by governments asserting that Latin America was at the forefront of the
global struggle to stop an armed communist takeover orchestrated by the Soviet
Union globally and Cuba regionally.

Across the world, aid from the superpowers was important but did not guarantee
results. Despite US economic aid and direct military intervention, anti-communist
regimes in South Vietnam, Cambodia, and Laos all fell to communist armies in
1975, and Thailand, Burma, Indonesia, and the Philippines remained both anti-
communist and authoritarian. Regimes on both sides of this ideological divide in
the region carried out brutal repression against their own people.

In South Asia, the India-Pakistan rivalry precipitated numerous shifts in Cold
War alliances. In the first decades of the Cold War, India—a leader of the Non-
Aligned Movement—had more cordial relations with communist countries than
it did with the United States. However, border disputes with China and concern
over Maoist revolutionaries inside India tempered the Indian political elite's enthusiasms for China. Ongoing Soviet support for India also expanded the rift between the Soviet Union and China. In contrast, Pakistan had closer ties to the
United States for a time after independence, although relations cooled when a
left-leaning government came to power in the 1970s and looked for development
aid from the Soviets. Relations between the United States and Pakistan improved
after an anti-communist military regime took power and found common cause
with the United States opposing Soviet plans in the region. Complicating international relations during this era, both India and Pakistan developed nuclear
weapons technology in the context of their own rivalry, rather than as part of any
broader Cold War plan guided by the United States or the Soviet Union.

## OPEC, Energy, and Geopolitics

The Middle East, with a significant share of the world's known oil reserves, played
an important role in global political and economic relations. Geostrategic calculations, Cold War confrontations, and ethnic and religious tensions exacerbated
by postwar decolonization led repeatedly to unrest in the region. In October
1973, war broke out for the second time in six years between Israel and neighboring Egypt and Syria. Israel received support from the United States and Western
Europe. In solidarity with Egypt and Syria, the Organization of Petroleum Exporting Countries (OPEC) accelerated its plan to shift the relationship between
oil producers and consumers, restricting oil production to create shortages and
increase prices.

What was OPEC and why did its actions matter? Petroleum was the greatest
single material factor differentiating the twentieth century economy from what
came before. Oil had replaced coal as the most important power source for global

**MAP 13.2** The Oil Crisis, 1973–74

industry. In 1960 four Middle Eastern oil producers—Iraq, Iran, Saudi Arabia, and Kuwait—as well as Venezuela, in South America, joined together to form OPEC. The organization's members committed to set production levels and coordinate policies to protect "permanent sovereignty over their natural resources in the interest of their national development." Soon thereafter, OPEC added Indonesia, Algeria, Nigeria, and Libya, all of which had recently won independence from European colonial powers. By 1973, Qatar, the United Arab Emirates, and Ecuador were also members.

Although founded as an economic organization, OPEC's membership also shared some common political goals, many of which challenged the power of Europe and the United States. In retaliation against Western support of Israel in the 1973 war, OPEC drastically curtailed production, which raised prices by diminishing the global supply of oil. Although the supply was interrupted only temporarily, OPEC's actions exposed the dependence of industrial nations. The United States—the world's largest consumer of oil—panicked, government rationing was instituted, and prices rose sharply. The global economy soon fell into recession.

This was the first of several "oil shocks" of the 1970s that drove a reconsideration of economic development policy among the industrial nations. Since the 1970s, alternative energy sources—nuclear, solar, wind, and others—and new technologies, such as hydraulic fracturing ("fracking"), have changed components of the geopolitics of energy and will continue to do so. However, global industry and transportation still rely fundamentally on petroleum, a nonrenewable resource, and the global appetite for fossil fuels continued to grow at a rapid pace into the twenty-first century.

## Revolution in Iran

Another challenge to the Cold War status quo emerged from the Middle East at the end of the 1970s. In Iran, as a mass uprising drove the ruling Shah, Mohammed Reza Pahlavi (1919–1980), into exile in 1979, memories of how he had gained autocratic power in 1953—with the aid of the US Central Intelligence Agency—spurred the opposition. Among the most committed activists in the anti-Shah movement was a Shi`a cleric, Ruhollah Khomeini (1902–1989), who had spent fifteen years in exile. During his years in Iraq and France, cassette tapes of his teachings—interpretations of Islamic tradition mixed with anti-American and anti-Semitic denunciations—circulated throughout Iran and beyond. Politically savvy, Khomeini reached out to other anti-Shah groups, even those whose members did not share his vision of Iran's future but who agreed that any change must start with removing the Shah.

**THE SHAH'S EXILE AND KHOMEINI'S RETURN, HASAN ISMA'ILZADAH, 1979.** This poster employs a traditional Iranian "storytelling" style of painting, popular in coffeehouses. Highly detailed paintings like this were used as storytelling aids, often around national or religious tales. Here, we see the events surrounding the 1979 revolution, with the Shah, suitcases packed, leaving the country while the Ayatollah Ruhollah Khomeini returns triumphantly from Paris.

Khomeini's faction, committed to a new state where fundamentalist interpretations of Islamic practice would guide all political, economic, and social life, won admirers and momentum in its bid to control the country's destiny when its militants stormed the US Embassy in protest of the decision to allow the exiled Shah to enter the United States for medical treatment. The militants took hostages and began to release information obtained in the ransacked embassy files about the ways in which members of rival political groups had "betrayed" the revolution by meeting with US officials. In the version of the revolution's history told by Khomeini, the new regime's political and spiritual leader, "All the tombstones [of those who died to make the revolution] belong to Muslims from the lower echelons of society: peasants, workers, tradesmen, committed religious scholars. Those who imagine that some force other than Islam could shatter the great barrier of tyranny are mistaken."

The new regime in Iran committed to a policy of nationalization of key resources and full employment for its citizens. One might expect that the emergence of an anti-American oil-producing state in the Middle East would benefit Soviet designs for the region, but the Soviets themselves were flummoxed by an Islamist uprising against the communist regime in Afghanistan.

## Afghanistan between Empires, Again

The Soviet invasion of Afghanistan, which began in 1979—the same year as the Iranian Revolution—evoked past imperialist aggression. The Russian Empire had been deeply involved in Afghanistan and this continued into the Soviet period. Long a strategic crossroads, Afghanistan had defied empire-builders' plans to subdue and control it. Its importance to both superpowers grew as its

Western neighbors Iran and Iraq became major oil producers while its southeastern neighbors India and Pakistan acquired nuclear weapons technology.

The Afghans faced many of the same issues by now familiar to readers of this
book: how to modernize the country's economy, what aspects of traditional culture
to retain, and how to do all this while facing powerful rivals. Inside Afghanistan,
factions disagreed over the country's future. One group attempted to alter many
Muslim cultural traditions, including some related to marriage customs and land
distribution, as it tried to move the country in a more Marxist, secular direction.
Unpopular with much of the population, these measures led to civil war, fueled by
popular discontent. Foreign governments, including Pakistan and the United
States, provided support for antigovernment forces.

Fearing chaos on its border and the loss of a key strategic ally, the Soviet Union
deployed tanks, aircraft, and more than one hundred thousand troops to shore up
its preferred leadership group. The war, which began in December 1979 and lasted
for nearly a decade, was more than a proxy war between Soviet and US allies. The
war in Afghanistan also fueled a different international struggle—a pan-Islamist
movement. Soviet aggression was denounced by both the United States *and* revolutionary Iran. Many *Mujahideen* (resistance fighters) took as their central goal
the overthrow not only of the current Soviet-backed secular government but any
secular state. From North Africa to Indonesia, the cause attracted Islamist resistance fighters to Afghanistan. Many of these fighters were seeking a broader
Islamic movement that would transcend what these individuals saw as the artificial
territorial boundaries of nation-states imposed on the Islamic world by external
forces. After ten years, the Soviets withdrew from Afghanistan without victory
and drained of vital resources. In the aftermath, outside forces funded different
factions in the struggle for Afghanistan, with Pakistan, Saudi Arabia, and Iran all
supporting different groups.

One of the pan-Islamic fighters drawn to Afghanistan was a young Saudi named
Osama bin Laden (1957–2011). Born into one of the world's wealthiest families—
a fortune made in oil, construction, and banking—bin Laden was a university
student when the Soviet Union invaded Afghanistan, but he abandoned his studies to join the fight against the Soviets. Although he saw some combat, bin Laden
spent most of the war working with Pakistani forces training insurgents and fun-
neling money to the resistance.

When the Soviets withdrew in 1989, bin Laden returned to Saudi Arabia, intent
on spreading the lessons he claimed to have learned in the war against the Soviets.
Asserting the need to protect and spread traditional Muslim values against all
destructive and immoral secular powers, he urged the Saudi government to reject
its alliance with the United States. Bin Laden claimed, like the Mujahideen, that
he would pursue Holy War against his enemies through a new organization he called

*al-Qaeda* ("the Base"), which he had founded in the last years of the Afghan war. As the Cold War ended, Soviet forces—and American aid to their adversaries—withdrew from Afghanistan. In that power vacuum, al-Qaeda began to recruit and train a stateless army for global combat and covert attacks on targets it deemed contrary to the interests of Islam, chief among them the United States.

## Transitions in the Communist World in the 1980s

While the Soviet Union was engaged in Afghanistan, it faced other challenges as well. Its centrally directed economy could not deliver the same quantity and variety of consumer goods as more market-oriented economies. Its most lucrative export was petroleum (the USSR was the world's largest producer), but supplies peaked in 1987, after which production began to decline sharply. Economic weaknesses long disguised by oil revenues emerged. The arms race and proxy wars of the Cold War had also drained resources. Sluggish economic growth undermined the legitimacy of communist government. People also had wearied of the authoritarian rule that accompanied Soviet-style communism. Its allies in the Warsaw Pact, and client states such as Cuba, also stagnated economically.

Similar to the situation in Afghanistan, one of the most important challenges to Soviet control in Eastern Europe came from a transnational religious movement, in this case the Roman Catholic Church. Karol Józef Wojtyła (1920–2005), elected Pope John Paul II in 1978, was the first non-Italian leader of the world's largest Christian denomination in more than four hundred years. His Polish ancestry and consistent anti-communist message inspired labor leaders in Poland—which even under communism was overwhelmingly Catholic—and in 1980, a union movement called Solidarity emerged to publicly oppose the communist government. Previously, when dissident movements in East Central Europe challenged Soviet-allied governments, as in Hungary (1956) and Czechoslovakia (1968), their governments unleashed violent crackdowns with Soviet military support. But this did not happen in Poland, in large part because of changes in Soviet leadership.

### Internal Reforms in the Soviet Union

In 1982, after almost twenty years as the leader of the Soviet Union, Leonid Brezhnev (1906–1982) died. Two hardline, and elderly, successors died in office within the next three years, destabilizing the leadership and accentuating the predicament facing the USSR. Emerging out of the succession crisis, Mikhail Gorbachev (1931– ) was named the new General Secretary in 1985. Eager—perhaps desperate—to reshape Soviet society, reinvigorate its economy, and retain its position as a global superpower, Gorbachev promised *perestroika* (institutional

*PERESTROIKA* **POSTER FOR THE TWENTY-SEVENTH COMMUNIST PARTY CONGRESS, USSR, 1987.** The text states, "The policy is acceleration—perestroika—to work actively, boldly, creatively, competently!" Amid a stagnant economy and political crisis, Soviet head of state Mikhail Gorbachev called for reform and openness (*perestroika* and *glasnost* in Russian). Gorbachev's policies contributed to the collapse of communist governments throughout Europe in 1989 and then the disintegration of the Soviet Union itself in 1991.

restructuring) and *glasnost* (opening to criticism and debate). Allowing events in Poland to play out without Soviet intervention was one result of these changes in policy.

## Reform in China

Like the USSR, China entered the 1980s facing leadership transition and policy reassessment. In 1976, following the death of Mao Zedong—who had led the PRC since its founding—a brief power struggle opened a path to leadership for Deng Xiaoping (1904–1997). Deng had impeccable military and Communist Party credentials dating back to the 1930s, and his remarkable political skill had enabled him to survive not one, or two, but three purges under Mao. As China's leader, he charted a radical new course. Instead of ideological fervor and isolation, Deng opened China to the world and embarked on an economic modernization campaign that valued pragmatism and experimentation over communist principles.

Although it is hard to imagine today, when Deng came to power, the PRC made almost nothing for sale in the international marketplace, comprising less than one percent of global imports and exports in the early 1970s. This changed abruptly. In 1979, China's foreign trade amounted to under thirty billion dollars. By 1985, it passed seventy billion; and by 2012, China was the world's largest trading nation, with international exchanges valued at almost four trillion dollars, accounting for some 10 percent of all exports worldwide.

Deng moved the country quickly away from Maoist collectivism toward what he called "Socialism with Chinese characteristics." In short, market forces and more private ownership took more prominent roles in a centrally directed economy. State-owned corporations remained powerful, but for the bulk of Chinese society, economic transformation was at hand. Underscoring both the commercial and international aspect of the changes, Deng left for the United States as soon as diplomatic ties were formally established on January 1, 1979, and signed deals to allow Boeing Aircraft and Coca-Cola to do business with China.

The sweeping changes made the Chinese economy much more dynamic, but also less stable: the lives of millions of Chinese changed, but not continuously and consistently for the better. Global markets put new pressures on wages and prices. Inflation, which had not been an issue in China since the 1940s, rose sharply. Deng's Special Economic Zones (SEZs) brought foreign goods, including luxury goods, into China; but few people could afford them. Corruption, nepotism, and patronage flourished. And what of political change? Would economic changes inspire political change? Perhaps an emerging class of property owners would demand political rights to match its new economic influence?

A crackdown on public protests in the summer of 1989 demonstrated the limits of the regime's tolerance for a movement designed to achieve a political opening to go along with economic change. Inspired by the death of a pro-reform official that spring, tens of thousands of Chinese students occupied Tiananmen Square, the center of the capital and the symbolic heart of China. For three weeks, the protesters ignored government demands to disperse. On June 4, 1989, Chinese troops cleared the square by force, killing hundreds, perhaps thousands, as they advanced.

## The Collapse of the Soviet Bloc

Reports of the massacre in China reached Europe as Poles were voting. The outcome of their election was startling. Despite rules designed to prevent Solidarity from winning, the movement took two hundred sixty out of two hundred sixty one open seats in the Polish legislature. The communist government could no longer govern without regard for the Solidarity delegates. Single-party communist rule had ended, and this time the Soviet Union did not respond with violence. Tolerance of the changes in Poland signaled to reformers throughout the Soviet bloc what might be possible. In November, protesters tore down the Berlin Wall, which had symbolized the Cold War since its construction in 1961. Communist governments in East Germany, Czechoslovakia, Hungary, Romania, Yugoslavia, and Albania soon followed Poland in collapse. Two years later, the Soviet Union itself dissolved, with fifteen independent states emerging. The superpower relationship that had defined—and threatened—the entire world for fifty years seemed to vanish.

## Explaining the End of the Cold War

The Cold War ended suddenly. Even during the summer of 1989, few predicted the dramatic political changes that were around the corner in Europe, let alone the Soviet collapse. The decades since have seen broad disagreement about what provoked the collapse of the USSR and the end of the Cold War. The Cold War became the realm of historians, who sought out new sources from former communist regimes and declassified documents from the US Government and elsewhere. Many explanations emerged to account for this sudden shift in how the world was organized.

Some scholars have heaped praise on US President Ronald Reagan (1911–2004). In this view, which historian Robert Kagan has called "the standard narrative," Reagan, stridently anti-communist, engaged in tough rhetoric and an arms race, bankrupting the Soviet economy and constantly pressuring the Soviets to reform and exposing the contradictions and falsehoods of communist regimes. More common among historians is the view taken by John Lewis Gaddis and others who give three individuals—Reagan, Gorbachev, and Pope John Paul II—central roles in the end of the Cold War. In this analysis, Reagan's insistence that US policy strive to defeat, not contain, communism finds a partner in Gorbachev, who rejected the authoritarian model of his predecessors. Gorbachev initiated reforms in the Soviet bureaucracy and refused to suppress antigovernment protesters in Eastern Europe, as his predecessors had done. Catalyzing the people of Eastern Europe was John Paul II—the first Polish pope. When he celebrated mass in Warsaw in 1979, a quarter of a million people attended. His message—"Don't be Afraid"—inspired the creation of the Solidarity movement the following summer.

Other scholars look to changing structural factors, rather than individual actors, as most important. Joseph Nye, among others, points to the clear failure of the Soviet economy to provide its citizens with the kind of prosperity enjoyed by many Western nations as a critical factor. In this view, the Soviet economy was already in shambles before Ronald Reagan took office, and its political system was unable to respond effectively. The Soviet Union continued to spend most of its budget on an arms race that predated Reagan. In part, these expenditures were the cost of the imperial sprawl of the Soviet Union. Attempting to control disparate and volatile regions and peoples drained Soviet resources, as the invasion of Afghanistan in 1979 demonstrated. Although the adversarial relationship to the United States played a role in this spending, it was not the only factor and could not be attributed to a sudden or important change by one leader or even a trio of them. In this view, economic and ideological rigidity had doomed the Soviet Union before John Paul, Reagan, or Gorbachev stepped on the world stage.

Stephen Cohen rebuts this line of thinking as "retrospective determinism," arguing that the Soviet Union, like any political system, could and did change over time. Cohen sees the major causes of the collapse as internal to the Soviet Union, including Gorbachev's decisions as leader. The Soviet economy was bad, but large states rarely collapse because of a bad economy alone, Cohen argues. He suggests that the Soviet Union was at its most democratic just before it dissolved and that far from being doomed, or evil, the Soviet Union was on the verge of sustainable, democratic reform, as Gorbachev opened more space for protest and dissent. When Gorbachev also accommodated American demands on arms control and Soviet troop deployments, however, many hardliners within the Soviet establishment saw these two phenomena as linked and threatening. According to this analysis, internal reactions to fluid circumstances, not destiny, and not external actors, brought down the USSR.[1]

## Towards a New Global Order

Regime change was also occurring in the non-communist world. Beginning in the 1970s and continuing through the 1980s, dozens of authoritarian governments in Europe, Asia, and Latin America changed their political systems to allow greater electoral competition and to permit civic organizations and political parties to operate more freely. Many factors caused this third wave of democratization around the globe. Exhaustion from long civil wars, bold actions and calls for reconciliation by religious and political leaders, pressure from international organizations and civil society groups, and global economic forces all played a role. No road map charts the path that Spain, Guatemala, Argentina, South Korea, the Philippines, South Africa, and dozens of other countries took to build more democratic societies, just as the transformations in the communist world were also a mix of context and contingency. Many of these countries also underwent economic transformations that, although not as dramatic as the turn away from communist authoritarianism, were profound in their own right.

Facing rapid population growth, rising energy prices, low growth in productivity, and high public debt, elites in many developing countries came to believe that prospects for economic stability and development anywhere and everywhere in the world depended on embracing free market open-economy principles

---

[1] Stephen Cohen, *Soviet Fates and Lost Alternatives: From Stalinism to the New Cold War* (New York: Columbia University Press, 2013); John Lewis Gaddis, *The Cold War: A New History* (New York: Penguin, 2006); Robert Kagan, *The Return of History and the End of Dreams* (New York: Vintage, 2009); John Patrick Diggins, *Ronald Reagan: Fate, Freedom, and the Making of History* (New York: W.W. Norton & Company, 2007). A useful overview of these debates is provided by Joseph Nye, "Who Caused the End of the Cold War?," *The Huffington Post*, March 18, 2010, http://www.huffingtonpost.com/joseph-nye/who-caused-the-end-of-the_b_350595.html

(FMOEP). They found common cause with decision-makers in private industry, international organizations, and political leaders in some of the world's most advanced economies, like the Reagan administration (1981–89) in the United States and the Thatcher government (1979–90) in Great Britain. The most important of these principles was that future global economic growth required governments to allow markets to allocate more resources, including public goods like drinking water, electricity, and transportation. A corollary principle was that economic well-being required greater participation in international markets and not reliance on and protection of domestic ones. The level of faith in the private sector and commitment to dismantling government programs and services varied, but this trend was evident in policy changes around the world. Tariffs were lowered and government monopolies were sold to private investors. Social welfare programs, public sector jobs, and public investment in infrastructure projects diminished.

## The End of History and Its Quick Return

In the momentous year of 1989, a US State Department official and scholar named Francis Fukuyama published an article titled "The End of History?" The question mark in the title is important because the author's thesis is speculative, but it presented a jaw-dropping idea to those who were living through those moments. Fukuyama mused that the world might be reaching "the end point of mankind's ideological evolution and the universalization of Western liberal democracy as the final form of human government."[2]

The 1990s quickly and violently challenged the "End of History" thesis in the genocidal war that accompanied the breakup of Yugoslavia. NATO forces, icons of the Cold War, bombed the region in 1995 and again in 1999 to try to curtail the "ethnic cleansing" of President Slobodan Milosevic, who was later arrested and tried by a United Nations special war crimes tribunal. Brutal ethnic violence killed or displaced millions of people in Somalia and the Central African nation of Rwanda as well.

Like all conflicts, the ones that shaped the post-Cold War world had deep roots that often grew in unpredictable ways. One example of this emerged from the mountains that divided Afghanistan and Pakistan, where Osama bin Laden trained with Pakistani army officers to prepare resistance fighters against the Soviets a decade earlier. The United States, which employed the Mujahideen as proxies in the Cold War, partly funded these training camps, but few in Washington (or Moscow) would have predicted that bin Laden's organization, al-Qaeda, would outlast the Soviet Union: but that is what happened.

---

[2]    Francis Fukuyama, "The End of History?," *The National Interest* 16 (Summer 1989): 3–18.

The Soviet Union lasted just two years after it withdrew from Afghanistan, and bin Laden shifted his struggle to a new fight against the United States. He built al-Qaeda on the idea that "Western," especially American, values and culture threatened Islam, going so far as to posit a Christian-Jewish conspiracy intended to eliminate Islam. Al-Qaeda embraced religion as its primary identity, but it was rooted also in anticolonialism. For al-Qaeda, the United States was a successor to the European imperialist regimes that had shaped the political geography, economic prospects, and social contours of the world's Muslims for generations. In the worldview of bin Laden and his followers, only by challenging Western cultural and economic hegemony could Muslims succeed.

When challenging overwhelming power, anti-imperial movements have employed many tactics, from Gandhi's passive resistance to full-scale warfare. Al-Qaeda, active in more than a dozen countries by 1992, used many tactics, including direct attacks on the American presence in these countries and also attacks in Western countries. Both were designed to persuade Western governments, in particular the United States, and their populations, that the cost of the West's continued presence in Islamic countries was too onerous to sustain. In 1992, al-Qaeda bombed a Yemeni hotel where US troops had been housed. The following year, al-Qaeda operatives exploded a bomb in the basement of New York City's World Trade Center, a failed attempt to bring down the towers. Attacks in Saudi Arabia, Kenya, and Tanzania in the 1990s were all attributed to al-Qaeda.

On September 11, 2001, al-Qaeda transformed itself from one among many militant groups to the central focus of American foreign policy and the embodiment of the challenges of the post-Cold War world. On that morning, al-Qaeda operatives hijacked four airplanes, crashing one into each tower of New York's World Trade Center and a third into the Pentagon, the headquarters of the US Military in Washington, DC. The fourth plane, apparently intended for the White House, crashed in rural Pennsylvania after passengers resisted the hijackers. Nearly three thousand people died in the attacks, and many more were injured. In the aftermath, thousands were sickened by the toxic dust and smoke that lingered in the air of lower Manhattan for weeks.

Hopes that the end of the Cold War would deliver a global "peace dividend"— a reduction of violence and shift of government expenditures from military outlays to investments in developing human and social capital—were shattered. In the weeks that followed, US leaders characterized these events as attacks by people who "hate our freedoms" and declared a "war on terror," invading and occupying both Afghanistan (2001) and Iraq (2003), whose governments were cited as state sponsors of transnational terrorist organizations like al-Qaeda. Warfare shredded both countries, as rivals jockeyed to control territory and resources while the invading coalition attempted to create the conditions under which stable, friendly governments would coalesce. Radical Islamists attempted to expand their influence in other countries with majority Muslim populations, from Indonesia to Yemen, while terrorists bombed US allies in London (2004) and Madrid (2005).

The US-led coalition of forces completed a withdrawal from Iraq at the end of 2011, although violence continued, and troops remained in Afghanistan. A different wave of demonstrations, protests, and political upheaval, sometimes called the Arab Spring, rocked North Africa and the Middle East starting in late 2010 and accelerating in the spring of 2011. Rooted in more than six decades of strife, another fundamental conflict in the region—the tension between the Israeli government and the claims of Palestinians—remained undiminished.

## Resilience and Limitations of the Political Order

These ongoing conflicts remind us of a number of key points about the post-Cold War world, some of which resonate with the lessons of earlier eras. Superior weaponry and troop strength do not determine long-term historical outcomes when violent conflicts arise. Warfare has always drained the resources of those who engage in it; the costs in "blood and treasure" cannot be borne in perpetuity. Long-term sovereignty depends on effectiveness and legitimacy. In a world organized around socially contracted popular sovereignty, these can only be built on local foundations rather than imposed from above or outside. Furthermore, much of the ongoing violence throughout the Muslim world was driven by conflicts between different groups of Muslims split by theological disputes and competing claims over material resources, as well as other religious and ethnic groups with resource disparities and differing visions of political and economic organization among them. Finally, states outside the region, including the United States, Russia, China, and the region's most important former European colonial powers (France and Great Britain) all maintained conflicting goals and interests in the region, even though they all agreed in theory that certain forms of Islamic radicalism were a common threat to their visions of the modern world.

This confrontation triggered profound debates about the resilience and potential limitations of the contemporary global political order of nation-states, especially about the extent to which rights claims (including, for example, freedom of speech or proscriptions against cruel and unusual punishment) can or should be limited by sovereign states in the pursuit of national security. Perplexing dilemmas about the rules of war between states and non-state actors lingered as well. During this same era, transformations in the global economy raised additional questions about the nature of sovereignty at the dawn of a new millennium.

## Economic Integration

In 1972, the Ford Motor Company launched a secret project named "Bobcat." The project's goal was to design, build, and sell a "world car," taking advantage of changes in transportation, communications, and manufacturing to reduce costs and the potential for disruption throughout the supply, production, and distribution chains. Construction workers plowed under onion fields and orange groves in Valencia, Spain, to break ground on a new assembly plant. Engineers in England, Germany, and the United States designed the vehicle. Parts came from factories located in numerous countries. The first Ford Fiesta rolled off the Spanish assembly line in 1976. Subsequent iterations of the vehicle—which became one of the best-selling automobiles in history—have been manufactured and sold in South America, South Africa, South Asia, Southeast Asia, China, and the United States.

Such highly integrated, international processes of production, distribution, and consumption became the norm over the four decades following the introduction of the Ford Fiesta. For commodities with lower thresholds to investment in the manufacturing base, such as consumer electronics and textiles, production could shift quickly and dramatically. Almost one hundred companies manufactured televisions in the United States during the 1950s, but that number declined to zero—not one—by the end of the twentieth century. Mexico became the largest exporter of televisions in the world. Then, in 2012, one US company announced to patriotic applause that it would begin assembling televisions in the United States. However, these units—just like the units being assembled in Mexico—would be made from parts manufactured in Asia. On both sides of the US-Mexico border, televisions would only receive final assembly before being shipped to retail stores. In both cases, the parts were made on the other side of the world.

As we noted previously, opening of economic relations between the United States and China, the collapse of communist regimes, and the reassessment of economic development strategies in non-communist states helped to create the conditions for increasing global economic integration. We have to add several additional pieces to the puzzle, however: the computer and communications revolution, regional economic integration and the establishment of the World Trade Organization.

## The European Union and the World Trade Organization

In 1957, a treaty brought together Belgium, Italy, West Germany, the Netherlands, Luxembourg, and France in the European Economic Community, or "Common Market." This charter was one of the first to use the term "supranational": above the nation. It required individual nation-states to concede to the broader organization power over certain issues formerly reserved for the member states' own governments while retaining full sovereignty in other areas. The steps toward European integration began with agreements on economic issues, such as trade and agricultural production standards, but then moved on to educational and environmental issues, the creation of a common currency—the Euro—and even discussions about foreign policy and collective security. In 1993, the organization changed its name to the European Union (EU) to better reflect its broad mandate. In 2012, Croatia became the twenty-eighth member of the EU, completing a process of application and negotiation that had taken almost ten years. Plans existed for further expanding the organization.

Other regional trading associations emerging in the same time frame focused mostly on lowering the costs of moving commodities and capital across borders and less on broad issues of political integration and shared sovereignty. Nonetheless, treaties such as the Association of Southeast Asian Nations Free Trade Agreement (1992) and North American Free Trade Agreement (1994) changed the economic relationships among signatory countries. They also sparked debate about the nature of sovereignty in the modern world, as individual countries created binding agreements that critics saw as ceding pieces of national sovereignty without the extensive public deliberations that such changes should require.

Each of these regional agreements moved in step with the revival of broader global trade negotiations originally envisioned in the days of the Bretton Woods meetings during the Second World War. In 1986, delegates arrived in Punta del Este, Uruguay to begin the most ambitious round of trade negotiations ever undertaken, covering global transactions in everything from staple foods, to plastic trinkets, to cutting-edge pharmaceuticals. By the time the negotiations were complete, more than one hundred countries had laid the foundation for the World Trade Organization (WTO), which was inaugurated in 1995. WTO delegates establish the terms by which member states permit goods, from staple foods to banking services, to move across national boundaries. By 2012, more than one hundred fifty WTO member states were responsible for 95 percent of international commerce. These negotiations and the organizations that emerged from them created the legal and diplomatic frameworks for further global economic integration. The computer and telecommunications revolutions provided the means by which this integration was carried out.

## The Internet

It is nearly impossible to imagine today, but when the Berlin Wall fell, almost no one learned the news via the Internet, a system that had its roots in discussions and experiments in data sharing and communications by researchers at universities, corporations, think tanks, and government agencies. The growing availability, capacity, and convenience of "personal" computers during the 1980s sparked

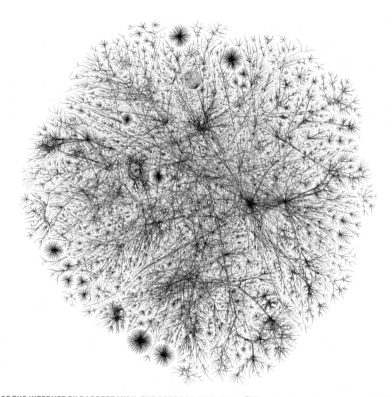

**MAP OF THE INTERNET BY BARRETT LYON, THE OPTE PROJECT, 2014.** "Where do you go when you go online?" As important as the Internet has become to our world, understanding how it works challenges the imagination. A single email message gets broken down into multiple data packets, each of which travels from its source across multiple pathways, some of which may be wires and others of which may be signals passed by satellites or radio towers. The data is then reconstituted at its destination. Barrett Lyon, an entrepreneur and artist, developed the Opte Project to create visual representations, like the one shown here, to map the pathways along which data packets flow around the world. This work is beautiful but also practical. The maps can suggest inefficiencies in the system or even the occurrence of natural disasters that disrupt the flow of data.

interest in using linked computation for commercial purposes, personal communications, and leisure activities. These trends came together in the 1980s, as closed research networks, often funded by government agencies, yielded to commercial enterprises linking private users to vast and powerful systems of hardware and ever-multiplying packets of data.

In 1990, only three million people worldwide had access to the Internet, and more than two million of these were in the United States. By the start of 1996—the year Larry Page and Sergey Brin began the research that would yield Google—there were still only sixteen million Internet users, just 0.4 percent of the world's population. About this time, early in the teaching careers of the authors of this book, we used to arrange special class sessions in the university computer lab, which began with an explanation of what the Internet was! In that one year, however, Internet use doubled, and it increased at an astounding pace over the following years. By December 2000, the number of users reached three hundred sixty-one million. Five years later, it was more than one billion. In 2012, it was estimated that nearly two and one-half billion people, over 35 percent of the world's population, used the Internet.

The globalization that accompanied the Internet revolution was of such a different quality that in some ways it constituted an entirely new way of interacting. Telephones and telegraphs had made transcontinental communication possible, even instantaneous, a century earlier, but the scale, variety, and declining cost of computing has been one of the great material revolutions in human history, from computer-aided design to MMORPG: massive multiplayer online role-playing games. It is a cliché, but no less true for being so, that the average mobile phone today has more computing power than machines that would have filled a room a half-century ago.

## The New Global Economy

The three trends of integration, deregulation, and computerization affected the global financial system, just as they did every other piece of the global economy. But in 2008, the system came close to collapse. Fueled principally by risky financial practices in the United States and Europe, many of the world's largest economies fell into deep recession. Lehman Brothers, one of the world's largest and oldest investment banks, collapsed. Trillions of dollars of consumer wealth disappeared and stock markets shed value. In Europe, many member states of the European Union struggled to pay their debts. Governments in Greece, Ireland, and Iceland came close to failure, while the economies of Spain and even Italy— among the world's ten largest economies—appeared in jeopardy. Jobless rates approached 50 percent in some European countries. Alluding to the 1929 global crash, some called this the "Great Recession." In the United States and Europe, this was termed "the global financial crisis."

However, this global crisis had very different impacts around the world. The world's financial system was indeed global, and the downturn in the United States and Europe affected the entire world; but even in 2009—the worst year of the recession—dozens of countries managed economic growth of greater than four percent, mostly in Asia and Africa. In 2010, China and India again grew at more than 10 percent per year. In this new decade, half of the world's largest economies were in Europe and North America, but none of the fastest growing economies were. China and India were on both lists: top ten in size *and* in growth. Many observers credited the continued growth in Asia with averting a true global economic catastrophe on the scale of the Great Depression.

**THE GLOBAL DISTRIBUTION OF WEALTH IN THE EARLY 21st CENTURY**

A country's GDP per capita as percentage of world average ($10,500) 2009:

LUX Country with GDP per capita among highest
ZIM Country with GDP per capita among lowest

- over 400%
- 200–400%
- 100–200%
- 50–100%
- 25–50%
- 10–25%
- under 10%

**MAP 13.3** The Global Distribution of Wealth in the Early Twenty-first Century

By 2010, after three decades of steady, rapid growth, China overtook Japan to become the world's second-largest economy. It was also the world's largest trading nation, exporting and importing more goods than any other country. All this trade made China wealthy: a favorable balance of trade gave it tremendous cash reserves, enabling it to expand its political influence, much of it to support its enormous demand for raw materials. Chinese companies—many of them state-owned or state-supported—invested in Africa, South America, and even the United States. China acquired mineral rights and signed trade agreements in exchange for investment and infrastructure projects.

India also emerged during this period as an economic giant, entering the world's top-ten economies in the 2000s. Like China, India relied on manufacturing for much of its growth, but India's experience of British colonialism enabled it to tap into the population's English-language skills as part of its economic plan, particularly in the global service sector, where outsourcing customer support services—help lines and call centers—was now technologically and logistically feasible.

These trends and statistics have led some analysts to suggest that the global economy, and the power that goes with it, may be moving in a new direction. In 2001, an analyst for the Goldman Sachs investment bank used demographic trends, natural resource stores, and recent economic growth to hypothesize that four national economies—Brazil, Russia, India, and China—would dominate the twenty-first century. As early as 2008, these countries attempted to use the perception of their growing clout to make joint statements and proposals on a variety of global issues on which they had common goals. Subsequently joined by South Africa, the BRICS (Brazil, Russia, India, China, and South Africa) ministers began to meet regularly at the United Nations and other global diplomatic gatherings. They have issued joint statements on issues ranging from unrest in the Middle East to global climate change. Together, these BRICS states have some three billion people, with a GDP on par with the United States or the European Union. Yet their common ground may shift; they have at least as many differences as commonalities, and the global economy changes ever more rapidly. Other pundits began to bundle together Mexico, Indonesia, Nigeria, and Turkey as the "MINT" countries, suggesting that these may be a new global vanguard, experiencing economic growth despite serious challenges to the efficacy of government and sovereignty itself, from forces as diverse as radical Islamists and narco-traffickers.

Are we returning to a distribution of global economic resources that looked like the situation in 1400, when India and China together accounted for two-thirds of the world's economic production? It appears unlikely. While China's economy may soon become (or may already be!) the world's largest, projections make it unlikely that it could again dominate production as it did in 1400. If the European Union is considered as a single economy—it functions as one in many ways—it is even larger than the US economy. Measured another way, China and India together account for about one-third of the world's population and are both among the world's ten largest economies, but together they account for just 14 percent of overall global economic output. Europe and North America, on the other hand, comprise about one-eighth of the global population, yet still account for well over half of the world's economic output. The North Atlantic dominance that we saw in the late nineteenth century is no longer so striking, but it still exists. At the same time, though, as the stories of BRICS and MINT demonstrate, the modern global economy presents potential to create wealth around the world. The astonishing economic growth of India, China, and other states in the last four decades has brought unprecedented opportunities—more people have been lifted out of poverty in China alone since 1949 than in the rest of the world in all of history—but also new challenges, both anticipated and unanticipated.

## The Down Side of the Economic Up Side

Rapid industrialization in India and China left these two countries reeling from its effects. For many, choking levels of air pollution came to symbolize China's economic growth. In January 2013, conditions became so bad—pollution levels in Beijing exceeded the World Health Organization's recommended limits by 500 percent—that they were labeled the "airpocalypse." But, the airpocalypse was soon repeated, becoming a recurring feature of life in the Chinese capital and other cities. While the dramatic photographs of air pollution captured public attention, experts suggested that water and soil pollution were even more serious problems, with even greater health risks.

In contrast to China's authoritarian one-party state, contemporary India has often been touted as "the world's largest democracy." India does indeed have competitive, representative politics but endures slowness and inefficiency in its complex, corrupt system. These factors contributed to the 2012 power outages, which affected 9 percent of the world's population. And, although not featured as prominently in international news reports, air pollution in India is even worse than in China.

The experiences of India and China raise crucial points about the environmental costs of economic growth. The scientific evidence supporting human contributions to climate change is robust, yet when considering international solutions, countries like China and India point out that the countries that industrialized in the nineteenth century and remain the world's wealthiest caused much of the damage to the environment, but countries that are industrializing now will bear disproportionately the costs of stricter controls on pollution. They also point out that any global climate treaties might lack sufficient enforcement capacity for all signatories, allowing some countries to delay implementation while others are forced to comply because they are smaller or weaker—not China or India certainly, but they claim to make this case for other countries playing catch-up in economic development.

Perhaps no country embodies these dilemmas of the modern global economy better than the Maldives, the smallest country in Asia by population—three hundred fifty thousand residents. The Maldives, a chain of islands off the coast of India that became independent in 1965, is the lowest country on the planet and is slowly disappearing as climate change raises water levels. The Maldives also has the highest GDP per capita in South Asia, a result of the growth in its tourism industry, which provides almost two-thirds of the country's foreign exchange and 90 percent of government income through various taxes. If you were to fly from New York to the islands for your vacation, you would be responsible for pumping almost two and one-half metric tons of carbon dioxide into the air. Yet, if everyone decided to forego vacations to places like the Maldives for any reason, even really good ones, much of the global economy would collapse, causing direct and immediate damage to those countries that are pulling themselves out of poverty through tourism. On the other hand, without a radical change in our collective behavior, the Maldives might not be here in the next century.

The Maldives illustrate the general trends that characterize this chapter. Between 1970 and 2010, many indicators of human development made tremendous positive strides. Using the United Nations Human Development Index (HDI)—an aggregate of health, education, and income—one sees only three countries out of one hundred thirty-five with a decline in HDI between 1970 and 2010. The average person on the planet was better educated, lived a longer and healthier life, and had a higher income in 2010 than in 1970. The data also show two less encouraging trends. First, the environmental costs of this improvement were high, measured in air pollution, soil erosion, water scarcity and depletion of resources like forest cover. Second, whereas life for the average person has improved according the basic indicators used to compile the HDI, the gap between the wealthy and the poor has increased both globally and within many of the world's countries. Both of these trends appear ominous. One challenge is at the material level, as the planet and its human population test the sustainability limits of the Biological New Regime that emerged with industrialization in the nineteenth century. The other challenge is political and social, raising questions about the efficacy and legitimacy of states premised on popular sovereignty and respect for the gamut of human rights if such inequalities remain entrenched.

## Conclusion

The last decades of the twentieth century witnessed remarkable changes to the global political and economic order. The 1970s were in many ways the height of the Cold War. Although still not engaging in direct military confrontation with each other, both the United States and the Soviet Union continued to deploy their own troops and proxies around the world, seeking the upper hand in their long face-off. Authoritarian regimes ruled many of the world's countries, communist and anti-communist. At the same time, bookend events in the 1970s—the change in US–China relations and the revolution in Iran—hinted at the tremendous changes that would emerge in the final two decades of the century.

Political and economic transformations characterized the 1980s. Cold War authoritarian regimes of both the left and right ceded power to representative governments, while a new push to open the global economy to market forces, accompanied by changes in technology, finance, and other business practices, upended systems of production, consumption, and distribution. Regional and global trade negotiations and organizations attempted to build a rational and stable framework for the new economy.

The end of the Cold War did not deliver on the promise of peace. Religious and ethnic strife gripped much of the world in the 1990s and into the new millennium. The pace of the global economy and the precipitous dismantling of regulation intersected in the broadest crisis in global markets since the Great Depression.

## TIMELINE

**1957**
European Economic Community formed

**1972**
Richard Nixon first US president to visit China

**1976**
Mao Zedong dies; first Ford Fiesta automobile produced

**1979**
Shah of Iran overthrown; USSR invades Afghanistan; United States establishes diplomatic relations with China; Margaret Thatcher elected Prime Minister of Britain

**1985**
Mikhail Gorbachev becomes leader of Soviet Union

**1960**
OPEC founded

**1973**
War in the Middle East; OPEC slashes oil production

**1978**
Karol Józef Wojtyła becomes first non-Italian pope in 400 years; Deng Xiaoping becomes leader of China

**1980**
Solidarity movement formed in Poland

Overall, the material quality of life improved for most of the planet's population between 1972 and 2012, but at a high cost to the environment and an increase in the gap between a wealthy cosmopolitan elite enjoying the fruits of globalization as never before and an anxious majority, a little healthier, a little wealthier, a little better educated, and very uncertain about its future.

## A Few Good Books

Reza Aslan. *Beyond Fundamentalism: Confronting Religious Extremism in the Age of Globalization*. New York: Random House, 2010.

Christian Caryl. *Strange Rebels: 1979 and the Birth of the Twenty-First Century*. New York: Basic Books, 2014.

Slavenka Drakulic. *How We Survived Communism and Even Laughed*. London: Hutchinson, 1991.

Philip Gourevitch. *We Wish to Inform You That Tomorrow We Will Be Killed with Our Families: Stories from Rwanda*. New York: Picador, 1999.

Carolyn Merchant. *Death by Nature: Women, Ecology, and the Scientific Revolution*. New York: Harper, 1990.

Orville Schell. *Discos and Democracy: China in the Throes of Reform*. New York: Anchor, 1989.

Daniel Yergin. *The Prize: The Epic Quest for Oil, Money, and Power*. Rev. ed. New York: Free Press, 2008.

*For additional resources, including maps, primary sources, visuals, web links, and quizzes, please go to **www.oup.com/us/carter***

**1989**
Soviet forces withdraw from Afghanistan; Tiananmen Square massacre, China; Berlin Wall breached; Communist governments ousted in Eastern and Central Europe; Francis Fukuyama publishes "The End of History?"

**1991–99**
Yugoslav Wars, widespread ethnic cleansing

**1995**
World Trade Organization founded

**2003**
US invades Iraq

**2010**
China becomes world's second-largest economy

**2013**
"Airpocalypse" in China

**1991**
Soviet Union dissolved

**1994**
Genocide in Rwanda kills over five hundred thousand people

**2001**
al-Qaeda attacks topple World Trade Center in New York

**2008–09**
Global financial crisis

**2012**
Massive power blackout in India; 2.5 billion people use the Internet

# Epilogue

W e began our story of how the world came to look the way it does with a vignette about fifteenth-century China and the world's largest ship, so we thought it appropriate to make our last vignette, from the twenty-first century, also about China and the world's largest ship. This story does not involve an emperor; its major actors are businessmen associated with the modern Chinese state, a "people's republic." The treasure crossing the seas is not textiles or spices but petroleum.

In September 2014, a Chinese business group supported by the PRC government leased the world's largest ship, capable of carrying over three million barrels of oil, enough energy to power a Toyota Prius from Earth to Neptune, or satisfy the energy demand of the entire East Coast of the United States for one day. The Chinese buyers did not want this massive ship to deliver oil to the marketplace, though (at least not right away). Their plan was to keep the tanker at sea until the price of oil rose high enough for them to make a better return on their investment and then deliver the crude oil to a refinery. So, they leased the supertanker *TI Europe* from the Belgian company that commissioned the vessel from a South Korean shipbuilder to place crude oil they bought from Russia into floating storage off the coast of Asia.

---

O ne goal we set for this book was to help readers understand how global political and economic organization in our day compares to the fifteenth century. This image of the petroleum market provides a useful snapshot of the terrain we have traversed across the pages of this book. When Zheng He sailed the Indian Ocean in the 1400s, he represented an empire whose ruler inherited his position and claimed political legitimacy as the "son of heaven." The Chinese sovereigns who helped sponsor the voyage of the *TI Europe* preside over much the same territory as Ming rulers, but the modern People's Republic of China, like all other states on earth today, takes a form of political organization that emerged in the eighteenth century and remains dominant in the early twenty-first century: the nation-state. Despite many and constant challenges to the territorial shape and organizational form of individual states, most political movements today accept the claim that sovereignty emerges from a relationship between ruler and ruled, rather than one between ruler and the heavens.

This connection is often expressed through both ideology and performance. In the early twenty-first century, most of the world's nation-states chose their leaders by popular election. Even in states with authoritarian governments and no meaningful popular participation (like the China that leased the *TI Europe*), rulers generally claim the right to rule because they represent the will of the people. The social contract idea may be imperfect or even badly broken, but it still dominates how the world's population and its elites talk and think about government. It also means that interactions among the world's sovereign states take place within a context of rights claims regardless of any given state's internal political order. In the modern world, war is often justified on grounds that the aggressors seek to liberate peoples who have been unable to exercise their rights claims against the current sovereign ruling over them.

The modern world is also interconnected on an unprecedented scale. It is worth repeating that globalization is not new, but the speed and scale of communications and transportation across the globe has transformed the nature of globalization in the recent past. The Columbian Exchange brought global interconnections, but the linkages were intermittent and limited prior to the nineteenth century. As steamships, railroads, and telegraphs gave way to airplanes, radios, and automobiles, goods, services, and information travelled ever greater distances at ever increasing speeds. In 1957, the philosopher Hannah Arendt (1906–1975) made the profound observation that the earth's peoples may have had a diverse past, but in the twentieth century, "For the first time in history, all peoples on earth have a common present.... Every country has become the almost immediate neighbor of every other country, and every man feels the shock of events which take place at the other end of the globe." In the decades since Arendt wrote that, the links connecting places and people have only become tighter.

The pace of production and consumption sparked by industrialization continues. From the middle of the twentieth century to the early twenty-first century, the world's population grew by approximately two and one-half times, but the global economy expanded by a factor of ten. This increase in economic activity has not been distributed evenly. Concentration levels of this wealth have fluctuated over time, both within and across states and regions, as has the gap between the world's richest and poorest peoples. However, a sharp contrast between the world's wealthy minority and its poor majority remains a troubling characteristic of the modern world.

Having completed this book, you will have a better idea of the many ways in which the world's fifteenth-century and twenty-first century political and economic orders differ and some of the ways they may not be so different. We also established another goal, however, which was to provide some understanding of how historical inquiry can be used to explain how and why these changes occurred. Throughout this book, we have explored the ways historians examine the choices individuals and groups had available to them, tried to explain as best we could our understanding of why they made certain choices and not others, and how the consequences (intended and unintended) of those choices forged the modern world.

Historians are often asked to explain the relevance of their work. There's a good chance you're reading this book as a requirement for a course at a college or university, and there's a good chance that you (or someone you know) has asked why studying history makes any sense at all. Fair question: why, in a rapidly changing present, worried about an uncertain future, should anyone take the time to learn about the past?

In a book called *The Idea of History*, the philosopher and historian R. G. Collingwood (1889–1943) laid out various theories about what history was—and what it was not—and how to practice historical inquiry. Collingwood argued that the goal of history was to understand why people in the past acted as they did; it was not enough to know simply what they did. A historian must walk in another's shoes, to understand the options that were then available, and to make sense of why one choice was made and not another.

To do this requires empathy, creativity, and self-reflection, but it also demands the rigorous analysis of quantitative and qualitative data. The methods of historical inquiry therefore fit the disciplines of both the social sciences and the humanities. Even the authors of this book disagree on which side of that divide they reside professionally. Whichever you consider most important, the tools of historians can help us understand how people have evaluated situations, made decisions, and responded to challenges. We can see the consequences of their actions or their failure to act. We can be inspired by people who acted nobly or with great wisdom or courage; we can be enraged by those who acted callously, or out of spite or hatred. But not all of us will respond in the same way, or take away the same understanding, of every historical era, trend, or event. This is due first to the way that each historian chooses to exercise creativity and empathy in selecting research topics; but it is also because of the data available and the analytical methods applied. As we noted in the Introduction, the sum total of all those choices explains how there can be so many different histories.

The task of historical inquiry is now both easier and more difficult than ever before. As we've tried to show throughout this book, historians rely on sources to make sense of the past. Until recently, most archival records resided in a handful of libraries, museums, or government buildings. Few people could reach those repositories; there weren't many of them; and travel was slow, limiting the number of people who could use these sources. But changes that have defined the modern world have also redefined what historians do. New technologies have changed the kinds of sources available to us and the ways historians do their work. Information exists on a scale previous generations could not imagine. Photos and moving pictures have transformed the conduct of historical inquiry, as has the availability of electronic records—emails, tweets, and web pages are now analyzed as part of the historical record.

More and more historical records are available electronically, including reproductions of very old, unpublished documents that archives around the world are making available electronically to the public. The Internet can give us instant access to more information than even the largest library, museum, or archive could provide just a generation ago. But this is not to say that it is easier to find "the truth." Access to more data does not automatically equate to improved historical understanding, especially because questions of who controls the flow of primary sources—what, how, and where data will be stored and accessed—are as controversial today as they ever have been. The historian's task remains the same, even if the tools and methods are changing.

Marc Bloch (1886–1944), like Collingwood, was a scholar during the tumultuous Three Decades' Crisis we wrote about in Chapters 10, 11, and 12. Bloch was a founder of the "*Annales* school," a group of historians who insisted that the value of historical inquiry did not lie in repeating stories about kings and queens but in analyzing big social structures and socially shared beliefs about how the world worked. Bloch and his colleagues tried to understand how places changed over centuries, even millennia, and how structures shaped the lives of people living in them. This emphasis on structures and underlying conditions led some critics of this approach to accuse these historians of denying the importance of human agency in shaping outcomes. But Marc Bloch's life belied the idea that he did not value individual human agency. When the Nazis invaded France, Bloch left his job as a professor of medieval history to join the Resistance. His book, *The Historian's Craft*, which has influenced generations of historians and remains a vital contemplation of what we do, was only published after Bloch was captured and killed by Nazi secret police.

Few of us will confront choices as stark as those Marc Bloch had to make, but his story says a lot about why we should all read, and practice, history. We started the book by noting that history is not the same as the past. We'll conclude by asserting that the most important thing about the study of history is really about the future. Using all of our skills, and mustering the best resources, we can do our best to learn about the choices people made in the past—what constrained their options, why they made their decisions, and what the consequences were. Doing so, perhaps we can learn something about making choices for ourselves, sensitive to the worlds of our fellow inhabitants on this planet. All choices are limited by environment, by technology, and by political, social, and economic constraints, but there are always decisions to be made. Understanding how and why different people made choices in different eras is an essential goal of the historian's craft. And if you believe—as we do—in the importance of human agency and the possibility of free will, then understanding these things might help each of us to make important decisions about the future.

The history of the past six centuries shows that human progress is not inevitable; but there have been some decisions, by the powerful and the humble, that made the world better for others, at least for a time, and at least in some ways. Other decisions helped to impoverish, marginalize, or destroy other human beings. We have at our disposal more tools, more resources, and more ideas than ever before about how to debate and understand world history. Perhaps if more of us engage in these debates, we can imagine and work toward a future of decisions that make the world better for ourselves and others.

# Credits

CHAPTER 12

p. 310: Courtesy of the Library of Congress; p. 310: © Michael Nicholson/Corbis; p. 320: © Sawada/Corbis; p. 324: © Bettmann/CORBIS; p. 329: AFP/Getty Images

CHAPTER 13

p. 336: Everett Collection/Newscom; p. 336: NASA; p. 344: Courtesy of the Library of Congress; p. 347: Courtesy of the Library of Congress; p. 356: Courtesy of the Library of Congress

# Index

Italicized page numbers indicate a photo, illustration, or timeline reference

Abbas, Safavid Shah, 67
Abbasid Caliphate, 27
Abdulmecid, Ottoman
    Sultan, 145
Abode of Islam (*dar al-Islam*), 35
abolition of serfdom, Russia, 225
abolition of slavery
    in Brazil, 212
    in Central America, 168
    in France, 156–157
    in Great Britain, 168
    in Mexico, 168, 194
    in Spanish America, 209
    World Antislavery Conference,
      199, 224
absolutism
    in China, 123–125
    Enlightened Absolutism, 148
    in France, 122, 139, 146
    in Russia, 122–123
Accra protests, Ghana, 282,
    283–284, 285, 307
Aceh sultanate (Indonesia), 60, 72
*Address to the German Nation* (Fichte),
    163–164, *171*
aerial bombing
    of China, by Japan, 301, *302*
    in World Wars I and II,
      264, 305, 315
    of Spain, by Germany, 300
Afghani, Jamal al-Din al-, 234, 239
Afghanistan
    Anglo-Russian rivalry and, 167
    global wealth distribution,
      358 (map)
    Mujahideen resistance fighters,
      345–346, 351
    Soviet invasion of, 344–345,
      349, 362
    Soviet withdrawal from,
      345, 352
    US occupation of, 352, 353
Africa. *See also* East Africa; Ghana;
    Kenya; South Africa; West Africa
    Christian dynasties in, 37
    cost of gaining
      independence, 321
    empires and trade, ca. 1770, 144
      (map)
    European exploitation of, 233
    export of slaves to Caribbean,
      55, 64

1500–1914, population movement,
    200 (map)
Islam religion in, 35
Italy's imperialism in, 300
Kingdom of Mutapa, 36–37
maize in West Africa, *114*
Mali empire, 5, 35, 36
rejection of the modern state in,
    243–245
"scramble for Africa", 226, 230
Songhai Kingdom, 20 (map),
    36–37, 43, 68 (map)
sovereignty struggles in, 237–238
Suez Canal, opening of, 216,
    225, 230
trade networks, 22, 35, 36–37
transatlantic slave trade, 118 (map),
    128–130, 132, *140*, 167, 182
transition to sedentary
    agriculture, 176
Wahehe Rebellion, 246
African slaves in the Americas
    European demand for plantation
      labor, 128
    growth of, in global labor
      force, 94
    in Portuguese territory, 55
    reconstructing the lives of, 100
    on sugarcane plantations,
      98–99, 100
    transport to the Americas, 64
Afro-Eurasian supercontinent. *See also*
    individual countries, continents,
    empires and dynasties
    Africa's placement into, 35–37
    agriculture, 25, 28, 54
      (map), 55, 97
    astronomy-related discoveries, 87
    autocratic hereditary imperial
      states in, 120
    Black Death, 28, 29, 32, 37
    collapse and transformation, 27–38
    Columbian Exchange, 47, 53, 54
      (map), 55–56, 96–98, 249, 266
    divergent rulership models, 140
    early modern land empires,
      68 (map)
    economic/political order, 21–25, 27
    ethnic/religious networks, 25
    famines, 27
    15th century trading networks, 20
      (map), 21–22

food production strategies,
    26 (map)
Ottoman Empire link, 33–35
political order, 22–24, 26 (map),
    33–35
religious diversity in, 24–25
state-making, 70–71, 120
weaponry, 70
agriculture
    Afro-Eurasian supercontinent, 25,
      28, 54 (map), 55, 97
    Americas, 55
    Columbian Exchange and,
      53, 55
    15th century food production
      strategies, 26 (map)
    1500s, global practices, 94, *114*
    granary system, China, 25
    hunting and gathering, transition
      to, 176
    indigenous skills with, 5
    mass production of, 6
    rural economies and, 94, *114*
    slave plantation production, 182
    world's fair exhibitions, 221
Ahuitzotl, Tenochtitlan ruler,
    40 (map), 45, 64
Ainslie, Robert, *142*
airplanes, 177, 268, 366
Akbar, Mughal emperor, 74, 88, 95
Alam II, Mughal Emperor, 117
Albuquerque, Afonso de, *18*, 21
al-Dawani, Jalal al-Din, 71
Alevism, Muslim sect, 96
Alexander VI (Pope), 58
Algerian War of Independence, 335
Algonquians, 127
Al-Idrisi, Muhammad, 22
*All Quiet on the Western Front*
    (Remarque), 264, *281*
All-African People's Conference
    (Ghana), 332–333, 335
Al-Masudi, Abu al Hasan, 22
al-Qaeda, 345–346, 351–353,
    363
Amazonas Theater, Manaus,
    Brazil, 226, 229
American Bison, 248–250, 252
American Committee for Armenian
    and Syrian Relief, 287
American Revolution, 151–152,
    167, 188

Americas. *See also* African slaves in the Americas; Aztec empire; Inca empire; indigenous peoples; Mexica; North America; Spanish America
  agriculture, 5, 55
  Andean resistance movement, 56
  Aztec empire, 38–39, 40 (map), 42
  Christian conversions in, 57
  colonial expansion era, 56–59
  Columbian Exchange, 47, 53, 54 (map), 55–56, 96–98, 249, 266
  Columbus's voyages to, 16, 38, 46 (map), 48, 49
  empires and states (ca. 1830), 160 (map)
  indigenous record-keeping, 38
  political organization of, 38–39, 42, 58
  raw materials/markets of, 181
  reconstructing the lives of African slaves, 100
  rejoining of Afro-Eurasia, 38
  Spanish presence in, 47–58
  transition to sedentary agriculture, 176
Amritsar (Jallianwala Bagh) Massacre, 288, *308*, 323
*An Inquiry into the Nature and Causes of Wealth of Nations* (Smith), 147, 170
anarcho-syndicalist movement, 246–247
Andean resistance movement (1560), 56
Anderson, Benedict, 164
Anglo-Belgian Indian Rubber Company, 235
Angola
  achievement of independence, 335
  Civil War, 313–314
  Cold War influence in, 333
  Cold War map, 312 (map)
  decolonization, 327 (map)
  independence of, 335
  MPLA poster, *310*
animal domestication, 97
animal gifts, *18*
*Annales* school, 368
"Answering the Question: What is Enlightenment?" (Kant), 146, 147
Anthony, Susan B., 210
archaeological excavations, 22
Arendt, Hannah, 366
Armenian genocide, 287, *287*, 308
*The Art of War* (Machiavelli), 70
Articles of Confederation, 150, 162, 173
Asia. *See also* Afro-Eurasian supercontinent; Central Asia; East Asia; South Asia; Southeast Asia
  Cold War conflicts, 340–341
  cost of gaining independence, 321
  direct trade with Spanish America, *114*
  European activity (ca. 1650), 61 (map)
  European exploitation of, 233

Europe's control of trade routes, 103
  globalization and, 56
  India textile exports to, 98
  manufactured goods, 102
  oceanic trade routes, 62
  opening of Tokyo University, 225
  overland trade routes, 22
  principal trade commodities, 103 (map)
  rice production and market, 95
  search for spices in, 104
  search for "western passage" to, 48, 58
  sovereignty struggles in, 237–238
  Timur's conquests in, 32–33
"Asian Tiger" economies, 331
Association of Southeast Asian Nations Free Trade Agreement (1992), 355
Atahualpa, Inca ruler, 50, 65
Ataturk, Mustafa Kemal, Republic of Turkey President, 286
Atlantic Charter, 318
Atlantic Slave Trade Database (Emory University), 131
Audubon, John James, 249
Augustine of Hippo (St. Augustine), 57
Aurangzeb, Mughal emperor, 74, 119
Auschwitz death camp, 311
Australia
  Centennial Exhibition display, 221
  1500–1914, population movement, 200 (map)
  First World War participation, 269
  post-WW II economic recovery, 294
  trade networks, 218
  world's fair exhibit, 221
Austria
  empires and trade, ca. 1770, 144 (map)
  exclusion from Germany, 206
  French war against, 155
  Ottoman influence, 72
  post-Napoleon, 165 (map)
  Seven Years' War participation, 135
  succession disputes in, 134
  voting rights expansion, post-WW I, 276
Austrian Habsburg Empire, 68 (map), 205 (map)
Austro-Hungarian Empire, 166–167, 230, 262–263, 271 (map)
automobiles, 177, 216, 354, 366
Aztec empire, 38–39, 40 (map), 42, 51, 65, 106. *See also* Mexica

Bacon, Francis, 87, 88, 89
Bakewell, Peter, 107
Balkan Wars, 260, 262–263, 273, *280*
Bandung Conference, 332, 335
Bass Ale, 217, 225
battle, major fields of global (1914–1945), 256 (map)
Battle of the Somme (WW I), 267
Beccaria, Cesare, 148

Behrendt, Steven, 131
Belgian Commission of Inquiry, 236
Belgian Congo. *See also* Congo Free State
  atrocities in, 251
  Leopold II rulership, 235–236
  Morel's books on, 236
  rubber plantations, 229, 236
  strategic competition in, 230
  women captives in, 235
Belgium
  Common Market member, 354
  emergence of, 166
  Germany's invasion of, 263, 303
  power rivalries, 230
  rule of Philip II, 79–80
  women's right to vote, 276
  World War I trench map, 266
  world's fair participation, 221
Bell, Alexander Graham, 221
Benjamin of Tudela, 25, 27
Berkman, Alexander, 247
Berlin Conference (1884), 226, 227, 230, 252
Berlin Wall, 316, 335, 348, 355, 363
Big Five Allies of World War II, 314–317
bin Laden, Osama, 345–346, 351–352
biological old regime, 25, 27, 89, 114, 176, 181
Birkenau death camp, 311
Bismarck, Otto von, 226, 227, 230
Black Code edict (Louis XIV), 132, *140*
Black Consciousness Day (Brazil), 117
Black Death (bubonic plague), 28, 29, 32, 37
*The Black Man's Burden* (Johnson), 233–234, 253
Black Shirts, 257
*blitzkrieg* ("lightning war") tactics, 264, 300, 303, 305
Bloch, Marc, 368
Bloody Sunday Massacre (1905), *260, 280*
Boer War, South Africa (1899–1902), 245 (map), 259
Bolívar, Simón, 161–162
Bolivia, 49, 160 (map), 174 (map), 294, 298
*The Book of Navigation* (Reis), 72
Bossuet, Jacques-Bénigne, 122
Bourbon Reforms, 133, 157–159
Boxer Uprising, China, 242–243, 244, 253
Boyar Duma (in Russia), 122
Brady, Matthew, 193
Brahe, Tycho, 87
Brazil
  abolition of slavery, 225
  Amazonas Theater, Manaus, 226, 229
  ban of slavery, 212
  Dutch-Portuguese rivalry in, 132
  path to independence, 159, 161
  rubber industry, 227, 229
  slave trade, 127, 139
  sugarcane production, 98, *115*
  21st century economic growth, 359
  wars of, 117

Bretton Woods Accords, 329, *334*
British Ceylon (Sri Lanka), rubber plantations, 229
British East India Company, 63–64, 112, 119, 125, 190
British North America
    breakup of, 148–152
    colonial society, 138
    *Common Sense* influence on, *198*
    Declaration of Independence, 13, 149, 154, 170, 215, 321
    Jamestown Colony, 59, *65*, 144 (map)
    Plymouth Colony, 59, 112
    post-Seven Years' War expansion, 135, 137–138
    revolt of the colonists, 149–150, 151–152
    slave labor in, 149
    thirteen colonies, 144 (map), 149, 152, *170*
    Virginia colony, 131
Brittain, Vera, 264
Brooke, Rupert, 264
bubonic plague (Black Death), 28, 29, 32, 37
Buddhism, 24–25, 32
Burke, Edmund, 156
Burma (Myanmar), 230, 304, 307, 319, 332, 341

Cabot, John (Giovanni Caboto), 46 (map), 58
Cairo Protests (1919), *282, 285*
Calico Acts (1701, 1721), 91, 93, 114, *115*
Calicut kingdom, India
    as trading hub, 20 (map), *60*
    voyages of exploration, 19, 46 (map)
California gold rush, United States, 214, *224*
"California School" of world history, 181
Calvin, John, 59
*Candide* (Voltaire), 147
Canton System (Qing Dynasty), 189–190, *196*
capitalism
    global capitalism alternatives, 246
    industrial capitalism criticism, 187–188
    Lenin on, 277, 278–279, *281*, 290
    Marx on, 201
    print capitalism, 164
Caribbean region
    British domination in, 148–149
    Chinese laborers in, 213
    Columbus's voyages to, 16, 47, 48, *64*
    death of indigenous population, 53
    expulsion of Jews, 132
    post-WW I economic overhaul, 293
    slave cemeteries, 55, 100
    slave trade, 55, *64*, 100, 127, 139
    Spanish settlements, 49
    sugarcane production, 98, 100, *101*, 213

US investments in, 250
    voyages to, 16, 45, 46 (map), 47, 48
    World War I participation, 274
Carnegie, Andrew, 218, 247
Carretta, Vincent, 130
Castro, Fidel, 313, 328
Catherine the Great, Russian Empress, 148
Celali Rebellion (1595), 96, *114*
Centennial Exhibition, Philadelphia, 220
Central America, 38, 161, 168, 200 (map), 250, 274
Central Asia, 35, 86, 110, 167, 189, 230, 259
Charles I, King of England, *89*
Charles V, Holy Roman Emperor, *50*, 76, 79, 81
Charter Oath (1868, Japan), 215
chemical weapons in World War I, 266–267, 306
Chiang Kai-shek, Chinese Nationalist Party leader, 290, 302, *308*, 317
Chile
    independence from Spain, 251
    post-WW I financial system reform, 294
    response to global economic collapse, 298
    world's fair exhibit, 221
China. *See also* Ming Dynasty; Qing Dynasty; Taiwan
    absolutism in, 123–125, 139
    agriculture, 25, 94
    anti-imperialist, nationalist protests, *282*
    Boxer Uprising, 242–243, 244, 253
    Chiang Kai-shek's rulership, 290, 302, *308*, 317
    communist models of political economy, 331
    Cultural Revolution, 340
    currencies, 95–96
    Deng Xiaoping's reforms, 347–348, *362*
    discoveries about World War II, 314–315
    early 19th century, global manufacturing control, 258
    1500–1914, population movement, 200 (map)
    first locomotive in, *172*
    formation of, 319, *334*, 337
    German imperialism in, 239
    granary system development, 25
    Han Dynasty, 23, 86–87
    industrialization in, 180
    Japan's invasion of, 301–302, *302*
    launch of *Tianqi* steamship, 173, 175, *197*
    legalization of Christianity, 191–192
    Macartney's mission to, 190, *196*
    Manchu Qing conquest of, 85
    Mandate of Heaven (*tianming*), 84, 85, 87, 124–125
    Mao Zedong's leadership, 290, 319, 341, 347, *362*
    mass unrest in, 260–261
    May Fourth Movement, 289, *308*

Ming to Qing Dynasties, 124 (map)
Mongol Yuan Dynasty, 28, 84
nationalist frustrations in, 289–290
Nationalist Party, 289
naval conflict with Japan, 239–242
navigation methods, 218
1914, civil war, 262
Nixon's visit to, *336*, 337, 339, 340, *362*
Opium Wars, *172*, 189–192, *196*, 204, 214
pollution "airpocalypse," 340, *343*
post-WW I financial system reform, 294
post-WW I protests, 273
printing technology development, 77
Qianlong Emperor, 125, 190, 191
religious issues in, 83–84
Russian imperialism in, 239
1700s, standard of living, 181
shipbuilding expertise, 5, 29
silver exports, 191
silver imports, 56, 60–61, 84–85, 102, 108
Song Dynasty, 27, 29
sovereignty issues, 238–242
Special Economic Zones, 348
statecraft development, 84
Sun Yat-sen's presidency, 260–261, 273, *281*, 289
support for Marxist groups, 313
Taiping War, 175, 192, 195, *197*
tax systems reform, *114*
testing of nuclear weapons, 340
*TI Europe* voyage sponsorship, 365, 366
trade networks, 22, 60, 62
transition to sedentary agriculture, 176
tribute system, 113
21st century reforms, 347–348, 357
UN recognition of, 340
US anti-Chinese xenophobia, 195
US "Ping-Pong Diplomacy" with, 340
US post-WW II relationship with, 339–340
voyages of Zheng He, *18, 19*, 21, 29–32, 34*t*, 365
Warlord Era, 261
World War I participation, 269
Yuan Dynasty, China, 28, 84
Chinese Civil War (1945–1949), 339
Chinese Communist Party, 289–290, *308*, 319, 337, 347, *362*
Chinese coolies, 213–214, *224*
Chinese Nationalist Party (KMT), 261, 290
Chinggis Khan (Mongol chieftan), 27
Christian missionaries, 45–47, 59, 63, 126, 128
Christian reformation, 74–77

Christianity. *See also* Roman
  Catholicism
  African dynasties, 37
  antislavery sentiment, 167
  in China, 63, 78, 84
  China's legalization of, 191–192
  empire-building tool, 24
  in Ethiopia, 37, 75
  15th century, second half, 37
  indigenous conversions, 48, 49, 57
  issues of faith, 59
  in Japan, 45–46, 63
  in Mughal Empire, 74
  North American conversions, 126
  Ottoman Empire, 33, 34
  Protestantism, 59, 63, 76, 81–82
  role in building states, 24–25
  Spanish Inquisition and, 79
  spreading in Asia, 21
  Treaty of Nanjing legalization of,
    191–192
  Voltaire's mocking of, 147
  wars with Islamic empires, 37, 57
  works of Luther, 79
Church of England, 81
Churchill, Winston
  comment on coming of war, 262
  concerns for slaughter in Kenya, 324
  dismissal of Gandhi, 323
  Iron Curtain speech, 315–316, 324
Civil War (US), 162, 197
  Brady's photographic
    documentation, 193
  causes, 193–194
  global industrialization and, 194
  post-war legal equality, 211
  post-war Reconstruction,
    194, 210–212
  pre-war abolition movement, 210
*Civilization and Its Discontents*
  (Freud), 248
Cixi, Empress Dowager, 242
climate change, global, 96
Clive, Lord, 116, 117
coal, 6, 177, 181–182, 290, 341–342
coffee and tea houses, 97
coffee roasting technology, 222–223
Cohen, Stephen, 350
Cold War
  Angola civil war, 310
  Asia, 340–341
  deaths from violent wars, 321
  East Asia, 318–321, 320, 339
  efforts at rejection of, 332–333
  explanation for end of, 349–350
  global conflicts, 312 (map)
  Iran/Guatemala, support
    of US, 328
  Korean War, 319
  Latin America, 340–341
  Nixon's overtures to PRC, 336
  Southeast Asia, 318–321, 320
  UN and growing
    confrontations, 318
  US-Soviet rivalry, 329
  violations of UN principles, 332
Cole, Jeffrey, 107
Collingwood, R. G., 367, 368
Colombia
  escaped slaves' communities, 131

independence from Spain, 251
  post-WW I financial system
    reform, 294
Colt firearms, 194
Columbian Exchange
  description, 53, 54 (map), 55–56
  global impact of, 47, 55, 96–98,
    249, 266, 366
  initial limitations of, 366
  map, 54 (map)
  origin of, 53, 64
  sugarcane introduction, 98
Columbus, Christopher, 16, 38, 46
  (map), 48, 49, 64
*Common Sense* (Paine), 198
communism. *See also* Chinese
  Communist Party
  as alternative in China, 289
  collapse of, 187
  European worker issues, 188
  Nazi Germany opposition to, 299
  Reagan's policy towards, 349
  US containment efforts, 319,
    334, 340
Communist International (Comintern),
  290, 308, 320
*The Condition of the English Working
  Class* (Engels), 187, 197
Condorcet, Nicolas de, 146–147,
  149, 210
Condorcet, Sophie de, 156
*The Conduct of Kings*
  (Ibn Ruzbihan), 71
Confucianism, 31, 69
*Confucius as a Reformer*
  (Kang Youwei), 242
Congo Free State, 235, 251, 252
Congo Reform Association, 235, 236
Congress of Berlin (1878), 227,
  229–230, 252, 263
Conquest, Robert, 291
Constitutional Convention (1787),
  150, 172, 173. *See also* US
  Constitution
containment policy, US, 316, 319, 326
Continental System (of Napoleon),
  158, 203
Convention People's Party, Ghana, 285
coolie trade, 213–214, 224
Copernicus, Nicolai, 87
Corn Laws (Great Britain), 203, 204
Cortés, Hernán, 40 (map), 46 (map),
  49–51, 50, 56, 64
Cossacks, 122
"The Crash." *See* New York Stock
  Exchange crash
Crimean War (1853–1856), 192–193,
  193, 197
Cuba
  Castro, Fidel, President, 313, 328
  Chinese coolies in, 213–214, 224
  escaped slaves' communities, 131
  Guevara's leadership of
    revolution, 328
  Soviet commitments in, 332
  Spanish settlements in, 49
  US control of, 233, 275
Cuitlahuac, Aztec ruler, 51
currencies
  boom-bust cycle and, 251

in China, 108–109
  Euro, common currency, 355
  global expansion of, 109–110
  gold standard, 293, 294, 295, 296
    (map), 298
  minting of silver coins, 108–109
  post-World War I, 293
  post-World War II, 329
*Current Anthropology* journal, 52
Czechoslovakia
  adult voting rights, 276
  creation of, 273
  Germany's absorption of, 302
  Prague Spring, Soviet suppression,
    328, 335
  Soviet collapse and, 346
  voting rights expansion, post-
    WW I, 276

Da Gama, Vasco, 21, 30,
  31–32, 43
*Daily Mail*, British newspaper, 259
Dalrymple, Dana, 291–292
Darling, Linda, 70
Darwin, Charles, 232, 247–248, 252
Dattel, Gene, 182
Dawes Plan, 244, 293, 308
De Gouges, Olympe, 156
death camps, World War II, 306, 310,
  311, 314, 317
*Declaration of Sentiments* (Stanton), 210
Declaration of the Rights of Man
  and Citizen (France), 154, 156,
  170
Declaration of United Nations, 315, 334
decolonization
  Africa/Asia (1945–1975),
    327 (map)
  Gandhi and India, 321–323,
    322 (map)
  Ghana, 285
  Kenya, 323–326, 324
  Philippines, 326
  superpowers and, 326, 328
Delhi Sultanate (India), 32
Deng Xiaoping, Chinese leader,
  347–348, 362
Denmark, 34, 303
Dessalines, Jean-Jacques, 157
Devereux, Stephen, 292
Díaz, Porfirio, President of Mexico,
  261–262
Díaz del Castillo, Bernal, 64
Diderot, Denis, 146
*A Discourse about the Provision of Money*
  (Machiavelli), 70
diseases, contagious
  bubonic plague (Black Death),
    28, 29, 32, 37
  flu pandemic, global deaths, 281
Dos Equis beer (Mexico), 217
Douglass, Frederick, 210
Dunant, Henry, 193
Dutch. *See also* Netherlands
  ceramics trading, 103
  Indonesian settlements, 319
  North American settlements, 127
  oceanic trade expansion, 59, 102,
    129–130
  rivalry with Portuguese in Brazil, 132

silver trade disruptions by, 84
slavery/slave trade, 199
South Africa settlements, 168
textile imports, 105
trade with Japan, 44, 63–64, 65
tulipmania craze, 110–111
voyages of exploration, 46 (map)
wars of, 117
world's fair exhibit, 223
Dutch Cape colony, 59
Dutch East India Company, 63–64, 98, 105, 112, 115, 133
Dutch Protestants, 63
Dutch Republic, 105
Dutch West India Company, 59
Dutch-Portuguese rivalry, 132
Dyer, Reginald, 288

East Africa
  Maji-Maji Rebellion, 243, 244–246, 245 (map), 253
  trade networks, 18, 22, 36–37, 84
  transatlantic slave trade route, 118 (map)
  Zheng He's voyage to, 29
East Asia
  Cold War in, 318–321, 320, 339
  Japanese rule in, 275–276, 301, 309
  Russian expansion in, 230
  1700–1900, population growth, 174 (map)
  trade networks, 18, 36–37, 97, 104, 228 (map)
  US containment policy in, 319
East India Company, 190–191, 230
Eastern Europe
  balance of power changes, 133–135
  communist models of political economy, 331
  John Paul II's influence in, 349
  Soviet control of, 330, 346
  Timurid expansion in, 32
  transnational religious movements, 346
  as tripwire for World War I, 273
  World War II, 315–316
Ecuador, 138, 294, 343
Edison, Thomas, 223
Egypt
  achievement of limited independence, 308
  Aswan High Dam project, 331
  British occupation, WW I, 283
  independence movement, 145, 169
  Napoleon's invasion of, 167
  1919, Cairo Protests, 282, 285
  Sha`rawi's leadership of women's protests, 283
  solidarity of OPEC with, 341
  Wafd [Delegation] Party, 283
Egyptian Feminist Union, 283, 308
1840–1889, 199–224
  abolition, immigration, free labor, 212–214
  coolie trade/meaning of slavery, 213–214
  food revolution, 217–218
  Japan's modernization, 214–216

major population movements, 200 (map)
new European states, 204–205, 207
Ottoman/Russian empire challenges, 207, 208 (map), 209
reform vs. revolution, 201–212
Second Industrial Revolution, 216–220
Spanish America, 209–210
timekeeping advances, 218–220
US, post-Civil War Reconstruction, 210–212
World Antislavery Conference, 199, 201
world's fairs, 220–223
1878–1910, 227–252
  American Bison, 248–250
  Boxer Uprising, 242–243, 244, 253
  challenging the modern order core, 246–250
  Ghost Dance ritual, 243, 244, 246, 249, 252
  human nature, question of, 247–248
  Maji-Maji Rebellion, 243, 244–246, 245 (map), 253
  neocolonialism, 250–251
  New Imperialism, 226, 229–234, 238–242, 243, 319
  Passenger Pigeons, 248–250
  questioning empire, 237–246
  redrawing map of the world, 229–237
  Sino-Japanese War, 239–242, 242
  working class agitation, 246–247
electric trolley systems, 229
Elizabeth I, Queen of England, 34, 81–82
Elkins, Caroline, 325
Elman, Benjamin, 241
Eltis, David, 131
empires/empire-building, 69–79. See also individual empires
  Christian reformation, 74–77
  defined, 23–24
  Islamic world, 71–74
  by Ivan IV, 75–76
  printed word, power of, 77–79
  ca. 1770, global trade, 144 (map)
  South Asian Muslim empire, 33
  use of religion in state-building, 24–25
  weaponry advances, 70
encomiendas system, 48, 49, 51, 57, 58
Encylopédie (ed. Diderot), 146
"The End of History" (Fukuyama), 351
Engels, Friedrich, 187, 197, 202, 224
England
  changing world of work, 184–187
  coffee and tea houses, 97
  first modern world's fair, 220
  Glorious Revolution, 120, 139, 141, 146
  Hansa League war with, 34
  Harrods of London, 217
  Hundred Years War, with France, 27–28, 43
  imports of South Asian cloth, 105
  incorporation of changing world, 125
  industrialization in, 180

limiting the power of the monarchy in, 120–122
London subway system, 186, 197
North American settlements, 58, 59, 65
Royal Observatory, Greenwich, 220
voyages of exploration, 46 (map), 58
weaponry, 79
as "workshop of the world," 179
world's fair exhibits, 221, 224
English Bill of Rights, 121, 146
English Civil War, 81–83, 85
Enlightened Absolutism, 148
Enlightenment
  Beccaria and, 148
  Condorcet on, 146–147
  critique of slavery, 167
  de Gouges on, 156
  defined/described, 146–147
  Kant on, 146, 147
  limited notions of progress, 153
  Marx and, 187
  political system challenges, 147–148, 149, 151, 167, 170
  Pombaline reforms, 143–144, 159
  US Constitution and, 150
  Voltaire on, 147
Equiano, Olaudah, 130, 141
Estates General (France), 122, 153
"Estimating Aboriginal American Population" (1966, Current Anthropology), 52
Ethiopia
  Christian practices in, 37, 75
  invasion of, 299–300
  Menelik II, ruler, 237–238, 238, 252
  Ottoman conquests in, 74
  Selassie, Haile, Emperor, 299, 328
  Soviet control of, 328
Europe. See also Afro-Eurasian super-continent; individual countries
  activity in Asia (ca. 1650), 61 (map)
  book printing advances, 78
  coffee and tea houses, 97
  conquests of indigenous peoples, 48–53
  early conceptions of the world, 48
  exploitation of Africa, Asia, 233
  fortifications and battles (1450–1750), 80 (map)
  India's textile link with, 104–105
  industrialization in, 180
  Japan export monopoly with, 105
  migrations to Spanish Americas, 55
  military expenditures, 258, 280
  New Imperialism, 231, 319
  1920s economic recession, 292
  post-WW I economic overhaul, 293
  potatoes, importance of, 97
  rivalries between empires, 167
  "scramble for Africa," 230
  silver production growth, 106
  sovereignty issues, 35
  "Springtime of the Nations," 202, 202
  technology/redistribution of wealth, 6
  voyages of exploration (ca. 1450), 46 (map)
  Wars of Religion, 79, 80 (map), 81–83

European Economic Community
("Common Market"), 354
European Recovery Plan (Marshall
Plan), 330, 334
European Union (EU), 354–355,
357, 359–360
Export-Led Industrialization, 331
*Exposition Universelle* (World Fair,
Paris), 199, 201, 223

Fallacy of the Predetermined Outcome
(Historian's Fallacy), 32
*A Farewell to Arms* (Hemingway),
264, 281
Fascio di Combattimento ("Combat
League"), 279
fascism
Grand Council of Fascism, 257, 281
Mussolini's promotion of, 257
1920s–1930s spread of, 298–299
WW II fight to end, 314–315
Fascist Party (Italy), 279
Febvre, Lucien, 78
Ferdinand II of Aragon (King of Spain),
37–38, 48, 79
Ferguson, Niall, 326
Fichte, Johann Gottlieb, 163–164,
171, 196
1500–1914, major population
movements, 200 (map)
1571–1701, 91–114. *See also*
globalization
Asian trade, principal commodities,
103 (map)
changing foodways, 96–98
global currency expansion, 109–110
global rural economies, 94–98
manufactured goods, 101–105
political economy, 112–113
silver supply, 106–109
sugar-slave plantation system, 98,
99 (map), 100, 101
textiles, 104–105
tulips (tulipmania), 110–112, 113
Fifteenth Amendment (US
Constitution), 211
firearms, 45, 51, 127, 144 (map), 194
First Calico Act (1701), 115
First Opium War (China), 172,
196, 214
First World War. *See* World War I
Fitch, John, 172, 173, 196. *See also*
*Perseverance* steamboat
Five Good Emperors (Rome,
96 CE–180 CE), 23
flu pandemic, global deaths, 281
food revolution, industrialization and,
217–218
foodways around the globe, 96–98
fourteen points (Wilson, 1918),
272–273, 281
1405–1510, 19–43. *See also*
Afro-Eurasian supercontinent
Afro-Eurasian political, economic
order, 21–25, 27
Aztec empire, 38–39, 40 (map), 42
Black Death, 28, 29, 32, 37
Central and South Asia struggle,
32–33
collapse/transformation, 27–38

food production, 26 (map)
Iberian Peninsula, 37–38
Inca empire, 41 (map), 42
Ottoman Empire, 33–35, 37, 42, 72
political/economic order, 21–25
sea voyages, exploration, 18, 19, 21,
29–32, 34t
1486–1639, 45–65
colonial expansion, 56–69
Columbian Exchange, 47, 53, 54
(map), 55–56, 96–98, 249, 266
competition from European
powers, 58–59
conquest era, 48–59
global connections, 60, 61 (map),
62–64
Iberian presence in the Pacific, 60,
62–63
Japan and the Dutch, 63–64
transition to colonial society, 56–58
voyages of exploration, 46 (map)
France
absolutism in, 122, 139, 146
anarcho-syndicalist movement, 246
Black Code, 132, 140
challenge of British commercial,
industrial superiority, 204
coffee and tea houses, 97
Common Market member, 354
Crimean War participation,
192–193
Declaration of the Rights of Man
and Citizen, 154, 156, 170
discoveries about World War II,
314–315
early 20th century, global
manufacturing control, 258
Estates General, 122, 153
fight for control of Calicut, 60
Germany's blitzkrieg in, 303
Hundred Years War, with England,
27–28
imports of South Asian cloth, 105
incorporation of changing
world, 125
industrialization in, 184, 185
invasion/occupation of
Indochina, 239
Louis XIV, reign of, 120, 122,
132–133, 140
North American settlements, 59
Paris, World's Fair, 199, 201, 223
post-Napoleon, 165 (map)
post-WW II hold on colonial
enterprises, 318
pre-WW I alliances, 263
Seven Years' War, 117, 119,
131–132, 135, 136 (map),
137–139, 148–149, 189
Southeast Asia territories of, 230
trade networks, 64
transatlantic slave trade role, 132
voyages of exploration, 46 (map)
war against Austria, 155
weaponry, 79
World War I participation, 263,
266, 269, 270, 273
World War II participation,
304–305

Franciscan missionaries, 59, 126
Franco, Francisco, 300
Franco-Prussian War, 206
Franz Ferdinand, Habsburg Archduke,
262–263
Frederick II (Frederick the Great),
Prussian King, 148
Frederick III, Elector of Saxony, 76
Frederick William I, Prussian "Soldier
King," 134
free market open-economy principles
(FMOEP), 350–351
free trade. *See also* individual free trade
agreements
Britain's advocacy for, 182
Smith's advocacy for, 147, 182
Treaty of Nanjing and, 191
US vision of, 315
World War II and, 329
French and Indian War. *See* Seven
Years' War
French Indochina. *See* Vietnam
French National Assembly, 154, 156
French Protestants, 59
French Revolution
global impact of, 145
promise of equal rights to
all men, 321
roots of, 153–154
significance of, 155–156, 321
Freud, Sigmund, 247–248, 253
Frick, Henry Clay, 247
Fukuyama, Francis, 351
Fumio, Yano, 255
Fundamental Law of 1906 (Russia), 260

Galilei, Galileo, 87
Gandhi, Mohandas K.
decolonization of India and,
321–323, 322 (map)
"Indian Home Rule" pamphlet,
288, 308
Indian National Congress
leadership, 288
passive resistance method, 352
quote on changing the world, 17
role in raising political
consciousness, 288–289
Garibaldi, Giuseppe, 206
Gellner, Ernest, 164
General Agreement on Tariffs and
Trade (GATT), 330
Geneva Conventions, 193
George III, King of England, 190
German Confederation, 165 (map),
205 (map)
German Democratic Republic (East
Germany), 316
German Empire, 195, 205 (map),
207, 299
German Federal Republic (West
Germany), 316
German Peasants War, 76, 88, 95
Germany. *See also* Hitler, Adolf; Nazi
Party, Germany
anti-imperialist, nationalist
protests, 282
Berlin Conference, 226, 227,
230, 252
Berlin Wall, 316, 335, 348, 355, 363

*blitzkrieg* ("lightning war") tactics, 264, 300, 303, 305
challenge of British commercial, industrial superiority, 204
compulsory male military service, 259
Congress of Berlin, 227, 229–230, 252, 263
Dawes Plan, 244, 293, *308*
early 20th century, global manufacturing control, 258
1871, formation of, 204, 205 (map), 206
exclusion of Austria, 206
fascism in, 314
home front deaths WW I, 268
invasion of Poland, 303, *309*
invasion of Soviet Union, 309, *309*
Italy, anti-communist treaty alliance, 302
Japan, anti-communist treaty alliance, 302
Krupp's role in unification, 195
military expenditures, 258
nationalist ideology of, 207
"New Course" of Wilhelm II, 263
1940, treaty with Japan, Italy, 304
railroad network, 216
response to global economic collapse, 298
rise of Hitler/Nazi Party, 299
role in Thirty Years' War, 81
unification of, 225, 232
voting rights expansion, post-WW I, 276
World War I participation, 263, 265–270, 272–274
world's fair exhibits, 221
WW II, death camps, Holocaust, 306, 309, *310*, 311, 313–314, 317
Germany-Soviet nonaggression pact, 303, *309*
Ghana
    Accra protests, *282*, 283, 285, 307
    All-African People's Conference, 332–333, 335
    Convention People's Party, 285
    Nkrumah's presidency, *282*, 285, *309*, 325
Ghost Dance, Native American ritual, 243, 244, 246, 249, 252
Glama-Stroberle, João, *142*
*glasnost*, 347, *347*
global economic growth, 357, 358 (map), 359–361
global financial crisis, 357
global population growth, 1700–1900, 174 (map)
global power relations, transformation of, 188–195
    Crimean War, 192–193, *193*
    Opium Wars, *172*, 189–192, *196*, 204, 214
    Taiping War, 175, 192, 195, *197*
    US slavery, industry, Civil War, 193–194
    weaponry developments, 195
global rural economies, 94–98
    changing foodways, 96–98

impact of silver on, 95
political-cultural-religious influences, 94
responses to globalization, 95–96
rice market, Southeast Asia, 95
rural elites and, 94–95
global wealth distribution, twenty-first century, 358 (map)
globalization. *See also* New Imperialism
    Asia and Western hemisphere, 56
    communication's impact on, 366
    examples of interconnections, 64–65
    1571–1701, first global economy, 91–114
    Internet's impact on, 355–357, 363, 368
    in Japan, 45
    manufactured goods and, 101–104
    new global economy, 357–360
    rural responses to, 95–96
    silver supply and, 106–109
    sovereigns and, 49
    technology's impact on, 221
    21st century, economy and, 357–360
    unpredictable economic outcomes of, 92–93
Glorious Revolution (1688), 120, 139, *141*, 146
*Godfather* movies, 23
gold standard, 293, 294, 295, 296 (map), 298
Goldman, Emma, 247
Gorbachev, Mikhail, 262, 346–347, 349–350
Government of India Act (1919), 288
*Gramática de la lengua española* (Spanish grammar book), 79
Gran Colombia, 161–162
Grand Council of Fascism (Italy), 257, *261*, 281
Grant, Kevin, 236
Great Britain. *See also* England; Ireland
    abolition of slave trade, 168, *224*
    aerial bombing by Germany, 264, 305
    anarcho-syndicalist movement, 246
    Bass Ale, 217, 225
    Boer War news coverage, 259
    Calico Act, 91, 93, 114, *115*
    casualties in WW I, 267
    control of India, 230
    Corn Laws, 203, 204
    Crimean War participation, 192–193
    discoveries about World War II, 314–315
    early 20th century, global manufacturing control, 258
    fight for control of Calicut, *60*
    First Opium war participation, 191
    Germany's antagonism of, 263
    Government of India Act, 288
    growth of factories, 182, 184, 186–187
    Hong Kong, establishment as colony, 191, *196*
    Indian textile imports, 91, 93
    industrialization to 1850, 178 (map)
    Marx's influence on, 203–204

Naoroji's praise of, 234
opposition to rule in India, 288–289
Peterloo Massacre, 204
post-WW I global imperialism, 288
post-WW II hold on colonial enterprises, 318
Qing Dynasty's rebuke of, 189–190
rebellions against rule of, 204
Reform Act of 1832, 204, *224*
rivalry with Russia, 167
Seven Years' War, 117, 119, 131–132, 135, 136 (map), 137–139, 148–149, 189
1763, empire map, 136 (map)
Stamp Act, 137, 138
Sugar Act, 137
trade with South Asia, 117
transatlantic slave trade role, 132
volunteerism for WW I, 263–264, 265
voting rights expansion, post-WW I, 276
World War I participation, 263–264, 265, 267
World War II participation, 303–304
Great Depression (1929), 12, 281, 286, 295–298, *308*, 315, 317, 331
Great Reforms, Tsarist Russia, 207
Great War. *See* World War I
Greater East Asia Co-Prosperity Sphere (Japan), 301
Greece
    economic collapse, 357
    gaining of independence, 145, *171*
    German occupation of, 303
    political/geographic changes, 221
    separation from Ottomans, 166, 169
    submarine purchases, 258
    US aid to, 319
    US anti-communist aid, 319
    World War I participation, 269
Gu Yanwu, Chinese political scholar, 87, 88, 89
Guangxu Emperor, China, 242
*The Guardian*, British newspaper, 259
Guatemala
    Cold War support for US, 328
    coup d'état in, 326–327
    post-WW I financial system reform, 294
Guevara, Ernesto "Che," 328
Gulag system, Soviet Union, 291, 328
Gulhane (Rose Bower) Edict, *142*, 145, *171*
Gutenberg, Johannes, 78

Habsburg Empire, 68 (map), 80 (map), 86, 205 (map), 262, 272
hairstyle decree, Qing Dynasty, 123, *140*
Haiti
    French sovereignty claims, *154*
    gaining of independence, 156–157, 168, *171*
    US occupation of, 274–275
*hajj*, pilgrimage to Mecca, 35–36, 77

Han Dynasty China (206 BCE–220 CE), 23, 86–87
Hanseatic League (Hansa), 34–35
Harris, Alice Seeley, 236
Harrison, John, 219
Harrods of London, 217
*Harvest of Sorrow* (Conquest), 291
Hegel, Georg, 187
Heineken beer, 217
Hemingway, Ernest, 264, *281*
Henry VIII, King of England, 81
hereditary monarchs, 37, 121
Hibiya Riots, Japan, *254*, 255, *280*
Hideyoshi, Toyotomi, Japanese ruler, 47
Hindus/Hinduism, 24, 32
Hironaka, Kono, *254*
*The Historian's Craft* (Bloch), 368
Hitler, Adolf
    Chiang pursuit of alliance with, 302
    Holocaust/targeting of Jews, 306,
        *309*, *310*, 313–314, 317
    *Mein Kampf* (*My Struggle*),
        299, *308*
    nonaggression pact with Stalin,
        303, 304
    rise to power, *309*
Ho Chi Minh (Nguyen Ai Quoc), 272,
    320, 321, 334
Hobbes, Thomas, 82–83, *89*, 121
Hobson, John, 277–278
Holland, William, *198*
Holocaust ("Final Solution"), WW II,
    306, *309*, *310*, 313–314, 317
*Holodomor* ("Extermination by
    Hunger") policy, Soviet Union,
    291
Homestead Strike (1892), 247, *252*
Hong Kong, establishment as British
    colony, 191, *196*
Hong Xiuquan, 192
Huancavelica, Peruvian Andes, 91, 107
human nature, question of, 247–248
Hundred Days' Reforms, Qing Dynasty,
    242, 253
Hundred Years War, 27–28, *43*
Hungarian Christians, 33
Hungary
    call for independence, 202–203
    collapse of communism in, 348
    German economic agreements
        with, 298
    rising inflation rates, 292
    Serbians in, 263
    Soviet invasion of, *335*
    Soviet suppression of uprisings,
        290, 328, 346
    voting rights expansion,
        post-WW I, 276
Hunt, Nancy Rose, 236
Hus, Jan, 77

Iberia (Iberian Peninsula)
    Catholic conversions, 63
    ceramic design motifs, 101
    Christian *vs.* Muslim conflicts, 57
    collapse in the Americas, 157–159,
        161–163
    political/economic profile, 37–38
    16th century Pacific expansion, 60,
        62–63

Ibn Battuta, 25, 27, 37
Ibn Ruzbihan, Fazlullah, 71
*The Idea of History* (Collingwood), 367
imperialism. *See also* New Imperialism
    of Britain, in South Africa, 288
    of Britain, in Southeast Asia, 30
    drivers of, 318
    of Europe, in the Americas, 231
    of France, in Indochina, 239
    Gandhi's view of, 322–323
    of Germany, in Africa, Asia, 195
    Hobson on, 277–278
    of Italy, in Africa, 300
    Johnson's denunciation of,
        233–234
    Kipling's portrayal of, 233
    Lenin's pamphlet on, 277, *281*
    of Russia, in China, 239
    slave labor and, 139, 158
"Imperialism, the Highest Stage of
    Capitalism" (Lenin), 277, *281*
Import Substitution
    Industrialization, 331
Inca empire, 41 (map)
    expansion of, 48
    rise to power, 42, 43
    silver production in, 91,
        107–108
    Spanish conquests in, 50, 51, 91
    Tupac Amaru II, ruler, 157–158
India. *See also* Gandhi, Mohandas K.
    Afghani on Britain's control
        of, 234
    Amritsar Massacre, 288, *308*, 323
    astronomy studies, 87
    Bandung Conference attendance,
        332
    Britain's control of, 230
    Delhi Sultanate, 32
    early 19th century, global
        manufacturing control, 258
    Gandhi, decolonization,
        and, 321–323
    Government of India Act, 288
    independence of, *334*
    Khan on Britain's control of, 234
    manufacture of calico cloth, *90*
    opposition to British rule in,
        288–289
    partition of, 322 (map)
    power grid development, 337, 339
    printing press in, 78
    Sepoy Mutiny *vs.* Britain, 204, *224*
    Seven Years' War participation, *136*
    tax code reform by Akbar, 95, *114*
    textile exports, *90*, 91, 93, 98
    trade networks, 22
    21st century economic growth, 359
*Indian Home Rule* (*Hind Swaraj*)
    (Gandhi), 288, 321
Indian National Congress, 288
Indian Ocean
    sea voyages, 19, 20 (map), 21, 30, 31
    trade networks, 5, 21–22, 32, 33, 36
India-Pakistan rivalry, 341
indigenous peoples. *See also*
    Native Americans
    agricultural production skills, 5
    anthropological studies of, 52–54
    Christian conversions of, 48, 49, 57

Columbus's initial contact with, 48
    concerns about treatment of, 49,
        52, 57
    dietary challenges, 97
    dying off of, 53, 55, *64*
    encomiendas imposed by Spain, 48
    European conquests of, 48–53
    Law of Burgos and, *64*
    Mexico's poor treatment of, 210
    Requerimiento and, 57–58
    rivalries/demographic
        transformation, 127
    as silver mine labor, 108
    societal transformation, 126–127
    Spain's reliance on, 51
    types of records kept by, 38, 52
industrial capitalism, criticism of,
    187–188
industrialization (Industrial
    Revolution). *See also* Second
    Industrial Revolution
    China's pollution "airpocalypse," 340
    cotton gin, 182, *196*
    Export-Led Industrialization, 331
    in France, *184*
    freedom and, 182–184
    Great Britain, to 1850, 178 (map)
    growth of factories, 177, 182, 184,
        185, 187, 219, 328
    Import Substitution
        Industrialization, 331
    internal combustion engines,
        216, 223
    of the military, 258–259
    models for development, 331–332
    railroads, 177, 216, 248, 366
    refrigeration technology, 177,
        218, 221
    revolutionary aspects of, 176–177
    rubber industry developments,
        227, 229
    scholarly debates about, 179–181
    slavery and, 182
    steam-driven machinery, 6, *172*,
        173, 176, 179, 221
    textile industry, spinning
        technology, 177, 178 (map),
        179
    US Civil War and, 194
*The Influence of Sea Power Upon
    History* (Mahan), 258
Intellectual Association of Egyptian
    Women, 283
internal combustion engines,
    216, 223
International Meridian Conference
    (1884), 218
International Monetary Fund (IMF),
    315, 329
International Red Cross, 193
International Trading Organization
    (ITO), 330
International Zheng He Society, 29–30
Internet, impact on globalization,
    355–357, *363*, 368
*The Interpretation of Dreams* (Freud),
    247–248, 253
Iran. *See also* Safavid Empire
    Cold War support for US, 328
    commitment to nationalization, 344

denunciation of Soviet
aggression, 344
Nadir Shah rise to power, *141*
oil production, 344–345
OPEC founding member, 343
revolution in, 343–344, 362
US-backed coup d'état in, 326, *335*
Iraq
creation of, 273
economic growth in, 357
Khomeini's exile in, 343
oil production, 344–345
OPEC founding member, 343
US invasion of, 352, *363*
US withdrawal from, 353
Ireland
civil war in, 82
economic collapse, 357
potatoes, importance of, 97
rebellions against British rule, 204
WW I enlistments, 265
Iron Curtain, 312 (map), 316, *324*
Iroquois Confederation, 127
Isabel, Brazilian Princess, 212
Isabella of Castile (Queen of Spain),
37–38, 48, 79
Islam religion, 32
*hajj*, pilgrimage to Mecca,
35–36, 77
Ottoman Empire, 33
role in building states, 24–25
Sunni *vs.* Shi`a division, 73, 74, 134
West and Central Africa, 35
Islamic empires
1500, world map, 73 (map)
math/astronomy contributions, 5
Mehmet II, military victories,
33–34, 37, 72
Sunni-Shi`a religion, 33
wars with Christians, 37, 57
Ismail I, Safavid Shah, 67, 69, 73, *88*
Italy
anarcho-syndicalist
movement, 246
Common Market member, 354
compulsory male military
service, 259
formation of, 204, 206
Garibaldi's military campaigns, 206
Germany's antagonism of, 263
Germany's anti-communist treaty
alliance with, 302
Grand Council of Fascism, 257, *261*
imperialism in Africa, 300
invasion of Ethiopia, *309*
Mussolini's promotion of fascism,
254, 257, 279
nationalist ideology of, 207
1940, treaty with China,
Germany, 304
unification of, 225
World War I participation, 269
world's fair exhibits, 221
Young Italy, secret society, 206
Ivan III, Grand Prince of Russia, 34–35
Ivan IV, Grand Prince of Moscow, 75

*The Jalalian Ethics* (al-Dawani), 71
Jamaica, 49, 131, 204
Jamestown Colony, 59, 65

Japan
advance into Southeast Asia, 319
aerial bombing of China, 301, *302*
annexation of Taiwan, 241
arrival of firearms in, 45
atomic bombing by US, 305, *309*
ban on trade with Portugal, 47,
63, 65
bombing of Pearl Harbor,
Hawaii, 304
Charter Oath, 215
in China (1931–1945), 303 (map)
China's naval conflict
with, 239–242
Christianity missionaries in, 45–46
compulsory male military
service, 259
conscription law, 216
Dutch trade with, 63–64, *65*
1870s–1930s, expansion of
influence, 240 (map)
export monopoly with Europe, 105
fascism in, 314
Germany's anti-communist treaty
alliance with, 302
as global power, 274–276
global power status, post-WW I,
274–276
Greater East Asia Co-Prosperity
Sphere, 301, *309*
Hibiya Riots, 254, 255, *280*
invasion of China, 301–302, *302*
Korea as formal colony of, 242
Meiji Constitution, 216, *225*, 275
Meiji ("Enlightened Rule")
government, 215
modernization of, 214–216
Nagasaki, Japan, *44*, 47, 61 (map), 63
1920s economic recession, 292
opening of Tokyo University, 225
Perry's naval mission to,
214–215, 224
printing press in, 78
response to global economic
collapse, 298
Saigo Takamori's rebellion, 216
Sakoku Edict, 47, 113, 215
Sapporo beer, 217
Shimabara Rebellion, 63
silver production in, 106
Sino-Japanese War, 239–242, *242*,
*253*, 255, 257, 258, *280*
sovereignty issues, 238–242
"Taisho Democracy" era, 275
Tokugawa clan, 47, 63, 215
trade network expansion, 62
Treaty of Portsmouth with Russia,
254, 255
"Twenty-one Demands"
of China, *281*
US role in recovery, 330
World War I participation, 269,
272–273, 276
World War II participation, 304
*The Japanese Graphic* magazine, 254, 255
Jefferson, Thomas, 151
Jesuit missionaries, 59
Jews/Judaism, 25
expulsion from French
Caribbean, 132

Holocaust, WW II, 306, *309*, *310*,
313–314, 317
home in Palestine, 286
in Iberian Peninsula, 37–38, 79
in Iraq, 25
in Ottoman Empire, 34
Rabbi Benjamin's travels, 25
John I, Portuguese king, 37
John Paul II, Pope, 346, 349
Johnson, H. T., 233–234
Judeo-Christian work ethic, 180
Juvenal, 22

Kagan, Robert, 349
Kang Youwei, 242
Kangxi Emperor, Qing Dynasty, 66, 67,
69, 89, 120, 124–125, *140*
Kant, Immanuel, 146, 147, 210
Kemmerer, Edwin K., 293–294
Kenya
animal gift from, *18*
arrest/release of Kenyatta, 325
Churchill's concerns for, 324–325
independence of, *335*
indigenous resistance to
Europeans, 324
Mau Mau Rebellion, *324*,
324–326, *335*
"self-determination" rhetoric
challenges, 323
voyages of exploration, 29
Kenyatta, Jomo, 325
Kepler, Johannes, 87
Khan, Sayyid Ahmad, 234, 239, *252*
khipus (Inca knotted textiles), 38, *39*
Khomeini, Ruhollah, 343–344, *344*
King Phillips' War (1675), 127, *140*
Kingdom of Mutapa, Africa, 36–37
Kipling, Rudyard, 233, *253*
Korea
anti-imperialist, nationalist
protests, *282*
as Japanese colony, 253
Japan's economic rule in, 301
North Korea, 85, 319, 331
printing technology development, 77
South Korea, 319, 326, 331,
350, 365
Korean War, 319, *335*
Krupp, Alfred, 195
Kuwait, 343

Landa, Diego de, 38
Landes, David, 180
Las Casas, Bartolomé de, 52, 57
Latin America
anarcho-syndicalist movement, 246
Cold War conflicts, 340–341
electric trolley systems, 229
Import Substitution
Industrialization, 331
military reorganization, 258
neocolonialism in, 250–251
oligarchic republics in, 209
post-WW I economic overhaul, 293
response to global economic
collapse, 297–298
trade networks, 103, 216
voting rights, 276
world's fair exhibits, 221

Laws of Burgos, 57, 64
League of Nations, 274, 286, 293,
    298–299, 317
legitimacy (of rulers)
    China's issues with, 84, 85, 87
    Cold War/communist
        governments, 346
    gaining/loss of, 88
    Hobbes/"Social Contract" theory
        of, 83
    Islamic rulers, 74
    Kangxi Emperor, 67, 69
    limiting factors, 23–24
    requirements, 23
    sovereignty and, 71, 82, 83, 353
Lehman Brothers, 357
Lenin, Vladimir
    anti-capitalist stance, 290
    Bolshevik leadership, 274, 277
    death of, 290
    description of global capitalism,
        278–279
    "Imperialism, the Highest Stage of
        Capitalism," 277, 281
Leo X, 21
Leopold II, Congo Free State King, 235
Levathes, Louise, 31–32
Leviathan (Hobbes), 82, 83, 89
Li Zicheng, 85
Lin Zexu, 191
Lincoln, Abraham, 194
Lisbon earthquake (1755), 142, 143, 147
literature produced by World War I, 264
Little Ice Age (17th century), 96, 114
Locke, John, 120–121, 140, 146,
    149, 318
López de Legazpi, Miguel, 63
Louis XIV, King of France, 120, 122,
    132–133, 140
Louis XVI, King of France, 153, 170
Luther, Martin, 59, 74–77, 79, 88. See
    also Protestant Christianity
Lyman, William, 217

Macartney, George, 190, 196
Machiavelli, Niccolò, 70–71, 74,
    83, 88
Macy's, New York, 217
Madero, Francisco, 261–262
Mahan, Alfred Thayer, 258
Maji-Maji Rebellion, East Africa, 243,
    244–246, 245 (map), 253
Mali Empire, West Africa, 5, 35, 35, 36,
    312 (map), 327 (map)
Malthus, Thomas, 147
Manchu hairstyle decree (Qing
    Dynasty), 123
Manchus. See Qing Dynasty
Mandate of Heaven (tianming), China,
    84, 85, 87, 124–125
Manhattan Island (NYC), 59
Manifesto of the Communist Party
    (Marx), 202, 224
Mansa Musa I, Emperor of Mali,
    35–36
manufactured goods, 101–105
Mao Zedong, 290, 319, 341, 347, 362.
    See also Chinese Communist Party
Marks, Robert, 27
Marshall, George, 330

Marshall Plan (European Recovery
    Plan), 330, 334
Martin, Henri-Jean, 78
Marx, Karl, 2, 187–188, 201–204,
    207, 224
Mary I, Queen of England, 81–82
The Matter, Form and Power of a
    Commonwealth, Ecclesiastical and
    Civil (Hobbes), 82
Mau Mau movement (Kenya), 324,
    324–326, 335
May Fourth Movement, China (1919),
    289, 308
Maya civilization, 38
Mayer, Luigi, 142
Mazzini, Giuseppe, 206, 224
McKinley, William, 247
McNeill, William, 180
Mecca, 29, 34, 35–36, 46 (map),
    72, 74, 97
Medina, 34, 72
Mehmed II, Ottoman sultan,
    33–34, 42, 72
Meiji Constitution (Japan), 216,
    225, 275
Meiji ("Enlightened Rule")
    government, Japan, 215
Mein Kampf (My Struggle) (Hitler),
    299, 308
Melo, Sebastião José de Carvalho e,
    Marquis of Pombal, 143
Menelik II, Ethiopian ruler,
    237–238, 238, 252
mercantilism, 112–113, 298
merchant guilds, 34
Mexica (Aztecs)
    Ahuitzotl's rulership, 44, 45, 64
    building of tributary states, 39–40
    civil engineering feats, 42
    empire expansion, 40 (map), 48
    founding of Tenochtitlan, 39, 40
        (map)
    Spanish conquest of, 51
Mexican Constitution, 277, 281
Mexican Revolution, 275, 281
Mexico, 160 (map). See also
    Tenochtitlan
    abolition of slavery, 168
    Acapulco trading center, 56, 58
    advocacy for scientific politics in,
        209
    Dos Equis beer, 217
    expansion era, 58
    1541 revolt, 56
    gaining of independence,
        159, 251
    influence of Científicos in, 225
    Philippine settlements, 62, 63
    poor treatment of indigenous
        peoples, 210
    post-WW I financial system
        reform, 294
    printing press, 78
    Puebla pottery, 102
    response to global economic
        collapse, 298
    1700–1900, population growth,
        174 (map)
    silver mining, 107, 108
    trade networks, 56, 92 (map)

    US war with, 194
    Valley of Mexico, 39, 40 (map), 45
Middle East. See also individual
    countries
    British strategy in, 269
    changes caused by Ottomans, 134
    Ming travels to, 84
    oil and global political, economic
        relations, 341–342
    political order struggles, 286–288
    term derivation, 15
    transition to sedentary
        agriculture, 176
millets, religious communities, 34, 72,
    86, 169
Milosevic, Slobodan, 351
Ming Dynasty, China
    ceramics, 101, 103
    Christian missionaries in, 63
    Confucianism, 31
    decline of, 84–85
    economic policies, 29
    Li Zicheng's rebellion, 85
    Mongol-China battles, 27
    rise to power, 27, 28–29, 42
    Single Whip reforms, 63
    suicide of emperor, 89
    trade networks, 32, 84
    voyages of Zheng He, 18, 19, 21,
        29–32, 34t, 365
    Yongle Emperor, 19, 28, 29
    Zhu Yuanzhang, Emperor, 84
missionaries, 45–47, 59, 63, 126, 128
Moctezuma I, Aztec emperor, 42
Moctezuma II, Aztec emperor, 50
Mohammed Reza Pahlavi, Shah
    of Iran, 343
monarchies, modernizing of
    in China, 123–125
    in England, 120–122
    in France, 122
    in Russia, 122–123
Mongol Empire
    China's expansion in, 69, 140, 189
    Chinggis Khan , chieftan, 27
    defeat of Abbasid Caliphate, 27
    Delhi Sultanate repulsion of, 32
    role of descendants of, 32
    Yuan Dynasty, China, 28, 84
Montchrestien, Antoine de, 112, 115
Montesinos, Antonio de, 52
Morel, Edmund, 236
Morgan, J. P., 218
The Morning Chronicle, British
    newspaper, 259
The Morning Post, British newspaper, 259
Mott, Lucretia, 199, 210
Mughal Empire
    Akbar, emperor, 74, 88, 95
    Aurangzeb, emperor, 74, 119
    boundaries, 16th–18th centuries,
        68 (map)
    ca. 1650, 61 (map)
    demise of power, 135
    formation of, 33, 74
    Sunni traditions in, 74
    Treaty of Allahabad,
        117–118, 141
    weaponry, 70
Muhammad, Prophet, 34, 35, 73

Mujahideen, 345–346, 351
Mussolini, Benito
  Black Shirts, supporters of, 257
  Grand Council of Fascism
    leadership, 257, *261*
  march on Rome, *281*
  promotion of fascism, *254*,
    257, 279
Muzaffar II, Sultan, 21

Nadir Shah, Shah of Iran, 134–135, *141*
Nagasaki, Japan, *44*, 47, 61 (map), 63
Naimark, Norman, 292
Naoroji, Dadabhai, 234, *252*
Napoleon Bonaparte, Emperor
  of France
  anti-British Continental System of,
    158, 203
  coup d'état in France, 155–156, *171*
  defeat of, 159, 189
  invasion of Egypt, 167
  invasion of Iberian Peninsula, 159
  Toussaint's suspicions of, 157
Napoleonic Wars, 145, 158–159,
  167–168, 203, 221
Nasser, Gamal Abdel, 326
*National Song* (Petőfi), 203
nationalist movements, 166–167,
  262–263, 321
Nationalist Party (China), 289
nation-states. *See also* states/
  state-building
  Balkan Peninsula's aspirations for,
    262–263
  conflicts, self-determination
    struggles, 286, 314
  consolidation in the Americas, 209
  debates about resilience,
    limitations, 353
  European Union formation,
    354–355
  as global capitalism alternative, 246
  growth of, 89
  Haiti as, 157
  impact on indigenous populations,
    210
  international stance against
    slaughter, 333
  Islamic world's artificial
    boundaries, 345
  as keystone of global political
    order, 170
  methods of construction, 205, 207
  post-Spanish America building,
    161, 162–163
  self-determination struggles, 286
  South Asia transition, 17
  US as, 157
  Western Eurasia dilemma, 164, 165
    (map), 166–167
  Wilson's advocacy for, 272
Native Americans
  alliances with colonists, 152
  extinction of buffaloes and, 249
  Ghost Dance ritual, 243, 244, 246,
    249, *252*
  King Phillip's War and, 127
  Sitting Bull, Lakota Chief, 244
  types of information sources,
    9, 10–11

Wounded Knee massacre of, 244
Wovoka, Paiute medicine man,
  244, 249, 252
NATO. *See* North Atlantic Treaty
  Organization
naval architecture, China, 29
navigation advances, 218–220
Nazi Party, Germany
  absorption of Austria,
    Czechoslovakia, 302
  Allied victories against, WW II,
    305, 315
  death camps, WW II, 306,
    *310*, 311, 314, 317
  destruction of Warsaw Ghetto,
    311, *354*
  Holocaust/targeting of Jews, 299,
    306, *309*, *310*, 311, 314, 317,
    325, 334
  new *Reich* (empire) goal, 302
  path in World War II, 303–304
  ultranationalist message of, 299
Nebrija, Antonio de, 79
"Negro village" attraction, *Exposition
  Universelle*, 199
Nehru, Jawaharlal, Indian Prime
  Minister, 332
neocolonialism, 250–251
Netherlands
  Common Market membership, 354
  fight for control of Calicut, 60
  Germany's blitzkrieg in, 303
  interests in War of Spanish
    Succession, 133
  post-WW II hold on colonial
    enterprises, 318
  role in Thirty Years' War, 81
  tulipmania in, 110–112, *113*, *115*
  voting rights expansion, post-WW
    I, 276
New Deal of Franklin Roosevelt,
  295, 297
New England Puritans, 59
New France, 58
New Imperialism
  Afghani/Khan, differences
    of opinion on, 234
  causes/consequences, debates
    about, 233–234
  China and, 238–242, 243
  contrasting view of, 233
  description, 226, 230–232
  factors in Europe's motivation
    for, 319
  global shadow cast by, 229–230
  Japan and, 238–242
New Spain. *See* Mexico
New Sweden (Delaware)
  Colony, 59
New Testament, *62*, 77, *88*
New York Stock Exchange
  crash (1929), 295, *308*
New Zealand, 200 (map), 218
Nguyen Ai Quoc. *See* Ho Chi Minh
Ngwale, Kinjikitile, 246
Nicholas II, Russian Tsar, 260
9/11. *See* World Trade Center (NYC),
  terrorist attacks
1905–1928, 255–281. *See also*
  World War I

China's embrace of fascism,
  289–290, 302
Hibiya Riots, Japan, *254*, 255, *280*
mass unrest in China, Russia,
  Mexico, 259–262
military industrialization, 258–259
new theories, grand strategy,
  258–259
"1914" poem (Brooke), 264
1919–1948, 283–308
  Accra protests, Ghana, 282, 283,
    285, 307
  Cairo Protests, Egypt, 282, 285
  challenges to British rule in India,
    288–289
  collapse of post-war order,
    294–302
  gold standard, 293, 294, 295, 296
    (map), 298
  Great Depression, 12, 281, 286,
    295–298, 315, 317, 331
  invasion of Ethiopia, 299–300
  mass killings, 305–306
  nationalism frustrations in China,
    289–290
  New Deal, 295, 297–298
  1920s global economy, 292–294
  1939, colonies and mandates, 284
    (map)
  redrawing global map, post-WW II,
    306–307
  Republic of Turkey, 286–288
  Soviet Union, 290–292
  Spanish Civil War, aerial bombing,
    300–301
  spread of fascism, 298–299
  World War II, path to, 303–305
1942–1975, 311–334
  Allies, new order plans, 314–321
  Angola Civil War, 313–314
  Cold War, East and Southeast Asia,
    318–321
  Cold War conflicts, 312 (map)
  decolonization, 321–326, 327, *327*
    (map)
  economic development,
    nonalignment, 328–333
  models for industrialization,
    331–332
  NATO formation, 316
  search for common ground, Big
    Five Allies, 316–318
  United Nations formation,
    317–318, *334*
  Warsaw Ghetto, 311, 313–314, *354*
1972–2012, 337–363
  al-Qaeda, 345–346,
    351–353, *363*
  China's reforms, 347–348
  Cold War, 1970s realism, 339–346
  Cold War, ending of, 349–350
  collapse of Soviet bloc, 348
  economic integration, 354–361
  global wealth distribution,
    358 (map)
  Iranian revolution, 343–344, 362
  Latin America and Asia, 340–341
  new global order, transition
    to, 350–353
  Oil Crisis, 342 (map)

1972–2012 (*Continued*)
    OPEC, energy, geopolitics, 341,
        342 (map), 343
    Soviet invasion of Afghanistan,
        344–345, 349, 362
    Soviet Union, internal reforms,
        346–347
    US occupation of Afghanistan,
        352, 353
Ninety-Five Theses (Luther), 74
Nixon, Richard, *336*, 337, 339, 340, *362*
Nkrumah, Kwame, *282*, 285, *309*, 325
Non-Aligned Movement, 332, *335*, 341
Non-Aligned Movement Conference
    (1961), 329
North America. *See also* British North
    America
    American Bison in, 248–250
    Columbian Exchange, 54 (map)
    conflicts among seaborne
        empires, 132
    empires and trade, ca. 1770, 144
        (map)
    English settlement attempts, 112
    English trade charters in, 59
    European demand for slave labor
        in, 128
    1500–1914, population movement,
        200 (map)
    firearms introduced in, 127
    horses introduced in, 126–127
    indigenous *vs.* European-origin
        peoples, 127
    material wealth concentration in, 6
    Passenger Pigeons in, 248–250
    Pueblo (Village) people, 126
    rejection of the modern state in,
        243–245
    resistance/rebellion in, 126–127
    Seven Years' War participation,
        135, 137–138
    17th century, global trade,
        92 (map)
    sugar cane cultivation, 99 (map)
    technology/redistribution of
        wealth, 6
    voyages of exploration, 46 (map), 48
North American Free Trade Agreement
    (NAFTA), 355
North Atlantic Treaty Organization
    (NATO), 312 (map), 316, 351
North Korea, 85, 319, 331
North Vietnam, *320*, 331, *335*
*Novum Organum Scientiarum* (New
    Instrument of Science) (Bacon),
    88, *89*

October Revolution, Russia, 274, *281*
oil (petroleum). *See* Organization
    of Petroleum Exporting
    Countries
oil and gas drilling technology, 216
Oil Crisis (1973–1974), 342 (map)
Opium Wars, *172*, 189–192, *196*,
    204, 214
Organization of Petroleum Exporting
    Countries (OPEC), 341, *342*,
    343, *362*
*Origin of Species* (Darwin), 247, *252*
Orthodox Christianity, 122

Ottoman Empire
    Abdulmecid sultanate, 145
    absolutism in, 139
    boundaries, 16th–18th centuries,
        68 (map)
    Celali Rebellion, 96, *114*
    contraction of, 208 (map)
    Crimean War participation,
        192–193
    defeat of Constantinople, 33, *43*
    diplomacy/wars of, 34
    economic crisis in, 110
    globalization's impact on
        rural life, 96
    Greece's separation from, 166, 169
    Gulhane (Rose Bower) Edict, *142*,
        145, *171*
    as key Afro-Eurasian link, 33–35
    Mehmed II, sultan, 33–34,
        37, 42, 72
    millet system, 34, 72, 86, 169
    Muslim dissent in, 169
    ongoing military campaigns, 96
    post-Napoleon, 165 (map)
    reform in, 168–169
    Reşid, Mustafa, Pasha, 145
    reversal of fortunes in, 134
    role in Thirty Years' War, 81
    Russia's wars with, 34, 134
    Selim I, sultan, 34
    Serbians in, 263
    submarine purchases, 258
    Suleiman I, sultan, 60, 72, *88*
    Tanzimat reforms, 145, 169, *171*,
        207, 224
    weaponry, 79
    World War I participation, 269,
        270, 272
Owen, Wilfred, 264, 280

Pachacuti Inca Yupanqui, Inca leader, 42
Paine, S. C. M., 241
Paine, Thomas, 198
Pakistan
    Bandung Conference, 332
    decolonization, 327 (map)
    independence of, 323, 334
    India-Pakistan border dispute, *336*
pamphlets, 74–75, 77, 149
Panama Canal, 228 (map),
    269–270, 274
Paris, World's Fair, 199, 201,
    223, *225*
Party of the Institutionalized
    Revolution (PRI),
    Mexico, 277
Pasteur, Louis, 217
pasteurization process, 217
*Pax Mongolica* (Mongolian Peace), 27
Peace of 1783, 135, 137
Peace of Westphalia (1648), 81
Peasant Reform, Russia, 207
Peltel, Feigele, 311–312
People of the Long House, 48
People's Movement for the Liberation
    of Angola (MPLA), *310*,
    313, *313*
perestroika (institutional
    restructuring), 346, 347
Perry, Matthew, 214–215, *224*

*Perseverance* steamboat, *172*, 173, *196*
Peru
    alliance with Spain, 51
    expansion of, 58
    financial system reform, 294
    rebellion/beheading of Viceroy, 59
    silver production, 107, 108, *114*
    surrender of Spanish Empire
        troops, 159, *171*
Peter the Great, Russian Tsar, 120,
    122–123, *123*, 133, *140*
Peterloo Massacre (Great Britain), 204
Petőfi, Sándor, 203
Philadelphia's world's fair, Centennial
    Exhibition, 220–222, 222, 223
Philip II, Spanish king, 62, 63, 79,
    81, 82
Philippines
    gaining of independence, 326
    Spanish settlements, 62
    trade networks, 32, 60, 101–102
    US control of, 233, 274
    World War II participation, 304
Phillip II, Spanish monarch, 62
*The Philosophy of Manufactures* (Ure),
    186–187, *196*
Picasso, Pablo, 300
*Plessy v. Ferguson* (1896), 212, *225*
Pliny the Elder, 22
Plymouth Colony, 59
Poland
    destruction of Warsaw Ghetto,
        311, *354*
    Germany's invasion of, 303, *309*
    interest in self-determination, 314
    post-WW I financial system
        reform, 294
    role in US-Soviet conflict, 315
    voting rights expansion, post-
        WW I, 276
*Politics Drawn from the Very Words of
    Holy Scripture* (Bossuet), 122
Polo, Marco, 19
Pombaline reforms (Portugal),
    143–144, 159
Pomeranian War. *See* Seven Years' War
Pomeranz, Kenneth, 180–181
population movements (1500–1914),
    200 (map)
Portugal
    defeat of Ceuta, Africa, 37, *42*
    enclave at Macau, 62, 65
    fight for control of Calicut, 60
    Indian Ocean trade, 60
    Japan's trade ban *vs.*, 47, 63, 65
    Lisbon earthquake, *142*, 143, 147
    1974 coup d'état, 313
    Pombaline reforms, 143–144, 159
    post-WW II hold on colonial
        enterprises, 318
    rivalry with Dutch in Brazil, 132
    rulership of John I, 37
    sea voyages, exploration, 19,
        30–31, 46 (map)
    seizure of Goa, South Asia, *43*
    seizure of Malacca, 60, *64*
    Seven Years' War participation, 135
    spice trade, 112
    Treaty of Tordesillas and, 58
    wars of, 117

potatoes, 53, 54 (map), 97
Potsdam Conference, 315, *334*
Prieto, Guillermo, 209
*The Prince* (Machiavelli), 70, *88*
Princip, Gavrilo, 262
printing presses, 77–78, *88*, 166
Protestant Christianity, 59, 63, 76,
    81–82. *See also* Dutch
    Protestants; French
    Protestants
Protestant Reformation, 76, 148
Prussia
    Franco-Prussian War, 206
    post-Napoleon, 165 (map)
    purchase of Krupp's canons,
        195, *197*
    Seven Years' War participation, 135
    succession disputes in, 134
Puerto Rico, 49, 159, 233, 274, 326
Puritans, 59

Qianlong Emperor, 125, 190, 191
Qing Dynasty (Manchu Qing Dynasty)
    absolutism in, 123–125
    boundaries, 16th–18th centuries,
        68 (map)
    Canton System, trade restrictions,
        189–190, *196*
    collapse of, 260, 261
    conquest of China, 85, 86–87
    economic expansion, 125
    hairstyle decree, 123, *140*
    Hundred Days' Reforms,
        242, 253
    Kangxi Emperor, *66*, 67, 69, *89*,
        120, 124–125, *140*
    leadership flexibility, 125
    Manchu decree on hairstyle,
        123, *140*
    Mandate of Heaven, 124–125
    "new Qing history," 86–87
    Opium Wars, *172*, 189–192, *196*,
        204, 214
    population growth, 124–125
    Qing Code, 124
    regions included in, 189
    self-strengthening program, 239
    trade map ca. 1770, 144 (map)
    weaponry, 79
Quakers, 167, 199
Qur`an, 32

*The Radicalism of the American
    Revolution* (Wood), 151–152
railroads, 177, 216, 248, 366
Razin, Stenka, 122
Reagan, Ronald, 349–351
Rebellion of the Barrios (Quito,
    Ecuador), 138, *141*, 157
Reconstruction, post-Civil War (US),
    194, 210–212
Reform Act of 1832 (Britain), 204, *224*
refrigeration technology, 177,
    218, 221
Remarque, Erich Maria, 264, *281*
Remington firearms, 194
Republic of Turkey. *See* Turkey/
    Republic of Turkey
Requerimiento (Requirement), 57–58
Reşid, Mustafa, Ottoman Pasha, 145

Revolutionary War. *See* American
    Revolution
Rhodes, Cecil, 218
Ricardo, David, 147
Ricci, Matteo, 78, *89*
Roaring Twenties, US, 294
Roca, Julio, 210
Rockefeller, John D., 218
Roman Catholicism, 59, 62, 63, 75, 78,
    81, 82, 132, 153
Romanov Dynasty (Russia), 139, 259
Roosevelt, Franklin, 295, 297
Roosevelt, Theodore, 255
Rousseau, Jean-Jacques, 83, 149, 210
Royal Observatory, England, 220
Russian Imperial Code, 123
Russian Revolution, 279
Russia/Russian Empire
    abolition of serfdom, 225
    Bloody Sunday Massacre, *260*, 280
    boundaries, 16th–18th centuries,
        68 (map)
    Boyar Duman, 122
    Central/East Asia expansion,
        230, 259
    Christian hierarchies in, 75
    civil war/revolution, 278 (map)
    Communist Party, 279
    defeat in Crimean War, 192–193
    empires and trade, ca. 1770, 144
        (map)
    1500–1914, population movement,
        200 (map)
    Fundamental Law of 1906, 260
    Great Reforms, 207, 209
    incorporation of changing
        world, 125
    mass unrest in, 259–260
    massive starvation in,
        291–292, *309*
    Menelik II, alliance with, 237
    October Revolution, 274, *281*
    Peter the Great, reign of, 120,
        122–123, 133–134, *140*
    post-Napoleon, 165 (map)
    railroad network, 216
    rivalry with Great Britain, 167
    Romanov Dynasty, 139, 259
    sale of Alaska to the US, 259
    Seven Years' War participation, 135
    Sino-Japanese War, 239–242, *242*,
        253, 255, 257, 258, 280
    Trans-Siberian Railway, 259, 280
    Treaty of Portsmouth with Japan,
        254, 255
    21st century economic growth, 359
    wars with Ottoman Empire,
        34, 134
    World War I participation, 263,
        265, 269, 270, 272
Russo-Persian War (1804–1813), *166*

Safavid Empire
    Abbas' leadership, 67
    boundaries, 16th–18th centuries,
        68 (map)
    collapse of, 134, 139, 169
    Ismail I's leadership, 67, 69, 73, *88*
    map location, 68 (map)
    resource/territorial disputes, 134

Shi`a religious tradition, 73
    weaponry, 79
Saigo, Takamori, 216
sakoku policy, Japan, 113
Sakoku Rei (Closed Country Edicts),
    Japan, 47
Sapporo beer (Japan), 217
Sardinia, 192–193
Sarmiento, Domingo Faustino, 209
Saudi Arabia, 286, 343, 345, 352
Say, Jean-Baptiste, 147
Scientific Method, 4, 87
"scramble for Africa" by Europe, *226*, 230
Second Calico Act (1721), 93
Second Industrial Revolution
    (industrialization), 216–220
    barbed wire fencing, 218
    coffee roasting technology, 222–223
    consumer credit, 217
    consumer goods expansion, 216–217
    engineering marvels, 216
    food revolution, 217–218
    industrial economy financiers, 218
    navigation advances, 218–220
    oil and gas drilling technology, 216
    refrigeration technology, 177, 218
    retail revolution, 217
    telephone, 221
    timekeeping advances, 218–220
Second Opium War (China), 191
Second World War. *See* World War II
Selassie, Haile, Ethiopian Emperor,
    299, 328
Selim I, Ottoman sultan, 34
Semper Augustus (tulip), 111
Sen, Tansen (Chinese historian), 30
Seneca Falls Convention, on women's
    rights, 199, 201, 210, 224
Sepoy Mutiny (India), 204, *224*
September 11, 2001. *See* World
    Trade Center (NYC), terrorist
    attacks
Sepúlveda, Juan Ginés de, 57
Serbia, 145, 208 (map), 230, 263, 269
Seven Years' War
    alternative names, 119
    description, aftermath, 117, 135,
        137–139, 148–149
    map, 136 (map)
    Qing Dynasty comparison, 189
1755–1839, 143–171
    American Revolution, 151–152, 188
    Bourbon reforms, 158–159
    Brazil's path to independence,
        159, 161
    breakup of British North America,
        148–152
    freedom and equality, 167–169
    French Revolution, 145,
        153–156, 321
    Haitian revolution, 156–157
    Iberian Empire's collapse, 157–159,
        161–163
    idea of the nation-state, 163–164,
        166–167
    Napoleonic Wars, 145, 158–159,
        167–168, 203, 221
    Spanish America, post-
        independence nations,
        161–163

1787–1868, 173–196. *See also*
industrialization
   changing world of work, 184–187
   Crimean War, 192–193, *193*, 197
   debates about the industrial
      revolution, 179–181
   freedom and industrialization,
      182–184
   global power relations,
      transformation of, 188–195
   industrial capitalism, criticism of,
      187–188
   industrial revolution story, 177,
      178 (map), 179
   Opium Wars, *172*, 189–192, *196*,
      204, 214
   revolutionary aspects of
      industrialization, 176–177
   US Civil War, 162, 193–194, *197*,
      210–212
   weaponry development, 195
   world population growth,
      174 (map)
Sha`rawi, Huda, 283
Sharps firearms, 194
Shimabara Rebellion (1637–1638), 63
Shuler, Kristrina, 100
Sieyès, Emmanuel Joseph, 153–154
silver
   Bourbon Reforms and, 158
   Chinese exports, 191
   Chinese imports, 56, 60–61,
      84–85, 102, 108, 190
   European production, 106
   global economy and, 92 (map),
      106–110, *114*
   Huancavelica production,
      91, 107–108
   Japanese production, 106
   from mine to mint to market,
      107–109
   Peruvian production, *114*
   Potosí production, *90*, 106–107
   processing advancements, 107
   supply disruptions, 191
   use of slave labor, 108
Singer, Isaac, 217
Single Whip reforms, Ming Dynasty, 63
Sino-Japanese War, 239–242, *242*, *253*,
   255, 257, 258, *280*
Sitting Bull, Lakota Chief, 244
1655–1765, 117–140
   Atlantic seaborne states, control
      issues, 125–131
   Central Eurasia, land-based
      empires, 133–135
   competition/conflicts, seaborne
      empires, 132–133
   England's monarchy, 120–122
   French, Russian, Chinese
      absolutism, 122–125
   modernizing monarchies, 120–125
   North American resistance and
      rebellion, 126–127
   path to World War Zero,
      131–135, 137–138
   Seven Years' War, 117, 135, 136
      (map), 137–139, 148–149
   slavery/slave trade, 127–131

slavery/slave trade, 127–130. *See also*
African slaves in the Americas
   in Barbados, *115*
   in Brazil, 127
   in British North America, 149
   in the Caribbean, 55, *64*, 100,
      127, 139
   cotton production and, 182,
      183 (map)
   Enlightenment critique of, 167
   escaped slaves' communities, 131
   Great Britain's ban of, 168
   Mexico's abolition of, 168
   Middle Passage, *129*, 130
   in North America, 131
   slave ship plans, *129*
   sources for studying, 130–131
   sugar-slave plantation system,
      98–99, 99 (map), 100, *101*
   transatlantic slave trade, 118 (map),
      128, 129–130, 132, 167, 182
   US Civil War and, 194
Smith, Adam, 147
Smith & Wesson firearms, 194
Snyder, Timothy, 292
social contract
   Burke's call for rewriting of, 156
   *Encylopédie* on, 146
   formation of states and, 121, 147,
      163, 167
   possible questions for inclusion,
      162
   US Constitution as example of,
      150
Social Contract (Locke), 138, 149
Social Contract theory of legitimacy
   (Hobbes), 83
Social Darwinism, 232–233
Social Security Act (1935), 297
Society of Jesus (Jesuits), 62
Somayaji, Nilakantha, 87
Song Dynasty, China, 27, 29
Songhai Empire, 20 (map), 36–37, *43*,
   68 (map)
Sonni Ali, Songhai king, 36
*The Sopranos* TV series, 23
Sorrieu, Frédéric, *202*
South Africa
   apartheid regime in, 313
   Boer War, 245 (map), 259
   British abolitionist activities
      in, 168
   discovery of diamonds, 230
   Dutch settlements, 168
   Ford automobiles in, 354
   Gandhi's activism in, 288
   Kemmerer's work in, 294
   meeting with BRICS ministers, 359
   1939, colonies and mandates, 284
      (map)
   Portuguese maize crops, 97
   post-WW I financial system
      reform, 294
   21st century economic growth, 359
South America
   campaigns *vs.* indigenous
      peoples, 210
   empires and trade, ca. 1770, 144
      (map)

1500–1914, population movement,
   200 (map)
OPEC membership, 343
Quito (Ecuador) rebellion,
   138–139
South Asia
   archaeological discoveries in, 22
   British East India Company in, 119
   Ibn Battuta's travels, 25
   independent nation-states, 17
   India-Pakistan rivalry, 341
   Ottoman links with, 34
   Portuguese seizure of Goa, *43*
   rhinoceros gift to, *18*
   Seven Years' War participation, 135
   sovereignty struggles in, 237
   struggles over, 32–33
   textile exports, 105
   trade networks, *18*, 64
   Treaty of Allahabad and,
      117–118
   Vijayanagara Hindu dynasty, 33
South China Sea, 19, 20 (map), 21–22,
   30, 36
South Korea, 319, 326, 331, 350, 365
Southeast Asia
   British/Dutch East India Company
      domination, 63–64
   Cold War in, 318–321, *320*, 339
   demand for textiles in, 104
   economy, fifteenth century, 32
   French territories in, 230
   indentured workers from, 213
   Japan's advance into, 319
   rice market, 95
   16th century trade expansion, 60
   sovereignty struggles, 237
   spice trade, 5, 22, 104
   trade networks, 60, 102, 104
sovereignty
   Africa/Asia struggles, 237–238
   Charles V's claims of, 79
   China/Japan struggles, 238–242
   China's issues with, 84, 87
   Christian dynasties, 37
   defined, 23
   Europe's issues with, 35
   Haiti, *154*
   legitimacy and, 71, 82, 83, 353
   Muslim ruler's claims of, 60
   Qing Dynasty claims of, 69
   Songhai Empire, 36
   South Asia's struggles, 237
   Southeast Asia's struggles, 237
   Spanish monarch's claims of, 57
   states/state-building and, 23–24
Soviet Union (USSR), 274
   collapse of, 187, 348
   commitments to Cuba, 332
   Communist International
      Party, 290
   consolidation of, 290
   debating famine in, 291–292
   democratic centralism in, 291
   discoveries about World War II,
      314–315
   establishment of, 274
   German invasion of, *309*
   *glasnost*, 347, *347*

Gorbachev's leadership, 262, 346–347, 349–350
Gulag (labor camp) system, 291, 328
interest in self-determination, 313
internal reforms in, 346–347
invasion of Afghanistan, 344–345, 349, 362
Iran's denunciation of aggression by, 344
from Lenin to Stalin, 290–291
perestroika, 346, 347
Stalin's industrialization of, 290–291
support for Marxist groups, 313
suppression of Prague Spring, 328, 335
Spain/Spanish Empire. See also Spanish America
aerial bombings, 300
Bourbon family control, 133
Caribbean settlements, 49
Christianization efforts, 48, 57
colonial expansion, 30
economic crisis in, 110
encomiendas system, 48, 49, 51, 57, 58
financing of Columbus, 38, 46 (map), 48
kidnap/execution of Atahualpa, 50, 65
Laws of Burgos, 57, 64
limited authority in North America, 126
"New Laws" (1542), 58, 65
Philippine settlements, 62, 63
post-Napoleon, 165 (map)
presence in the Americas, 47–58
Requerimiento, 57–58
role in Thirty Years' War, 81
Seven Years' War participation, 135
trade network expansion, 62
voyages of Columbus, 16, 38, 46 (map), 48
weaponry, 79
weaponry of, 51
Spanish America
autonomous economic system, 105
British control of slave trade in, 132
Chinese coolies in, 213–214, 224
Christian missionaries in, 128
citizen and nation in, 209–210
conflict vs. accommodation in, 56, 95
direct trade with Asia, 102, 114
freedom gained by slaves in, 168
indigenous labor force in, 108, 158
nation and citizen in, 209–210
post-independence nation-building, 161, 162–163
Rebellion of the Barrios, 138, 141, 157
silver production, 56, 91, 96
Spanish Civil War, 300–301, 309
Spanish Inquisition, 79
Special Economic Zones (SEZs), China, 348
spice trade, 98, 112
"Springtime of the Nations" in Europe (1848), 202, 202

Stalin, Josef
collectivization of agriculture, 291
comment on WW II losses, 316
death of, 335
industrialization of Soviet Union, 290–291
nonaggression pact with Hitler, 303
Stamp Act (1765), 137, 138
Stanford, Leland, 218
Stanton, Elizabeth Cady, 199, 210–211, 211
states/state-building. See also nation-states
China's statecraft development, 84, 86
defined, 22–23
Machiavelli and, 70
political advice literature on, 70–71`
religion's role in building, 24
sovereignty and, 23–24
Tilly on "stateness," 70
steam engine technology, 6, 172, 173, 176, 221
steamships, 175, 177, 194, 366
Steer, George L., 300
Stuart Dynasty, Great Britain, 82, 121. See also Mary, Queen of England
Suez Canal, 216, 225, 230, 326
Sugar Act, 137
sugar-slave plantation system, 98, 99 (map), 100, 101
Suleiman the Magnificent, Ottoman sultan, 60, 72, 88
Sultan Husayn, Safavid Shah, 134
Sun Yat-sen, President of China, 260–261, 273, 281, 289
Sunni Islam, 33, 34, 72, 73, 74, 134
Sunni-Shi`a Islam, 33, 34, 67, 73, 74, 134
Sweden, 81, 135

Taiping War (1850–1864), 175, 192, 195, 197
"Taisho Democracy" era, Japan, 275
Taiwan
anti-communist development, 326
Asian Tiger economy in, 331
decolonization, 327 (map)
Japan in, 240 (map), 241, 275, 303 (map)
Nationalists flight to, 339
trade networks, 104–105, 298
US protection of, 339–340
Tan Ta Sen, 29–30
Tandeter, Enrique, 107
Tanzimat reforms, Ottoman Empire, 145, 169, 171, 207, 224
Tauger, Mark, 292
Tehran Conference, 315
telephone, 221
Tenochtitlan (Mexica capital)
Ahuitzotl's assumption of power, 45, 64
location, 40 (map), 46 (map)
Mexica's founding of, 39
Moctezuma II's leadership, 50
surrender to Cortés, 50, 51, 64

Testament of Youth (Brittain), 264
textile spinning technology, 177, 179
Third Carnatic War. See Seven Years' War
Third Estate (France), 153–154
Third Silesian War. See Seven Years' War
Thirty Years' War (1618–1648), 81, 132, 134
Three Decades Crisis, 285
TI Europe voyage, 365, 366
Tianqi steamship, China, 173, 175, 197
Tilly, Charles, 70, 71n1
Timbuktu, Africa, 20 (map), 36
timekeeping advances, 218–220
The Times, British newspaper, 259
Timur (aka Tamerlane)/Timurid Dynasty, 32–33, 134
Tlacaelel I, Aztec politician, 42
"To the Christian Nobility of the German Nation" (Luther), 79
Tokugawa clan, Shogun of Japan, 47, 63, 215
"The Tokyo Riot Graphic" (Japanese Graphic magazine), 255
Topkapi Palace, Istanbul, 142, 145
Toussaint L'Ouverture, François, 157
A Tract on Political Economy (Montchrestien), 112, 115
trade networks. See also voyages of exploration
Africa, 22, 35, 36–37
Afro-Eurasia, 20 (map), 21–22, 35, 36–37
Australia, 218
China, 22, 60, 62
Dutch, 44, 63–64, 65
East Africa, 18, 22, 36–37, 84
East Asia, 18, 36–37, 97, 104, 228 (map)
empires/global trade (1874–1914), 228 (map)
France, 64
global foodways, 96–98
Indian Ocean, 5, 21–22, 32, 33, 36
Ming Dynasty, China, 32, 84
Philippines, 32, 60, 101–102
1770, global trade, 144 (map)
16th century expansion, 60
South Asia, 18, 64
Southeast Asia, 60, 102, 104
spice trade, 98, 112
Taiwan, 104–105, 298
tripling of global trade (1820–1850), 184, 196
Vietnam, 60, 189
West Africa, 36, 59, 64
"Tragic Week," Buenos Aires, 276
transatlantic slave trade, 118 (map), 128–130, 129–130, 132, 140, 167, 182
transportation
airplanes, 177, 268
automobiles, 177, 216, 354, 366
railroads, 177, 216, 248, 366
rapid transit systems, 185
trolley systems, electric, 229
Trans-Siberian Railway, 259, 280

*A Treatise on Holy War* (Prime Minister of Persia), *166*
Treaty of Adrianople, 208 (map)
Treaty of Allahabad, 117–118, *141*
Treaty of Berlin, 208 (map)
Treaty of Bucharest, 208 (map)
Treaty of Frankfurt, 206
Treaty of Karlowitz, 208 (map)
Treaty of Kuchuk-Kainarji, 208 (map)
Treaty of Lausanne, 208 (map)
Treaty of London, 208 (map)
Treaty of Nanjing, 191–192, *196*
Treaty of Paris (1783), 152, *170*
Treaty of Passarowitz, 208 (map)
Treaty of Portsmouth, *254*, 255
Treaty of Ryswick (1697), 100
Treaty of Tordesillas (1494), 58
Treaty of Versailles, 275
Treblinka death camp, 311, 314
tribute system, China, 113
trolley systems, electric, 229
Truman, Harry, 316
tulips (tulipmania), 110–112, *113*, *115*
Tupac Amaru II, Inca ruler, 157–158
Tupac Amaru Rebellion, 158
Turkey/Republic of Turkey
    anti-imperialist, nationalist protests, 282
    Celali Rebellion, 96, *114*
    emergence of, 286–288, *308*
    Mediterranean coast, Alanya fortress, 72 (map)
    non-Turk struggles under Ottomans, 287
    political struggles, 286–288
    popularity of tulips, 110
    US aid to, 319
    US containment policy in, 319
2015, world map, 338 (map)

underground (public transport) construction, London, *186*
Union of Soviet Socialist Republics (USSR). *See* Soviet Union
United Nations (UN)
    admittance of East and West Germany, 316
    arrest of Slobodan Milosevic, 351
    Atlantic Charter basis, 318
    BRICS ministers' meetings, 359
    China, permanent seat holder, 318–319
    Cold War violations, 332
    condemnation of North Korea, 319
    Declaration of United Nations, 315, *334*
    formation of, 317–318, *334*
    founding principles of, 318, 332
    principles of, 318
    recognition of PRC, 340
    war crimes tribunals, 351
United Nations Charter, 317, 318
United Nations Human Development Index (HDI), 361
United Nations Security Council, 317, 319
United States (US). *See also* British North America; Civil War; Native Americans
    anarcho-syndicalist movement, 246

anti-Chinese xenophobia, 195
Articles of Confederation, 150, 162, 173
atomic bombing of Japan, 305, *309*
ban on Chinese immigrants, 212
California gold rush, 214, *224*
Caribbean investments, 250
Centennial Exhibition, 220
challenge of British commercial, industrial superiority, 204
Constitutional Convention, 150, 172, 173
containment policy, 316, 319, 326
control of Philippines, Cuba, Puerto Rico, 233
coup d'état in Guatemala, 326–327
coup d'état in Iran, 326, 335
currency system, 110
Dawes Plan, 293
Declaration of Independence, 13, 149, 154, 170, 215, 321
discoveries about World War II, 314–315
early 20th century, global manufacturing control, 258
global power status, post-WW I, 274–276
gold rush, 214, *224*
interest in self-determination, 313
invasion of Iraq, 352, *363*
massacre of Native Americans, 244
New Imperialism of, *226*
1919, "Red Summer," 276
1933, peak unemployment, *309*
North American Free Trade Agreement, 355
occupation of Afghanistan, 352, 353
OPEC's power challenges, 343
Philadelphia world's fair, 220–222, *222*, 223
"Ping-Pong Diplomacy" with China, 340
post-Civil War rebuilding of, 210–212
power broker role, post-WW I, 272
pursuit of "Life, Liberty, and the Pursuit of Happiness," 169
"Remember the Maine" rally call, 259
response to global economic collapse, 298
Roaring Twenties, 294
role in Japan's recovery, 330
Russia's sale of Alaska to, 259
voting rights expansion, post-WW I, 276
"war on terror" declaration, 352
World War I participation, 269–270, 272
World War II participation, 304–305, *309*
Yung Wing's visit to, 195
Universal Declaration of Human Rights (1948), 318, *334*
Ure, Andrew, 186–187
US Centennial Exhibition (Philadelphia World's Fair), 220–222, *222*, 223

US Central Intelligence Agency (CIA), 313
US Constitution, 163, 170, 194, 277. *See also* Constitutional Convention
US War for Independence. *See* American Revolution
USS *Maine*, 259

Vanderbilt, Cornelius, 218
Venezuela, 49
Victoria, Queen of England, 230
Vietnam, 303 (map)
    communist models of political economy, 331
    decolonization, 327 (map)
    European-built schools, 233
    French control of, 272, 321
    Japanese occupation, 304
    national independence movement, 319, 320–321
    rubber plantations, 229
    trade networks, 60, 189
    US "strategic hamlets" in, 325
    World War II participation, 320
Vietnam War, *320*, 335
Vietnamese Declaration of Independence, 321, *334*
Vijayanagara Hindu dynasty (South Asia), 33
Virginia colony, 131
Virginia Company, 112
Voltaire, 146
voyages of exploration
    of Cabot, 46 (map), 58
    of Columbus, 16, 38, 46 (map), 48
    of Cortés, 40 (map), 46 (map), 49–51, *50*, 56, 64
    of Da Gama, 21, *30*, 31–32, *43*
    1485–1600, 46 (map)
    of Zheng He, *18*, *19*, 21, 29–32, *30*, *34t*, 365
Vries, Peter, 180

Wade, Geoff, 30
Wafd [Delegation] Party, Egypt, 283
Wafdist Women's Central Committee, 283
Wahehe Rebellion (1891–1898), 246
War of Spanish Succession, 133, *141*
war on terror declaration, US, 352
Wars of Religion, 79, 80 (map), 81–83
Warsaw Ghetto, 311, 313–314, *354*
Warsaw Pact, 312 (map), 316, 339, 346
Washington, George, 151
"The Way of Subjects" pamphlet (Japan Ministry of Education), 301
weaponry
    Afro-Eurasian continent, 70
    Civil War, US, 193, 194
    of Krupps, 195
    of Spain, 51
    in World War I, 265–266
West Africa
    maize agriculture, 97, *114*
    Mali empire, 5, 26, 35, *35*, 312 (map), 327 (map)
    Songhai Empire, 43

trade networks, 36, 59, 64
transatlantic slave trade, 128, 129–130
West India Company, 59
Western Eurasia
  Congress of Berlin participation, 227
  nation-state dilemma, 164, 165 (map), 166–167
  1914–1923, redrawn map, 271 (map)
  trade route links, 33
whale hunters, Arctic Circle, 48
*When China Ruled the Seas: The Treasure Fleet of the Dragon Throne, 1405–1433* (Levathes), 31n3
"The White Man's Burden" (Kipling), 233, 253
Whitney, Eli, 182, *196*
Wilhelm II, German Kaiser, 263
Wilhelm of Prussia, Emperor of Germany, 206
William of Orange, 121
Williams, George Washington, 235–236
Wilson, Woodrow, 272–273, *281*
Winchester firearms, 194
Witbooi, Hendrik, 238
Wojtyła, Karol Józef (Pope John Paul II), 346, 349
women's rights
  constitutional amendment for, 211
  Seneca Falls Convention on, 199, 201, 210, *224*
Wood, Gordon, 151–152
World Antislavery Conference, 199, 201, *224*
World Bank, 315, 329
World Trade Center (NYC), terrorist attacks, 352
World Trade Organization (WTO), 315, 354–355, *363*
World War I
  Australia's participation, 269
  Bolshevik withdrawal from, 274
  British recruitment poster for India, *270*
  British volunteerism for WW I, 263–264, 265
  celebrations for the war, 265

chemical weapons used in, 266–267, 306
China's participation, 269
death/destruction statistics, 270, 272
Dominions of the British Empire participation, 269
economic consequences, 292–294
Egypt's participation, 269
France's participation, 263, *266*, 269, 270, 273
Gandhi/India and, 288–289
Germany's participation, 263, 265–270, 272–274, 306
global stakes of, 269
Great Britain's participation, 263–264, 265, 267
"home front" struggles, 267–269
Italy's participation, 269
Japan's participation, 269, 272–273, 276
literature produced by, 264
major fields of battle, 256 (map)
nightmarish aspects of, 266–267
onset of, 263–264
Ottoman participation, 269, 270, 272
Polish post-war self-determination, 314
pre-war global alliances, 262–263
Russia's participation, 263, 265, 269, 270, 272
settlements/treaties ending the war, 272–274, *281*
treaties ending, 315
trench map, France and Belgium, 266 (map)
US humanitarian aid to Armenia, *287*
US participation, 269–270, 272
weaponry/ammunition issues, 265
World War II. *See also* Nazi Party; Germany
  air power strategy, 264, 304, 305
  atomic bombing of Hiroshima, Nagasaki, 305
  Big Five Allies post-war planning, 314–317
  France's participation, 304–305
  Germany's participation, 303–306
  Italy's participation, 304–305

Japan's participation, *302*, 304, 305
major fields of battle, 256 (map)
Nazi death camps, 306, *310*, 311, 314, 317
onset in Europe, *302*
path to, 303–305
post-war economics, 307
post-war global ruins, 308
post-war Three Decades Crisis, 285
Soviet Union's participation, 304
US participation, 304–305
Vietnam's participation, 320
World War Zero. *See* Seven Years' War
world's fairs
  Centennial Exhibition, Philadelphia, 220–222, *222*, 223
  *Exposition Universelle*, Paris, 199, 201, 223
  "living museums" feature, *198*
Wounded Knee, massacre of Native Americans, 2244
Wovoka, Paiute medicine man, 244, 249, *252*
Wu Sangui, Ming general, 85
WW I. *See* World War I
WW II. *See* World War II
Wycliffe, John, 77

Yalta Conference, 315
Yongle Emperor (China), 19, 28, 29
Young Czech movement (Prague), 203
Young Italy, secret society, 206, 224
Yrigoyen, Hipólito, 276
Yuan Dynasty, China, 28, 84
Yuan Shikai, President of China, 261
Yucatán peninsula, 38, 49
Yukichi, Fukuzawa, 238, 252
Yung Wing, 195, *197*

Zeng Guofan, Chinese Governor-General, 175, 192, 195
zeppelins, 268
Zheng He, *18, 19,* 21, 29–32, *30,* 34t, 365
Zhou Enlai, 336
Zhu Xi, 87
Zhu Yuanzhang, Ming Emperor, 84
Zumbi of Palmares, 117, 127, *141*
Zwingli, Huldrych, 59